McDougal, Littell

Reading Literature

Purple Level
Yellow Level
Blue Level
Orange Level
Green Level
Red Level
GOLD LEVEL

Three Zebras. Mara Abboud.

McDougal, Littell

Reading Literature

The McDougal, Littell English Program

Gold Level

Jacqueline L. Chaparro, Ed. D.

Judith L. Joyce

Rena Moran

Mary Ann Trost

McDougal, Littell & Company

Evanston, Illinois

New York   Dallas   Sacramento   Raleigh

Consultants

Deanne L. Azbell, Teacher, Eastmoor Middle School, Columbus, Ohio

Adele Bennett, R.S.M., Intermediate Reading Coordinator, Resurrection School, Chicago, Illinois

Sherryl Broyles, Specialist in Reading and Language Arts, Los Angeles Unified School District, Los Angeles, California

Gerald W. Casey, English Language Arts Coordinator, Red Clay Consolidated School District, Wilmington, Delaware

Cathryn S. Chellis, Teacher, Monroe Traditional Middle School, Columbus, Ohio

Rosalind E. Engel, Professor in Child Development, Iowa State University, Ames, Iowa

Claire Ward Kondig, Assistant Principal, Thurmont Middle School, Thurmont, Maryland

Diane J. Leventhal, Communications Coordinator, Norristown Area School District, Norristown, Pennsylvania

Charles P. Martin, Communications Coordinator, Chichester School District, Boothwyn, Pennsylvania

Dr. Jane Matanzo, Curriculum Specialist, Frederick County Board of Education, Frederick, Maryland

Nina Kay Miller, Teacher, Francis Case Elementary School, Ellsworth Air Force Base, South Dakota

Joyce Bahr Nordstrom, Supervisor, Language Arts, Denver Public Schools, Denver, Colorado

Mary Kay Rummel, Ph.D., National Language Arts Consultant, Fridley, Minnesota

Dixie Lee Spiegel, Associate Professor, Reading and Language Arts, University of North Carolina at Chapel Hill, Chapel Hill, North Carolina

Betty Stanton, Teacher, Dallas Independent School District, Dallas, Texas

ISBN 0-86609-225-0

Copyright © 1989 by McDougal, Littell & Company
Box 1667, Evanston, Illinois 60204

CONTENTS

UNIT 1
Timeless Tales

FICTION   POETRY   DRAMA

UNIT 2
Meeting Challenges

FICTION   POETRY   NONFICTION

UNIT 3
Finding a Place

UNIT 4
Learning About Life

FICTION   POETRY   NONFICTION

Handbook for Reading and Writing

Dear Student,

You are about to embark on an adventure—the adventure of reading fine literature. You will travel through time and space, visiting cities of the past and worlds of the future. You will meet fascinating characters who face exciting challenges. This book and your imagination will guide you.

Reading Literature will introduce you to a wide variety of literature. You will read stories, poems, plays, and works of nonfiction in their original forms. These works have been written by world-famous authors such as Lewis Carroll, Joan Aiken, Isaac Asimov, Jean Craighead George, Langston Hughes, Yoshiko Uchida, Lloyd Alexander, and Nikki Giovanni. Some of the works may make you laugh and others may make you cry. All of them should make you think.

Literature is your inheritance. Great writers of the past and present have left you a wealth of ideas, experiences, and feelings. Through reading, you can share and enjoy these riches.

Reading Literature can stretch your mind, sharpen your senses, and enrich your life. You will improve your reading, thinking, and vocabulary skills. You will discover how professional writers write, and you will learn to use a similar process for your own writing. Most of all, you will have the thrill of losing yourself in literature and finding there the wondrous challenge that is life.

Sincerely,
The Authors and Editors

UNIT ONE

FICTION   POETRY   DRAMA

Timeless Tales

Carnival Evening, 1886, HENRI ROUSSEAU.
Philadelphia Museum of Art: The Louis E. Stern Collection.

Reading Fiction

What Makes a Story?

A story is a work of **fiction.** That is, it comes from the story-teller's imagination. Some stories are told aloud. They may change a bit each time they are told. Other stories are carefully written for readers to enjoy. All stories, whether spoken or written, share three common elements.

The Elements of a Story

Every story has characters, a setting, and a plot. These are the threads the storyteller weaves together to make a story.

Characters. The people and animals in a story are called the **characters.** Some characters are more important than others. They are called **main characters.** The story centers around them.

Setting. When and where a story takes place is called the **setting.** A story may be set in a real or imaginary place. It may be set in past, present, or future time. Sometimes the setting is clearly stated, usually at the beginning of the story. At other times, you must use the story details to figure out the setting.

Plot. The series of events in a story is called the **plot.** The plot usually centers around a problem and the action that the characters take to solve the problem. The action builds toward an important moment, or climax. This may be a decision, or a discovery, or an event, for example. The **climax** is the turning point of the story. Then the problem is solved, and the story comes to a close.

Part 1

Stories from Oral Tradition

Some stories popular today were first told thousands of years ago. These stories belong to **oral tradition.** That is, they have been passed by word of mouth from generation to generation. Many of these stories were eventually written down.

One type of story that comes from oral tradition is the folk tale. A **folk tale** is a simple story about human or animal characters. It is usually set in the distant past. Some folk tales are legends. **Legends** are made-up stories that attempt to explain something that really happened or that tell about someone who really lived. Other folk tales teach lessons about life. Folk tales are told in every country around the world. Versions of the same story may be found in many different countries.

A character in a folk tale often represents one human quality. He or she may be clever or brave or greedy, for example. The plot often involves a **conflict,** or struggle, between good and evil. The use of humor and magic is common in folk tales.

How to Read a Folk Tale

The tales you will read in Unit 1 come from several countries. Some are retellings of folk tales from oral tradition. Others are modern stories that use folk-tale plots and characters.

As you read each tale, picture the setting and action. Learn about the characters. Pay attention to what they say and do, to what other characters say about them, and to what the writer tells you directly. Notice how one plot event leads to another. Be on the lookout for surprises. As you read, try to discover why these stories are called "timeless tales."

Comprehension Skills

Time Order and Cause and Effect

How many times have you heard someone say "Tell me what happened next" or "Why did you do that?" In literature, as in life, events are often related. Knowing how events are connected will help you understand what you read.

Time Order

Events in stories are often connected by **time order.** That is, one event follows another event in time. Words or phrases such as *first, then, while, the next day,* and *at last* signal the time order, or **sequence,** of events. Writers do not always use clue words. Often they simply tell things in the order that they happen. How is time order shown in these sentences from "The Wise Old Woman"?

Gradually there were fewer and fewer old people in the village and *soon* they disappeared altogether. *Then* the young lord was pleased.

Cause and Effect

Events can also be connected by **cause and effect.** That is, one event is the reason that another event happens. The event that happens first in time is the **cause.** What follows is the **effect.** The effect can be an event or a change in the way a character behaves or thinks.

Clue words often point out causes and their effects. Some of these clue words and phrases are *because, therefore, since, in order that, so/that,* and *if/then.* Notice how cause and effect are shown in this sentence from "The Wise Old Woman."

"If you cannot perform this task," the lord threatened, "I shall come to conquer your village."

Failure to perform the task has to happen first. This would be the cause. The lord's conquering the village would be the effect. The clue word is *if*.

An effect might not follow the cause right away. Sometimes the effect happens later in the story. A story may even begin with an effect. Then the events of the plot explain the causes.

As you read, look for the ways events and ideas are connected. Sometimes events are stated out of sequence. Look for clue words to help you. Picture the order of events in your mind. Then ask yourself, "What might happen because of this event? What caused this event or change to happen?"

Exercises: Using Time Order and Cause and Effect

A. Read this paragraph. Tell what happened first, second, and last. Name any clue words. Tell what caused the last event.

> Then Tyl left them, and all that day the shoemaker could not keep from telling everyone he met about his good fortune. So it wasn't long before the news reached his rich neighbor Lucas Koop.

B. A **time line** is a way of picturing the order in which things happen. This time line for "The Ugly Duckling" sums up the plot in a few words. Draw your own time line to show the order of main events in a familiar tale such as "Cinderella."

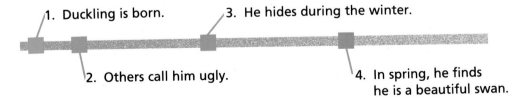

1. Duckling is born.
2. Others call him ugly.
3. He hides during the winter.
4. In spring, he finds he is a beautiful swan.

$\mathcal{V}$ocabulary Skills

Words and Their Parts

As you read, you will come across words whose meanings you do not know. You can learn ways to help you figure out these unknown words. One way of attacking a new word is to divide and conquer it. To do this, look carefully at how the word is put together. You can understand some words by figuring out their parts.

Prefixes and Suffixes

A word without any parts added is called a **base word.** Parts may be added to the beginning or the end of the base word.

Prefix. A word part added to the beginning of a base word is a **prefix.** The prefix changes the meaning of the base word.

Suffix. A word part added to the end of a base word is a **suffix.** A suffix can change or add to the meaning of a word. It may also change the part of speech of a word. For example, the suffix *-ness* changes the adjective *kind* to the noun *kindness.*

Some words are made up of three or even more parts. There may be a base word, one or more prefixes, and one or more suffixes within the same word. Look at this long word. Notice how it can be broken down.

	prefix	+	base word	+	suffix
unmistakable =	*un-*	+	*mistake*	+	*-able*

The prefix *un-* means "not"; the suffix *-able* means "can be." By combining these meanings with the base word, you see that *unmistakable* means "cannot be mistaken."

Notice that in *unmistakable,* the letter *e* is missing from the word *mistake.* Often, the spelling of the base word changes when a suffix is added to it. However, the spelling of the base word does not change when a prefix is added.

When you read an unknown word, try taking the word apart. See if the word is a base word with word parts added. If it is, figure out the meaning of each part. Then add the meanings together.

Compound Words

Sometimes two base words are combined to form a compound word. Often you can figure out the meaning of the compound from the meanings of the two base words. For instance, an *eyelid* is a lid for the eye. However, the compound word might have a different meaning from the one you would expect from combining its parts. For example, an *eyetooth* has nothing to do with eyes. If combining the two base words does not give you a meaning that makes sense as you read, look up the word in a dictionary.

Exercise: Examining Parts of a Word

Identify the parts of each underlined word in these sentences. Then explain the meaning of the whole word.

1. All the <u>townsfolk</u> agreed that the <u>unreasonable</u> lord had made a <u>dreadful</u> decree.

2. The whole <u>countryside</u> was in danger since the wizard had <u>unfortunately</u> <u>misplaced</u> his magic book.

Duke Pishposh of Pash

JAY WILLIAMS

Think about a trick you played on someone. Did you get into trouble? Notice how Tyl's tricks get him both in and out of trouble.

On a day in early spring, Prince William of Orange rode into the city of Delft. He was the leader of the armies of the Netherlands, and he was on his way to Amsterdam to meet with his captains. As he passed through the square on his way to the burgomaster's house, he heard a commotion. A small crowd of people had surrounded a man in a bright red jacket—some arguing at the tops of their voices, and some laughing.

The prince rode to the spot and commanded them to be silent. They recognized him immediately and fell back quietly.

"What is happening here?" he asked.

One man stepped forward. "Your Highness," said he, "I am a cheese merchant. This fellow in the red coat told me he had a perfect way of getting rid of mice. He said the gadget was guaranteed to work every time, and so I bought it for a hundred florins. This is what he gave me. It's a swindle!" He held out a hammer and a block of wood. "He told me to put each mouse on the block of wood and hit it with the hammer."

Prince William could not help laughing. "He was right; it will work every time. But you are right, too; it was a swindle."

He looked at the man in the red jacket. "What is your name?" he said.

"Tyl Uilenspiegel, Your Highness," said Tyl with a low bow.

"I have heard of you," said the prince, frowning. "Return this man's money and come with me."

Tyl did not dare to disobey, so he gave the money back and followed the prince to the burgomaster's house.

There Prince William said sternly, "You are a rogue and a trickster. Can you give me one reason why I should not send you to prison?"

"It's not my fault, Your Highness," said Tyl. "It's just that everyone I meet is so foolish. All I have to do is ask, and people give me money. Why, I'll wager I can get the richest man in Delft to give me anything I want."

"I don't believe it," said the prince. "If you can do such a thing, I'll set you free."

"Very well," Tyl said. "All I need is five gold pieces to start with."

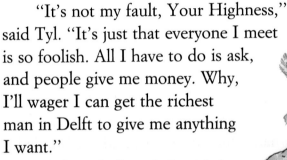

The prince gave them to him and said, "I must stay in Delft for two days. That is all the time you have."

"It's enough," said Tyl.

The richest man in Delft was named Lucas Koop. He was suspicious and bad-tempered and stingy. He lived in a fine house and spent one-half of his time counting his money, and the other half dreaming of ways to get more. Next door to Lucas Koop's big house was a little house belonging to a poor shoemaker, Jan Brouwer. Jan was hard-working and kind and the biggest gossip in town.

That night a ragged beggar with a patch over one eye knocked at the shoemaker's door. "I have traveled many miles, and I have no money," he said. "Please let me warm myself at your fire for a little while."

"Come in, come in," said the shoemaker. "You must be hungry, too, and you're just in time for supper. We haven't much, but what there is, you're welcome to share."

In came Tyl—for of course it was he. The shoemaker's wife greeted him, and the shoemaker's two children stared at him curiously. He warmed himself before the fire and told them stories of his travels, and they listened in wonder, for they had never been away from Delft. Then they all sat down to a simple meal of bread and sausages, and if there wasn't much food, there was plenty of friendliness to season it.

After dinner Tyl said, "I thank you, good people. Now I must be on my way again."

"Nonsense!" said Jan Brouwer. "The night is cold and dark, and I wouldn't think of turning you out. We haven't any spare beds, but you are welcome to sleep before the fire." He filled a bag with straw, placed it near the hearth, and gave Tyl a blanket. Tyl curled up on the straw and slept soundly, for he had spent the night in many worse places.

In the morning they had bread and milk for breakfast, and then Tyl stood up, looking suddenly much taller and more dignified. "I have something to tell you," he said to the shoemaker. "I am no beggar, but Duke Pishposh of Pash. Every spring I travel about in disguise, looking for people who are kind and generous, and when I find them, I reward them for each thing they give me. You have given me five things—a roof over my head, a good dinner, a fire, a bed, and breakfast. Here are five gold pieces."

He put the money into the shoemaker's hand. The poor man stared, and his wife and children stared, too, for they had never before seen so much gold all at once.

Then Tyl left them, and all that day the shoemaker could not keep from telling everyone he met about his good fortune. So it wasn't long before the news reached his rich neighbor Lucas Koop.

That night Tyl, still dressed in beggar's rags and wearing a patch over one eye, knocked at the door of Lucas Koop's house. A servant appeared.

"The night is cold, and my way is hard," said Tyl. "Please may I come in and warm myself?"

The servant bowed. "My master has given orders that any ragged beggar—especially one with a patch over his eye— should be admitted. Come in, and I will take you to him."

Tyl grinned to himself and followed the servant into a paneled room full of splendid furniture and rich paintings. A fire was burning in a big tiled stove, and Lucas Koop was standing before it. When he saw Tyl, he came forward to greet him, trying to smile although he had no practice at it.

"Welcome!" he croaked. "Glad to see you. I'm always kind to beggars, and anyone will tell you that I am the most generous man in the world. I'm sure you must be hungry—"

"That's right," said Tyl.

"Then come this way." And Koop led him into a dining room where, at a long table, a feast was spread.

"What handsome silver dishes these are," said Tyl.

"Do you like them? Please take one as a gift," Koop said.

After he had eaten as much as he could hold, Tyl said, "Now I must be on my way again."

"No, no," said Koop. "You are my guest. I have a bedroom specially prepared for you." He showed Tyl a room in which there was a big four-poster bed, spread with linen sheets and heaped with feather quilts. On a table beside the bed were a bowl of fruit, a pitcher of wine, a silver goblet.

"What a beautiful goblet," said Tyl.

"Do you like it? Please take it as a gift," said Koop. "Anything in the house is yours. Help yourself." And in his head, he added up the number of gold pieces he would get the next morning from Duke Pishposh of Pash.

But the next morning, his guest was gone. So were the silver dish, the silver goblet, a gold tobacco box, a pewter candlestick, and a great many other expensive things. On the table was a note that said, "Come to the burgomaster's house for your reward. Duke Pishposh of Pash."

Full of joy, Lucas Koop scurried to the burgomaster's house. There he found Prince William of Orange having breakfast with the beggar, who no longer had a patch over his eye and wore a red jacket instead of rags.

"Here is the rich man I was telling you about," said Tyl to the prince as Lucas Koop came in. "He gave me the things in this sack." And he showed Prince William the silver dish, the silver goblet, the tobacco box, the candlestick, and all the rest.

"Is it true?" the prince asked.

"Yes, Your Highness," answered Koop.

"There you are," said Tyl. "And what's more, I didn't even have to ask him for anything. He gave me a splendid dinner and a soft bed and told me to help myself to anything in the house. Isn't that so?"

"Of course," said Lucas Koop. "Now, where is my reward?"

Tyl rose and stretched out his hand. "You already have everything anyone could want," he said solemnly. "Your reward is the comfortable feeling that you have done a good deed."

"What?" shrieked Koop. "Is that all?"

"You have my thanks as well," said Tyl.

Lucas Koop jumped up and down in fury. "I don't want your

thanks. You gave five gold pieces to Jan Brouwer. I ought to have five hundred!"

"Jan Brouwer let me in because he thought I was a poor beggar," Tyl replied. "So he deserved the money. But you let me in because you thought I was a rich duke, so you don't deserve a thing."

"I agree," said Prince William. "You are a little too greedy, Master Koop. You may go, and Tyl may keep what you gave him."

Koop saw that the prince was not to be trifled with. He turned and silently went home. Then the prince said to Tyl, "You are free. You have won your bet."

"Thank you, Your Highness," said Tyl, picking up the sackful of treasures. "But to tell the truth, I won my bet two days ago."

"What do you mean?" asked the prince.

"You are richer than Lucas Koop, and so when you arrived, you became the richest man in Delft. Two days ago I asked you for five gold pieces, and you gave them to me without a murmur." He hoisted the sack over his shoulder. "Good-bye, Your Highness," he said with a smile. "You see, it's just as I said. It's not my fault—I only ask, and people give me whatever I want."

Jay Williams (1914-1978) was a comedian, a soldier, and a press agent before he became a writer. Williams is best known as a coauthor of the Danny Dunn science fiction books. He wrote for people of all ages. Many of his story ideas came from his interest in history, fencing, caves, and archery.

Other books: *The Tournament of the Lions*
The Hawkstone

Developing Comprehension Skills

1. What wager does Tyl make with the prince?

2. Tyl visits Jan *before* he visits Lucas Koop. Why is this time order important?

3. Why does Lucas Koop offer his possessions to Tyl?

4. How does Tyl trick the prince?

5. Imagine that you are the prince. When you realize that you too have been tricked, how will you feel?

6. **Focus on Thinking: Identifying Cause and Effect.** One event can be the reason for another event. The first event is the **cause;** the second is the **effect.** What causes Tyl to make the wager? What is the effect of his winning?

Reading Fiction

1. **Understanding Characters in Folk Tales.** A **trickster,** or a clever player of tricks, is a common character in folk tales. Often tricksters use disguises. What disguises does Tyl use?

2. **Identifying the Setting.** The time and place in which a story happens is called the **setting.** Where and when is this story set? Is this setting real or imaginary?

3. **Analyzing Plot.** The series of events in a story is called the **plot.** In many folk tales, the plot takes a surprise turn at the end. In this story, when do you find out that Tyl wins the bet with the prince? When does Tyl actually win the bet?

Speaking and Listening

Playing a Role. To play the role of a character, you should think, act, and speak as if you were that character. Imagine that Tyl is on trial for his first trick. Choose a role to play in the trial. You can be a witness, a lawyer for or against Tyl, the victim, the judge, Tyl, or a member of the jury. Let the jury decide Tyl's guilt or innocence.

Writing in Response to Literature

The prince claims that Tyl is a rogue, but Tyl claims to be an innocent person. What is your opinion of Tyl? Write a paragraph that explains why you feel as you do.

Whose advice do you value most? Discover with the young lord how valuable the advice of others can be.

The Wise Old Woman

YOSHIKO UCHIDA

Many long years ago, there lived an arrogant and cruel young lord who ruled over a small village in the western hills of Japan.

"I have no use for old people in my village," he said haughtily. "They are neither useful nor able to work for a living. I therefore decree that anyone over seventy-one must be banished from the village and left in the mountains to die."

"What a dreadful decree! What a cruel and unreasonable lord we have," the people of the village murmured. But the lord fearfully punished anyone who disobeyed him, and so villagers who turned seventy-one were tearfully carried into the mountains, never to return.

Gradually there were fewer and fewer old people in the village and soon they disappeared altogether. Then the young lord was pleased.

"What a fine village of young, healthy, and hard-working people I have," he bragged. "Soon it will be the finest village in all of Japan."

Now there lived in this village a kind young farmer and his aged mother. They were poor, but the farmer was good to his

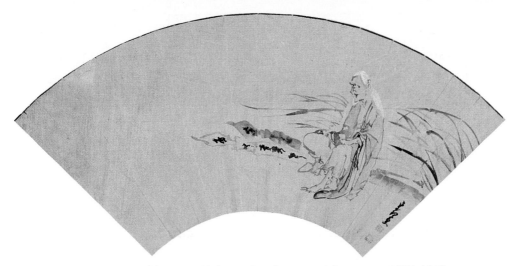

Japanese Fan: An Old Woman Sitting on Two Overturned Graveposts, 1615–1868.
Freer Gallery of Art, Smithsonian Institution, Washington, D.C. 98.135f

mother, and the two of them lived happily together. However, as the years went by, the mother grew older, and before long she reached the terrible age of seventy-one.

"If only I could somehow deceive the cruel lord," the farmer thought. But there were records in the village books and everyone knew that his mother had turned seventy-one.

Each day the son put off telling his mother that he must take her into the mountains to die, but the people of the village began to talk. The farmer knew that if he did not take his mother away soon, the lord would send his soldiers and throw them both into a dark dungeon to die a terrible death.

"Mother—" he would begin, as he tried to tell her what he must do, but he could not go on.

Then one day the mother herself spoke of the lord's dread decree. "Well, my son," she said, "the time has come for you to take me to the mountains. We must hurry before the lord sends his soldiers for you." And she did not seem worried at all that she must go to the mountains to die.

"Forgive me, dear mother, for what I must do," the farmer said sadly, and the next morning he lifted his mother to his shoulders and set off on the steep path toward the mountains. Up and up he climbed, until the trees clustered close and the path was gone. There was no longer even the sound of birds, and they heard only the soft wail of the wind in the trees. The son walked slowly, for he could not bear to think of leaving his old mother in the mountains. On and on he climbed, not wanting to stop and leave her behind. Soon, he heard his mother breaking off small twigs from the trees that they passed.

"Mother, what are you doing?" he asked.

"Do not worry, my son," she answered gently. "I am just marking the way so you will not get lost returning to the village."

The son stopped. "Even now you are thinking of me?" he asked wonderingly.

The mother nodded. "Of course, my son," she replied. "You will always be in my thoughts. How could it be otherwise?"

At that, the young farmer could bear it no longer. "Mother, I cannot leave you in the mountains to die all alone," he said. "We are going home and no matter what the lord does to punish me, I will never desert you again."

So they waited until the sun had set and a lone star crept into the silent sky. Then in the dark shadows of night, the farmer carried his mother down the hill and they returned quietly to their little house. The farmer dug a deep hole in the floor of his kitchen and made a small room where he could hide his mother. From that day, she spent all her time in the secret room and the farmer carried meals to her there. The rest of the time, he was careful to work in the fields and act as though he lived alone. In this way, for almost two years, he kept his mother safely hidden and no one in the village knew that she was there.

Then one day there was a terrible commotion among the villagers, for Lord Higa of the town beyond the hills threatened to conquer their village and make it his own.

"Only one thing can spare you," Lord Higa announced. "Bring me a box containing one thousand ropes of ash and I will spare your village."

The cruel young lord quickly gathered together all the wise men of his village. "You are men of wisdom," he said. "Surely you can tell me how to meet Lord Higa's demands so our village can be spared."

But the wise men shook their heads. "It is impossible to make even one rope of ash, sire," they answered. "How can we ever make one thousand?"

"Fools!" the lord cried angrily. "What good is your wisdom if you cannot help me now?"

And he posted a notice in the village square offering a great reward of gold to any villager who could help him save their village.

But all the people in the village whispered, "Surely it is an impossible thing, for ash crumbles at the touch of the finger. How could anyone ever make a rope of ash?" They shook their heads and sighed, "Alas, alas, we must be conquered by yet another cruel lord."

The young farmer, too, supposed that this must be, and he wondered what would happen to his mother if a new lord even more terrible than their own came to rule over them.

When his mother saw the troubled look on his face, she asked, "Why are you so worried, my son?"

So the farmer told her of the impossible demand made by Lord Higa if the village was to be spared, but his mother did not seem troubled at all. Instead she laughed softly and said, "Why, that is not such an impossible task. All one has to do is soak ordinary rope in salt water and dry it well. When it is burned, it will hold its shape and there is your rope of ash! Tell the villagers to hurry and find one thousand pieces of rope."

The farmer shook his head in amazement. "Mother, you are wonderfully wise," he said, and he rushed to tell the young lord what he must do.

"You are wiser than all the wise men of the village," the lord said when he heard the farmer's solution, and he rewarded him with many pieces of gold. The thousand ropes of ash were quickly made and the village was spared.

In a few days, however, there was another great commotion in the village as Lord Higa sent another threat. This time he sent a log with a small hole that curved and bent seven

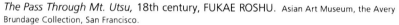

The Pass Through Mt. Utsu, 18th century, FUKAE ROSHU. Asian Art Museum, the Avery Brundage Collection, San Francisco.

times through its length, and he demanded that a single piece of silk thread be threaded through the hole. "If you cannot perform this task," the lord threatened, "I shall come to conquer your village."

The young lord hurried once more to his wise men, but they all shook their heads in bewilderment. "A needle cannot bend its way through such curves," they moaned. "Again we are faced with an impossible demand."

"And again you are stupid fools!" the lord said, stamping his foot impatiently. He then posted a second notice in the village square asking the villagers for their help.

Once more the young farmer hurried with the problem to his mother in her secret room.

"Why, that is not so difficult," his mother said with a quick smile. "Put some sugar at one end of the hole. Then, tie an ant to a piece of silk thread and put it in at the other end. He will weave his way in and out of the curves to get to the sugar and he will take the silk thread with him."

"Mother, you are remarkable!" the son cried, and he hurried off to the lord with the solution to the second problem.

Once more the lord commended the young farmer and rewarded him with many pieces of gold. "You are a brilliant man and you have saved our village again," he said gratefully.

But the lord's troubles were not over even then, for a few days later Lord Higa sent still another demand. "This time you will undoubtedly fail and then I shall conquer your village," he threatened. "Bring me a drum that sounds without being beaten."

"But that is not possible," sighed the people of the village. "How can anyone make a drum sound without beating it?"

This time the wise men held their heads in their hands and moaned, "It is hopeless. It is hopeless. This time, Lord Higa will conquer us all."

The young farmer hurried home breathlessly. "Mother, Mother, we must solve another terrible problem or Lord Higa will conquer our village!" And he quickly told his mother about the impossible drum.

His mother, however, smiled and answered, "Why, this is the easiest of them all. Make a drum with sides of paper and put a bumblebee inside. As it tries to escape, it will buzz and beat itself against the paper and you will have a drum that sounds without being beaten."

The young farmer was amazed at his mother's wisdom. "You are far wiser than any of the wise men of the village," he

Equestrian Portrait of Hosokawa Sumimoto.
Eisei Library, Tokyo.

said, and he hurried to tell the young lord how to meet Lord Higa's third demand.

When the lord heard the answer, he was greatly impressed. "Surely a young man like you cannot be wiser than all my wise men," he said. "Tell me honestly, who has helped you solve all these difficult problems?"

The young farmer could not lie. "My lord," he began slowly, "for the past two years I have broken the law of the land. I have kept my aged mother hidden beneath the floor of my house, and it is she who solved each of your problems and saved the village from Lord Higa."

He trembled as he spoke, for he feared the lord's displeasure and rage. Surely now the soldiers would be summoned to throw him into the dark dungeon. But when he glanced fearfully at the lord, he saw that the young ruler was not angry at all. Instead, he was silent and thoughtful, for at last he realized how much wisdom and knowledge old people possess.

"I have been very wrong," he said finally. "And I must ask the forgiveness of your mother and of all my people. Never again will I demand that the old people of our village be sent to the mountains to die. Rather, they will be treated with the respect and honor they deserve and share with us the wisdom of their years."

And so it was. From that day, the villagers were no longer forced to abandon their parents in the mountains, and the village became once more a happy, cheerful place in which to live. The terrible Lord Higa stopped sending his impossible demands and no longer threatened to conquer them, for he, too, was impressed. "Even in such a small village there is much wisdom," he declared, "and its people should be allowed to live in peace."

And that is exactly what the farmer and his mother and all the people of the village did for all the years thereafter.

Yoshiko Uchida (born 1921), the daughter of Japanese immigrants, grew up in California. She bases some of her stories on Japanese folk tales she heard from her family. Others have come from people she interviewed in Japan. Uchida won an award for helping to bring about a greater understanding of the Japanese-American culture.
Other books: *A Jar of Dreams*
Samurai of Gold Hill

Developing Comprehension Skills

1. What is the young lord's reason for sending the old people away?

2. Why does the farmer take his mother to the mountains? Why does he bring her back even though he might be punished?

3. Who is Lord Higa? What will happen if the village does not meet his demands?

4. Explain why the young lord is angry with the wise men. Why is the old woman able to solve the village's problems?

5. What causes Lord Higa to spare the village? What causes the young lord to spare the mother? How are the two causes alike?

6. **Focus on Thinking: Problem Solving.** There may be more than one way to solve a problem. One step in problem solving is to consider possible solutions. If the young lord never changes his decree, what problem will he face at age seventy-one? What are some possible solutions?

Reading Fiction

1. **Recognizing the Theme.** Works of literature usually present a **theme,** that is, a message about life. In folk tales, the theme is often a lesson that characters learn. Who teaches the lesson in this story? What is the lesson?

2. **Examining Plot.** You remember that the events in a story make up its **plot.** The events in many folk tales include nearly impossible tasks for characters to perform. Name the tasks that are important to the plot of this tale. Explain how one task is performed.

3. **Recognizing Characteristics of Folk Tales.** In folk tales, things often happen in threes. There may be three wishes, or three children, or three tasks, for example. In what way is three important in this tale? Explain how the number three plays a part in another tale you know.

Writing in Response to Literature

Think of someone you know who is old. In what ways is this person important or valuable to you? Write a paragraph that explains your feelings.

How do pets show their loyalty? See how a dog's loyalty results in this Puerto Rican legend about a landmark.

The Stone Dog

PURA BELPRÉ

 In Puerto Rico many years ago near the Condado Lagoon,[1] there lived a poor fisherman. He lived alone in a hut. His only companion was his dog.

The fisherman and his dog were devoted to each other. They might be seen strolling on the white sandy beach. Or they might be seen coming through the tangle of vines along the road that led to San Juan. However, there was one place where nobody saw them together. That was in the fisherman's boat. The man never took the dog along with him.

But the dog was always beside his master as the fisherman made his little boat ready to sail. When the man pulled out to sea each morning, the dog would scamper up on the high ridge that separated the Condado Lagoon from the open sea. There he would sit and watch all day. The dog never moved until late afternoon when he saw the little boat return. Then he would race back to the shore to greet his master. And together the man and the dog would set off for San Juan to sell the fresh-caught fish.

---

1. **Condado Lagoon** (kōn dä'dō lə gün'): the body of water enclosed by a coral reef in San Juan, Puerto Rico.

Casa Campestre, late 19th century, MANUEL JORDAN. Institute of Puerto Rican Culture, San Juan.

As the years went by, the fisherman grew older. So did the faithful dog. The fisherman still went out to sea. The dog still watched for his return, sitting on the high ridge above the lagoon.

One morning early in September, the fisherman was getting his little boat ready. All at once the dog began to bark and howl. He circled around the fisherman and tugged at his trousers. The fisherman could not remember when he had seen his dog act so strangely. He patted the dog's back, thinking the dog wanted to play. But nothing made any difference. The dog kept barking. The fisherman laughed and continued getting ready. Finally he gave the dog another pat. Then the man climbed into the boat and sailed away. The dog went to his watching place, still barking and howling.

There were other fishing boats out that morning. The sky was blue and the breeze soft and fresh.

Suddenly the soft breeze changed. It began to blow wildly. The fisherman's boat was seized by the wind and whirled around. The sky darkened. Rain began to fall.

"It's a hurricane!" said the fisherman. "A hurricane blowing onshore!"

The man thought of his dog at once. Had the dog left the ridge and run home? Or was he still sitting there? The fisherman tried to steer his boat and turn it toward the shore. Suddenly a great wave swept over his head and tossed the boat away.

When dawn came next morning, the hurricane was over. The sky was blue once more. The sea was so calm it was hard to believe it was the same sea that had roared and raged the night before. When the sun rose over the mountains, the families of the other fishermen ran to the shore. They watched for the return of the boats. They waited and waited, but none returned.

Then the people went slowly back to their homes to endure their grief and start a new life. As they rebuilt their village, no one gave a thought to the fisherman's dog.

Several months later a group of villagers was out gathering sea grapes.[2] They noticed what appeared to be the figure of a dog sitting high on the ridge above the lagoon.

"Look," said one. "Isn't that the old fisherman's dog?"

"How could it be, after all this time?" said another.

To prove his point, the first man climbed the ragged stony ridge to get hold of the dog. But when he reached the spot, he found only a rock—a rock shaped like a dog. The man came

---

2. **sea grapes** (sē grāps): a type of tropical shrub with glossy heart-shaped leaves, small green flowers, and purplish berries.

down quickly. But as soon as the people looked up again, they saw the stone dog. His head was held high. His body was alert, as if ready to spring into the sea. He just sat there on top of the ridge, waiting, waiting. . . .

And there he sits today for anyone to see.

Actual photo of the Stone Dog as it looks today off the shores of the Condado Lagoon, San Juan, Puerto Rico. Copyright © Edgar Bertran, San Juan.

Pura Belpré (1899-1982) was born and raised in Puerto Rico. She was the first Hispanic librarian to work in a New York City Public Library. She used storytelling and puppet theater to teach Puerto Rican folklore to children. Belpré retold tales that she remembered from her youth. Many of these tales can be found in her books.

Other books: *Perez and Martina*
Santiago

Developing Comprehension Skills

1. What does the dog usually do when the fisherman is out at sea?

2. What is the dog trying to tell the fisherman by its strange actions? How does the fisherman respond?

3. Identify clue words that show time order in the second paragraph on page 31.

4. What happens to the fisherman? What appears to happen to the dog? Find details to support your answers.

5. Legends are stories that combine fact and fiction. This legend was told to explain a real landmark. Which part of the story could only be fiction, or imaginary?

6. **Focus on Thinking: Locating Details.** The many bits of description that make up a whole story are called details. Details can suggest ideas. Find details in the story that support the idea that animals sense danger or changes in weather before humans do.

Reading Fiction

1. **Relating Character to Plot.** The way characters feel about each other affects events in the plot. How do the characters' feelings affect the plot in "The Stone Dog"?

2. **Evaluating Setting.** You know that the time and the place in which a story happens is called the setting. Describe the setting of "The Stone Dog." Could the story happen in some other place? If so, what details about the place would have to be the same?

Study and Research

Using an Atlas. An **atlas** is a book of maps. Use an atlas to locate a map of the islands in the Caribbean Sea. Find the island of Puerto Rico and then locate the city of San Juan. What body of water lies to the north of Puerto Rico? What body of water lies to the west?

Writing in Response to Literature

Why do you think people value pets? Write a paragraph that gives your reasons. Use examples from your own experience or from stories you have read.

What qualities do you look for in a friend? Discover what Kim learns about his friends.

The Beggar in the Blanket

A Vietnamese Tale Retold by GAIL B. GRAHAM

Many hundreds of years ago, two brothers lived in a village at the edge of the forest. Their names were Kim and De.

Kim was the elder, and he was very industrious. He had worked hard all his life, and now he was one of the richest men in the village.

De was inclined to be lazy. He worked when he needed something to eat or a new pair of sandals, but he never worked very hard, and he never worked for very long. He lived all alone because he couldn't afford to feed a wife.

Kim had a number of friends who were as rich and as hard-working as he was. Kim's friends kept him so busy that he hardly ever had time to think about his poor, lazy younger brother.

But Kim's wife was a gentle and thoughtful woman, and she felt sorry for De.

"It's been more than a month since we've seen your brother," she said to Kim one night. "Why don't you ask him to come and have dinner with us?"

Kim was surprised. "What would Nguyen and Ton and

Cao and Duc and all my other friends think if they came in and found that good-for-nothing brother of mine sitting at our table?" he asked. "They would be insulted! They would never come to my house again!"

"So much the worse for them," replied his wife. "Friends are not the same as a brother."

"And it's a good thing they're not!" Kim retorted. "The whole village would starve if all my friends were as lazy as De."

Kim's wife could see that it was no use arguing with her stubborn husband. Nevertheless she vowed that she would make Kim understand the value of a brother, even a poor and lazy brother like De.

The next evening Kim came home to find his wife weeping and trembling.

"A terrible thing has happened," she sobbed. "While you were away, a beggar came to our door and tried to rob us. I chased him with my broom, and he dropped his sack and tried to run away. But he stumbled over a stick of wood, and he fell . . . and he hit his head against the hearthstone. He's . . . he's dead."

Kim was horrified. "Where is he?"

His wife pointed toward the corner. "I wrapped him up in that old blanket," she said. "It wasn't my fault! He was trying to rob us. But the Mandarin will never believe me; he'll think that I murdered a helpless old beggar! We are ruined!" And she wept harder than ever.

Kim sat down and tried to think. He thought and thought, but all he could think about was the terrible humiliation of having to go before the Mandarin and admit that his wife had killed a poor old beggar.

"I have an idea," Kim's wife said at last. "If you get one of your friends to help you, you can carry the beggar into the

forest and bury him. No one will miss an old beggar, and even if they do, they won't think to suspect us."

Kim couldn't think of a better plan, so he snatched up his coat and hurried away to seek help from his friend Nguyen.

Nguyen listened politely to everything Kim said. But when Kim asked for help, Nguyen shook his head.

"I'd like to help you," he replied slowly. "But you see, I am so old and so weak that I really wouldn't be any help at all. Why don't you go and ask Ton?"

Kim crossed the road and rapped at Ton's door.

"Kim!" exclaimed Ton. "I was just thinking about you. Come in. Will you have a cup of tea?"

"I need your help," said Kim. And he explained what had happened.

As Kim spoke, Ton began to squirm and grimace as if he were in pain. At last Ton collapsed onto the floor. He drew his knees up to his chin and moaned.

"If only you had come at some other time!" groaned Ton.

"I'd be happy to help you, but I've got terrible pains in my stomach! I'm much too sick to carry anything!"

Kim walked out into the night. I'll go and see Cao, he thought. Surely he will help me.

But Cao's house was dark and still. Cao and his whole family had gone to the next village for a visit.

It's a good thing I have so many friends, thought Kim. Duc will be home, and I know I can count on him.

Lights glowed in all the windows of Duc's house. Duc himself opened the door and bade Kim come in and warm himself by the fire.

Kim told Duc about the beggar. Duc was very sympathetic and understanding. He agreed that Kim's wife was not to blame, and he thought that the plan to bury the beggar in the forest was a very clever plan.

"Then you'll help me!" cried Kim.

Duc looked surprised. "Help you? Oh, I can't possibly help you," he said quickly. "You see, my wife isn't feeling very well this evening, and I don't want to leave her alone in the house."

There was nothing for Kim to do but return home and tell his wife that not one of his friends would help him.

"Fine friends!" she snorted. "They'll come to your house and eat your rice and drink up your tea, but where are they when you need them? It's a lucky thing for us that you have a brother! Don't just stand there, go and fetch De!"

Kim blinked. "Why should De be willing to help me?" he asked his wife. "What have I ever done for him?"

"Little enough," she replied. "But he's your brother. If he won't help you, no one will."

Much to Kim's surprise, De readily agreed to help him bury the beggar. The two brothers carried the rolled-up blanket deep into the forest and buried it beneath a tree. Then they went home to bed.

Kim's wife woke him at dawn.

"Kim!" she whispered. "There are three messengers from the Mandarin at our door!"

Kim dressed hurriedly and went out to see what the messengers wanted.

"You and your wife must come with us," said the first messenger.

"You have been summoned to appear before the Mandarin," said the second messenger.

"Make haste!" warned the third messenger. "The Mandarin must not be kept waiting!"

Kim and his wife marched obediently along behind the three messengers to the Mandarin's palace. They were led into a small bare chamber and told to wait. An hour passed. At last Kim and his wife were ordered to enter the Mandarin's court.

Nguyen and Ton and Duc were already there, standing at either side of the Mandarin's throne. Kim's heart sank. He knew in an instant that his friends had betrayed him.

The Mandarin looked sternly down at Kim.

"Your wife murdered a helpless beggar," said the Mandarin. "Last night you went to the homes of each of these three honest men and tried to persuade them to help you hide the beggar's body."

Kim stared at the floor and said nothing.

"These three honest men followed you into the forest," continued the Mandarin. "They watched you bury the beggar beneath a tree. And then they dug up the body and brought it here to me."

Four servants came forward and placed the rolled-up blanket at the Mandarin's feet.

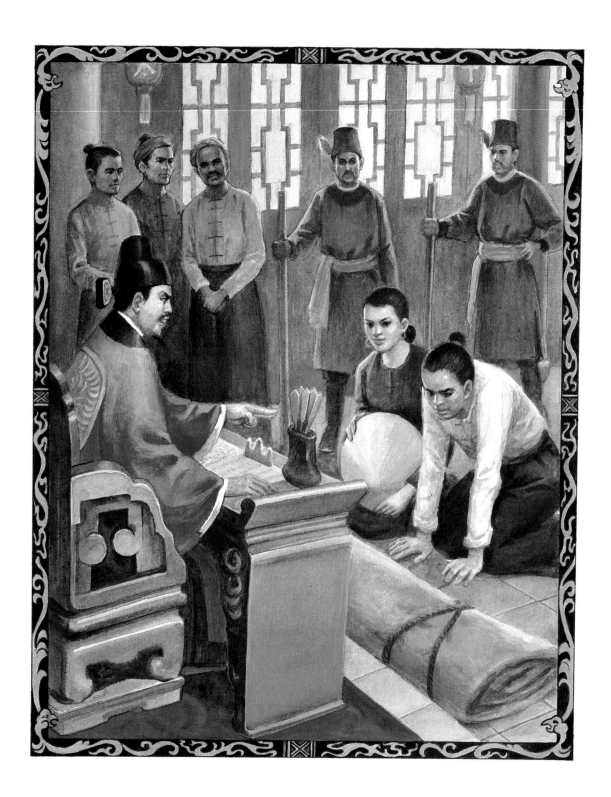

"Unroll the blanket!" commanded the Mandarin.

It was done. A murmur of surprise swept through the room. For there was no beggar inside the blanket! Instead it was filled with sticks and stones.

The Mandarin glared at Nguyen and Ton and Duc. "You swore that this man and his wife had murdered a helpless beggar!" he said angrily. "You claimed a reward. Well, where is the beggar?"

Nguyen and Ton and Duc were silent.

"Where is the beggar?" thundered the Mandarin.

Kim's wife stepped forward and bowed. "Your Excellency," she said. "There is no beggar. I invented the story because I wanted to prove to my husband that the love of his poor brother was more valuable than the love of his rich friends."

The Mandarin was so impressed with her cleverness and so pleased that there hadn't been a murder that he bade all of them go back to their village. But Nguyen and Ton and Duc were so ashamed of themselves that they could scarcely hold their heads up. And Kim never forgot the lesson that he had learned from the beggar in the blanket.

Gail B. Graham worked as a writer and reporter in the Virgin Islands, Hong Kong, Japan, and Vietnam. Graham spent hundreds of hours in Saigon libraries and bookstores finding information for her Vietnamese tales. During the war in Vietnam, she was captured by the Viet Cong. An article she wrote at that time appears in the U.S. *Congressional Record.* She also writes under the pen name of Gail Barclay.

Developing Comprehension Skills

1. Why does Kim refuse to invite his brother to his house for dinner?

2. How does Kim's wife feel about his attitude toward his brother? What does she vow?

3. How does Kim react to the news of the murder? Who is he most worried about?

4. How does Kim try to solve his problem? Why does he finally go to his brother for help?

5. At the end of the story, why are Kim's friends ashamed? Do you think they should be ashamed? Why or why not?

6. **Focus on Thinking: Finding Reasons for Actions.** Often you must think beyond a character's words to find the real reason for an action. Look beyond the excuses that Kim's friends give him. What do you think are their reasons for refusing to help?

Reading Fiction

1. **Understanding Surprise Endings.** Some folk-tale plots end with a surprise. There may be a clue that a surprise is coming. In this story, the reader is led to believe that the blanket hides a body. What clue early in the story hints that a surprise may be coming?

2. **Identifying the Theme.** What Kim learns is the theme of this folk tale. What is that theme? Who teaches the lesson?

3. **Judging a Character.** You can learn about characters from their actions and from other characters. What do you learn about De from Kim? What do you learn from De's own actions? Which source do you think gives a truer picture of De?

Critical Thinking

Evaluating. To **evaluate** means to judge the worth of something. Evaluate the wife's plan to teach Kim a lesson. First list the good and bad points of her plan. Then decide if the plan was a good one.

Writing in Response to Literature

Suppose Kim asked you to help bury the beggar. Would you help? Write your answer in a letter to Kim.

Language and Literature

Vocabulary

Prefixes. Knowing the meanings of prefixes can help you understand word meanings. You read that Tyl did not dare *disobey* the Prince. The base word *obey* means "to follow the orders of." The prefix *dis-* means "the opposite of." *Disobey* means "the opposite of obey" or "not to follow orders."

Here are the meanings of some other common prefixes.

re- (back; again) *mis-* (wrong)
pre- (before) *un-* (not; opposite of)

Exercise. Answer each question below. Explain your choice.

1. Does the stone dog misplace or replace the living dog?
2. Was Kim's brother usually unemployed or reemployed?
3. Does the cruel lord mistreat or pretreat the old people?
4. Does Tyl prearrange, disarrange, or rearrange his trick?

Developing Writing Skills

Writing a Description. Think about the settings of the folk tales you read. Choose one setting. Pretend that you are a person living in that country at that time. Who would you choose to be? Describe yourself and what you do.

Prewriting. Think about where you live. Decide who you are and what you do. List as many descriptive words and phrases about yourself as you can. Jot down details about your job, home, and clothing. Circle the details you plan to use.

Drafting. Begin by introducing yourself. Tell what you do. Use your notes to write sentences that describe the way you look and live.

Revising and Sharing. Add details to improve your description. When your word picture is clear, illustrate it. Share your two types of pictures.

The Fools of Chelm and the Stupid Carp

ISAAC BASHEVIS SINGER

In Chelm, a city of fools, every housewife bought fish for the Sabbath.[1] The rich bought large fish, the poor small ones. They were bought on Thursday, cut up, chopped, and made into gefilte fish[2] on Friday, and eaten on the Sabbath.

One Thursday morning the door opened at the house of the community leader of Chelm, Gronam Ox, and Zeinvel Ninny entered, carrying a trough full of water. Inside was a large, live carp.

"What is this?" Gronam asked.

"A gift to you from the wise men of Chelm," Zeinvel said. "This is the largest carp ever caught in the Lake of Chelm, and we all decided to give it to you as a token of appreciation for your great wisdom."

"Thank you very much," Gronam Ox replied. "My wife, Yente Pesha, will be delighted. She and I both love carp. I read

---

1. **Sabbath** (sab′ əth): Saturday, the day of rest and worship in the Jewish faith.
2. **gefilte fish** (gə fil′ tə fish): cakes of chopped fish, onion, egg, and seasonings. The cakes are boiled and served cold.

in a book that eating the brain of a carp increases wisdom, and even though we in Chelm are immensely clever, a little improvement never hurts. But let me have a close look at him. I was told that a carp's tail shows the size of his brain."

Gronam Ox was known to be nearsighted, and when he bent down to the trough to better observe the carp's tail, the carp did something that proved he was not as wise as Gronam thought. He lifted his tail and smacked Gronam across the face.

Gronam Ox was flabbergasted. "Something like this never happened to me before," he exclaimed. "I cannot believe this carp was caught in the Chelm lake. A Chelm carp would know better."

"He's the meanest fish I ever saw in my life," agreed Zeinvel Ninny.

Even though Chelm is a big city, news traveled quickly there. In no time at all the other wise men of Chelm arrived at the house of their leader, Gronam Ox. Treitel Fool came, and Sender Donkey, Shmendrick Numskull, and Dopey Lekisch.

Fish in the Air, 1970, IVAN GENERALIĆ. Collection of the Artist.

Gronam Ox was saying, "I'm not going to eat this fish on the Sabbath. This carp is a fool, and malicious to boot. If I eat him, I could become foolish instead of cleverer."

"Then what shall I do with him?" asked Zeinvel Ninny.

Gronam Ox put a finger to his head as a sign that he was thinking hard. After a while he cried out, "No man or animal in Chelm should slap Gronam Ox. This fish should be punished."

"What kind of punishment shall we give him?" asked

Treitel Fool. "All fish are killed anyhow, and one cannot kill a fish twice."

"He shouldn't be killed like other fish," Sender Donkey said. "He should die in a different way to show that no one can smack our beloved sage, Gronam Ox, and get away with it."

"What kind of death?" wondered Shmendrick Numskull. "Shall we perhaps just imprison him?"

"There is no prison in Chelm for fish," said Zeinvel Ninny. "And to build such a prison would take too long."

"Maybe he should be hanged," suggested Dopey Lekisch.

"How do you hang a carp?" Sender Donkey wanted to know. "A creature can be hanged only by its neck, but since a carp has no neck, how will you hang him?"

"My advice is that he should be thrown to the dogs alive," said Treitel Fool.

"It's no good," Gronam Ox answered. "Our Chelm dogs are both smart and modest, but if they eat this carp, they may become as stupid and mean as he is."

"So what should we do?" all the wise men asked.

"This case needs lengthy consideration," Gronam Ox decided. "Let's leave the carp in the trough and ponder the matter as long as is necessary. Being the wisest man in Chelm, I cannot afford to pass a sentence that will not be admired by all the Chelmites."

"If the carp stays in the trough a long time, he may die," Zeinvel Ninny, a former fish dealer, explained. "To keep him alive we must put him into a large tub, and the water has to be changed often. He must also be fed properly."

"You are right, Zeinvel," Gronam Ox told him. "Go and find the largest tub in Chelm and see to it that the carp is kept alive and healthy until the day of judgment. When I reach a decision, you will hear about it."

Of course Gronam's words were the law in Chelm. The five wise men went and found a large tub, filled it with fresh water, and put the criminal carp in it, together with some crumbs of bread, challah,[3] and other tidbits a carp might like to eat. Shlemiel, Gronam's bodyguard, was stationed at the tub to make sure that no greedy Chelmite wife would use the imprisoned carp for gefilte fish.

It just so happened that Gronam Ox had many other decisions to make and he kept postponing the sentence. The carp seemed not to be impatient. He ate, swam in the tub, became even fatter than he had been, not realizing that a severe sentence hung over his head. Shlemiel changed the water frequently, because he was told that if the carp died, this would be an act of contempt for Gronam Ox and for the Chelm Court of Justice. Yukel the water carrier made a few extra pennies every day by bringing water for the carp. Some of the Chelmites who were in opposition to Gronam Ox spread the gossip that Gronam just couldn't find the right type of punishment for the carp and that he was waiting for the carp to die a natural death. But, as always, a great disappointment awaited them. One morning about half a year later, the sentence became known, and when it was known, Chelm was stunned. The carp had to be drowned.

Gronam Ox had thought up many clever sentences before, but never one as brilliant as this one. Even his enemies were amazed at this shrewd verdict. Drowning is just the kind of death suited to a spiteful carp with a large tail and a small brain.

That day the entire Chelm community gathered at the lake to see the sentence executed. The carp, which had become

---

3. **challah** (hä′lə): a type of rich white bread.

almost twice as big as he had been before, was brought to the lake in the wagon that carried the worst criminals to their death. The drummers drummed. Trumpets blared. The Chelmite executioner raised the heavy carp and threw it into the lake with a mighty splash.

A great cry rose from the Chelmites: "Down with the treacherous carp! Long live Gronam Ox! Hurrah!"

Gronam was lifted by his admirers and carried home with songs of praise. Some Chelmite girls showered him with flowers. Even Yente Pesha, his wife, who was often critical of Gronam and dared to call him fool, seemed impressed by Gronam's high intelligence.

In Chelm, as everywhere else, there were envious people

who found fault with everyone, and they began to say that there was no proof whatsoever that the carp really drowned. Why should a carp drown in lake water? they asked. While hundreds of innocent fish were killed every Friday, they said, that stupid carp lived in comfort for months on the taxpayers' money and then was returned sound and healthy to the lake, where he is laughing at Chelm justice.

But only a few listened to these malicious words. They pointed out that months passed and the carp was never caught again, a sure sign that he was dead. It is true that the carp just might have decided to be careful and to avoid the fisherman's net. But how can a foolish carp who slaps Gronam Ox have such wisdom?

Just the same, to be on the safe side, the wise men of Chelm published a decree that if the nasty carp had refused to be drowned and was caught again, a special jail should be built for him, a pool where he would be kept prisoner for the rest of his life.

The decree was printed in capital letters in the official gazette of Chelm and signed by Gronam Ox and his five sages—Treitel Fool, Sender Donkey, Shmendrick Numskull, Zeinvel Ninny, and Dopey Lekisch.

Isaac Bashevis Singer (born 1904) came to America from Poland in 1935. Singer writes in his own native language, Yiddish. Then his stories are translated into other languages. Many of his stories are set in Poland. Singer uses humor to make points about human nature. He received the Nobel Prize for Literature in 1978.

Other books: *The Golem*
A Crown of Feathers

© 1986 Layle Silbert

Developing Comprehension Skills

1. What does the carp do to Gronam Ox?

2. Why does Gronam Ox take the carp's action as an insult?

3. What problem must Gronam Ox solve? Give two reasons why he takes so long.

4. How does Gronam Ox finally decide to punish the carp? In your opinion, is this really a punishment? Why or why not?

5. **Focus on Thinking: Drawing a Conclusion.** When you make a decision based on pieces of information, you are **drawing a conclusion.** Consider what you know about Gronam Ox. Find information that shows what most Chelmites think about him and his decisions. What conclusion can you draw about most Chelmites?

Reading Fiction

1. **Understanding Character.** Names in folk tales can suggest qualities of the characters. Explain what the names in this story suggest about the characters.

2. **Recognizing Humor.** Writers sometimes create humor by narrating foolish events in a very serious manner. Give an example of a foolish event that is treated seriously in this story.

3. **Examining Description.** The word choices an author makes can create humor. Find several adjectives that are used to describe the carp's personality. How do these words add to the humor of this story?

Critical Thinking

Examining a Generalization. A statement made about a whole group is called a **generalization.** Generalizations are not always true. Test a generalization by deciding if it is true for everyone in the group. The author calls Chelm a "city of fools." This generalization implies that everyone in the city of Chelm is a fool. Is everyone in Chelm a fool, or are there exceptions? Explain your answer.

Writing in Response to Literature

Imagine for a moment that you are the carp in the story. How do you feel about the way the Chelmites treat you? Write your view of their actions and decisions.

The Cat and the Golden Egg

LLOYD ALEXANDER

Quickset, a silver-gray cat, lived with Dame Agnes, a poor widow. Not only was he a cheerful companion, but clever at helping the old woman make ends meet. If the chimney smoked, he tied a bundle of twigs to his tail, climbed up the flue, and cleaned it with all the skill of the town sweep. He sharpened the old woman's knives and scissors, and mended her pots and pans neatly as any tinker. Did Dame Agnes knit, he held the skein of yarn; did she spin, he turned the spinning wheel.

Now, one morning Dame Agnes woke up with a bone-cracking rheumatism. Her joints creaked, her back ached, and her knees were so stiff she could no way get out of bed.

"My poor Quickset," she moaned, "today you and I must both go hungry."

At first, Quickset thought Dame Agnes meant it was the rheumatism that kept her from cooking breakfast, so he answered:

"Go hungry? No, indeed. You stay comfortable; I'll make us a little broiled sausage and soft boiled egg, and brew a pot of tea for you. Then I'll sit on your lap to warm you, and soon you'll be good as new."

Before Dame Agnes could say another word, he hurried to the pantry. But, opening the cupboard, he saw only bare shelves: not so much as a crust of bread or crumb of cheese; not even a dry bone or bacon rind.

"Mice!" he cried. "Eaten every scrap! They're out of hand, I've been too easy on them. I'll settle accounts with those fellows later. But now, mistress, I had best go to Master Grubble's market and buy what we need."

Dame Agnes thereupon burst into tears. "Oh, Quickset, it isn't mice, it's money. I have no more. Not a penny left for food or fuel."

"Why, mistress, you should have said something about that before now," replied Quickset. "I never would have let you come to such a state. No matter, I'll think of a way to fill your purse again. Meantime, I'll have Master Grubble give us our groceries on credit."

"Grubble? Give credit?" Dame Agnes exclaimed. "You know the only thing he gives is short weight at high prices. Alas for the days when the town had a dozen tradesmen and more: a baker, a butcher, a greengrocer, and all the others. But they're gone, thanks to Master Grubble. One by one, he's gobbled them up. Schemed and swindled them out of their businesses!

And now he's got the whole town under his thumb, for it's deal with Grubble or deal with no one."

"In that case," replied Quickset, "deal with him I will. Or, to put it better, he'll deal with me."

The old woman shook her head. "You'll still need money. And you shall have it, though I must do something I hoped I'd never have to do."

"Go to the linen chest," Dame Agnes went on. "At the bottom, under the good pillowslips, there's an old wool stocking. Fetch it out and bring it to me."

Puzzled, Quickset did as she asked. He found the stocking with a piece of string tied around the toe and carried it to Dame Agnes, who undid the knot, reached in and drew out one small gold coin.

"Mistress, that's more than enough," said Quickset. "Why did you fret so? With this, we can buy all we want."

Instead of being cheered by the gold piece in her hand, Dame Agnes only sighed:

"This is the last of the small savings my dear husband left to me. I've kept it all these years, and promised myself never to spend it."

"Be glad you did keep it," said Quickset, "for now's the time you need it most."

"I didn't put this by for myself," Dame Agnes replied. "It was for you. I meant to leave it to you in my will. It was to be your legacy, a little something until you found another home. But I see I shall have to spend it. Once gone, it's gone, and that's the end of everything."

At this, Dame Agnes began sobbing again. But Quickset reassured her:

"No need for tears. I'll see to this matter. Only let me have that gold piece a little while. I'll strike such a bargain with

Master Grubble that we'll fill our pantry with meat and drink a-plenty. Indeed, he'll beg me to keep the money and won't ask a penny, that I promise."

"Master Grubble, I fear, will be more than a match even for you," Dame Agnes replied. Nevertheless, she did as Quickset urged, put the coin in a leather purse, and hung it around his neck.

Quickset hurried through town to the market, where he

found Master Grubble sitting on a high stool behind the counter. For all that his shelves were loaded with victuals of every kind, with meats, and vegetables, and fruits, Grubble looked as though he had never sampled his own wares. There was more fat on his bacon than on himself. He was lean-shanked and sharp-eyed, his nose narrow as a knife blade. His mouth was pursed and puckered as if he had been sipping vinegar, and his cheeks as mottled as moldy cheese. At sight of Quickset, the storekeeper never so much as climbed down from his stool to wait on his customer, but only made a sour face; and, in a voice equally sour, demanded:

"And what do you want? Half a pound of mouse tails? A sack of catnip? Out! No loitering! I don't cater to the cat trade."

Despite this curdled welcome, Quickset bowed and politely explained that Dame Agnes was ailing and he had come shopping in her stead.

"Sick she must be," snorted Master Grubble, "to send a cat marketing, without even a shopping basket. How do you mean to carry off what you buy? Push it along the street with your nose?"

"Why, sir," Quickset answered, "I thought you might send your shop boy around with the parcels. I'm sure you'll do it gladly when you see the handsome order to be filled. Dame Agnes needs a joint of beef, a shoulder of mutton, five pounds of your best sausage, a dozen of the largest eggs—"

"Not so fast," broke in the storekeeper. "Joints and shoulders, is it? Sausage and eggs? Is that what you want? Then I'll tell you what I want: cash on the counter, paid in full. Or you, my fine cat, won't have so much as a wart from one of my pickles."

"You'll be paid," Quickset replied, "and very well paid.

But now I see your prices, I'm not sure I brought enough money with me."

"So that's your game!" cried Grubble. "Well, go and get enough. I'll do business with you then, and not before."

"It's a weary walk home and back again," said Quickset. "Allow me a minute or two and I'll have money to spare. And, Master Grubble, if you'd be so kind as to lend me an egg."

"Egg?" retorted Grubble. "What's that to do with paying my bill?"

"You'll see," Quickset answered. "I guarantee you'll get all that's owing to you."

Grubble at first refused and again ordered Quickset from the shop. Only when the cat promised to pay double the price of the groceries, as well as an extra fee for the use of the egg, did the storekeeper grudgingly agree.

Taking the egg from Master Grubble, Quickset placed it on the floor, then carefully settled himself on top of it.

"Fool!" cried Grubble. "What are you doing? Get off my egg! This cat's gone mad, and thinks he's a chicken!"

Quickset said nothing, but laid back his ears and waved his tail, warning Grubble to keep silent. After another moment, Quickset got up and brought the egg to the counter:

"There, Master Grubble, that should be enough."

"What?" shouted the storekeeper. "Idiot cat! You mean to pay me with my own egg?"

"With better than that, as you'll see," answered Quickset. While Grubble fumed, Quickset neatly cracked the shell and poured the contents into a bowl. At this, Grubble ranted all the more:

"Alley rabbit! Smash my egg, will you? I'll rub your nose in it!"

Suddenly Master Grubble's voice choked in his gullet. His

eyes popped as he stared into the bowl. There, with the broken egg, lay a gold piece.

Instantly, he snatched it out. "What's this?"

"What does it look like?" returned Quickset.

Grubble squinted at the coin, flung it onto the counter and listened to it ring. He bit it, peered closer, turned it round and round in his fingers, and finally blurted:

"Gold!"

Grubble, in his fit of temper, had never seen Quickset slip the coin from the purse and deftly drop it into the bowl. Awestruck, he gaped at the cat, then lowered his voice to a whisper:

"How did you do that?"

Quickset merely shook his head and shrugged his tail. At last, as the excited storekeeper pressed him for an answer, he winked one eye and calmly replied:

"Now, now, Master Grubble, a cat has trade secrets just as a storekeeper. I don't ask yours, you don't ask mine. If I told you how simple it is, you'd know as much as I do. And if others found out—"

"Tell me!" cried Grubble. "I won't breathe a word to a living soul. My dear cat, listen to me," he hurried on. "You'll have all the victuals you want. For a month! A year! Forever! Here, this very moment, I'll have my boy take a cartload to your mistress. Only teach me to sit on eggs as you did."

"Easily done," said Quickset. "But what about that gold piece?"

"Take it!" cried Grubble, handing the coin to Quickset. "Take it, by all means."

Quickset pretended to think over the bargain, then answered:

"Agreed. But you must do exactly as I tell you."

Grubble nodded and his eyes glittered. "One gold piece from one egg. But what if I used two eggs? Or three, or four, or five?"

"As many as you like," said Quickset. "A basketful, if it suits you."

Without another moment's delay, Grubble called his boy from the storeroom and told him to deliver all that Quickset ordered to the house of Dame Agnes. Then, whimpering with pleasure, he filled his biggest basket with every egg in the store.

His nose twitched, his hands trembled, and his usually sallow face turned an eager pink.

"Now," said Quickset, "so you won't be disturbed, take your basket to the top shelf and sit on it there. One thing more, the most important. Until those eggs hatch, don't say a single word. If you have anything to tell me, whatever the reason, you must only cluck like a chicken. Nothing else, mind you. Cackle all you like; speak but once, and the spell is broken."

"What about my customers? Who's to wait on them?" asked Grubble, unwilling to lose business even in exchange for a fortune.

"Never fear," said Quickset. "I'll mind the store."

"What a fine cat you are," purred Grubble. "Noble animal. Intelligent creature."

With that, gleefully chuckling and licking his lips, he clambered to the top shelf, hauling his heavy burden along with him. There he squatted gingerly over the basket, so cramped that he was obliged to draw his knees under his chin and fold his arms as tightly as he could; until indeed he looked much like a skinny, long-beaked chicken hunched on a nest.

Below, Quickset no sooner had taken his place on the stool than Mistress Libbet, the carpenter's wife, stepped through the door.

"Why, Quickset, what are you doing here?" said she. "Have you gone into trade? And can that be Master Grubble on the shelf? I swear he looks as if he's sitting on a basket of eggs."

"Pay him no mind," whispered Quickset. "He fancies himself a hen. An odd notion, but harmless. However, since Master Grubble is busy nesting, I'm tending shop for him. So, Mistress Libbet, how may I serve you?"

"There's so much our little ones need," Mistress Libbett sighed unhappily. "And nothing we can afford to feed them. I was hoping Master Grubble had some scraps or trimmings."

"He has much better," said Quickset, pulling down one of the juiciest hams and slicing away at it with Grubble's carving knife. "Here's a fine bargain today: only a penny a pound."

Hearing this, Master Grubble was about to protest, but caught himself in the nick of time. Instead, he began furiously clucking and squawking:

"Cut-cut-cut! Aw-cut!"

"What's that you say?" Quickset glanced up at the agitated storekeeper and cupped an ear with his paw. "Cut more? Yes, yes, I understand. The price is still too high? Very well, if you insist: two pounds for a penny."

Too grateful to question such generosity on the part of Grubble, Mistress Libbet flung a penny onto the counter and seized her ham without waiting for Quickset to wrap it. As she hurried from the store, the tailor's wife and the stonecutter's daughter came in; and, a moment later, Dame Gerton, the laundrywoman.

"Welcome, ladies," called Quickset. "Welcome, one and all. Here's fine prime meats, fine fresh vegetables on sale today. At these prices, they won't last long. So, hurry! Step up!"

As the delighted customers pressed eagerly toward the counter, Master Grubble's face changed from sallow to crimson, from crimson to purple. Cackling frantically, he waggled his head and flapped his elbows against his ribs.

"Cut-aw-cut!" he bawled. "Cut-cut-aw! Cuck-cuck! Cock-a-doodle-do!"

Once more, Quickset made a great show of listening carefully:

"Did I hear you a-right, Master Grubble? Give all? Free? What a generous soul you are!"

With that, Quickset began hurling meats, cheese, vegetables, and loaves of sugar into the customers' outstretched baskets. Grubble's face now turned from purple to bilious green. He crowed, clucked, brayed, and bleated until he sounded like a barnyard gone mad.

"Give more?" cried Quickset. "I'm doing my best!"

"Cut-aw!" shouted Grubble and away went a chain of sausages. "Ak-ak-cut-aak!" And away went another joint of beef. At last, he could stand no more:

"Stop! Stop!" he roared. "Wretched cat! You'll drive me out of business!"

Beside himself with fury, Master Grubble forgot his cramped quarters and sprang to his feet. His head struck the ceiling and he tumbled back into the basket of eggs. As he struggled to free himself from the flood of shattered yolks, the shelf cracked beneath him and he went plummeting headlong into a barrel of flour.

"Robber!" stormed Grubble, crawling out and shaking a fist at Quickset. "Swindler! You promised I'd hatch gold from eggs!"

"What's that?" put in the tailor's wife. "Gold from eggs? Master Grubble, you're as foolish as you're greedy."

"But a fine cackler," added the laundrywoman, flapping her arms. "Let's hear it again, your cut-cut-awk!"

"I warned you not to speak a word," Quickset told the storekeeper, who was egg-soaked at one end and floured at the other. "But you did. And so you broke the spell. Why, look at you, Master Grubble. You nearly turned yourself into a dipped pork chop. Have a care. Someone might fry you."

With that, Quickset went home to breakfast.

As for Master Grubble, when word spread that he had been so roundly tricked, and so easily, he became such a laughingstock that he left town and was never seen again. At the urging of the townsfolk, Dame Agnes and Quickset took charge of the market, and ran it well and fairly. All agreed that Quickset was the cleverest cat in the world. And, since Quickset had the same opinion, it was surely true.

Lloyd Alexander (born 1924) has loved hero tales since he first read about King Arthur. While in the army, he grew to love the country of Wales. His interest in Welsh folklore led to his writing a set of fantasy books known as the Prydain chronicles. *The High King* won a Newbery Medal. *The Black Cauldron* was made into a movie.

Other books: *Coll and His White Pig*
Time Cat

Developing Comprehension Skills

1. What do you learn about Quickset's personality at the beginning of the story?

2. Why is Master Grubble's market the only store in town? How does this affect his prices?

3. Draw a time line like the one on page 7 to show the order of events in Quickset's trick. List at least four main events.

4. Why does Quickset tell Master Grubble that the spell will be broken if Grubble speaks?

5. Is Quickset a good judge of character? How do you know?

6. **Focus on Thinking: Recognizing an Effect.** An **effect** is the result of another event or action. After Quickset's trick, everyone laughs at Master Grubble. What effect does their laughter have on him?

Reading Fiction

1. **Appreciating Description.** You can learn about characters from the writer's description of them. Find the paragraph that describes Master Grubble when Quickset first sees him. What details of his appearance fit his personality?

2. **Recognizing Elements of a Folk Tale.** In many folk tales, animals are important characters. They are given qualities of people. In what ways is Quickset more like a person than a cat?

Study and Research

Using an Encyclopedia. Encyclopedias are useful resources for finding information. They are often found in the reference section of the library. Read the entry for *monopoly* in an encyclopedia. Then answer these questions: Is Master Grubble's business a monopoly? What is the effect of a monopoly on a consumer?

Writing in Response to Literature

Making someone a laughingstock can be seen as funny or as cruel. Write about a time when you saw or experienced this type of behavior. Explain how you felt.

Which was your favorite fairy tale when you were growing up? Have fun with this modern version of a traditional tale.

Dragon, Dragon

JOHN GARDNER

There was once a king whose kingdom was plagued by a dragon. The king did not know which way to turn. The king's knights were all cowards who hid under their beds whenever the dragon came in sight, so they were of no use to the king at all. And the king's wizard could not help either because, being old, he had forgotten his magic spells. Nor could the wizard look up the spells that had slipped his mind, for he had unfortunately misplaced his wizard's book many years before. The king was at his wit's end.

Every time there was a full moon the dragon came out of his lair and ravaged the countryside. He frightened maidens and stopped up chimneys and broke store windows and set people's clocks back and made dogs bark until no one could hear himself think.

He tipped over fences and robbed graves and put frogs in people's drinking water and tore the last chapters out of novels and changed house numbers around.

He stole spark plugs out of people's cars, and put firecrackers in people's cigars, and stole the clappers from all the church bells, and sprung every bear trap for miles around so the bears could wander wherever they pleased.

And to top it all off, he changed around all the roads in the kingdom so that people could not get anywhere except by starting out in the wrong direction.

"That," said the king in a fury, "is enough!" And he called a meeting of everyone in the kingdom.

Now it happened that there lived in the kingdom a wise old cobbler who had a wife and three sons. The cobbler and his family came to the king's meeting and stood way in back by the door, for the cobbler had a feeling that since he was nobody important there had probably been some mistake, and no doubt the king had intended the meeting for everyone in the kingdom except his family and him.

"Ladies and gentlemen," said the king when everyone was present, "I've put up with that dragon as long as I can. He has got to be stopped."

All the people whispered amongst themselves, and the king smiled, pleased with the impression he had made.

But the wise cobbler said gloomily, "It's all very well to talk about it—but how are you going to do it?"

And now all the people smiled and winked as if to say, "Well, King, he's got you there!"

The king frowned.

"It's not that His Majesty hasn't tried," the queen spoke up loyally.

"Yes," said the king, "I've told my knights again and again that they ought to slay that dragon. But I can't force them to go. I'm not a tyrant."

"Why doesn't the wizard say a magic spell?" asked the cobbler.

"He's done the best he can," said the king.

The wizard blushed, and everyone looked embarrassed. "I used to do all sorts of spells and chants when I was younger," the wizard explained. "But I've lost my spell book, and I begin to fear I'm losing my memory too. For instance, I've been trying for days to recall one spell I used to do. I forget, just now, what the deuce it was for. It went something like—

> Bimble,
> Wimble,
> Cha, Cha
> CHOOMPF!

Suddenly, to everyone's surprise, the queen turned into a rosebush.

"Oh dear," said the wizard.

"Now you've done it," groaned the king.

"Poor Mother," said the princess.

"I don't know what can have happened," the wizard said nervously, "but don't worry, I'll have her changed back in a jiffy." He shut his eyes and racked his brain for a spell that would change her back.

But the king said quickly, "You'd better leave well enough alone. If you change her into a rattlesnake, we'll have to chop off her head."

Meanwhile the cobbler stood with his hands in his pockets, sighing at the waste of time. "About the dragon . . ." he began.

"Oh yes," said the king. "I'll tell you what I'll do. I'll give the princess's hand in marriage to anyone who can make the dragon stop."

"It's not enough," said the cobbler. "She's a nice enough girl, you understand. But how would an ordinary person support her? Also, what about those of us that are already married?"

The Medieval Castle, 1985, BILL BELL. Photograph: Jaro Art Galleries, New York City.

"In that case," said the king, "I'll offer the princess's hand, or half the kingdom, or both—whichever is most convenient."

The cobbler scratched his chin and considered it. "It's not enough," he said at last. "It's a good enough kingdom, you understand, but it's too much responsibility."

"Take it or leave it," the king said.

"I'll leave it," said the cobbler. And he shrugged and went home.

But the cobbler's eldest son thought the bargain was a good one, for the princess was very beautiful and he liked the idea of having half the kingdom to run as he pleased. So he said to the king, "I'll accept those terms, Your Majesty. By tomorrow morning the dragon will be slain."

"Bless you!" cried the king.

"Hooray, hooray, hooray!" cried all the people, throwing their hats in the air.

The cobbler's eldest son beamed with pride, and the second eldest looked at him enviously. The youngest son said timidly, "Excuse me, Your Majesty, but don't you think the queen looks a little unwell? If I were you, I think I'd water her."

"Good heavens," cried the king, glancing at the queen who had been changed into a rosebush, "I'm glad you mentioned it!"

Now the cobbler's eldest son was very clever and was known far and wide for how quickly he could multiply fractions in his head. He was perfectly sure he could slay the dragon by somehow or other playing a trick on him, and he didn't feel that he needed his wise old father's advice. But he thought it was only polite to ask, and so he went to his father, who was working as usual at his cobbler's bench, and said, "Well, Father, I'm off to slay the dragon. Have you any advice to give me?"

The cobbler thought a moment and replied, "When and if you come to the dragon's lair, recite the following poem.

> *Dragon, dragon, how do you do?*
> *I've come from the king to murder you.*

Say it very loudly and firmly and the dragon will fall, God willing, at your feet."

"How curious!" said the eldest son. And he thought to himself, "The old man is not as wise as I thought. If I say something like that to the dragon, he will eat me up in an instant. The way to kill a dragon is to out-fox him." And keeping his opinion to himself, the eldest son set forth on his quest.

When he came at last to the dragon's lair, which was a cave, the eldest son slyly disguised himself as a peddler and knocked on the door and called out, "Hello there!"

"There's nobody home!" roared a voice.

The voice was as loud as an earthquake, and the eldest son's knees knocked together in terror.

"I don't come to trouble you," the eldest son said meekly. "I merely thought you might be interested in looking at some of our brushes. Or if you'd prefer," he added quickly, "I could leave our catalog with you and I could drop by again, say, early next week."

"I don't want any brushes," the voice roared, "and I especially don't want any brushes next week."

"Oh," said the eldest son. By now his knees were knocking together so badly that he had to sit down.

Suddenly a great shadow fell over him, and the eldest son looked up. It was the dragon. The eldest son drew his sword, but the dragon lunged and swallowed him in a single gulp, sword and all, and the eldest son found himself in the dark of the dragon's belly. "What a fool I was not to listen to my wise old father!" thought the eldest son. And he began to weep bitterly.

"Well," sighed the king the next morning, "I see the dragon has not been slain yet."

"I'm just as glad, personally," said the princess, sprinkling the queen. "I would have had to marry that eldest son, and he had warts."

Now the cobbler's middle son decided it was his turn to try. The middle son was very strong and was known far and wide for being able to lift up the corner of a church. He felt perfectly sure he could slay the dragon by simply laying into him, but he thought it would be only polite to ask his father's advice. So he went to his father and said to him, "Well, Father, I'm off to slay the dragon. Have you any advice for me?"

The cobbler told the middle son exactly what he'd told the eldest.

"When and if you come to the dragon's lair, recite the following poem.

> *Dragon, dragon, how do you do?*
> *I've come from the king to murder you.*

Say it very loudly and firmly, and the dragon will fall, God willing, at your feet."

"What an odd thing to say," thought the middle son. "The old man is not as wise as I thought. You have to take these dragons by surprise." But he kept his opinion to himself and set forth.

When he came in sight of the dragon's lair, the middle son spurred his horse to a gallop and thundered into the entrance swinging his sword with all his might.

But the dragon had seen him while he was still a long way off, and being very clever, the dragon had crawled up on top of

The Medieval Castle (detail), 1985, BILL BELL. Photograph: Jaro Art Galleries, New York City.

the door so that when the son came charging in, he went under the dragon and on to the back of the cave and slammed into the wall. Then the dragon chuckled and got down off the door, taking his time, and strolled back to where the man and the horse lay unconscious from the terrific blow. Opening his mouth as if for a yawn, the dragon swallowed the middle son in a single gulp and put the horse in the freezer to eat another day.

"What a fool I was not to listen to my wise old father," thought the middle son when he came to in the dragon's belly. And he too began to weep bitterly.

That night there was a full moon, and the dragon ravaged the countryside so terribly that several families moved to another kingdom.

"Well," sighed the king in the morning, "still no luck in this dragon business, I see."

"I'm just as glad, myself," said the princess, moving her mother, pot and all, to the window where the sun could get at her. "The cobbler's middle son was a kind of humpback."

Now the cobbler's youngest son saw that his turn had come. He was very upset and nervous, and he wished he had never been born. He was not clever, like his eldest brother, and he was not strong, like his second-eldest brother. He was a decent, honest boy who always minded his elders.

He borrowed a suit of armor from a friend of his who was a knight, and when the youngest son put the armor on, it was so heavy he could hardly walk. From another knight he borrowed a sword, and that was so heavy that the only way the youngest son could get it to the dragon's lair was to drag it along behind his horse like a plow.

When everything was in readiness, the youngest son went for a last conversation with his father.

"Father, have you any advice to give me?" he asked.

"Only this," said the cobbler. "When and if you come to the dragon's lair, recite the following poem.

> *Dragon, dragon, how do you do?*
> *I've come from the king to murder you.*

Say it very loudly and firmly, and the dragon will fall, God willing, at your feet."

"Are you certain?" asked the youngest son uneasily.

"As certain as one can ever be in these matters," said the wise old cobbler.

And so the youngest son set forth on his quest. He traveled over hill and dale and at last came to the dragon's cave.

The dragon, who had seen the cobbler's youngest son while he was still a long way off, was seated up above the door, inside the cave, waiting and smiling to himself. But minutes passed, and no one came thundering in. The dragon frowned, puzzled, and was tempted to peek out. However, reflecting that patience seldom goes unrewarded, the dragon kept his head up

out of sight and went on waiting. At last, when he could stand
it no longer, the dragon craned his neck and looked. There at
the entrance of the cave stood a trembling young man in a suit
of armor twice his size, struggling with a sword so heavy he
could lift only one end of it at a time.

At sight of the dragon, the cobbler's youngest son began to
tremble so violently that his armor rattled like a house caving
in. He heaved with all his might at the sword and got the
handle up level with his chest, but even now the point was
down in the dirt. As loudly and firmly as he could manage, the
youngest son cried—

> *Dragon, dragon, how do you do?*
> *I've come from the king to murder you.*

"What?" cried the dragon, flabbergasted. "You? *You?*
Murder *Me???*" All at once he began to laugh, pointing at the
little cobbler's son. *"He he he ho ha!"* he roared, shaking all
over, and tears filled his eyes. *"He he he ho ho ho ha ha!"*
laughed the dragon. He was laughing so hard he had to hang
onto his sides, and he fell off the door and landed on his back,
still laughing, kicking his legs helplessly, rolling from side to
side, laughing and laughing and laughing.

The cobbler's son was annoyed. "I *do* come from the king
to murder you," he said. "A person doesn't like to be laughed
at for a thing like that."

"He he he!" wailed the dragon, almost sobbing, gasping for
breath. "Of course not, poor dear boy! But really, *he he,* the
idea of it, *ha ha ha!* And that simply ri*dic*ulous *poem!*" Tears
streamed from the dragon's eyes, and he lay on his back
perfectly helpless with laughter.

"It's a good poem," said the cobbler's youngest son
loyally. "My father made it up." And growing angrier he

The Medieval Castle (detail), 1985, BILL BELL. Photograph: Jaro Art Galleries, New York City.

shouted, "I want you to stop that laughing, or I'll—I'll—" But the dragon could not stop for the life of him. And suddenly, in a terrific rage, the cobbler's son began flopping the sword end over end in the direction of the dragon. Sweat ran off the youngest son's forehead, but he labored on, blistering mad, and at last, with one supreme heave, he had the sword standing on its handle a foot from the dragon's throat. Of its own weight the sword fell, slicing the dragon's head off.

"He he ho huk," went the dragon—and then he lay dead.

The two older brothers crawled out and thanked their younger brother for saving their lives. "We have learned our lesson," they said.

Then the three brothers gathered all the treasures from the dragon's cave and tied them to the back end of the youngest brother's horse, and tied the dragon's head on behind the treasures, and started home. "I'm glad I listened to my father," the youngest son thought. "Now I'll be the richest man in the kingdom."

There were hand-carved picture frames and silver spoons and boxes of jewels and chests of money and silver compasses and maps telling where there were more treasures buried when these ran out. There was also a curious old book with a picture of an owl on the cover, and inside, poems and odd sentences and recipes that seemed to make no sense.

When they reached the king's castle, the people all leaped for joy to see that the dragon was dead, and the princess ran out and kissed the youngest brother on the forehead, for secretly she had hoped it would be him.

"Well," said the king, "which half of the kingdom do you want?"

"My wizard's book!" exclaimed the wizard. "He's found my wizard's book!" He opened the book and ran his finger along under the words and then said in a loud voice, "Glmuzk, shkzmlp, blam!"

Instantly the queen stood before them in her natural shape, except she was soaking wet from being sprinkled too often. She glared at the king.

"Oh dear," said the king, hurrying toward the door.

John Gardner (1933–1982) grew up on a dairy farm in Batavia, New York. He became a professor of medieval literature and creative writing. Gardner is best known for the books he wrote for adults. These include poems, tales, novels, and essays. He died in a motorcycle accident at the age of forty-nine.

Other books: *Gudgekin the Thistle Girl*
The King of the Hummingbirds and Other Tales

Developing Comprehension Skills

1. What is the king's problem? Why can neither the knights nor the wizard solve the problem?

2. Name several terrible deeds the dragon does. Which deed finally causes the king to call a meeting?

3. What plan does each of the older sons use to attack the dragon? How does each plan reflect that son's particular talent?

4. How does each son react to his father's advice? Why does the youngest son follow the advice?

5. In the story, the father is described as wise. Do you think his actions and statements are those of a wise person? Tell why or why not.

6. **Focus on Thinking: Understanding Cause.** An event may have more than one cause. What final events cause the dragon to die?

Reading Fiction

1. **Recognizing Elements of a Folk Tale.** In this tale, the youngest of three brothers saves the day. The successful youngest child is a common character in folk tales. Name two other ways this tale is like traditional tales.

2. **Understanding a Modern Tale.** Modern writers sometimes create humor by changing the elements of folk tales. They may also include details that do not fit the time period. Find three ways this tale is unlike traditional tales.

3. **Appreciating Humor.** Picturing a scene in your mind helps you appreciate its humor. Reread the dragon's death scene. What details make it humorous?

Speaking and Listening

Interpreting a Character. You can interpret, or express understanding of a character, by acting as if you were that character. Pretend that you are a character in this story. Tell what happens to you. Use *I* and *me* instead of *he* or *she*.

Writing in Response to Literature

What do you think the queen will say to the king after the story ends? Write a short conversation that they might have.

Language and Literature

Vocabulary

Suffixes. You can unlock the meanings of some words by combining the meanings of the base word and the suffix. For example, Gronam Ox called the carp *malicious*. The base word *malice* means "ill will." Since the suffix *-ous* means "full of," *malicious* means "full of ill will."

Learn the meanings of these common suffixes.

-ous (full of)   *-less* (without)   *-able* (can be; having)

Exercise. Replace each phrase in parentheses with a single word. The word should combine the underlined base word with a suffix from above. Then read the paragraph using the new words.

Tic's life was often (full of peril). Once, he and his brother Tac, a (having respect) wizard, were ordered to amuse the king. (Without fear) Tic lay down in a (having comfort) box, which Tac split in half. When Tac later introduced Tic as his half brother, the king was (without speech).

Developing Writing Skills

Presenting an Opinion. What is mildly funny to one person may be hilarious to someone else. Which of the last three stories do you think is the funniest? Write your opinion and support it with reasons.

Prewriting. Decide which story you felt was funniest. Picture in your mind the funny scenes. Find and jot down the details in the story that you feel create the humor.

Drafting. Give your opinion in a topic sentence. Then use the examples and details from your notes to explain your opinion. End by summing up your feelings.

Revising and Sharing. Your opinion should be clearly stated. Make sure you have at least three examples to support it. Share your opinion.

Reading Poetry

What Is Poetry?

Poetry is a form of literature that uses words in a special way. The words can tell a story or describe a picture. They can express an idea or a feeling. A poem can even have a special sound, like music. Because it is written in lines, poetry has a special look. The language, sound, and look of poetry create its magic.

The Elements of Poetry

Certain elements or features found in poetry make it easy to identify. These elements include form, rhyme, and rhythm.

Form. The form of a poem is the way it looks on a page. The words in poetry are arranged in lines. These lines may or may not be complete sentences. Groups of lines are called **stanzas.** Stanzas in poetry are like paragraphs in other kinds of writing.

Rhyme. Words that end in the same syllable sound are said to **rhyme.** *Unfair* and *prepare* rhyme, for example. Some poems use rhyming words at the ends of lines. This use of rhyme can form a pattern. Patterns of rhyme are often repeated throughout a poem.

Read the first stanza from "Paul Revere's Ride" by Henry Wadsworth Longfellow. Which lines rhyme with each other?

Listen, my children, and you shall hear
Of the midnight ride of Paul Revere,
On the eighteenth of April, in Seventy-five;
Hardly a man is now alive
Who remembers that famous day and year.

Rhythm. Like music, a poem has a beat or rhythm. **Rhythm** is the pattern of strong beats you hear when you read a poem aloud. An even beat gives the poem a musical sound. Some poems have an even, regular beat. In others, the rhythm sounds more like normal conversation.

Read aloud these lines from "Dorlan's Home Walk" by Arthur Guiterman. Tap out the rhythm as you read. How many strong beats do you hear in each line? Do you notice a pattern to the rhythm?

> The ninth; last half; the score was tied,
>   The hour was big with fate,
> For Neal had fanned and Kling had flied
>   When Dorlan toed the plate.

Narrative Poetry

Storytellers of long ago found that rhyme and rhythm made their stories easier to remember. For this reason, they often told stories in the form of poems. A poem that tells a story is called a **narrative poem.** It has features of both a story and a poem. As a story, a narrative poem has characters, a setting, and a plot. As a poem, it may have patterns of rhyme and rhythm.

How to Read Narrative Poems

When you read a narrative poem, try to picture the setting and characters. Make sure you understand what is happening as the plot unfolds. Listen for a pattern in the rhythm. Listen also to the sounds of the words. Look for a pattern of rhyming words. Notice how the rhyme and rhythm affect the way you feel. Most of all, enjoy the tale each poet tells.

When were you tricked into doing something? In this poem, see who gets tricked and who gets a treat.

The Walrus and the Carpenter

LEWIS CARROLL

The sun was shining on the sea,
    Shining with all his might:
He did his very best to make
    The billows smooth and bright—
And this was odd, because it was   5
    The middle of the night.

The moon was shining sulkily,
    Because she thought the sun
Had got no business to be there
    After the day was done—   10
"It's very rude of him," she said,
    "To come and spoil the fun!"

The sea was wet as wet could be,
    The sands were dry as dry.
You could not see a cloud, because   15
    No cloud was in the sky:
No birds were flying overhead—
    There were no birds to fly.

The Walrus and the Carpenter
    Were walking close at hand;   20
They wept like anything to see
    Such quantities of sand:
"If this were only cleared away,"
    They said, "it *would* be grand!"

"If seven maids with seven mops
    Swept it for half a year,
Do you suppose," the Walrus said,
    "That they could get it clear?"
"I doubt it," said the Carpenter,
    And shed a bitter tear.   30

"O Oysters, come and walk with us!"
    The Walrus did beseech.
"A pleasant walk, a pleasant talk,
    Along the briny beach:
We cannot do with more than four,   35
    To give a hand to each."

The eldest Oyster looked at him
    But never a word he said:
The eldest Oyster winked his eye,
    And shook his heavy head—   40
Meaning to say he did not choose
    To leave the oyster-bed.

But four young Oysters hurried up,
    All eager for the treat:
Their coats were brushed, their faces washed, 45
    Their shoes were clean and neat—

And this was odd, because, you know,
    They hadn't any feet.

Four other Oysters followed them,
    And yet another four: 50
And thick and fast they came at last,
    And more, and more, and more—
All hopping through the frothy waves,
    And scrambling to the shore.

The Walrus and the Carpenter   55
    Walked on a mile or so,
And then they rested on a rock
    Conveniently low:
And all the little Oysters stood
    And waited in a row.   60

"The time has come," the Walrus said,
    "To talk of many things:

Of shoes—and ships—and sealing-wax—
　　Of cabbages—and kings—
And why the sea is boiling hot—　　　　　65
　　And whether pigs have wings."

"But wait a bit," the Oysters cried,
　　"Before we have our chat;
For some of us are out of breath,
　　And all of us are fat!"　　　　　　　70
"No hurry!" said the Carpenter.
　　They thanked him much for that.

"A loaf of bread," the Walrus said,
　　"Is what we chiefly need:
Pepper and vinegar besides　　　　　　75
　　Are very good indeed—
Now, if you're ready, Oysters dear,
　　We can begin to feed."

"But not on us!" the Oysters cried,
　　Turning a little blue.　　　　　　　80
"After such kindness, that would be
　　A dismal thing to do!"
"The night is fine," the Walrus said.
　　"Do you admire the view?"

"It was so kind of you to come!　　　　85
　　And you are very nice!"
The Carpenter said nothing but
　　"Cut us another slice.
I wish you were not quite so deaf—
　　I've had to ask you twice!"　　　　90

"It seems a shame," the Walrus said,
    "To play them such a trick,
After we've brought them out so far,
    And made them trot so quick!"
The Carpenter said nothing but   95
    "The butter's spread too thick!"

"I weep for you," the Walrus said:
    "I deeply sympathize."
With sobs and tears he sorted out
    Those of the largest size,   100
Holding his pocket-handkerchief
    Before his streaming eyes.

"O Oysters," said the Carpenter,
    "You've had a pleasant run!
Shall we be trotting home again?"   105
    But answer came there none—
And this was scarcely odd, because
    They'd eaten every one.

Lewis Carroll (1832–1898) was the pen name for
Charles Lutwidge Dodgson, a mathematician from
England. He wrote the well-known classic *Alice in
Wonderland* to entertain a friend's daughter, Alice.
"The Walrus and the Carpenter" came from the
sequel *Through the Looking Glass*. Carroll's books have
been translated into almost every language.

Developing Comprehension Skills

1. What odd thing is happening in the first stanza?

2. What invitation do the Walrus and the Carpenter extend to the oysters?

3. Near the end, the Walrus cries for the oysters. Meanwhile, what is he doing to them? Do his actions suit his words?

4. What do you think of the Walrus? Is he clever, ordinary, funny, or cruel? Give reasons for your opinion.

5. **Focus on Thinking: Examining the Details.** Details, or small bits of information, can make writing serious or ridiculous. Examine the details in this poem and decide if the poem is serious or ridiculous. Give examples to support your answer.

Reading Poetry

1. **Recognizing Rhyme Patterns.** In some poems, each stanza has the same pattern of rhyme. Which lines rhyme in the first stanza of this poem? Is this pattern repeated in any other stanzas? If so, in which ones?

2. **Hearing Rhythm.** In many poems you can hear a rhythm, or pattern of strong beats. Read these lines aloud, and decide which words should receive a strong beat.

> The sea was wet as wet could be,
> The sands were dry as dry.

Find another pair of lines in the poem that has the same pattern of strong beats.

3. **Understanding Narrative Poetry.** Like any story, a narrative poem has characters and a setting. Identify the characters and setting of this poem.

Speaking and Listening

Reading Poems Aloud. Humorous poems are even more enjoyable when they are read aloud. Work in groups to prepare an oral reading of this poem. Decide on a proper tone of voice for each speaker. As you read, let your voice bring out the repeated sounds and the regular rhythm of the poem.

Writing in Response to Literature

The old oyster chooses not to join the Walrus and the Carpenter. Write what he might say when he hears what happened.

The Cremation of Sam McGee

ROBERT SERVICE

Dawn Over the Yukon, 1907, TED HARRISON. Illustration from *The Cremation of Sam McGee*. By permission of Wm. Morrow & Company, New York City.

There are strange things done in the midnight sun
　By the men who moil for gold;
The Arctic trails have their secret tales
　That would make your blood run cold;
The Northern Lights have seen queer sights,　　5
　But the queerest they ever did see
Was that night on the marge of Lake Lebarge
　I cremated Sam McGee.

Now Sam McGee was from Tennessee,
    where the cotton blooms and blows. 10
Why he left his home in the South to roam
    'round the Pole, God only knows.
He was always cold, but the land of gold
    seemed to hold him like a spell;
Though he'd often say in his homely way 15
    that he'd "sooner live in Hell."

On a Christmas Day we were mushing our way
    over the Dawson trail.
Talk of your cold! through the parka's fold
    it stabbed like a driven nail. 20
If our eyes we'd close, then the lashes froze
    till sometimes we couldn't see,
It wasn't much fun, but the only one
    to whimper was Sam McGee.

And that very night, as we lay packed tight 25
    in our robes beneath the snow,
And the dogs were fed, and the stars o'erhead
    were dancing heel and toe,
He turned to me, and "Cap," says he,
    "I'll cash in this trip, I guess; 30
And if I do, I'm asking that you
    won't refuse my last request."

Well, he seemed so low that I couldn't say no;
    then he says with a sort of moan,
"It's the cursed cold, and it's got right hold 35
    till I'm chilled clean through to the bone.

Yet 'taint being dead—it's my awful dread
    of the icy grave that pains;
So I want you to swear that, foul or fair,
    you'll cremate my last remains."   40

A pal's last need is a thing to heed,
    so I swore I would not fail;
And we started on at the streak of dawn;
    but God! he looked ghastly pale.
He crouched on the sleigh, and he raved all day   45
    of his home in Tennessee;
And before nightfall a corpse was all
    that was left of Sam McGee.

There wasn't a breath in that land of death,
    and I hurried, horror-driven,   50
With a corpse half hid that I couldn't get rid,
    because of a promise given;
It was lashed to the sleigh, and it seemed to say:
    "You may tax your brawn and brains,
But you promised true, and it's up to you   55
    to cremate these last remains."

Now a promise made is a debt unpaid,
    and the trail has its own stern code.
In the days to come, though my lips were dumb,
    in my heart how I cursed that load!   60
In the long, long night, by the lone firelight,
    while the huskies, round in a ring,
Howled out their woes to the homeless snows—
    Oh God, how I loathed the thing!

And every day that quiet clay 65
    seemed to heavy and heavier grow;
And on I went, though the dogs were spent
    and the grub was getting low.
The trail was bad, and I felt half mad,
    but I swore I would not give in; 70
And I'd often sing to the hateful thing,
    and it hearkened with a grin.

Till I came to the marge of Lake Lebarge,
    and a derelict there lay;
It was jammed in the ice, but I saw in a trice 75
    it was called the *Alice May*.
And I looked at it, and I thought a bit,
    and I looked at my frozen chum;
Then "Here," said I, with a sudden cry,
    "is my cre-ma-tor-eum!" 80

Ice Fog Over the Lake, 1907, TED
HARRISON. Illustration from *The Cremation
of Sam McGee.* By permission of Wm. Morrow &
Company, New York City.

The Cremation of Sam McGee 91

Some planks I tore from the cabin floor,
    and I lit the boiler fire;
Some coal I found that was lying around,
    and I heaped the fuel higher;
The flames just soared, and the furnace roared— 85
    such a blaze you seldom see,
And I burrowed a hole in the glowing coal,
    and I stuffed in Sam McGee.

Then I made a hike, for I didn't like
    to hear him sizzle so; 90
And the heavens scowled, and the huskies howled,
    and the wind began to blow.
It was icy cold, but the hot sweat rolled
    down my cheeks, and I don't know why;
And the greasy smoke in an inky cloak 95
    went streaking down the sky.

I do not know how long in the snow
    I wrestled with grisly fear;
But the stars came out and they danced about
    ere again I ventured near; 100
I was sick with dread, but I bravely said,
    "I'll just take a peep inside.
I guess he's cooked, and it's time I looked."
    Then the door I opened wide.

And there sat Sam, looking cool and calm, 105
    in the heart of the furnace roar;
And he wore a smile you could see a mile,
    and he said, "Please close that door.

It's fine in here, but I greatly fear
    you'll let in the cold and storm—   110
Since I left Plumtree, down in Tennessee,
    it's the first time I've been warm.''

There are strange things done in the midnight sun
    By the men who moil for gold;
The Arctic trails have their secret tales   115
    That would make your blood run cold;
The Northern Lights have seen queer sights,
    But the queerest they ever did see
Was that night on the marge of Lake Lebarge
    I cremated Sam McGee.   120

Robert Service (1874–1958) left England at the age of twenty to work as a bank clerk in Canada. He spent many years in the Yukon Territory. Living there gave him ideas for his poems about miners and trappers of the Northwest. During World War I, Service went back to England to work as a newspaper reporter and ambulance driver.

Developing Comprehension Skills

1. Which lines explain why Sam stays in the cold Arctic?

2. What is Sam's last wish? Why does he make this request?

3. Who is the narrator of this poem? Why does he agree to do what Sam asks? What do his reasons and actions show about his personality?

4. Draw a time line to show the order of main events in the story.

5. Reread lines 97 to 104. What do you expect to happen next? How is what really happens different from what you expect?

6. **Focus on Thinking: Inferring a Character's Feelings.** You can **infer,** or figure out, a character's feelings from the character's words and actions. Cap willingly makes the promise to Sam. How does he feel about his promise as the story goes on? Find two phrases that show his feelings.

Reading Poetry

1. **Identifying Rhyme Pattern.** Look for a pattern of rhyming words at the ends of lines in this poem. Which lines in each stanza rhyme? Some poems also have **internal rhyme.** That is, words within the same line rhyme. Find two lines that have internal rhyme.

2. **Identifying Climax.** A narrative poem has a plot. The events of the plot build to the most exciting moment, or the **climax.** What is the climax of this poem?

3. **Examining Repetition.** The first stanza of this poem is repeated at the end of the poem. Why do you think the author chose to repeat the stanza?

Critical Thinking

Comparing Poems. To **compare** means to find what two or more different things have in common. Reread both narrative poems. Then list at least three ways in which the poems are alike.

Writing in Response to Literature

What feeling do you get from this poem? Do you feel that it is humorous, or eerie, or both? Write a paragraph that explains how the poem affects you. Use phrases from the poem in your explanation.

Language and Literature

Vocabulary

Multiple Word Parts. When you read an unfamiliar word, look for a familiar base word within it. Then study any prefixes and suffixes that are combined with that base. Figure out the meaning of the new word by adding the meanings of the prefixes and suffixes to the base.

Combining the meaning of all the parts may not always give the correct meaning. For instance, *disappoint* does not mean "not to appoint." It means "not to satisfy." When you figure out a meaning, see if it makes sense in the sentence. If it does not, look up the word in a dictionary.

Exercise. Use the meanings of the word parts to explain the meaning of each word below. Which words might describe the Walrus? Which describe Sam McGee? Which describe neither?

dishonorable	untruthful	reheatable
uncomfortable	mistrustful	unmerciful

Developing Writing Skills

Retelling a Story. Some nursery rhymes are really narrative poems. As narrative poems, they have characters, setting, and a plot. Rewrite a common nursery rhyme as a story.

Prewriting. Choose a nursery rhyme, such as "Little Miss Muffet," that tells a story. List the main events of the plot. Invent details about the characters and reasons for their actions. Decide whether your story will be funny or serious.

Drafting. Introduce your characters and setting. Tell the events in the correct time order. Add details to complete your story.

Revising and Sharing. Make sure you have told the most important events of the nursery rhyme. Decide if any new information is needed. Share your stories with another class.

Reading Drama

What Is Drama?

Any story in this book could be written as a drama, or play. **Drama** is a form of literature meant to be acted out for an audience. When drama is performed on stage, actors and actresses play the parts of the characters. They tell the story through their words and actions.

The Elements of Drama

Like any story, a play has characters, a setting, and a plot. The characters with the most important parts are the **main characters.** They usually do most of the speaking. The characters with less important parts are called **minor characters.** They help keep the plot moving forward. When a play is acted out, the **scenery,** or decorations on stage, helps show the setting. The plot of a play, like the plot of any story, usually deals with a problem that must be solved.

Besides characters, setting, and plot, plays also have special features. These features make drama different from other types of literature.

Cast of Characters. Most written drama begins with a list of the names of all the characters. The characters are usually listed in the order they appear in the play. Sometimes a detail identifying the character follows his or her name.

Dialogue. A play is written almost entirely in dialogue. **Dialogue** means the words or conversations that the characters say to one another. Lines of dialogue give written drama a special look. A character's name appears first on the page. His or her lines, or dialogue, follow the name.

Stage Directions. Besides dialogue, the play also includes short sets of directions. These are called **stage directions.** The purpose of these directions is to guide actors in performing the play. These directions also help the reader to picture what would be happening on stage. Some stage directions tell the actors how to speak their lines. Some explain when, where, and how to move on stage. Others suggest the objects, or **props,** that the actors need on stage. Still others give ideas about scenery, lighting, or costumes. In this book, stage directions are printed in italics inside parentheses, as in the following example.

> **Town Clerk** *(writing with a flourish).* Quillow, the Toymaker. Now, I will read the minutes of the last meeting.

Acts and Scenes. A long play is often divided into sections called **acts.** Acts in plays are like chapters in books. Acts are divided further into **scenes.** Each scene tells what happens in just one time and place. Shorter plays may not be divided into acts and scenes.

How to Read Drama

The key to reading a play is to picture what would happen on stage. Use the hints in the stage directions to help you. Keep track of who the characters are and how they are related to one another. Figure out what problem the main characters are trying to solve. Decide if the play is funny or serious. This will help you imagine how the dialogue would sound if you heard it spoken aloud.

Recall a situation in which you felt powerless. Then read to find out how imagination can make someone powerful.

The Great Quillow

Based on the story by JAMES THURBER
Adapted by Moyne Rice Smith

CHARACTERS

Lamplighter	Tailor	Candlemaker	Quillow,
Town Crier	Butcher	Cobbler	*the Toymaker*
Town Clerk	Candymaker	Carpenter	Hunder,
Blacksmith	Baker	Locksmith	*the Giant*

The action of the play takes place in a village square above which rises a hill. The narrow houses of New Moon Street have pointed roofs and red chimneys. The only props on stage are a small bench up center and a street lamp down right, at the end of the street.

The time sequence, which covers several days, will be indicated only by lighting and the music of the bells which we hear when the clock in the tower strikes the hours.

The village clock strikes seven as the curtains open on the dusk of the village square. After a moment the Lamplighter *enters with his long staff.*

As he lights the street lamp, the stage lights creep up a little.

Town Crier (*circling from rear of audience to front of stage down right, ringing his bell and chanting*). Town meeting tonight. Town meeting tonight. Town meeting tonight. . . .

Lamplighter (*stopping down center stage and turning to* Crier). What good is a town meeting when the Giant Hunder sits above our village and curses it? What can we do? He has plundered the villages of the far countryside. And today the earth shook when he strode onto our hillside. He pulled up four trees to make room to sit down!

Town Crier. And when he called to us our doors shook and our windows rattled!

Lamplighter. What demands has he made?

Town Crier. The Town Clerk has gone to hear Hunder's will. We meet now to hear his demands. (*He continues off down left and around back of audience, his bell ringing softly.*) Town meeting tonight. Town meeting tonight. Town meeting tonight. . . .

(*The* Lamplighter *stays on stage and is joined now by the line of* Villagers *who follow the* Town Clerk *from the rear of the audience onto stage from down right. The* Crier *has circled the auditorium and has joined the rear of the procession.*)

Town Clerk (*as he enters, carrying scroll and quill, and takes his place on the bench up center*). There are 99 other men in the town, but it's the Town Clerk this, and the Town Clerk that, and the Town Clerk everything!

(*The* Villagers, *who are the* Town Councilors, *arrange themselves in small groups. They mutter and whisper to each other.* Quillow *has followed them in and sits cross-legged on the edge of the stage, down far right.*)

Town Clerk. Town meeting will come to order! Town meeting will come to order! (*They quiet down.*) I will now call the roll.

Blacksmith. We're all here. You can see that!

Town Clerk (*as each name is called, the* Councilors *answer impatiently*). Tailor, Butcher, Candymaker, Blacksmith, Baker, Candlemaker, Lamplighter, Cobbler, Carpenter, Locksmith, Town Crier. (*He looks over his spectacles at* Quillow.) We have a visitor tonight, as usual. (*All turn and look amusedly at* Quillow.) Quillow, the Toymaker. I will make the proper entry in the minutes.

Blacksmith. Never mind the minutes. Read us the demands of Hunder the Giant. (*cries of* Hear! Hear!)

Town Clerk (*writing with a flourish*). Quillow, the Toymaker. Now, I will read the minutes of the last meeting.

Candymaker. Let's dispense with the minutes of the last meeting. (*cries of* Hear! Hear!)

Town Clerk. It must be properly moved and duly seconded.

Tailor (*quickly*). I do so properly move.

Butcher. And I duly second.

Blacksmith. Now read the demands of Hunder the Giant! (*cries of Hear! Hear!*)

Town Clerk. Next comes unfinished business. (*all sigh*) We have before us a resolution to regulate the speed of merry-go-rounds. . . .

Blacksmith. Dispense with it!

Town Clerk. It must be properly moved and duly seconded.

Candymaker. I do so properly move. . . .

Baker. And I duly second!

Town Clerk (*unrolling scroll*). We come now to the business of the day. I have here the demands of Hunder the Giant. The document is most irregular. It does not contain a single "greeting" or "whereas" or "be it known by these presents." (*reads*) "I, Hunder, must have three sheep every morning." (*All:* Three sheep!)

Butcher (*aghast*). Why, that would use up all the sheep in the valley in a week and a fortnight, and there would be no mutton for our own people!

Town Clerk. "I, Hunder, must have a chocolate a day as high and as wide as a spinning wheel." (*general dismay*)

Candymaker. Why, that would exhaust all the chocolate in my storeroom in three days!

Town Clerk. "I, Hunder, must have a new jerkin made for me in a week and a fortnight."

Tailor (*gasps*). Why, I would have to work night and day to make a jerkin in a week and a fortnight for so large a Giant, and it would use up all the cloth on my shelves and in my basement.

Town Clerk. "I, Hunder, must have a new pair of boots within a week and a fortnight."

Cobbler (*moans*). Why, I would have to work night and day to make a pair of boots for so large a Giant in a week and a fortnight, and it would use up all the leather in my workshop and in my back room.

Town Clerk. "I, Hunder, must have an apple pie each morning made of a thousand apples."

Baker. Why, that would use up all the apples and flour and shortening in town in a week and a fortnight; and it would take me night and day to make such a pie, so that I could bake no more pies or cakes or cookies, or blueberry muffins or cinnamon buns or cherry boats or strawberry tarts or plum puddings for the people of the town.

Town Clerk. "I, Hunder, must have a house to live in by the time a week and a fortnight have passed."

Carpenter (*sobs*). Why, I would have to work night and day to build a house for so large a Giant in a week and a fortnight. And all my nephews and uncles and cousins would have to help me, and it would use up all the wood and pegs and hinges and glass in my shop and in the countryside.

Locksmith. I will have to work night and day to make a brass key large enough to fit the keyhole in the front door of the house of so large a Giant. It will use up all the brass in my shop and in the community.

Candlemaker. And I will have to make a candle for his bedside so large it will use up all the wick and tallow in my shop and the world!

Town Clerk. This is the final item. "I, Hunder, must be told a tale each day to keep me amused."

Quillow (*who has sat all this time with his arms folded and his eyes shut, now opens his eyes and raises his hand*). I will be the teller of tales. I will keep the Giant amused.

Candymaker. Does anyone have any idea of how to destroy the Giant? (*The* Councilors *think, and then in turn are inspired with a great idea.*)

Lamplighter. I could creep up on him in the dark and set fire to him with my lighter.

Quillow. The fire of your lighter would not harm him any more than a spark struck by a colt-shoe in a meadow.

Blacksmith. Quillow is right. But I could build secretly at night an enormous catapult which would cast a gigantic stone and crush Hunder.

Quillow. He would catch the stone as a child catches a ball, and he would cast it back at the town and squash all our houses.

Tailor. I could put needles in his suit.

Cobbler. I could put nails in his boots.

Candlemaker. I could put gunpowder in his candles.

Candymaker. I could put oil in his chocolates.

Butcher. I could put stones in his mutton.

Baker. I could put tacks in his pies.

Locksmith. I could make the handle of his brass key as sharp as a sword.

Carpenter. I could build the roof of his house insecurely so that it would fall on him.

Quillow. The plans you suggest would merely annoy Hunder as the gadfly annoys the horse and the flea annoys the dog.

Blacksmith. Perhaps the Great Quillow has a plan of his own. (*all laugh*)

Candymaker. Has the Great Quillow a plan? (*He does not answer.*)

(*The* Councilors *go out slowly and sadly, muttering about their heavy tasks of the night.* Quillow *sits alone thinking. Suddenly his face lightens. He pantomimes the suggestion of the doll he is going to make. He skips off gleefully as the lights dim to off.*

The only light on the stage now is that of the street lamp. The town clock strikes five and the Lamplighter *enters and puts out the street light, as the stage lights rise for morning.*)

Town Crier (*enters on tiptoe*). Sh! Don't wake the Giant.

Lamplighter. Sh! His food may not be ready.

Town Crier (*softly*). Five o'clock, and all's well! (*He circles to the rear of the audience. The* Villagers *tiptoe on, wearily carrying their foodstuffs. They line up across the front of the stage, backs to the audience, facing the hill with the sleeping* Giant.)

Baker. The pie is baked.

Candymaker. The chocolate is made.

Butcher. The sheep are dressed.

Locksmith. I worked all night on the great brass key.

Blacksmith. I helped him with my hammer and anvil.

Candlemaker. I have scarcely begun the enormous candle.

Carpenter. I am weary of sawing and planing.

Tailor. My fingers are already stiff, and I have just started the Giant's jerkin.

Cobbler. My eyes are tired, and I have hardly begun to make his boots.

Town Crier. Where is Quillow? Where is that foolish little fellow?

Lamplighter. He was in his shop at midnight, making toys.

All. Toys!

Locksmith. He could have helped with the key.

Baker. The pie.

Butcher. The sheep.

Cobbler. The boots.

(Quillow *appears smiling and bowing.*)

Blacksmith. Well!

Quillow. Good morning.

Blacksmith. I worked all night with my

hammer and anvil helping the locksmith with the great brass key. The Lamplighter tells us YOU spent the night making toys!

Quillow (*cheerily*). Making toys, and thinking up a tale to amuse the Giant Hunder.

Blacksmith. And a hard night you must have spent hammering out your tale.

Locksmith. And twisting it.

Carpenter. And leveling it.

Baker. And rolling it out.

Tailor. And stitching it up.

Cobbler. And fitting it together.

Candlemaker. And building it around a central thread.

Butcher. And dressing it up.

Candymaker. And making it not too bitter and not too sweet.

Hunder (*awakening, his head and shoulders appear above the hillside, up center*). HO! HO! (*He claps his hands and the* Villagers *fall backwards. He roars with laughter.*) Bring me my sheep, my pie, my chocolate! (*The* Villagers *lug their food-stuffs across the stage, climb on the bench, and heave them up to the* Giant.) Tell me your silly names, and what you do. (Hunder *gnaws greedily at his food, as the* Villagers *quickly tell their trades, each bowing as he speaks.*)

Hunder. You! You with the white hair, who are you?

Quillow. I am Quillow, the teller of tales.

Hunder. Bow!

Quillow. Wow! (*The others are aghast at his impudence.*)

Hunder (*scowls with fury, then suddenly laughs*). You are a fairly droll fellow. Perhaps your tales will amuse me. If they do not, I will put you in the palm of my hand and blow you so far it will take men five days to find you. Now, the rest of you, be off to your work. (*The* Villagers *sneak off in terror, as* Hunder *continues to eat.*) Now, you, tell me a tale.

Quillow (*sits cross-legged*). Once upon a time, a Giant came to our town from a thousand leagues away, stepping over the hills and rivers. He was so mighty a Giant that he could stamp upon the ground with his foot and cause the cows in the fields to turn flip-flops in the air and land on their feet again.

Hunder. Garf! I can stamp upon the ground with my foot and empty a lake of its water.

Quillow. I have no doubt of that, O Hunder. But the Giant who came over the hills and rivers many and many a year ago was a lesser Giant than Hunder. He was weak. He fell ill of a curious malady.

Hunder. Rowf! That Giant was a goose, that Giant was a grasshopper. Hunder is never sick. (*smites his chest*)

Quillow. This other Giant had no ailment of the chest or the stomach or the mouth or the ears or the eyes or the arms or the legs.

Hunder. Where else can a Giant have an ailment?

Quillow (*dreamily*). In the mind, for the mind is a strange and intricate thing. In lesser men than Hunder, it is subject to mysterious maladies.

Hunder. Wumf! Hunder's mind is strong like the rock! (*smites his forehead*)

Quillow. No one to this day knows what brought on this dreadful disease in the mind of the other Giant. He suffered no pain. His symptoms were marvelous and dismaying. First he heard the word. For fifteen minutes one morning, beginning at a quarter of six, he heard the word.

Hunder. Harumph! What was the word the Giant heard for fifteen minutes one day?

Quillow. The word was "woddly." All words were one word to him. All words were "woddly."

Hunder. All words are different to Hunder. And do you call this a tale you have told me? A blithering goose of a Giant hears a word and you call that a tale to amuse Hunder? I hear all words. This is a good chocolate; otherwise I should put you in the palm of my hand and blow you over the housetops.

Quillow (*as the town clock strikes six*). I shall bring you a better tale tomorrow. No one knows to this day what caused the weird illness in the mind of the other Giant. (Hunder *growls, yawns, and sinks his great head onto his arms and goes to sleep.* Quillow *smiles and goes to downstage right.*)

Quillow (*calling softly*). Town Crier! Town Crier! (*The* Town Crier *tiptoes on.*) Call the people. Tell them

Quillow has a plan to destroy the Giant Hunder. Call them quietly.

Town Crier (*circling the audience and crying softly*). Town meeting in the village square. Town meeting in . . .

(*As the lights dim into dusk, the* Villagers *enter quietly and form a group around* Quillow.)

Blacksmith. What is this clown's whim that brings us here like sheep?

(Quillow *whispers to the group. They nod and whisper to each other conspiratorially.*)

Lamplighter. It will never work.
Candymaker. It is worth trying.
Town Crier. I have a better plan. Let all the women and all the children stand in the streets and gaze sorrowfully at the Giant, and perhaps he will go away.

Candymaker. Let us try Quillow's plan. He has a magic, the little man.

(*The lights dim to off. The* Villagers *quietly move to either side of the stage and sit. As the lights rise for morning, the* Villagers *are discovered in their places, with* Quillow *sitting cross-legged on the bench below the hillside.*)

Hunder (*awakening with great noises*). Tell me a tale, smallest of men, and see to it that I do not nod, or I shall put you in the palm of my hand and blow you through yonder cloud.

Quillow. Once upon a time, there was a King named Anderblusdaferafan, and he had three sons named Ufabrodoborobe, Quamdelrodolanderay and Tristolcomofarasee.

Hunder. Why did this King and his sons have such long and difficult names?

Quillow. Ah, it was because of the King's mother, whose name was Isoldasadelofandaloo. One day as the King and his sons were riding through the magical forest, they came upon a woddly. Woddly woddly woddly woddly. Woddly, woddly, woddly. . . .

Hunder (*bellows*). Say it with words! You say naught but woddly!!

Quillow. Woddly woddly woddly woddly. . . .

Hunder (*roars*). Can this be the malady come upon me? Or do you seek to frighten Hunder?

Quillow. Woddly woddly woddly. Woddly woddly woddly.

Hunder (*in terror, shouts at the* Villagers. *He points to each one as he asks a question and grows more and* *more horrified as each one answers his question with* Woddly, woddly). You, Blacksmith, tell me your name. (*to another*) What is the time of day? . . . Where are you going? . . . How are you feeling? . . . (*etc.*) All talk! All talk! Say words!

(*The* Villagers *carry on conversations with each other using only the word* Woddly.)

Hunder (*silencing them with his roaring*). It is the malady! I have heard the word! It is the malady! What am I to do to cure the malady? (*The town clock strikes six.*)

Quillow. I was telling you how the King and his three sons rode through the magical forest. . . .

Hunder. I heard the word. All men said the word.

Quillow. What word?

Hunder. Woddly.

Quillow. That is but the first symptom, and it has passed. Look at the chimneys of the town. Are they not red?

Hunder. Yes, the chimneys are red. Why do you ask if the chimneys are red?

Quillow. So long as the chimneys are red, you have no need to worry, for when the second symptom is upon you, the chimneys of the town turn black.

Hunder. I see only red chimneys, but what could have caused Hunder to hear the word?

Quillow (*as the lights dim*). Rest well. I will tell you another tale tomorrow. (*As* Hunder *goes to sleep,* Quillow *signals to the* Villagers. *They quietly move to the chimneys which they pretend to paint. They remove the red cutouts and when they have finished and have returned to their places, the lights come up again for morning.*)

Hunder (*stirs, rubs eyes, yawns, stretches, and then stares*). The chimneys! The chimneys are black! The malady is upon me again. Teller of tales, tell me what I must do. The chimneys are black! Look, teller of tales, name me fairly the color of yonder chimneys.

Quillow. The chimneys are red, O Hunder. The chimneys are red. See how they outdo the red rays of the sun.

Hunder. The rays of the sun are red, but the chimneys of the town are black.

Quillow. You tremble, and your tongue hangs out, and these are indeed the signs of the second symptom. But still there is no real danger, for you do not see the blue men. Or do you see the blue men, O Hunder?

Hunder. I see the men of the town staring at me. But their faces are white and they wear clothes of many colors. Why do you ask me if I see blue men?

Quillow. When you see the blue men, it is the third and last symptom of the malady. If that should happen, you must rush to the sea and bathe in the waters or your strength will become the strength of a kitten. Perhaps if you fast for a day and a night, the peril will pass.

Hunder. I will do as you say, teller of tales, for you are wise beyond the manner of men. Bring me no food today, tell me no tale. (*He moans and covers his eyes and sleeps.*)

(*The light dims and the* Villagers *softly steal behind the screens so that when the morning light rises there is no one visible except* Quillow, *the sleeping* Giant, *and the* Town Crier.)

Quillow (*as the town clock strikes five*). Cry the hour. Cry all's well.

Town Crier. Five o'clock! Five o'clock and all's well!

Hunder (*awakens and looks cautiously at the village*). The chimneys are still black, but I see no blue men. (*grins, smites his chest and roars*) HO, Councilors! Bring me my sheep and my pie and my chocolate, for I have a vast hunger. Behold I am still a whole man! I have heard the word and I have seen the black chimneys, but I have not beheld the blue men.

Quillow. That is well, for he who beholds the blue men must bathe in the yellow waters in the middle of the sea, or else he will dwindle first to the height of the pussy willow, then to the height of the daffodil, then to the height of the violet, until finally he becomes a small voice in the grass, lost in the thundering of the crickets.

Hunder. But I shall remain stronger than the rock and taller than the oak.

Quillow. If you are stronger than the rock and taller than the oak, then stamp on the ground and make yonder cow in the field turn a flip-flop.

Hunder (*gleefully*). Behold, I will make the cow turn twice in the air. (*stamps heavily*)

(*The blue men slide over the village walls and dance up and down in the air.*)

Hunder (*cries in anguish*). The blue men! The blue men have come! The world is filled with little blue men!

Quillow. I see no blue men, but you have begun to shrink like the brook in dry weather, and that is the sign of the third symptom.

Hunder (*shaking with terror*). The sea! The sea! Point me to the sea!

Quillow. It is many leagues to the east. Run quickly toward the rising sun and bathe in the yellow waters in the middle of the sea.

(*Bellowing with anguish,* Hunder *disappears behind his hillside. As his roaring diminishes, the* Villagers *enter.*)

Villagers (*lifting* Quillow *to their shoulders*).
THE GREAT QUILLOW!

James Thurber (1894–1961) wrote about the problems of ordinary people. Many of his stories and cartoons first appeared in *The New Yorker* magazine. *The Great Quillow* is a Thurber story that Moyne Rice Smith has adapted into a play.

Other books: *The Night the Ghost Got In*
The Thurber Carnival

Developing Comprehension Skills

1. What is the purpose of the first town meeting?

2. Why are the other villagers angry with Quillow on the morning after the first town meeting?

3. Briefly explain Quillow's plan. Why do the villagers go along with his plan?

4. Most villagers think only about how Hunder's demands affect them personally. How is Quillow's thinking different from theirs?

5. **Focus on Thinking: Understanding Cause and Effect.** In literature, events or actions often cause a change in a character's thinking. What does Quillow's story cause Hunder to think? What is the effect of the story on Hunder's actions?

Reading Drama

1. **Identifying the Main Characters in Drama.** The most important characters in a play are the main characters. Who are the main characters in this play? How do you know?

2. **Appreciating Dialogue.** In drama, the story is told through the **dialogue,** or what the characters say. Reread the section in which Quillow first tells Hunder about the other giant. How does the rest of the plot depend on this dialogue?

3. **Recognizing Stage Directions.** Brief directions enclosed in parentheses are called **stage directions.** Some tell actors how to say lines. Some explain how to move. Others are directions about props or lighting. Find examples of three different kinds of stage directions in the play.

Speaking and Listening

Giving a Dramatic Reading. Work with a group to present a reading of part or all of this play. Choose a character and practice reading that character's lines aloud. Let your voice express the character's feelings. Practice with the group. Then present your reading to the class.

Writing in Response to Literature

Quillow uses the power of a story to defeat a giant. Write about a time when a story affected you strongly.

Language and Literature

Vocabulary

Compound Words. You can usually understand the meaning of a compound word by combining the meanings of its base words. The word *keyhole,* for example, means "a hole for a key." Sometimes a compound word has a new meaning that does not combine its parts. To *hoodwink* means "to trick," not "to shut a hat's eyelid." When the combined meanings of the base words do not make sense, look up the word in a dictionary.

Exercise. Find six compound words in the paragraph below. Try defining each word by combining the meanings of its base words. Use a dictionary if the combined meanings do not make sense.

> The news about Lord Ord has spread like wildfire. He left the townspeople spellbound when he defeated Ig, the grumpy giant. Lord Ord captured the headstrong giant one afternoon by tickling him with crabgrass.

Developing Writing Skills

Comparing Stories. *The Great Quillow* is a folk tale written as a play. Compare the plot to a similar plot from the fiction section of this unit.

Prewriting. Choose a tale in which the hero, like Quillow, has to solve a difficult problem. List ways in which the two plots are alike. Reread the stories if necessary.

Drafting. In your topic sentence, tell which tales you are comparing. Then tell ways in which the plots are alike. As you write, decide if you need to begin a new paragraph. Each paragraph should cover only one main idea.

Revising and Sharing. Make sure each paragraph gives one main idea. Change or drop any sentences that do not support that idea. Compare your final paper with a classmate's for ideas.

Unit 1 *R*eview

Using Your Skills in Reading Fiction

Read this paragraph from "The Magic Purse of the Swamp Maiden" by Yoshiko Uchida. What is the setting? What character is introduced? What is the first event in the plot?

Long ago in a small village of Japan, there lived a young farmer who was very, very poor. In the spring of the year, the people of his village planned a pilgrimage to the great shrine of Ise, and for weeks ahead, there was talk of nothing else.

Using Your Skills in Reading Poetry

Read the first stanza from the narrative poem "Casabianca" by Felicia Hemans. Which lines rhyme with each other? How many strong beats do you hear in the first line? How many do you hear in the second line? What character is introduced? Give one detail about the setting.

The boy stood on the burning deck,
Whence all but he had fled;
The flame that lit the battle's wreck,
Shone round him o'er the dead.

Using Your Skills in Reading Drama

Read these lines of dialogue from the play *The Pied Piper of Hamelin,* based on a poem by Robert Browning. Name the characters. Explain what information each stage direction is giving. Tell what is happening in the plot.

Piper. Be careful what you promise, your Honor. I shall keep you to your bargain. Will you give me one thousand guilders?

Mayor. One thousand? Why, Piper, if you can free Hamelin of rats, I'll give you fifty thousand guilders!

Piper (*holding up his hand in protest*). No! One thousand guilders is my price—no more, no less. Is it a bargain, your Honor?

Mayor (*impatiently*). Of course, of course!

Using Your Comprehension Skills

List in correct time order three events that happen in the following paragraph. Identify any word that is a clue to the time order. Explain how two events are connected by cause and effect. What clue word tells you this?

> Before it left town, the dragon ate three of the village's finest citizens. Therefore the village fathers sent for Hamil, the world-famous dragon slayer.

Using Your Vocabulary Skills

Look carefully at each word below. Find the base word or words in each. Identify any prefixes or suffixes that have been added. Then give the meaning of the whole word.

misuse   thoughtless   disagreeable   rattlesnake

Using Your Writing Skills

Choose one of the writing assignments below. Follow directions.

1. Explain in a paragraph why you think this unit is called "Timeless Tales."

2. Write your own "timeless tale" in story or poem form.

How Writers Write

Understanding the Process of Writing

Look at the paintings on pages 69 and 115. What do these paintings, which look so very different, have in common? Both are the work of artists who went through a process, or series of steps, to achieve the end result. As the artists were painting, they each made many decisions about form, color, and details. The decisions and the results were different, but each process resulted in a work of art.

Writing is a creative process just like painting. Every piece of literature you read is the end result of a process that the writer went through. This process can be divided into four stages: **prewriting, drafting, revising,** and **sharing**. Together these stages make up the **process of writing**.

Understanding the process of writing will help you appreciate the literature you read. You will be able to look at a story or poem and think about the decisions the author made in creating that work. You too can use this process just as professional writers do.

New Mexico Sunset,
1978, LINDA
LOMAHAFTEWA.
Private Collection.

Prewriting

Writers do not just sit down and start writing. First they must figure out what to write and how best to write it. This thinking and planning stage, called **prewriting,** takes time. The following steps will help you work through the thinking and planning you must do before you write.

1. Choose and limit a topic. What are you going to write about? You may be assigned a topic. You may be free to choose your own topic. If so, where will your idea for a topic come from?

Professional writers are always on the lookout for writing ideas. Elaine Konigsburg, author of *From the Mixed-Up Files of Mrs. Basil E. Frankweiler,* says, "Ideas for my stories come from things that have happened to our family and from things that I have read." Some writers, like Margaret and H. A. Rey, authors of the *Curious George* series, keep folders or notebooks of ideas. They say:

We collect material for a story long before we begin to write. Mr. Rey, who draws the illustrations, keeps a folder marked "Ideas." All sorts of things go into it—newspaper clippings, photos, a funny story heard at a party, and so on. As it turns out, only a small part of what we file is used in the story, but a full file helps.

Lloyd Alexander, author of *Time Cat*, talks about a slightly different way of finding ideas:

One thing I had learned during those seven years was to write about things I knew and loved. Our cats delighted me. So did music . . . I was writing out of my own life and experience.

Nikki Giovanni, a poet, says, "You start with an idea, because even a feeling is an idea. If you can't put a feeling into words, then you can't feel it."

To get ideas for your topic, start with what you know. Think about things you like to do. Also think of what you would like to know more about. Make a list of possible topics. Circle the one you find most exciting or feel that you have the most to say about.

After you choose a topic, brainstorm about it. Think of everything you can say. Let your ideas flow freely, and jot down every one. Write your topic in the middle of the page, and cluster your ideas around it. Talk about your topic with others.

Next, you need to narrow or limit your topic to fit the length of your writing. Are you writing a paragraph or three pages? Your topic should be specific enough to handle well in the length you choose. You will probably need to focus your thinking on a part of the topic. For example, if you choose to write a short poem about a vacation you had, focus on a single moment or sight. If you are writing an article about eagles, limit the topic to nesting habits or diet, for example. Once you begin writing, you may find that you need to write a longer work, or further limit your topic.

2. Decide on your purpose. Why are you writing? Do you want your readers to learn about something? Do you want them to laugh? Do you want them to think about a problem? Do you want them to imagine a sight or understand the way you feel? Your reason for writing will determine what and how you write.

3. Decide on your audience. When you talk, you probably choose details and language to suit your listeners. When you write, you make the same kinds of choices. Think about who your readers will be. Are they very young children, or adults, or your friends? You want them to enjoy and understand your work. You can vary your writing to suit your readers.

Many writers try to picture their readers as they write. Robert Cormier says: "I have an intelligent reader in mind, and I don't compromise that." On the other hand, William Pené du Bois, author of *Twenty-One Balloons,* has a different reader in mind: "I feel I write for the lazy ones. I want things to happen fast. I would like to entertain."

4. Gather information. Sometimes you may choose a topic that is personal. Then you can write about your experiences and thoughts from memory. At other times, you will need to do some research to write well. You must find facts on which to base an article or report. If you are writing fiction, you should research real people and places. If your setting is Antarctica, for example, research will help you describe the setting and actions more accurately.

Jean Craighead George, author of fiction and nonfiction works

Author Yoshiko Uchida writes several drafts of her stories. She enjoys explaining to students the steps she takes in the process of writing. © June Finfer, Chicago.

about animals, explains how she learns more about her subject: "I read scientific papers, lives of animals, and even weather reports."

Holling C. Holling, a writer of nature stories, takes many notes during his research. He explains how he keeps track of them:

> When I need to do extensive research for writing or illustrating, I generally use loose-leaf or unlined paper for collecting my information. When I am ready to use this amassed data, I label each item plainly. . . . I use the wall space near my desk for an over-sized bulletin board. Here I can pin up loose pages from the notebooks or any other bits I have accumulated during my research. These can be arranged and rearranged. . . .

Like Mr. Holling, be sure to take notes while you research. These notes will help you remember what you have learned. When you feel that you have learned enough about your topic, you can begin the next step.

5. Organize your ideas. You want your readers to be able to follow your ideas easily. Help the readers by presenting your writing in a sensible order.

Read through your notes. Cross out details that are not needed. Next, arrange your remaining notes in order. For a story, use time order. For a description, order your details as you would notice them. For a paragraph meant to persuade, arrange your ideas in order of importance.

As you organize your ideas, you may realize that you need more information. If so, do more research now. You may even decide that you want to change your topic slightly.

Many writers arrange their ideas in an outline. Later, their outlines help them stay "on track" in their writing. Outlines help writers to think logically. Other writers do not make a formal outline. Carol Ryrie Brink, author of *Caddie Woodlawn*, writes:

> It is a very good idea to make an outline of what you expect to write. But, if I have my plot clearly in mind, I do not always make an outline. What I do is write out scenes or parts of scenes as they come to me clearly and freshly. These are not necessarily in order, but I put them aside, like unstrung beads.

Drafting

Once you have done your thinking and planning, you are ready to begin your first draft. A **draft** is a rough version of what you are writing. It is often full of small errors, but it does not need to be perfect. It is your first chance to get your ideas down so that you can take a good look at them.

When you write your draft, you turn your notes into sentences and paragraphs. Try to follow your outline as you write. Leave space between the lines for later corrections.

Wilson Rawls, author of *Where the Red Fern Grows*, explains about writing drafts:

> Do not worry about grammar and punctuation on your first draft. The important thing is to get your story down on paper. Your

first work will probably need a lot of rewriting. You can worry about grammar and punctuation then.

Writer Dorothy Sterling writes her first draft in a different way:

> I do my rough draft in my head. Sometimes I sit at the typewriter all morning and don't write a word. Or I write a sentence, cross it out, and start over again—and again—and again.

Writing requires constant thinking. You may often change your mind while you are writing. You may need to change entire paragraphs if your ideas are not working well together. Do not be afraid to change your plans at any time during the writing process.

Remember that different people write in different ways. It is important to find the way that works best for you.

Revising

When you revise, you look for ways to improve your writing. First you focus on ideas and the way you have stated them. You might change the way you organized details by moving sentences or paragraphs. You may need to add facts or take out unnecessary information. You can make sentences clearer by adding precise nouns, strong action verbs, or descriptive adjectives and adverbs. Make your corrections or additions in the spaces you left between lines. You can use the proofreading symbols shown on page 123.

If you are working on a word processor, you can delete or add words or change positions of sentences while your draft is on the screen. Then print out your draft and revise it on paper once more.

Read your draft slowly and carefully. Ask yourself questions about the writing. If you write nonfiction, for example, ask these questions:

1. Did I organize my ideas clearly and logically? Do the ideas flow together smoothly?

2. Did I stick to my topic? Should I add any details? Should any be left out?

3. Does every sentence express a complete thought? Is every word the best word to express my meaning?

4. Is the writing interesting? Will others want to read it?

Your paper may begin to look messy. Professional writers are used to this. Look at the example below of a marked-up draft from Yoshiko Uchida's *In Between Miya*. If your paper becomes too hard to read, recopy the draft on a clean sheet of paper.

This sample of manuscript from *In Between Miya* shows how author Yoshiko Uchida revises her writing. The Kerlan Collection, University of Minnesota, Minneapolis.

When at last it was July, Miya could scarcely wait for the
And /or VACATION to begin on the twentieth ⊙
rainy season to ~~come to an~~ end. She despised the gloomy wet days
when all of Japan seemed a soggy sponge, soaking up every bit of
water the heavens ~~ever~~ held. The days were cold and leaden, and
the roads oozed with mud. ~~A cold dampness seeped into everything.~~
Shoes grew moldy; books smelled musty, and their pages stuck together. Even the quilts felt clammy, and Miya thought longingly
of the charcoal foot warmer that Mother slipped into the quilts
during the winter. ~~Mother's laundry never dried, and~~ if the sun
Mother
appeared (even /for) a few hours, ~~she~~ hurried to put up the bamboo
while Miya took all the shoes from
poles and hung out her wash ~~to dry. If the sun came out while~~
a
~~Miya was home, her first task was to hurry to~~ the shoe box and
them out to dry ⊙
put ~~out everyone's shoes to dry out.~~

You might want someone else to read your paper during this stage. Joan Aiken, author of many stories and poems, says this about revising:

> Every writer needs a sounding-board reader. My sister and I perform this function for each other. We read each other's books in manuscript, first draft, and vigorously criticize. I find this an essential stage of the process.

One trick that many authors use during the revision stage is to leave their writing alone for a while, and then go back to it with a "fresh eye."

Proofreading. You have made your additions and corrections. Your writing says what you want it to say. Now make sure that little errors do not distract your readers. Read your writing again. Look for mistakes in spelling, grammar, punctuation, and capitalization. Mark your changes with the proofreading symbols shown on page 123.

After you have corrected the errors, ask someone else to proofread your work. Another reader may find your errors more easily than you can.

Preparing the Final Copy. Now you need to write or type your final copy. You want it to look as neat as possible. Remember to make every correction that is marked on your draft paper. Then check yourself by reading your writing one last time.

Sharing Your Work

Professional writers seek publishers to print their work. You, too, can share your work with other people. You might read it aloud to the class, or read it onto a tape. You may wish to put it on a bulletin board or in a class folder. Perhaps you could have someone act it out, or you might illustrate it yourself.

Poet Nikki Giovanni says:

> A poem is like a song. You don't read a song, you sing it, and you have to hear it to appreciate it. The same thing applies to poetry. It should be read aloud.

Writer Jay Williams sums up the whole writing process in this way:

> It is very hard work thinking up ideas and getting a story to sound real. It is also hard work imagining just how people talk, and making them talk and move just the way you want them to, inside your head and then on paper. But it isn't hard work when you take pleasure in what you're doing—and I do.

As you use the process of writing to create your own works, you may begin to feel the way Matt Christopher feels: "Since I began writing, every day is a new adventure."

Proofreading Symbols

Symbol	Meaning	Example
∧	insert	Gardners
≡	capitalize	i
/	make lowercase	Version
∼	transpose (switch positions)	evalaute
✐	omit letters, words	of the story
¶	make new paragraph	¶The setting is
⊙	insert a period	before but the way

Somebody Just Like You ...

Somebody just like you wrote the poems on these pages. Somebody your age painted the pictures. Someone in the same grade as you wrote the story.

Does either of the poems describe your feelings? Do you think the story and the paintings are exciting?

It is important for you to remember that writing can be good no matter how old the author is. You do not have to grow up to create an important piece. In fact, you don't have to get a day older.

The tools for writing are in this book, and you have already learned how to use them. The ideas are already in your head, and the feelings are already in your heart.

Blue

Loneliness is blue.
It smells like a rainy day.
It feels like an icy window.
It looks like a blank face.

Corby Koehler
Taft Junior High School
Cedar Rapids, Iowa

What Counts

My face may be wrinkled
My nose may be small,
My hands may be bony
My body too tall.

My ears may be big
My fingernails long,
My voice may be hoarsey
When I sing a song.

My hair may be stringy
My legs not so straight,
But it's the person inside me
That makes me so great.

Jorie Cooper
Maple Dale School
Fox Point, Wisconsin

Surviving

I remember it was Saturday when the actual blizzard began. As I looked out my frosted window, I could barely see an inch in front of my face. Winds whipped and lashed outside, blowing the snow furiously.

It gave me a sense of security just being in my warm home. In the kitchen I heard the radio blaring away. Dozens and dozens of cancellations were given. Dancing classes, stores, restaurants, organizations, factories, and more were cancelled.

Two days went by. The radio droned on with cancellations. Now the schools were closed. I felt like getting out of the house. Looking at tremendous snowdrifts began to bore me. I began to resent the deep, crisp snow that trapped me. I felt alone and helpless, and wondered if the blizzard would ever end.

The blizzard gradually died, and we could get outside. The snow was beautifully resting, sculptured by the wind. Now it was time to dig out. Soon activity on the streets began. Life returned to the barren wasteland. The blizzard of '85 was over.

Elizabeth Amabile
S.S. Peter and Paul School
Williamsville, New York

UNIT TWO

FICTION   POETRY   NONFICTION

Meeting Challenges

Diamond Shoal (detail), 1905, WINSLOW HOMER.
Collection of IBM Corporation, Armonk, New York.

Reading Fiction

Conflict

As you read a story, what makes you want to keep reading? Chances are that you have become interested in the plot. You want to find out how the characters meet a challenge, solve a problem, or get themselves out of trouble. The plots of most stories center around a conflict. A **conflict** is a struggle between opposing forces. There are two main kinds of conflict in stories: external and internal.

External Conflict

A struggle between a character and an outside force is an **external conflict**. Characters may face several types of outside forces. The outside force may be another character. In "The Cat and the Golden Egg," for instance, there is a conflict between the cat Quickset and Master Grubble. The conflict may be between a character and the community. That is, the character may look, act, or think differently from the rest of society. In "Duke Pishposh of Pash," Tyl's ideas of right and wrong are in conflict with the beliefs of the people around him. The outside force may also be a force of nature. For example, in "The Cremation of Sam McGee," Sam struggles against the arctic cold.

Internal Conflict

A struggle that takes place in a character's mind is an **internal conflict**. For example, a character might have to decide between right and wrong or between two solutions to a problem. Sometimes a character must deal with his or her own mixed feelings or thoughts. Early in "The Wise Old Woman," the farmer faces an internal conflict. He must decide whether to abandon his mother or to risk his own life to save her.

The Importance of Conflict

Conflict is a necessary part of every story. In short stories there is usually one major conflict. In longer stories there may be several conflicts. Sometimes minor conflicts result from a character's efforts to deal with the major conflict.

Conflict adds excitement and suspense to a story. The conflict usually becomes clear early in the story. As the plot unfolds, the reader starts wondering what will happen next and how the characters will handle the conflict. Many readers enjoy trying to predict the final outcome.

The excitement usually builds to a high point, or climax. The **climax** is the turning point of the story. Something happens that causes the conflict to be settled. The reader then learns the final outcome and the story ends.

Reading for Conflict

As you read a story, identify the main characters. Decide what conflict, or problem, they face. Look for the steps they take to settle the conflict. See if these steps cause other conflicts. Watch for clues and try to predict what the characters will do. Enjoy the buildup of suspense. Put yourself in the story. Decide if you would solve the conflict as the characters do.

Comprehension Skills

Main Idea

Literature presents challenges for both the writer and the reader. The writer faces the challenge of putting ideas into words. The reader faces the challenge of understanding what the writer is trying to say.

Writers of both fiction and nonfiction organize their ideas in paragraphs. A **paragraph** is a group of sentences about one idea. This idea is the **main idea**. The main idea can be stated directly or it can be implied.

Stated Main Idea

In some paragraphs, the main idea is stated in one sentence called the **topic sentence**. The topic sentence is often the first sentence, but it may be any sentence in the paragraph. The other sentences add **supporting details**. That is, they explain or tell more about the main idea. Sometimes a writer uses more than one paragraph to develop a main idea.

Notice how the first sentence expresses the main idea in this paragraph from *Nadia the Willful* by Sue Alexander. The other sentences give specific details to tell more about this idea.

> Nadia began to speak of Hamed. She told of walks she and Hamed had taken, and of talks they had had. She told how he had taught her games, told her tales and calmed her when she was angry. She told many things that she remembered, some happy and some sad.

Implied Main Idea

Sometimes the main idea is not stated in a topic sentence. Instead, it is **implied**, or suggested. In this case, you must think about the details and decide what main idea connects them. Reread the paragraph before the last sentence of "The Stone Dog" on pages 32 and 33. What main idea is implied in this paragraph?

In poetry, ideas are often implied. Like a paragraph, groups of lines may express one idea. The poem as a whole may express one or more than one idea.

Finding the Main Idea

Whenever you read, you are reading for ideas. Stop occasionally and ask yourself these questions.

1. What is the main idea of this paragraph? Is it stated in a topic sentence?

2. How do the other sentences support this idea?

3. If a main idea is not stated, what idea is implied?

Exercise: Understanding the Main Idea

Identify the main idea of each paragraph below.

1. Pelé took his soccer ball everywhere. He would practice kicking it as he walked down the street. He would dribble it or aim it at a telephone pole. He could do almost anything with it.

2. My English teacher gave me a book of Robert Burns's poems. I wore it out as I carried it with me wherever I went. If Burns, a plowboy in Scotland, could do it, I, a plowboy in Kentucky, could do it. That's the way I looked at it.

Vocabulary Skills

Context Clues

Do you know what *hubris* means? Suppose you read, "One weakness in the main character is hubris, or pride." You could figure out from the context that *hubris* means "pride." The **context** is the sentence or paragraph in which a word appears. When writers use unusual words, they often include clues to the meaning in the context. The words and phrases that help explain a word are called **context clues**. There are several kinds of context clues.

Definition or Restatement Clues. A writer may define or restate a new word in a different way. This context clue is called a **definition** or **restatement** clue.

1. A photograph of a *marabou* won the first prize. A marabou is a type of stork.

2. The canoe had an *outrigger*, a sort of balancing pole, fastened to one side.

Some words and phrases that signal definition or restatement clues are *or, that is, in other words*, and *also called*. Punctuation marks such as commas and dashes can also be clues.

Example Clues. A writer may use examples to help explain a word. The word itself may be an example of something more familiar.

1. The store sells men's *haberdashery*, such as hats, shirts, and socks.

2. Roots of some vegetables, such as a *rutabaga*, can be eaten.

Signals of example clues include *such as, for example, for instance, like, and other,* and *especially.*

Comparison and Contrast Clues. In a **comparison** clue, a writer compares a new word to something simpler to understand. Key signal words include *like, as, similar to,* and *than.*

Her apologies poured as *profusely* as oil gushing from a well.

In a **contrast** clue, the writer includes an idea opposite in meaning. The contrast helps explain the word.

She expected to feel *anxious,* but she felt calm.

The word *but* signals that *anxious* must be the opposite of *calm.* The words *however, yet, although, on the other hand,* and *different from* can also signal contrast clues.

Inference Clues. There may not be one single clue to a word's meaning. However, the reader can sometimes piece together several ideas in the context to **infer,** or figure out, what a word means. The context below gives several hints to the meaning of *devastated.*

The storm devastated our neighborhood. Four houses were destroyed, and all the trees were uprooted. The roof of the corner store collapsed, and the power lines snapped.

Exercise: Using Context Clues. Use context clues to explain the underlined words.

1. The tourists were ready to <u>disembark</u>, or leave the ship.
2. As a child, Tom had many <u>ailments</u> such as mumps and measles.
3. The light rain became a <u>deluge</u> that flooded our street.
4. The lawyer's <u>proposal</u> was like other offers she had made.
5. Although its mother is graceful, the new colt is <u>ungainly</u>.

When you really miss someone what do you do? Discover how Nadia deals with her loss of a loved one.

Nadia the Willful

SUE ALEXANDER

In the land of the drifting sands where the Bedouin[1] move their tents to follow the fertile grasses, there lived a girl whose stubbornness and flashing temper caused her to be known throughout the desert as Nadia the Willful.

Nadia's father, the sheik Tarik, whose kindness and graciousness caused his name to be praised in every tent, did not know what to do with his willful daughter.

Only Hamed, the eldest of Nadia's six brothers and Tarik's favorite son, could calm Nadia's temper when it flashed. "Oh, angry one," he would say, "shall we see how long you can stay that way?" And he would laugh and tease and pull at her dark hair until she laughed back. Then she would follow Hamed wherever he led.

One day before dawn, Hamed mounted his father's great white stallion and rode to the west to seek new grazing ground for the sheep. Nadia stood with her father at the edge of the oasis and watched him go.

Hamed did not return.

---

1. **Bedouin** (bed'oo win): a nomadic tribe of Arabs.

Nadia rode behind her father as he traveled across the desert from oasis to oasis, seeking Hamed.

Shepherds told them of seeing a great white stallion fleeing before the pillars of wind that stirred the sand. And they said that the horse carried no rider.

Passing merchants, their camels laden with spices and sweets for the bazaar, told of the emptiness of the desert they had crossed.

Tribesmen, strangers, everyone whom Tarik asked, sighed and gazed into the desert, saying, "Such is the will of Allah."[2]

At last Tarik knew in his heart that his favorite son, Hamed, had been claimed, as other Bedouin before him, by the drifting sands. And he told Nadia what he knew— that Hamed was dead.

Bedouins, 1905–1906, JOHN SINGER SARGENT.
The Brooklyn Museum, Purchased by Special Subscription.

Nadia screamed and wept and stamped the sand, crying, "Not even Allah will take Hamed from me!" until her father could bear no more and sternly bade her to silence.

Nadia's grief knew no bounds. She walked blindly through the oasis neither seeing nor hearing those who would console her. And Tarik was silent. For days he sat inside his tent, speaking not at all and barely tasting the meals set before him.

Then, on the seventh day, Tarik came out of his tent. He called all his people to him, and when they were assembled, he

---

2. **Allah** (ä lä′): the Arabic word for *God.*

spoke. "From this day forward," he said, "let no one utter Hamed's name. Punishment shall be swift for those who would remind me of what I have lost."

Hamed's mother wept at the decree. The people of the clan looked at one another uneasily. All could see the hardness that had settled on the sheik's face and the coldness in his eyes, and so they said nothing. But they obeyed.

Nadia, too, did as her father decreed, though each day held something to remind her of Hamed. As she passed her brothers at play she remembered games Hamed had taught her. As she walked by the women weaving patches for the tents, and heard them talking and laughing, she remembered tales Hamed had told her and how they had made her laugh. And as she watched the shepherds with their flock she remembered the little black lamb Hamed had loved.

Each memory brought Hamed's name to Nadia's lips, but she stilled the sound. And each time that she did so, her unhappiness grew until, finally, she could no longer contain it. She wept and raged at anyone and anything that crossed her path. Soon everyone at the oasis fled at her approach. And she was more lonely than she had ever been before.

One day, as Nadia passed the place where her brothers were playing, she stopped to watch them. They were playing one of the games that Hamed had taught her. But they were playing it wrong.

Without thinking, Nadia called out to them. "That is not the way! Hamed said that first you jump this way and then you jump back!"

Her brothers stopped their game and looked around in fear. Had Tarik heard Nadia say Hamed's name? But the sheik was nowhere to be seen.

Bedouin Women, 1905–1906, JOHN SINGER SARGENT. The Brooklyn Museum, Purchased by Special Subscription.

"Teach us, Nadia, as our brother taught you," said her smallest brother.

And so she did. Then she told them of other games and how Hamed had taught her to play them. And as she spoke of Hamed she felt an easing of the hurt within her.

So she went on speaking of him.

She went to where the women sat at their loom and spoke of Hamed. She told them tales that Hamed had told her. And she told how he had made her laugh as he was telling them.

At first the women were afraid to listen to the willful girl and covered their ears, but after a time, they listened and laughed with her.

"Remember your father's promise of punishment!" Nadia's mother warned when she heard Nadia speaking of Hamed.

"Cease, I implore you!"

Nadia knew that her mother had reason to be afraid, for Tarik, in his grief and bitterness, had grown quick-tempered and sharp of tongue. But she did not know how to tell her mother that speaking of Hamed eased the pain she felt, and so she said only, "I will speak of my brother! I will!" And she ran away from the sound of her mother's voice.

She went to where the shepherds tended the flock and spoke of Hamed. The shepherds ran from her in fear and hid behind the sheep. But Nadia went on speaking. She told of Hamed's love for the little black lamb and how he had taught it

Landscape with Goatherd, 1905, JOHN SINGER SARGENT. Oil on canvas, 24¼" × 31⅞". The Metropolitan Museum of Art, New York City, Gift of Mrs. Francis Ormond.

to leap at his whistle. Soon the shepherds left off their hiding and came to listen. Then they told their own stories of Hamed and the little black lamb.

The more Nadia spoke of Hamed, the clearer his face became in her mind. She could see his smile and the light in his eyes. She could hear his voice. And the clearer Hamed's voice and face became, the less Nadia hurt inside and the less her temper flashed. At last, she was filled with peace.

But her mother was still afraid for her willful daughter. Again and again she sought to quiet Nadia so that Tarik's bitterness would not be turned against her. And again and again Nadia tossed her head and went on speaking of Hamed.

Soon, all who listened could see Hamed's face clearly before them.

One day, the youngest shepherd came to Nadia's tent calling, "Come, Nadia! See Hamed's black lamb, it has grown so big and strong!"

But it was not Nadia who came out of the tent.

It was Tarik.

On the sheik's face was a look more fierce than that of a desert hawk, and when he spoke, his words were as sharp as a scimitar.

"I have forbidden my son's name to be said. And I promised punishment to whoever disobeyed my command. So shall it be. Before the sun sets and the moon casts its first shadow on the sand, you will be gone from this oasis—never to return."

"No!" cried Nadia, hearing her father's words.

"I have spoken!" roared the sheik. "It shall be done!"

Trembling, the shepherd went to gather his possessions.

And the rest of the clan looked at one another uneasily and muttered among themselves.

In the hours that followed, fear of being banished to the desert made everyone turn away from Nadia as she tried to tell them of Hamed and the things he had done and said.

And the less she was listened to, the less she was able to recall Hamed's face and voice. And the less she recalled, the more her temper raged within her, destroying the peace she had found.

By evening, she could stand it no longer. She went to where her father sat, staring into the desert, and stood before him.

"You will not rob me of my brother Hamed!" she cried, stamping her foot. "I will not let you!"

Tarik looked at her, his eyes colder than the desert night.

But before he could utter a word, Nadia spoke again. "Can you recall Hamed's face? Can you still hear his voice?"

Tarik started in surprise, and his answer seemed to come unbidden to his lips. "No, I cannot! Day after day I have sat in this spot where I last saw Hamed, trying to remember the look, the sound, the happiness that was my beloved son—but I cannot."

And he wept.

Nadia's tone became gentle. "There is a way, honored father," she said. "Listen."

And she began to speak of Hamed. She told of walks she and Hamed had taken, and of talks they had had. She told how he had taught her games, told her tales and calmed her when she was angry. She told many things that she remembered, some happy and some sad.

And when she was done with the telling, she said gently, "Can you not recall him now, Father? Can you not see his face? Can you not hear his voice?"

Tarik nodded through his tears, and for the first time since Hamed had been gone, he smiled.

"Now you see," Nadia said, her tone more gentle than the softest of the desert breezes, "there is a way that Hamed can be with us still."

The sheik pondered what Nadia had said. After a long time, he spoke, and the sharpness was gone from his voice.

"Tell my people to come before me, Nadia," he said. "I have something to say to them."

When all were assembled, Tarik said, "From this day forward, let my daughter Nadia be known not as Willful, but as Wise. And let her name be praised in every tent, for she has given me back my beloved son."

And so it was. The shepherd returned to his flock, kindness and graciousness returned to the oasis, and Nadia's name was praised in every tent. And Hamed lived again—in the hearts of all who remembered him.

Sue Alexander (born 1933) began writing stories for her friends at the age of eight. She particularly enjoys writing fantasy stories. She likes to excite the imagination of young people. Many of her works have appeared in magazines such as *Weekly Reader*. Alexander has also written book reviews.

Other books: *Nadir of the Streets*
Witch, Goblin, and Sometimes Ghost

Developing Comprehension Skills

1. What is the main idea of the third paragraph?

2. What happens to Hamed?

3. How do Nadia and Tarik each react to Hamed's death at first? What does Tarik do a week later?

4. How and why does Nadia disobey her father? Why does she finally talk with him about the decree?

5. Nadia has to face the fact of death. How might this change her feelings about life and people?

6. **Focus on Thinking: Analyzing Change of Attitude.** The way a person thinks and feels about something is called an **attitude**. How does Tarik's attitude toward Nadia change during the story?

Reading Fiction

1. **Understanding Conflict.** A problem that a character struggles with in a story is called a **conflict**. Describe the conflict Nadia has in her mind. Describe a conflict she has with someone else.

2. **Relating Setting to Plot.** Where the story is set can affect the plot. How does the desert setting affect the plot of this story? How does it make Tarik's punishment of the shepherd a harsh one?

3. **Understanding Minor Characters.** Characters who are not as important as the main characters are called **minor characters**. The writer often uses these characters to develop the plot. Why is the shepherd a minor character? How is he used to develop the plot?

Study and Research

Using Cross References. Some encyclopedia articles end with a list of topics called **cross-references**. The list refers you to other articles in the encyclopedia related to the topic.

Look up *Bedouin* in an encyclopedia. Read the article, and then look up one cross-reference. Summarize the information that you find.

Writing in Response to Literature

"Nadia the Willful" becomes "Nadia the Wise." Does Nadia become any less willful? Write your opinion. Give reasons to support it.

*Can you remember a time
when you thought you were in
danger? Read about the danger
that Mako faces.*

Ghost of the Lagoon

ARMSTRONG SPERRY

The island of Bora Bora, where Mako lived, is far
away in the South Pacific. It is not a large island—
you can paddle around it in a single day—but the
main body of it rises straight out of the sea, very
high into the air like a castle. Waterfalls trail down the faces of
the cliffs. As you look upward you see wild goats leaping from
crag to crag.

Mako had been born on the very edge of the sea, and most
of his waking hours were spent in the waters of the lagoon,
which was nearly enclosed by the two outstretched arms of the
island. He was very clever with his hands; he had made a
harpoon that was as straight as an arrow and tipped with five-
pointed iron spears. He had made a canoe, hollowing it out of a
tree. It wasn't a very big canoe—only a little longer than his
own height. It had an outrigger, a sort of balancing pole,
fastened to one side to keep the boat from tipping over. The
canoe was just large enough to hold Mako and his little dog,
Afa. They were great companions, these two.

One evening Mako lay stretched at full length on the

Marc in the Cove, 1986, HANK PITCHER. Collection of Mr. and Mrs. Jeffrey Hayden. Photograph: Jessica Darraby Gallery, Los Angeles.

pandanus[1] mats, listening to Grandfather's voice. Overhead, stars shone in the dark sky. From far off came the thunder of the surf on the reef.

The old man was speaking of Tupa, the ghost of the lagoon. Ever since the boy could remember, he had heard tales of this terrible monster. Frightened fishermen, returning from the reef at midnight, spoke of the ghost. Over the evening fires old men told endless tales about the monster.

Tupa seemed to think the lagoon of Bora Bora belonged to him. The natives left presents of food for him out on the reef: a

---

1. **pandanus** (pan dā′ nas): a shrub or tree having daggerlike leaves, common to Southeast Asia.

dead goat, a chicken, or a pig. The presents always disappeared mysteriously, but everyone felt sure that it was Tupa who carried them away. Still, in spite of all this food, the nets of the fishermen were torn during the night, the fish stolen. What an appetite Tupa seemed to have!

Not many people had ever seen the ghost of the lagoon. Grandfather was one of the few who had.

"What does he really look like, Grandfather?" the boy asked for the hundredth time.

The old man shook his head solemnly. The light from the cook fire glistened on his white hair. "Tupa lives in the great caves of the reef. He is longer than this house. There is a sail on his back, not large but terrible to see, for it burns with a white fire. Once when I was fishing beyond the reef at night I saw him come up right under another canoe—"

"What happened then?" Mako asked. He half rose on one elbow. This was a story he had not heard before.

The old man's voice dropped to a whisper. "Tupa dragged the canoe right under the water—and the water boiled with white flame. The three fishermen in it were never seen again. Fine swimmers they were, too."

Grandfather shook his head. "It is bad fortune even to speak of Tupa. There is evil in his very name."

"But King Opu Nui has offered a reward for his capture," the boy pointed out.

"Thirty acres of fine coconut land and a sailing canoe, as well," said the old man. "But who ever heard of laying hands on a ghost?"

Mako's eyes glistened. "Thirty acres of land and a sailing canoe. How I should love to win that reward!"

Grandfather nodded, but Mako's mother scolded her son for such foolish talk. "Be quiet now, son, and go to sleep.

Grandfather has told you that it is bad fortune to speak of Tupa. Alas, how well we have learned that lesson! Your father—" She stopped herself.

"What of my father?" the boy asked quickly. And now he sat up straight on the mats.

"Tell him, Grandfather," his mother whispered.

The old man cleared his throat and poked at the fire. A little shower of sparks whirled up into the darkness.

"Your father," he explained gently, "was one of the three fishermen in the canoe that Tupa destroyed." His words fell upon the air like stones dropped into a deep well.

Mako shivered. He brushed back the hair from his damp forehead. Then he squared his shoulders and cried fiercely, "I shall slay Tupa and win the king's reward!" He rose to his knees, his slim body tense, his eyes flashing in the firelight.

"Hush!" his mother said. "Go to sleep now. Enough of such foolish talk. Would you bring trouble upon us all?"

Mako lay down again upon the mats. He rolled over on his side and closed his eyes, but sleep was long in coming.

The palm trees whispered above the dark lagoon, and far out on the reef the sea thundered.

The boy was slow to wake up the next morning. The ghost of Tupa had played through his dreams, making him restless. And so it was almost noon before Mako sat up on the mats and stretched himself. He called Afa, and the boy and his dog ran down to the lagoon for their morning swim.

When they returned to the house, wide-awake and hungry, Mako's mother had food ready and waiting.

"These are the last of our bananas," she told him. "I wish you would paddle out to the reef this afternoon and bring back a new bunch."

The boy agreed eagerly. Nothing pleased him more than such an errand, which would take him to a little island on the outer reef half a mile from shore. It was one of Mako's favorite playgrounds, and there bananas and oranges grew in great plenty.

"Come, Afa," he called, gulping the last mouthful. "We're going on an expedition." He picked up his long-bladed knife and seized his spear. A minute later he dashed across the white sand where his canoe was drawn up beyond the water's reach.

Afa barked at his heels. He was all white except for a black spot over each eye. Wherever Mako went, there went Afa also. Now the little dog leaped into the bow of the canoe, his tail wagging with delight. The boy shoved the canoe into the water and climbed aboard. Then, picking up his paddle, he thrust it into the water. The canoe shot ahead. Its sharp bow cut through the green water of the lagoon like a knife through cheese. And so clear was the water that Mako could see the coral gardens, forty feet below him, growing in the sand. The shadow of the canoe moved over them.

A school of fish swept by like silver arrows. He saw scarlet rock cod with ruby eyes, and the head of a conger eel peering out from a cavern in the coral. The boy thought suddenly of Tupa, ghost of the lagoon. On such a bright day it was hard to believe in ghosts of any sort. The fierce sunlight drove away all thought of them. Perhaps ghosts were only old men's stories, anyway!

Mako's eyes came to rest upon his spear—the spear that he had made with his own hands—the spear that was as straight and true as an arrow. He remembered his vow of the night before. Could a ghost be killed with a spear? Some night when all the village was sleeping, Mako swore to himself, he would find out! He would paddle out to the reef and challenge

The Landscape of Tahiti, 1892, PAUL GAUGUIN.
Helsinki Atheneum. Photograph: Giraudon/Art Resource, New York City.

Tupa! Perhaps tonight. Why not? He caught his breath at the thought. A shiver ran down his back. His hands were tense on the paddle.

As the canoe drew away from shore, the boy saw the coral reef that above all others had always interested him. It was of white coral—a long, slim shape that rose slightly above the surface of the water. It looked very much like a shark. There was a ridge on the back that the boy could pretend was a dorsal fin, while up near one end were two dark holes that looked like eyes!

Times without number the boy had practiced spearing this make-believe shark, aiming always for the eyes, the most vulnerable spot. So true and straight had his aim become that the spear would pass right into the eyeholes without even touching the sides of the coral. Mako had named the coral reef "Tupa."

This morning as he paddled past it, he shook his fist and called, "Ho, Mister Tupa! Just wait till I get my bananas. When I come back, I'll make short work of you!"

Afa followed his master's words with a sharp bark. He knew Mako was excited about something.

The bow of the canoe touched the sand of the little island where the bananas grew. Afa leaped ashore and ran barking into the jungle, now on this trail, now on that. Clouds of seabirds whirled from their nests into the air with angry cries.

Mako climbed into the shallow water, waded ashore, and pulled his canoe up on the beach. Then, picking up his banana knife, he followed Afa. In the jungle the light was so dense and green that the boy felt as if he were moving underwater. Ferns grew higher than his head. The branches of the trees formed a green roof over him. A flock of parakeets fled on swift wings. Somewhere a wild pig crashed through the undergrowth while Afa dashed away in pursuit. Mako paused anxiously. Armed only with his banana knife, he had no desire to meet the wild pig. The pig, it seemed, had no desire to meet him, either.

Then ahead of him the boy saw the broad green blades of a banana tree. A bunch of bananas, golden ripe, was growing out of the top.

At the foot of the tree he made a nest of soft leaves for the bunch to fall upon. In this way the fruit wouldn't be crushed. Then with a swift slash of his blade he cut the stem. The bananas fell to the earth with a dull thud. He found two more bunches.

Then he thought, *I might as well get some oranges while I'm here. Those little rusty ones are sweeter than any that grow on Bora Bora.*

Afterglow, Tautira River, Tahiti about 1891, JOHN LA FARGE. National Gallery of Art, Washington, D.C., Adolph Caspar Miller Fund.

So he set about making a net of palm leaves in which to carry the oranges. As he worked, his swift fingers moving in and out among the strong green leaves, he could hear Afa's excited barks off in the jungle. That was just like Afa, always barking at something: a bird, a fish, a wild pig. He never caught anything, either. Still, no boy ever had a finer companion.

The palm net took longer to make than Mako had realized. By the time it was finished and filled with oranges, the jungle was dark and gloomy. Night comes quickly and without warning in the islands of the Tropics.

Mako carried the fruit down to the shore and loaded it into the canoe. Then he whistled to Afa. The dog came bounding out of the bush, wagging his tail.

"Hurry!" Mako scolded. "We won't be home before the dark comes."

The little dog leaped into the bow of the canoe, and Mako came aboard. Night seemed to rise up from the surface of the water and swallow them. On the distant shore of Bora Bora, cook fires were being lighted. The first star twinkled just over the dark mountains. Mako dug his paddle into the water, and the canoe leaped ahead.

The dark water was alive with phosphorus. The bow of the canoe seemed to cut through a pale, liquid fire. Each dip of the paddle trailed streamers of light. As the canoe approached the coral reef the boy called, "Ho, Tupa! It's too late tonight to teach you your lesson. But I'll come back tomorrow." The coral shark glistened in the darkness.

And then suddenly Mako's breath caught in his throat. His hands felt weak. Just beyond the fin of the coral Tupa there was another fin—a huge one. It had never been there before. And—could he believe his eyes? It was moving.

The boy stopped paddling. He dashed his hand across his

eyes. Afa began to bark furiously. The great white fin, shaped like a small sail, glowed with phosphorescent light. Then Mako knew. Here was Tupa—the real Tupa—ghost of the lagoon!

His knees felt weak. He tried to cry out, but his voice died in his throat. The great shark was circling slowly around the canoe. With each circle it moved closer and closer. Now the boy could see the phosphorescent glow of the great shark's sides. As it moved in closer he saw the yellow eyes, the gill slits in its throat.

Afa leaped from one side of the canoe to the other. In sudden anger Mako leaned forward to grab the dog and shake him soundly. Afa wriggled out of his grasp as Mako tried to catch him, and the shift in weight tipped the canoe on one side. The outrigger rose from the water. In another second they would be overboard. The boy threw his weight over quickly to balance the canoe, but with a loud splash Afa fell over into the dark water.

Mako stared after him in dismay. The little dog, instead of swimming back to the canoe, had headed for the distant shore. And there was the great white shark—very near.

"Afa! Afa! Come back! Come quickly!" Mako shouted.

The little dog turned back toward the canoe. He was swimming with all his strength. Mako leaned forward. Could Afa make it? Swiftly the boy seized his spear. Bracing himself, he stood upright. There was no weakness in him now. His dog, his companion, was in danger of instant death.

Afa was swimming desperately to reach the canoe. The white shark had paused in his circling to gather speed for the attack. Mako raised his arm, took aim. In that instant the shark charged. Mako's arm flashed forward. All his strength was behind that thrust. The spear drove straight and true, right into the great shark's eye. Mad with pain and rage, Tupa whipped about, lashing the water in fury. The canoe rocked back and forth. Mako struggled to keep his balance as he drew back the spear by the cord fastened to his wrist.

He bent over to seize Afa and drag him aboard. Then he stood up, not a moment too soon. Once again the shark charged. Once again Mako threw his spear, this time at the other eye. The spear found its mark. Blinded and weak from loss of blood, Tupa rolled to the surface, turned slightly on his side. Was he dead?

Mako knew how clever sharks could be, and he was taking no chances. Scarcely daring to breathe, he paddled toward the still body. He saw the faintest motion of the great tail. The shark was still alive. The boy knew that one flip of that tail could overturn the canoe and send him and Afa into the water, where Tupa could destroy them.

Swiftly, yet calmly, Mako stood upright and braced himself firmly. Then, murmuring a silent prayer to the Shark God, he threw his spear for the last time. Downward, swift as sound, the spear plunged into a white shoulder.

Peering over the side of the canoe, Mako could see the great fish turn over far below the surface. Then slowly, slowly, the great shark rose to the surface of the lagoon. There he floated, half on one side.

Tupa was dead.

Mako flung back his head and shouted for joy. Hitching a strong line about the shark's tail, the boy began to paddle toward the shore of Bora Bora. The dorsal fin, burning with the white fire of phosphorus, trailed after the canoe.

Men were running down the beaches of Bora Bora, shouting as they leaped into their canoes and put out across the lagoon. Their cries reached the boy's ears across the water.

"It is Tupa—ghost of the lagoon," he heard them shout. "Mako has killed him!"

That night as the tired boy lay on the pandanus mats listening to the distant thunder of the sea, he heard Grandfather singing a new song. It was the song that would be sung the next day at the feast that King Opu Nui would give in Mako's honor. The boy saw his mother bending over the cook fire. The stars leaned close, winking like friendly eyes. Grandfather's voice reached him now from a great distance, "Thirty acres of land and a sailing canoe. . . ."

Armstrong Sperry (1897–1976) worked as an illustrator for ten years. Then he decided to combine his drawings with his own stories. He got many ideas from his journeys all over the world. For two years, Sperry lived in the South Sea Islands, which inspired him to write many stories, including the award-winning *Call It Courage*.

Other books: *Little Eagle*
The Rain Forest

Developing Comprehension Skills

1. Who or what is the "ghost of the lagoon"? Why are people afraid of it?

2. For what two reasons does Mako first decide to kill Tupa?

3. Why is Mako so accurate with his spear?

4. Explain how Mako finally meets Tupa.

5. What is Mako's final reason for killing Tupa? Do you think he could have killed Tupa without this new reason? Why or why not?

6. **Focus on Thinking: Predicting.** You can use clues in a story to predict what might happen next. Reread the last paragraph. Predict what will happen to Mako in the near future.

Reading Fiction

1. **Relating Conflict to Plot.** Most plots center around a conflict or problem. What main problem does Mako face?

2. **Appreciating Description.** One way of describing is to make a comparison. The writer compares phosphorescent water to "pale, liquid fire." Find another description in the story that uses comparison.

3. **Identifying the Climax.** The turning point of a story is the **climax**. At this exciting moment, characters often make a decision or take action to solve a problem. What is the climax of this story?

Speaking and Listening

Addressing an Audience. When you address an audience, slow down your rate of speaking. Pronounce words carefully, and speak so that everyone can hear you. Stand up straight and look at your audience.

Just as Mako's friends will brag about him, brag about someone you know. Address your class using the hints above.

Writing in Response to Literature

Mako overcomes his fear when he must save Afa. Write about a time when you overcame your own fear for some reason.

From

Where the Red Fern Grows

WILSON RAWLS

Did you ever work to earn money for something you really wanted? Find out what a young boy must do to get what he wants.

It all started one day while I was hoeing corn down in our field close to the river. Across the river, a party of fishermen had been camped for several days. I heard the old Maxwell car as it snorted and chugged its way out of the bottoms. I knew they were leaving. Throwing down my hoe, I ran down to the river and waded across at a place called the Shannon Ford. I hurried to the camp ground.

It was always a pleasure to prowl where fishermen had camped. I usually could find things: a fish line, or a forgotten fish pole. On one occasion, I found a beautiful knife stuck in the bark of a sycamore tree, forgotten by a careless fisherman. But on that day, I found the greatest of treasures, a sportsman's magazine, discarded by the campers. It was a real treasure for a country boy. Because of that magazine, my entire life was changed.

I sat down on an old sycamore log, and started thumbing through the leaves. On the back pages of the magazine, I came to the "For Sale" section—"Dogs for Sale"—every kind of dog. I read on and on. They had dogs I had never heard of, names I couldn't make out. Far down in the right-hand corner,

I found an ad that took my breath away. In small letters, it read: "Registered redbone coon hound pups—twenty-five dollars each."

The advertisement was from a kennel in Kentucky. I read it over and over. By the time I had memorized the ad, I was seeing dogs, hearing dogs, and even feeling them. The magazine was forgotten. I was lost in thought. The brain of an eleven-year-old boy can dream some fantastic dreams.

How wonderful it would be if I could have two of those pups. Every boy in the country but me had a good hound or two. But fifty dollars—how could I ever get fifty dollars? I knew I couldn't expect help from Mama and Papa.

I remembered a passage from the Bible my mother had read to us: "God helps those who help themselves." I thought of the words. I mulled them over in my mind. I decided I'd ask God to help me. There on the banks of the Illinois River, in the cool shade of the tall white sycamores,

Young Master (detail), 1966, KEN DANBY.
Private Collection. Photograph: Gallery Moos, Toronto.

I asked God to help me get two hound pups. It wasn't much of a prayer, but it did come right from the heart.

When I left the camp ground of the fishermen, it was late. As I walked along, I could feel the hard bulge of the magazine jammed deep in the pocket of my overalls. The beautiful silence that follows the setting sun had settled over the river bottoms. The coolness of the rich, black soil felt good to my bare feet.

It was the time of day when all furried things come to life. A big swamp rabbit hopped out on the trail, sat on his haunches, stared at me, and then scampered away. A mother gray squirrel ran out on the limb of a burr oak tree. She barked a warning to the four furry balls behind her. They melted from sight in the thick green. A silent gray shadow drifted down from the top of a tall sycamore. There was a squeal and a beating of wings. I heard the tinkle of a bell in the distance ahead. I knew it was Daisy, our milk cow. I'd have to start her on the way home.

I took the magazine from my pocket and again I read the ad. Slowly a plan began to form. I'd save the money. I could sell stuff to the fishermen: crawfish, minnows, and fresh vegetables. In berry season, I could sell all the berries I could pick at my grandfather's store. I could trap in the winter. The more I planned, the more real it became. There was the way to get those pups—save my money.

I could almost feel the pups in my hands. I planned the little doghouse, and where to put it. Collars I could make myself. Then the thought came, "What could I name them?" I tried name after name, voicing them out loud. None seemed to fit. Well, there would be plenty of time for names.

Right now there was something more important—fifty dollars—a fabulous sum—a fortune—far more money than I had ever seen. Somehow, some way, I was determined to have

Gilley's House (detail), 1976, BOB TIMBERLAKE. Heritage Company, Lexington, North Carolina.

it. I had twenty-three cents—a dime I had earned running errands for my grandpa, and thirteen cents a fisherman had given me for a can of worms.

The next morning I went to the trash pile behind the barn. I was looking for a can—my bank. I picked up several, but they didn't seem to be what I wanted. Then I saw it, an old K. C. Baking Powder can. It was perfect, long and slender, with a good tight lid. I took it down to the creek and scrubbed it with sand until it was bright and new-looking.

I dropped the twenty-three cents in the can. The coins

looked so small lying there on the shiny bottom, but to me it was a good start. With my finger, I tried to measure how full it would be with fifty dollars in it.

Next, I went to the barn and up in the loft. Far back over the hay and up under the eaves, I hid my can. I had a start toward making my dreams come true—twenty-three cents. I had a good bank, safe from the rats and from the rain and snow.

All through that summer I worked like a beaver. In the small creek that wormed its way down through our fields, I caught crawfish with my bare hands. I trapped minnows with an old screen-wire trap I made myself, baited with yellow corn bread from my mother's kitchen. These were sold to the fishermen, along with fresh vegetables and roasting ears. I tore my way through the blackberry patches until my hands and feet

Flat Bottom, 1971, KEN DANBY. Private Collection. Photograph: Gallery Moos, Toronto.

were scratched raw and red from the thorns. I tramped the hills seeking out the huckleberry bushes. My grandfather paid me ten cents a bucket for my berries.

Once Grandpa asked me what I did with the money I earned. I told him I was saving it to buy some hunting dogs. I asked him if he would order them for me when I had saved enough. He said he would. I asked him not to say anything to my father. He promised me he wouldn't. I'm sure Grandpa paid little attention to my plans.

That winter I trapped harder than ever with the three little traps I owned. Grandpa sold my hides to fur buyers who came to his store all through the fur season. Prices were cheap: fifteen cents for a large opossum hide, twenty-five for a good skunk hide.

Little by little, the nickels and dimes added up. The old K. C. Baking Powder can grew heavy. I would heft its weight in the palm of my hand. With a straw, I'd measure from the lip of the can to the money. As the months went by, the straws grew shorter and shorter.

The next summer I followed the same routine.

"Would you like to buy some crawfish or minnows? Maybe you'd like some fresh vegetables or roasting ears."

The fishermen were wonderful, as true sportsmen are. They seemed to sense the urgency in my voice and always bought my wares. However, many was the time I'd find my vegetables left in the abandoned camp.

There never was a set price. Anything they offered was good enough for me.

A year passed. I was twelve. I was over the halfway mark. I had twenty-seven dollars and forty-six cents. My spirits soared. I worked harder.

Another year crawled slowly by, and then the great day

came. The long hard grind was over. I had it—my fifty dollars! I cried as I counted it over and over.

As I set the can back in the shadowy eaves of the barn, it seemed to glow with a radiant whiteness I had never seen before. Perhaps it was all imagination. I don't know.

Lying back in the soft hay, I folded my hands behind my head, closed my eyes, and let my mind wander back over the two long years. I thought of the fishermen, the blackberry patches, and the huckleberry hills. I thought of the prayer I had said when I asked God to help me get two hound pups. I knew He had surely helped, for He had given me the heart, courage, and determination.

Early the next morning, with the can jammed deep in the pocket of my overalls, I flew to the store. As I trotted along, I whistled and sang. I felt as big as the tallest mountain in the Ozarks.

Arriving at my destination, I saw two wagons were tied up at the hitching rack. I knew some farmers had come to the store, so I waited until they left. As I walked in, I saw my grandfather behind the counter. Tugging and pulling, I worked the can out of my pocket and dumped it out in front of him and looked up.

Grandpa was dumbfounded. He tried to say something, but it wouldn't come out. He looked at me, and he looked at the pile of coins. Finally, in a voice much louder than he ordinarily used, he asked, "Where did you get all this?"

"I told you, Grandpa," I said, "I was saving my money so I could buy two hound pups, and I did. You said you would order them for me. I've got the money and now I want you to order them."

Grandpa stared at me over his glasses, and then back at the money.

"How long have you been saving this?" he asked.

"A long time, Grandpa," I said.

"How long?" he asked.

I told him, "Two years."

His mouth flew open and in a loud voice he said, "Two years!"

I nodded my head.

The way my grandfather stared at me made me uneasy. I was on needles and pins. Taking his eyes from me, he glanced back at the money. He saw the faded yellow piece of paper sticking out from the coins. He worked it out, asking as he did, "What's this?"

I told him it was the ad, telling where to order my dogs.

He read it, turned it over, and glanced at the other side.

I saw the astonishment leave his eyes and the friendly-old-grandfather look come back. I felt much better.

Dropping the paper back on the money, he turned, picked up an old turkey-feather duster, and started dusting where there was no dust. He kept glancing at me out of the corner of his eye as he walked slowly down to the other end of the store, dusting here and there.

He put the duster down, came from behind the counter, and walked up to me. Laying a friendly old work-calloused hand on my head, he changed the conversation altogether, saying, "Son, you need a haircut."

I told him I didn't mind. I didn't like my hair short; flies and mosquitoes bothered me.

He glanced down at my bare feet and asked, "How come your feet are cut and scratched like that?"

I told him it was pretty tough picking blackberries barefoot.

He nodded his head.

It was too much for my grandfather. He turned and walked away. I saw the glasses come off, and the old red handkerchief come out. I heard the good excuse of blowing his nose. He stood for several seconds with his back toward me. When he turned around, I noticed his eyes were moist.

In a quavering voice, he said, "Well, Son, it's your money. You worked for it, and you worked hard. You got it honestly, and you want some dogs. We're going to get those dogs. . . ."

He walked over and picked up the ad again, asking, "Is this two years old, too?"

I nodded.

"Well," he said, "the first thing we have to do is write this outfit. There may not even be a place like this in Kentucky any more. After all, a lot of things can happen in two years."

Seeing that I was worried, he said, "Now you go on home. I'll write to these kennels and I'll let you know when I get an answer. If we can't get the dogs there, we can get them someplace else. And I don't think, if I were you, I'd let my Pa know anything about this right now. I happen to know he wants to buy that red mule from Old Man Potter."

I told him I wouldn't, and turned to leave the store.

As I reached the door, my grandfather said in a loud voice, "Say, it's been a long time since you've had any candy, hasn't it?"

I nodded my head.

He asked, "How long?"

I told him, "A long time."

"Well," he said, "we'll have to do something about that."

Walking over behind the counter, he reached out and got a sack. I noticed it wasn't one of the nickel sacks. It was one of the quarter kind.

My eyes never left my grandfather's hand. Time after time, it dipped in and out of the candy counter: peppermint sticks, jawbreakers, horehound, and gumdrops. The sack bulged. So did my eyes.

Handing the sack to me, he said, "Here. First big coon you catch with those dogs, you can pay me back."

I told him I would.

On my way home, with a jawbreaker in one side of my mouth and a piece of horehound in the other, I skipped and hopped, making half an effort to try to whistle and sing, and couldn't for the candy. I had the finest grandpa in the world and I was the happiest boy in the world.

Wilson Rawls (1913–1984) grew up in the Ozark Mountain region of Oklahoma. Books were always an important part of his life. He worked as a carpenter and a road builder, writing stories in his spare time. His most famous story, *Where the Red Fern Grows*, was first published as a series of episodes in *The Saturday Evening Post* magazine. In 1974 the story was made into a movie.

Another book: *Summer of the Monkeys*

Developing Comprehension Skills

1. What is the main idea of the third paragraph? Of the fourth paragraph?

2. Why is earning fifty dollars such a difficult goal for the boy to accomplish?

3. How does the boy earn money? How long does it take him to reach his goal?

4. What do you think Grandpa's thoughts are when he first sees the money? Why might he think that way? What might he think when he learns the truth?

5. **Focus on Thinking: Inferring Reasons.** To **infer**, use the facts you have to figure out something that is not stated. Infer the reason why Grandpa gives the boy so much candy.

Reading Fiction

1. **Examining Characters.** You can get to know a character from his or her thoughts, actions, and words. What quality does the boy show by working so long for his goal? What other qualities does he show? Explain your answers.

2. **Understanding Point of View.** A writer decides who will narrate the story; that is, from whose **point of view** the story will be told. Who tells this story? How do you know?

Speaking and Listening

Having a Group Discussion. A discussion is a way to share ideas. To have a good group discussion, listen carefully to others. Share your own ideas. Keep the discussion on the topic.

Organize a group discussion. Brainstorm for ways someone your age can earn money in your community. Select the ten best ideas of your group.

Writing in Response to Literature

The boy in the story responds to a very small newspaper advertisement. Suppose you were advertising the puppies. Make up a new advertisement for the puppies that might draw more customers.

Language and Literature

Vocabulary

Definition and Restatement Clues. You often find that a word may be defined or stated in another way in context, that is, in the same sentence or paragraph. Words such as *or, that is, also called, which is,* and *in other words* signal the definition. Punctuation marks such as commas and dashes can also be clues.

Exercise. Using context clues, explain the underlined words.

1. Mako received <u>kudos</u>, or praise, for his bravery.
2. Tupa the shark was <u>ravenous</u>, that is, extremely hungry.
3. Grandpa and the boy shared a <u>confidence</u>, or secret.
4. Nadia's family were <u>nomads</u>. They were people who wander from place to place.
5. Tarik composed a <u>lament</u>—a song of mourning—for Hamed.

Developing Writing Skills

Writing About Story Elements. The setting of a story often affects the plot. Explain how the settings affect the challenges that Nadia, Mako, and the boy from the Ozarks each face.

Prewriting. Think about the challenge each character faces. Summarize that challenge. List details about the setting of each story. Decide how the setting affects each challenge.

Drafting. Organize your paper by stories. Describe one setting, state the challenge, and link the two together. Start a new paragraph and discuss the next story in the same way. End with a general conclusion about how setting affects plot.

Revising and Sharing. Read carefully to make sure that your statements are complete and accurate. In a small group, choose one story to discuss. Share the ideas that everyone in the group has written.

Have you ever felt like an outsider? See how Hattie deals with her feelings of shyness and loneliness.

Hatsuno's Great-Grandmother

FLORENCE CRANNELL MEANS

 Hatsuno Noda walked alone in the crowd of girls and boys pouring out of school. She held her head so straight that her chubby black braids spatted her trim shoulders, and her step was so brisk that you would have thought she enjoyed walking by herself. Hatsuno could not bear to let anyone guess how lonesome she felt in the throng.

Brother Harry and six-year-old brother Teddy were deep in clumps of their schoolmates, but the girls from Hattie's class streamed by her without pausing. Behind her Patty White, whom she liked best of all, skipped along between Sue and Phyllis, giggling and talking. Hattie wondered what they were talking about. Often they were chattering about Hattie's secret dream; but today it sounded as if they were discussing the Mother's Day tea next month. This morning the teacher had appointed Patty chairman of the decorating committee.

Hattie could have helped decorate. Her slim fingers knew how to fold amazing Japanese paper birds, flowers, dolls. And at the old school the teacher would have had her do colored drawings on the blackboard, along with Tommy Lin, who was Chinese, and Consuelo, who was Mexican. The three drew better than any of the "plain Americans." But in this new school, where almost all were "plain Americans," no one knew what Hattie's fingers could do.

No, the girls were not talking about the tea.

"If you join now," Patty was saying, "you can go up to camp this summer—"

Oh, if only Patty were saying it to Hatsuno! But she wasn't. She broke off as she danced past with the others.

"Hi, Hattie!" she called, wrinkling her uptilted nose in a smile and tossing back her thistledown curls.

Hattie smiled a small, stiff smile, though she ached to shout "Hi!" and fall in step with Patty. Then maybe Patty would think to ask her.

"Join"—"camp": those words were the keys to one of Hattie's dearest dreams.

Hatsuno had never been in the mountains. All her life she had lived where she could see them, stretching like a purple wall across the end of the dingy downtown street. They were beautiful, with snow-capped peaks shining pink and lavender and gold in the sunrise, and Hatsuno had always longed to explore them; but though they looked so near, they were miles and miles away.

The new school had given her hope. In the new school there was a Camp Fire group; and every summer it spent a few days at a camp far up in the mountains. Hattie had seen pictures of its bark-covered lodges climbing steeply among the tall evergreens beside a sparkling stream. She had heard Patty tell of the campfires and the horse-back rides. For Patty was a Camp Fire girl, and Patty's mother was the guardian of the

The Silent Seasons—Fall, 1967, WILL BARNET. Oil on canvas, 43½" × 33"
Whitney Museum of American Art, New York City. Purchase with Funds from
Mr. and Mrs. Daniel H. Silverberg (73.48). Photograph by Geoffrey Clements.

group. Yet, friendly though Patty was, she never spoke of
Hattie's joining. And Hattie was far too shy to bring up the
subject.

In her old home she had not been so shy; but the old
house had grown too small, and they had had to move to a
larger one. Hattie, the first Noda baby, had been followed by
five boys, and, as Harry said, each child shrunk the house a
little bit more. This spring brought not only a new baby but a
new grandmother, and the house was as small as Hattie's year-
before-last coat. Even Mother couldn't let out its hems enough
to make it do.

Mother could manage almost anything. During the depression, when Father was out of work, Mother had kept the children neat as wax and even stylish. She was always up, working, when Hattie woke in the morning, always up, mending and making over, when Hattie went to sleep at night. Mother was proud that even in the bad years Denver had few Japanese Americans "on relief": almost as few as in jail.

Even Mother could not stretch the house enough for the new baby and Great-Grandmother. So the Nodas had moved, uprooting the children from neighborhood and school. The new school was pleasant; Hattie's teacher, Miss Bender, was lovely; Patty White was the prettiest girl Hattie had ever met. But Hattie didn't fit in.

So here she was, walking home alone, with Camp Fire and the mountains as far away as ever. Teddy overtook her, making noises like a machine gun—like a railway train—like an airplane. Teddy's face was as round as a button, his eyes as black as coal, his teeth as white as rice.

"Last one home's a lame duck!" he chirped at her.

She did not hurry as once she would have done. Home was a changed place now; changed by Grandmother as well as by the new house.

Though Great-Grandmother had come from Japan ten years ago, Hattie had never seen her till this month. Great-Grandmother had lived with Aunt Kiku in San Francisco, until Aunt Kiku's death had left Grandmother alone.

She was not at all what Hattie had expected; not at all like grandmothers in books, comfortable, plump people who loved to spoil their grandchildren. No, Grandmother was not that kind.

Hattie slowly opened the door, which still quivered from Teddy's banging it. Little gray Grandmother sat stiffly erect, only her head bent toward the sock she was darning, her small feet dangling.

"How do you do, Grandmother?" said Hattie.

"How do you do, Elder Daughter?" Grandmother responded. There is no easy way to say "granddaughter" in Japanese.

Under their folded lids Grandmother's eyes traveled down Hattie. Hattie, feeling prickly, smoothed her hair, straightened her collar, twitched her checked skirt, and finally shifted her weight to one knee as Grandmother reached her feet.

"A cold day for bare legs," Grandmother observed. Hattie thought her look added, *And a great girl twelve years old should wear long stockings.*

Self-consciously Hattie's eyes pulled free from Grandmother's. "Oh," she cried, "Dicky's climbed on the piano again." She ran over and replaced the box of satiny white wood in which her latest—and last—doll always stood on view, fairly safe from the six boys. It was an enchanting doll, with glossy black hair and a silk kimono. "The other boys at least keep off the piano," Hattie scolded, "but not Dicky."

Grandmother's cool eyes seemed to say, *Boys have to be excused, since they're so much more important than girls. And why should a great girl of twelve care about dolls?*

Hattie hurried on into the good-smelling kitchen. "Mother," she complained, "Grandmother doesn't understand that we're Americans, not Japanese. I bet she'd like me to flop down on my knees and bump my head on the floor the way you used to have to, and say, 'Honorable Grandmother, I have returned.'"

"Wash your hands," said Mother, "and help me get dinner on the table."

Hattie slapped her shoes down hard, as she went to the

sink to wash. She wished her heels weren't rubber; they didn't make enough noise to express her feelings.

"Of course you will give proper courtesy to the old," Mother said quietly.

"Why? She doesn't even like me." The question was useless. Hattie had grown up knowing that politeness to the old was as much a law as honesty, industry, self-control—and minding parents.

Mother only said, "Stop and buy grapefruit on your way from school. Be sure to pick out heavy ones."

"Of course," Hattie grumbled. Hadn't she known how to choose good fruit and vegetables since she was nine?

Dinner was Japanese American. Seven Nodas—and Grandmother—crowded around an ordinary American table; but the utensils were chopsticks instead of knives and forks. The fish soup and the pickled radish were Japanese; the *pakkai* were American spareribs and the fluffy white rice was international. Bread and butter were pure American, and the dessert was Japanese gelatin, too firm to quiver. "It's not so nervous as American jelly," Harry said, and made Teddy laugh till his eyes went shut.

Only Grandmother seemed all Japanese; in the way she sipped her soup and tea, with a noise that was polite in Japan but not in America; in the way she refused bread and butter; in the way she greeted an old neighbor of the Nodas', who came in as they were finishing the meal.

Grandmother shuffled across the room, toeing in, because for sixty-five of her seventy-five years she had worn clogs; and she bowed the deep bow of old Japan, her withered hands sliding down to her knees. Why couldn't Grandmother be more American?

The neighbor had come to remind them that tonight was

the festival called Buddha's[1] Birthday. Grandmother's eyes brightened at the news. But Mother apologized: she could not go with Grandmother, for Saburo the new baby was feverish, and she could never bear to leave her babies when they were sick. Father? He had to work tonight. Thoughtfully Grandmother looked at Hattie. Hattie excused herself and hurried back to school.

Right up to the time school opened, she kept seeing Grandmother's eyes brighten and grow dull. If Hattie had been with Patty and the others on the schoolground, as she longed to be, she might have forgotten Grandmother. But sitting lonesomely at her desk, pretending to read, she could not forget.

Maybe it was good, after all, to have a rule about being kind to old people whether they like you or not. Hattie thought of Mother, taking care of her and her brothers when they were young and helpless. How dreadful if, when Mother grew old and helpless, they did not take turn about and care for her! Hattie frowned at her book, thinking.

"Mad, Hattie? My, but you're scowling!" teased Patty, pausing as she came in from the schoolground.

Hattie shook her head and smiled. If only Patty would sit down beside her and say the thrilling words, "Oh, Hattie, wouldn't you like to join Camp Fire?" If she would even say, "Can't you come over after school?"

But after school Hattie walked home alone, as usual, stopping for the grapefruit on her way. When she had put them in the home cooler, she hunted up Grandmother, and ducked her head in a shy bow. "Grandmother," she said, "if you want

---

1. **Buddha** (bood′ ə, boō′ də): a religious philosopher and teacher who lived in India and founded the Buddhist faith.

Portrait of a Woman, date unknown, BARON VON STILLFRIED. Société de Géographie, Paris.

to go to Buddha's Birthday tonight, I'm sure Mother will let Harry and me go with you."

The Nodas were Methodists, so the Buddhist church was strange to Hattie and Harry. Tonight it was crowded, and all through the program small children trotted in and out and climbed over people's feet, with nobody minding. There were songs and dances and pantomimes, graceful kimonos, stately poses, dignified steps; and voices in the high falsetto which was the proper tone for Japanese actors, but which gave Hattie a funny, embarrassed feeling. "Such squeaky doors!" Harry whispered comically.

Coming home by street-car and bus, the three arrived so late that the house was all sleeping. Harry bade Grandmother good-night and stumbled drowsily to his room, but Grandmother lingered, eyes bright and cheeks flushed.

Hattie hunted for something to say. "The dancing was lovely," she said. "And the kimonos."

"I have one old kimono," Grandmother said, turning toward her door. With Hattie at her heels, she opened a dresser drawer and took out a silken bundle which she unfolded and held out, smiling faintly at Hattie's gasp of admiration.

"Chrysanthemums, for your aunt's name, Kiku, Chrysanthemum," said Grandmother. Gorgeous blossoms in many rich colors grew across the heavy blue crepe. "It was the only one saved from the great San Francisco fire. She wrapped it round one of her doll boxes." Grandmother motioned toward the drawer and a white wood box that lay there.

"Could I see?" Hattie stuttered.

"You may," Grandmother answered.

When Hattie slid open the box the breath of the Orient puffed out into her nostrils. She lifted the bag that protected the doll's hair and face, and gazed at the miniature lady, exquisitely moulded, and robed in brocades, padded, corded, embroidered. Clasping the box to her chest with one hand, Hattie pulled out a chair for Grandmother. "I don't know much about the doll festival," she coaxed shyly. "Here in Denver we don't."

She curled up on the floor at Grandmother's feet. "O Kiku San brought her doll set with her," Grandmother said, "when she married and came to America. This one is more than a hundred years old. We were taught to take care of things. The girls' festival—O Hina Matsuri—was a great day. It was play, but it taught us history and manners."

Looking from the doll to Grandmother, Hattie listened with all her might. She missed some words, for the Japanese the Nodas used at home was simple, and, to Hattie's relief, there had been no Japanese Language School for some years now. Still, she could follow the story, and it made pictures for her in the quiet night: little-girl-Grandmother wearing enchanting kimonos, in charming rooms carpeted with cushiony mats; spending long hours learning to serve tea just so, to arrange flowers just so, to paint the difficult Japanese letters just so; learning to hold her face and voice calm no matter how she felt. Girl-Grandmother, writing poems with her friends and going to view the full moon, valuing beauty above riches. Grandmother, hearing

The Other Side, 1986, JOSEPH RAFFAEL.
Photograph: Nancy Hoffman Gallery, New York.

about America, and longing to go where life was free for women. Grandmother, never able to come until she was too old to fit herself into this new land.

When the parlor clock struck one, Grandmother stopped short. "A girl of twelve should be asleep!" she said severely.

Next morning Hattie wondered if she had dreamed that companionable midnight visit, for Grandmother looked coldly at Hattie's bare knees and said, "Since you must run and jump like a boy, I suppose those ugly short clothes are necessary." But even while Hattie was biting her lip uncomfortably, Grandmother added, "Hatsuno, the chrysanthemum kimono and the doll are to be yours. After all, you are our only girl."

Home was beginning to seem homelike again.

That was fortunate for Hattie, since neighborhood and school were still strange. It was a relief to go back to their old district on Sundays, to the Japanese Methodist Church. And once Mother took the older children to an evening carnival at their old school. On the way they stopped at the store where they used to buy Japanese food, dishes, cloth. Clean and bright itself, it was jammed in among grimy second-hand stores and pawn shops. It was queer, Hattie thought, but no matter how clean people were, or what good citizens, if they happened to be born Chinese or Japanese or Mexican, they were expected to live down on these dirty, crowded streets, with the trucks roaring past. Yes, the new neighborhood and school were far pleasanter than the old—if only Hatsuno could fit in.

As Mother's Day approached, Hattie felt lonelier than ever. When she came into school two days before the tea, Patty, Sue, and Phyllis were huddled round the teacher's desk. Miss Bender smiled approvingly at Hattie, who was already top student in Seventh Grade. Patty smiled, too, and looked at her expectantly. Hattie's heart thumped with the wish to push herself in amongst them. But how could she? She smoothed her starched skirt under her, sat down, and pretended to clean out her desk.

"It's such a late spring," Miss Bender was saying, "the lilacs aren't out. But I'll bring sprays of cherry-blossoms. And we must find out how many mothers to expect. I hope your mother is coming, Hattie."

"No, ma'am," Hattie said soberly. "The baby has chickenpox, and Mother just won't leave a sick baby."

"Haven't you an aunt or grandmother who could come in her place?"

Oh, dear! Grandmother would be so different from the rest. What would Patty think of her? Then Hattie's head came up. "I'll ask Great-Grandmother," she said.

She thought Grandmother would refuse. She hoped Grandmother would refuse. Instead, Grandmother asked, "Every girl should have mother or grandmother at this tea?"

"Yes, Grandmother."

"And your mother will not leave the baby. Elder daughter, you went with me to Buddha's Birthday. I go with you to school."

Hattie swallowed a lump in her throat. Grandmother was doing this because she thought Hattie wished it. Tea— Grandmother would sip it in Japanese fashion. Would she notice if the girls giggled? She would hide the fact if she did. Hattie thought of Grandmother's long training in the concealment of pain or disappointment. Well, that was a good heritage for anybody. Hattie would use it now. "Thank you, Grandmother," she said. "I will come and get you Friday, after school."

When the two came into the schoolroom that afternoon, the mothers were all there and having their tea, and it seemed to Hattie that everyone stopped talking and turned to gaze. Well, she and Grandmother must look pretty funny, Hattie thought.

Hattie was dressed like the other girls, in white sweater and short white skirt, her white anklets folded neatly above her oxfords, and her black hair out of its braids and done in another favorite style of the season. Grandmother, as short and slim as Hattie, wore a dress nicely made over from a kimono, but looking a little strange; and her gray hair was combed straight back from the withered little face with its slanting eyes.

Politely Hattie introduced Miss Bender to Grandmother, and pulled up one of the visitor's chairs, since Grandmother had never been to a tea where people stood up and balanced the dishes on their hands. Patty brought her a plate, Phyllis the sandwiches, Sue a cup of tea. Then Patty returned, pulling her mother after her. "Mom," she said, "here's Hattie. And here's her great-grandma." Patty dropped her mother's hand and stood beaming.

Hattie looked anxiously at Grandmother. She could not speak a word of English, nor the others a word of Japanese. But, instead of words, Seventh Grade and its mothers were bringing sandwiches and cakes till Grandmother's plate was heaped. And Grandmother sat there, as stately and self-possessed and smiling as if she went to seven teas a week.

Hattie studied her more closely. Others might think Grandmother's little face a mask, but Hattie saw that the eyes were bright again, and that the wrinkled cheeks were pink. Grandmother liked it! Grandmother felt happy and at home!

Maybe even a great-grandmother could be lonesome, especially when she was too old to learn the ways of a new land. Thinking so happily of Grandmother that she forgot all about her own shyness, Hattie squeezed Patty's arm, just as she might have squeezed Teddy's on some rare occasion when he was sweet instead of maddening.

Patty squeezed back—quickly, as if she had been waiting for the chance. "Mother!" she stuttered, in a voice that matched her fluff of curls. "Mother, I think maybe I was mistaken. I think Hattie might like to—" She looked eagerly up into her mother's questioning eyes—"You ask her, Mother!" she begged.

"About Camp Fire? Hattie, would you like to join our Camp Fire group?"

Hattie was silent from pure joy and astonishment.

"If I got your name in this week," Mrs. White continued, "you could go to camp with us. A camp in the mountains; do you know about it?"

"Oh, yes, ma'am, I know," Hattie said with shining eyes. "Oh, yes, ma'am!"

Florence Crannell Means (1891–1980) was one of the earliest writers of literature about minority groups. She lived among the people she wrote about in order to better understand them. Means won an award for *The Moved-Outers*, a book about the struggles of American-born Japanese during World War II.

Other books: *Reach for a Star*
Our Cup Is Broken

Developing Comprehension Skills

1. Give two reasons why Hattie wants to join the Camp Fire group.

2. What are the major changes in Hattie's home life? How do the changes make her feel?

3. Early in the story, how does Hattie feel about her great-grandmother? Why does she go with Grandmother to the Buddha Birthday festival?

4. Why does Grandmother show her doll to Hattie? In what way does Hattie begin to see Grandmother that night?

5. How does Hattie expect the girls to react to her great-grandmother at the tea? Do you think her fears are realistic?

6. **Focus on Thinking: Identifying Effects.** One event can cause several effects. What does the tea cause Hattie to realize about Grandmother? What other effects does the tea have on Hattie?

Reading Fiction

1. **Analyzing Conflict.** Conflict between characters can have several causes. Give two causes of conflict between Hattie and Grandmother.

2. **Comparing Characters.** When you compare characters, look at their ways of thinking. In what ways are Hattie and her great-grandmother alike?

3. **Examining Details.** Literature can introduce you to other cultures. Find three details in this story that mention or describe old Japanese customs.

Study and Research

Skimming. To decide if a book or article will be useful in your research, use the method of fast reading called **skimming**. When you skim, let your eyes travel quickly down the page. Look for titles, headings, words in dark print, pictures, and captions.

Look up *Japan* in an encyclopedia. Skim the article to see what kinds of information are offered. Read a section that interests you, and summarize it for the class.

Writing in Response to Literature

Hattie at various times feels shy, lonely, and embarrassed. These are common feelings. Write about a time when you experienced one of these feelings.

Did you ever make a decision that your parents thought was wrong? See how Kennie stands behind a decision that he believes is right.

My Friend Flicka

MARY O'HARA

Report cards for the second semester were sent out soon after school closed in mid-June.

Kennie's was a shock to the whole family.

"If I could have a colt all for my own," said Kennie, "I might do better."

Rob McLaughlin glared at his son. "Just as a matter of curiosity," he said, "how do you go about it to get a *zero* in an examination? Forty in arithmetic; seventeen in history! But a *zero*? Just as one man to another, what goes on in your head?"

"Yes, tell us how you do it, Ken," chirped Howard.

"Eat your breakfast, Howard," snapped his mother.

Kennie's blond head bent over his plate until his face was almost hidden. His cheeks burned.

McLaughlin finished his coffee and pushed his chair back. "You'll do an hour a day on your lessons all through the summer."

Nell McLaughlin saw Kennie wince as if something had actually hurt him.

Lessons and study in the summertime, when the long

winter was just over and there weren't hours enough in the day for all the things he wanted to do!

Kennie took things hard. His eyes turned to the wide-open window with a look almost of despair.

The hill opposite the house, covered with arrow-straight jack pines, was sharply etched in the thin air of the eight-thousand-foot altitude. Where it fell away, vivid green grass ran up to meet it; and over range and upland poured the strong Wyoming sunlight that stung everything into burning color. A big jack rabbit sat under one of the pines, waving his long ears back and forth.

Ken had to look at his plate and blink back tears before he could turn to his father and say carelessly, "Can I help you in the corral with the horses this morning, Dad?"

"You'll do your study every morning before you do anything else." And McLaughlin's scarred boots and heavy spurs clattered across the kitchen floor. "I'm disgusted with you. Come, Howard."

Howard strode after his father, nobly refraining from looking at Kennie.

"Help me with the dishes, Kennie," said Nell McLaughlin as she rose, tied on a big apron, and began to clear the table.

Kennie looked at her in despair. She poured steaming water into the dishpan and sent him for the soap powder.

"If I could have a colt," he muttered again.

"Now get busy with that dish towel, Ken. It's eight o'clock. You can study till nine and then go up to the corral. They'll still be there."

At supper that night Kennie said, "But Dad, Howard had a colt all of his own when he was only eight. And he trained it and schooled it all himself; and now he's eleven, and Highboy is three, and he's riding him. I'm nine now and even if you did

give me a colt now I couldn't catch up to Howard because I couldn't ride it till it was a three-year-old and then I'd be twelve."

Nell laughed. "Nothing wrong with that arithmetic."

But Rob said, "Howard never gets less than seventy-five average at school, and hasn't disgraced himself and his family by getting more demerits than any other boy in his class."

Kennie didn't answer. He couldn't figure it out. He tried hard; he spent hours poring over his books. That was supposed to get you good marks, but it never did. Everyone said he was bright. Why was it that when he studied he didn't learn? He had a vague feeling that perhaps he looked out the window too much, or looked through the walls to see clouds and sky and hills and wonder what was happening out there. Sometimes it wasn't even a wonder, but just a pleasant drifting feeling of nothing at all, as if nothing mattered, as if there was always plenty of time, as if the lessons would get done of themselves. And then the bell would ring, and study period was over.

If he had a colt. . . .

When the boys had gone to bed that night Nell McLaughlin sat down with her overflowing mending basket and glanced at her husband.

He was at his desk as usual, working on account books and inventories.

Nell threaded a darning needle and thought, "It's either that whacking big bill from the vet for the mare that died or the last half of the tax bill."

It didn't seem just the auspicious moment to plead Kennie's cause. But then, these days, there was always a line between Rob's eyes and a harsh note in his voice.

"Rob," she began.

He flung down his pencil and turned around.

"Darn that law!" he exclaimed.

"What law?"

"The state law that puts high taxes on pedigreed stock. I'll have to do as the rest of 'em do—drop the papers."

"Drop the papers! But you'll never get decent prices if you don't have registered horses."

"I don't get decent prices now."

"But you will someday if you don't drop the papers."

"Maybe." He bent again over the desk.

Rob, thought Nell, was a lot like Kennie himself. He set his heart. Oh, how stubbornly he set his heart on just some one thing he wanted above everything else. He had set his heart on horses and ranching way back when he had been a crack rider at West Point; and he had resigned and thrown away his army career just for the horses. Well, he'd got what he wanted. . . .

She drew a deep breath, snipped her thread, laid down the sock, and again looked across at her husband as she unrolled another length of darning cotton.

To get what you want is one thing, she was thinking. The three-thousand-acre ranch and the hundred head of horses. But to make it pay—for a dozen or more years they had been trying to make it pay. People said ranching hadn't paid since the beef barons ran their herds on public land; people said the only prosperous ranchers in Wyoming were the dude ranchers; people said. . . .

But suddenly she gave her head a little rebellious, gallant shake. Rob would always be fighting and struggling against something, like Kennie; perhaps like herself, too. Even those first years when there was no water piped into the house, when every day brought a new difficulty or danger, how she had loved it! How she still loved it!

She ran the darning ball into the toe of a sock, Kennie's sock. The length of it gave her a shock. Yes, the boys were growing up fast, and now Kennie—Kennie and the colt. . . .

After a while she said, "Give Kennie a colt, Rob."

"He doesn't deserve it." The answer was short. Rob pushed away his papers and took out his pipe.

"Howard's too far ahead of him, older and bigger and quicker, and has his wits about him, and—"

"Ken doesn't half try, doesn't stick at anything."

She put down her sewing. "He's crazy for a colt of his own. He hasn't had another idea in his head since you gave Highboy to Howard."

"I don't believe in bribing children to do their duty."

"Not a bribe." She hesitated.

"No? What would you call it?"

She tried to think it out. "I just have the feeling Ken isn't going to pull anything off, and"—her eyes sought Rob's—"it's time he did. It isn't the school marks alone, but I just don't want things to go on any longer with Ken never coming out at the right end of anything."

"I'm beginning to think he's just dumb."

"He's not dumb. Maybe a little thing like this—if he had a colt of his own, trained him, rode him—"

Rob interrupted. "But it isn't a little thing, nor an easy thing, to break and school a colt the way Howard has schooled Highboy. I'm not going to have a good horse spoiled by Ken's careless ways. He goes woolgathering. He never knows what he's doing."

"But he'd love a colt of his own, Rob. If he could do it, it might make a big difference in him."

"If he could do it! But that's a big if."

At breakfast next morning Kennie's father said to him, "When you've done your study come out to the barn. I'm going in the car up to section twenty-one this morning to look over the brood mares. You can go with me."

"Can I go, too, Dad?" cried Howard.

McLaughlin frowned at Howard. "You turned Highboy out last evening with dirty legs."

Howard wriggled. "I groomed him—"

"Yes, down to his knees."

"He kicks."

"And whose fault is that? You don't get on his back again until I see his legs clean."

The two boys eyed each other, Kennie secretly triumphant

and Howard chagrined. McLaughlin turned at the door, "And, Ken, a week from today I'll give you a colt. Between now and then you can decide what one you want."

Kennie shot out of his chair and stared at his father. "A— a spring colt, Dad, or a yearling?"

McLaughlin was somewhat taken aback, but his wife concealed a smile. If Kennie got a yearling colt he would be even up with Howard.

"A yearling colt, your father means, Ken," she said smoothly. "Now hurry with your lessons. Howard will wipe."

Kennie found himself the most important personage on the ranch. Prestige lifted his head, gave him an inch more of height and a bold stare, and made him feel different all the way through. Even Gus and Tim Murphy, the ranch hands, were more interested in Kennie's choice of a colt than anything else.

Howard was fidgety with suspense. "Who'll you pick, Ken? Say—pick Doughboy, why don't you? Then when he grows up he'll be sort of twins with mine, in his name anyway. Doughboy, Highboy, see?"

The boys were sitting on the worn wooden step of the door which led from the tack room into the corral, busy with rags and polish, shining their bridles.

Ken looked at his brother with scorn. Doughboy would never have half of Highboy's speed.

"Lassie, then," suggested Howard. "She's black as ink, like mine. And she'll be fast—"

"Dad says Lassie'll never go over fifteen hands."

Nell McLaughlin saw the change in Kennie, and her hopes rose. He went to his books in the morning with determination and really studied. A new alertness took the place of the day-dreaming. Examples in arithmetic were neatly written out, and as she passed his door before breakfast she often heard the

monotonous drone of his voice as he read his American history aloud.

Each night, when he kissed her, he flung his arms around her and held her fiercely for a moment, then, with a winsome and blissful smile into her eyes, turned away to bed.

He spent days inspecting the different bands of horses and colts. He sat for hours on the corral fence, very important, chewing straws. He rode off on one of the ponies for half the day, wandering through the mile-square pastures that ran down toward the Colorado border.

And when the week was up he announced his decision. "I'll take that yearling filly of Rocket's. The sorrel with the cream tail and mane."

His father looked at him in surprise. "The one that got tangled in the barbed wire? That's never been named?"

In a second all Kennie's new pride was gone. He hung his head defensively. "Yes."

"You've made a bad choice, son. You couldn't have picked a worse."

"She's fast, Dad. And Rocket's fast—"

"It's the worst line of horses I've got. There's never one amongst them with real sense. The mares are hellions and the stallions outlaws; they're untamable."

"I'll tame her."

Rob guffawed. "Not I, nor anyone, has ever been able to really tame any one of them."

Kennie's chest heaved.

"Better change your mind, Ken. You want a horse that'll be a real friend to you, don't you?"

"Yes." Kennie's voice was unsteady.

"Well, you'll never make a friend of that filly. She's all cut and scarred up already with tearing through barbed wire after that mother of hers. No fence'll hold 'em—"

"I know," said Kennie, still more faintly.

"Change your mind?" asked Howard briskly.

"No."

Rob was grim and put out. He couldn't go back on his word. The boy had to have a reasonable amount of help in breaking and taming the filly, and he could envision precious hours, whole days, wasted in the struggle.

Nell McLaughlin despaired. Once again Ken seemed to have taken the wrong turn and was back where he had begun; stoical, silent, defensive.

But there was a difference that only Ken could know. The way he felt about his colt. The way his heart sang. The pride and joy that filled him so full that sometimes he hung his head so they wouldn't see it shining out of his eyes.

He had known from the very first that he would choose that particular yearling because he was in love with her.

The year before, he had been out working with Gus, the big Swedish ranch hand, on the irrigation ditch, when they had noticed Rocket standing in a gully on the hillside, quiet for once, and eying them cautiously.

"Ay bet she got a colt," said Gus, and they walked carefully up the draw. Rocket gave a wild snort, thrust her feet out, shook her head wickedly, then fled away. And as they reached the spot they saw standing there the wavering, pinkish colt, barely able to keep its feet. It gave a little squeak and started after its mother on crooked, wobbling legs.

"Yee whiz! Luk at de little *flicka*!" said Gus.

"What does *flicka* mean, Gus?"

"Swedish for little gurl, Ken."

Ken announced at supper, "You said she'd never been named. I've named her. Her name is Flicka."

The first thing to do was to get her in. She was running with a band of yearlings on the saddleback, cut with ravines and gullies, on section twenty.

They all went out after her, Ken, as owner, on old Rob Roy, the wisest horse on the ranch.

Ken was entranced to watch Flicka when the wild band of youngsters discovered that they were being pursued and took off across the mountain. Footing made no difference to her. She floated across the ravines, always two lengths ahead of the others. Her pink mane and tail whipped in the wind. Her long delicate legs had only to aim, it seemed, at a particular spot, for her to reach it and sail on. She seemed to Ken a fairy horse.

He sat motionless, just watching and holding Rob Roy in,

when his father thundered past on Sultan and shouted, "Well, what's the matter? Why didn't you turn 'em?"

Kennie woke up and galloped after.

Rob Roy brought in the whole band. The corral gates were closed, and an hour was spent shunting the ponies in and out and through the chutes, until Flicka was left alone in the small round corral in which the baby colts were branded. Gus drove the others away, out the gate, and up the saddleback.

But Flicka did not intend to be left. She hurled herself against the poles which walled the corral. She tried to jump them. They were seven feet high. She caught her front feet over the top rung, clung, scrambled, while Kennie held his breath for fear the slender legs would be caught between the bars and snapped. Her hold broke; she fell over backward, rolled, screamed, tore around the corral. Kennie had a sick feeling in the pit of his stomach, and his father looked disgusted.

One of the bars broke. She hurled herself again. Another went. She saw the opening and, as neatly as a dog crawls through a fence, inserted her head and forefeet, scrambled through, and fled away, bleeding in a dozen places.

As Gus was coming back, just about to close the gate to the upper range, the sorrel whipped through it, sailed across the road and ditch with her inimitable floating leap, and went up the side of the saddleback like a jack rabbit.

From way up the mountain Gus heard excited whinnies, as she joined the band he had just driven up, and the last he saw of them they were strung out along the crest running like deer.

"Yee whiz!" said Gus, and stood motionless and staring until the ponies had disappeared over the ridge. Then he closed the gate, remounted Rob Roy, and rode back to the corral.

Rob McLaughlin gave Kennie one more chance to change his mind. "Last chance, son. Better pick a horse that you have some hope of riding one day. I'd have got rid of this whole line of stock if they weren't so fast that I've had the fool idea that someday there might turn out one gentle one in the lot—and I'd have a race horse. But there's never been one so far, and it's not going to be Flicka."

"It's not going to be Flicka," chanted Howard.

"Perhaps she might be gentled," said Kennie; and Nell, watching, saw that although his lips quivered, there was fanatical determination in his eye.

"Ken," said Rob, "it's up to you. If you say you want her we'll get her. But she wouldn't be the first of that line to die rather than give in. They're beautiful, and they're fast, but let me tell you this, young man, they're *loco!*"

Kennie flinched under his father's direct glance.

"If I go after her again I'll not give up whatever comes; understand what I mean by that?"

"Yes."

"What do you say?"

"I want her."

They brought her in again. They had better luck this time. She jumped over the Dutch half door of the stable and crashed inside. The men slammed the upper half of the door shut, and she was caught.

The rest of the band was driven away, and Kennie stood outside of the stable, listening to the wild hoofs beating, the screams, the crashes. His Flicka inside there! He was drenched with perspiration.

"We'll leave her to think it over," said Rob when dinnertime came. "Afterward we'll go up and feed and water her."

But when they went up afterward there was no Flicka in the barn. One of the windows, higher than the mangers, was broken.

The window opened onto a pasture an eighth of a mile square, fenced in barbed wire six feet high. Near the stable stood a wagonload of hay. When they went around the back of the stable to see where Flicka had hidden herself they found her between the stable and the hay wagon, eating.

At their approach she leaped away, then headed east across the pasture.

"If she's like her mother," said Rob, "she'll go right through the wire."

"Ay bet she'll go over," said Gus. "She yumps like a deer."

"No horse can jump that," said McLaughlin.

Kennie said nothing because he could not speak. It was, perhaps, the most terrible moment of his life. He watched Flicka racing toward the eastern wire.

A few yards from it she swerved, turned, and raced diagonally south.

"It turned her! It turned her!" cried Kennie, almost sobbing. It was the first sign of hope for Flicka. "Oh, Dad! She has got sense. She has! She has!"

Flicka turned again as she met the southern boundary of the pasture, again at the northern; she avoided the barn. Without abating anything of her whirlwind speed, following a precise, accurate calculation and turning each time on a dime, she investigated every possibility. Then, seeing that there was no hope, she raced south toward the range where she had spent her life, gathered herself, and shot into the air.

Each of the three men watching had the impulse to cover his eyes, and Kennie gave a sort of a howl of despair.

Twenty yards of fence came down with her as she hurled herself through. Caught on the upper strands, she turned a complete somersault, landing on her back, her four legs dragging the wires down on top of her, and tangling herself in them beyond hope of escape. . . .

Kennie followed the men miserably as they walked to the filly. They stood in a circle watching, while she kicked and fought and thrashed until the wire was tightly wound and knotted about her, cutting, piercing, and tearing great three-cornered pieces of flesh and hide. At last she was unconscious, streams of blood running on her golden coat, and pools of crimson widening and spreading on the grass beneath her.

With the wire cutter which Gus always carried in the hip pocket of his overalls he cut all the wire away, and they drew her into the pasture, repaired the fence, placed hay, a box of oats, and a tub of water near her, and called it a day.

"I don't think she'll pull out of it," said McLaughlin.

Next morning Kennie was up at five, doing his lessons. At six he went out to Flicka.

She had not moved. Food and water were untouched. She was no longer bleeding, but the wounds were swollen and caked over.

Kennie got a bucket of fresh water and poured it over her

mouth. Then he leaped away, for Flicka came to life, scrambled up, got her balance, and stood swaying.

Kennie went a few feet away and sat down to watch her. When he went in to breakfast she had drunk deeply of the water and was mouthing the oats.

There began then a sort of recovery. She ate, drank, limped about the pasture, stood for hours with hanging head and weakly splayed-out legs, under the clump of cottonwood trees. The swollen wounds scabbed and began to heal.

Kennie lived in the pasture too. He followed her around; he talked to her. He, too, lay snoozing or sat under the cottonwoods; and often, coaxing her with hand outstretched, he walked very quietly toward her. But she would not let him come near her.

Often she stood with her head at the south fence, looking off to the mountain. It made the tears come to Kennie's eyes to see the way she longed to get away.

Still Rob said she wouldn't pull out of it. There was no use putting a halter on her. She had no strength.

One morning, as Ken came out of the house, Gus met him and said, "De filly's down."

Kennie ran to the pasture, Howard close behind him. The right hind leg which had been badly swollen at the knee joint had opened in a festering wound, and Flicka lay flat and motionless, with staring eyes.

"Don't you wish now you'd chosen Doughboy?" asked Howard.

"Go away!" shouted Ken.

Howard stood watching while Kennie sat down on the ground and took Flicka's head on his lap. Though she was conscious and moved a little she did not struggle nor seem frightened. Tears rolled down Kennie's cheeks as he talked to her and petted her. After a few moments Howard walked away.

"Mother, what do you do for an infection when it's a horse?" asked Kennie.

"Just what you'd do if it was a person. Wet dressings. I'll help you, Ken. We mustn't let those wounds close or scab over until they're clean. I'll make a poultice for that hind leg and help you put it on. Now that she'll let us get close to her, we can help her a lot."

"The thing to do is see that she eats," said Rob. "Keep up her strength."

But he himself would not go near her. "She won't pull out of it," he said. "I don't want to see her or think about her."

Kennie and his mother nursed the filly. The big poultice was bandaged on the hind leg. It drew out much poisoned matter, and Flicka felt better and was able to stand again.

She watched for Kennie now and followed him like a dog, hopping on three legs, holding up the right hind leg with its huge knob of a bandage in comical fashion.

"Dad, Flicka's my friend now; she likes me," said Ken.

His father looked at him. "I'm glad of that, son. It's a fine thing to have a horse for a friend."

Kennie found a nicer place for her. In the lower pasture the brook ran over cool stones. There was a grassy bank, the size of a corral, almost on a level with the water. Here she could lie softly, eat grass, drink fresh running water. From the grass, a twenty-foot hill sloped up, crested with overhanging trees. She was enclosed, as it were, in a green, open-air nursery.

Kennie carried her oats morning and evening. She would watch for him to come, eyes and ears pointed to the hill. And one evening Ken, still some distance off, came to a stop and a wide grin spread over his face. He had heard her nicker. She had caught sight of him coming and was calling to him!

He placed the box of oats under her nose, and she ate while he stood beside her, his hand smoothing the satin-soft skin under her mane. It had a nap as deep as plush. He played with her long, cream-colored tresses, arranged her forelock neatly between her eyes. She was a bit dish-faced, like an Arab,[1] with eyes set far apart. He lightly groomed and brushed her while she stood turning her head to him whichever way he went.

He spoiled her. Soon she would not step to the stream to drink but he must hold a bucket for her. And she would drink, then lift her dripping muzzle, rest it on the shoulder of his blue

---

1. **Arab** (ar'əb): a breed of swift, graceful horses native to the country of Arabia.

chambray shirt, her golden eyes dreaming off into the distance, then daintily dip her mouth and drink again.

When she turned her head to the south and pricked her ears and stood tense and listening, Ken knew she heard the other colts galloping on the upland.

"You'll go back there someday, Flicka," he whispered. "You'll be three, and I'll be eleven. You'll be so strong you won't know I'm on your back, and we'll fly like the wind. We'll stand on the very top where we can look over the whole world and smell the snow from the Neversummer Range. Maybe we'll see antelope. . . ."

This was the happiest month of Kennie's life.

With the morning Flicka always had new strength and would hop three-legged up the hill to stand broadside to the early sun, as horses love to do.

The moment Ken woke he'd go to the window and see her there, and when he was dressed and at his table studying he sat so that he could raise his head and see Flicka.

After breakfast she would be waiting at the gate for him and the box of oats, and for Nell McLaughlin with fresh bandages and buckets of disinfectant. All three would go together to the brook, Flicka hopping along ahead of them as if she were leading the way.

But Rob McLaughlin would not look at her.

One day all the wounds were swollen again. Presently they opened, one by one, and Kennie and his mother made more poultices.

Still the little filly climbed the hill in the early morning and ran about on three legs. Then she began to go down in flesh and almost overnight wasted away to nothing. Every rib showed; the glossy hide was dull and brittle and was pulled over the skeleton as if she were a dead horse.

Gus said, "It's de fever. It burns up her flesh. If you could stop de fever she might get vell."

McLaughlin was standing in his window one morning and saw the little skeleton hopping about three-legged in the sunshine, and he said, "That's the end. I won't have a thing like that on my place."

Kennie had to understand that Flicka had not been getting well all this time; she had been slowly dying.

"She still eats her oats," he said mechanically.

They were all sorry for Ken. Nell McLaughlin stopped disinfecting and dressing the wounds. "It's no use, Ken," she said gently, "you know Flicka's going to die, don't you?"

"Yes, Mother."

Ken stopped eating. Howard said, "Ken doesn't eat anything any more. Don't he have to eat his dinner, Mother?"

But Nell answered, "Leave him alone."

Because the shooting of wounded animals is all in the day's work on the western plains, and sickening to everyone, Rob's voice, when he gave the order to have Flicka shot, was as flat as if he had been telling Gus to kill a chicken for dinner.

"Here's the Marlin, Gus. Pick out a time when Ken's not around and put the filly out of her misery."

Gus took the rifle. "*Ja* boss. . . ."

Ever since Ken had known that Flicka was to be shot he had kept his eye on the rack which held the firearms. His father allowed no firearms in the bunkhouse. The gun rack was in the dining room of the ranch house, and going through it to the kitchen three times a day for meals, Ken's eye scanned the weapons to make sure that they were all there.

That night they were not all there. The Marlin rifle was missing.

When Kennie saw that he stopped walking. He felt dizzy.

He kept staring at the gun rack, telling himself that it surely was there—he counted again and again—he couldn't see clearly. . . .

Then he felt an arm across his shoulders and heard his father's voice.

"I know, son. Some things are awful hard to take. We just have to take 'em. I have to, too."

Kennie got hold of his father's hand and held on. It helped steady him.

Finally he looked up. Rob looked down and smiled at him and gave him a little shake and squeeze. Ken managed a smile too.

"All right now?"

"All right, Dad."

They walked in to supper together.

Ken even ate a little. But Nell looked thoughtfully at the ashen color of his face and at the little pulse that was beating in the side of his neck.

After supper he carried Flicka her oats but he had to coax her, and she would only eat a little. She stood with her head hanging but when he stroked it and talked to her she pressed her face into his chest and was content. He could feel the burning heat of her body. It didn't seem possible that anything so thin could be alive.

Presently Kennie saw Gus come into the pasture carrying the Marlin. When he saw Ken he changed his direction and sauntered along as if he was out to shoot some cottontails.

Ken ran to him. "When are you going to do it, Gus?"

"Ay was goin' down soon now, before it got dark. . . ."

"Gus, don't do it tonight. Wait till morning. Just one more night, Gus."

"Vell, in de morning den, but it got to be done, Ken. Yer fader gives de order."

"I know. I won't say anything more."

An hour after the family had gone to bed Ken got up and put on his clothes. It was a warm moonlit night. He ran down to the brook, calling softly. "Flicka! Flicka!"

But Flicka did not answer with a little nicker; and she was not in the nursery nor hopping about the pasture. Ken hunted for an hour.

At last he found her down the creek, lying in the water. Her head had been on the bank, but as she lay there the current of the stream had sucked and pulled at her, and she had had no strength to resist; and little by little her head had slipped down until when Ken got there only the muzzle was resting on the bank, and the body and legs were swinging in the stream.

Kennie slid into the water, sitting on the bank, and he hauled at her head. But she was heavy, and the current dragged like a weight; and he began to sob because he had no strength to draw her out.

Then he found a leverage for his heels against some rocks in the bed of the stream and he braced himself against these and pulled with all his might; and her head came up onto his knees, and he held it cradled in his arms.

He was glad that she had died of her own accord, in the cool water, under the moon, instead of being shot by Gus. Then, putting his face close to hers, and looking searchingly into her eyes, he saw that she was alive and looking back at him.

And then he burst out crying and hugged her and said, "Oh, my little Flicka, my little Flicka."

The long night passed.

The moon slid slowly across the heavens.

The water rippled over Kennie's legs and over Flicka's body. And gradually the heat and fever went out of her. And

the cool running water washed and washed her wounds.

When Gus went down in the morning with the rifle they hadn't moved. There they were, Kennie sitting in water over his thighs and hips, with Flicka's head in his arms.

Gus seized Flicka by the head and hauled her out on the grassy bank and then, seeing that Kennie couldn't move, cold and stiff and half-paralyzed as he was, lifted him in his arms and carried him to the house.

"Gus," said Ken through chattering teeth, "don't shoot her, Gus."

"It ain't fur me to say, Ken. You know dat."

"But the fever's left her, Gus."

"Ay wait a little, Ken. . . ."

Rob McLaughlin drove to Laramie to get the doctor, for Ken was in violent chills that would not stop. His mother had him in bed wrapped in hot blankets when they got back.

He looked at his father imploringly as the doctor shook down the thermometer.

"She might get well now, Dad. The fever's left her. It went out of her when the moon went down."

"All right, son. Don't worry. Gus'll feed her, morning and night, as long as she's—"

"As long as I can't do it," finished Kennie happily.

The doctor put the thermometer in his mouth and told him to keep it shut.

All day Gus went about his work, thinking of Flicka. He had not been back to look at her. He had been given no more orders. If she was alive the order to shoot her was still in effect. But Kennie was ill, McLaughlin making his second trip to town taking the doctor home, and would not be back till long after dark.

After their supper in the bunkhouse Gus and Tim walked down to the brook. They did not speak as they approached the filly, lying stretched out flat on the grassy bank, but their eyes were straining at her to see if she was dead or alive.

She raised her head as they reached her.

"By the powers!" exclaimed Tim. "There she is!"

She dropped her head, raised it again, and moved her legs and became tense as if struggling to rise. But to do so she must use her right hind leg to brace herself against the earth. That was the damaged leg, and at the first bit of pressure with it she gave up and fell back.

"We'll swing her onto the other side," said Tim. "Then she can help herself."

"Ja. . . ."

Standing behind her, they leaned over, grabbed hold of her left legs, front and back, and gently hauled her over. Flicka was as lax and willing as a puppy. But the moment she found herself lying on her right side, she began to scramble, braced herself with her good left leg, and tried to rise.

"Yee whiz!" said Gus. "She got plenty strength yet."

"Hi!" cheered Tim. "She's up!"

But Flicka wavered, slid down again, and lay flat. This time she gave notice that she would not try again by heaving a deep sigh and closing her eyes.

Gus took his pipe out of his mouth and thought it over. Orders or no orders, he would try to save the filly. Ken had gone too far to be let down.

"Ay'm goin' to rig a blanket sling fur her, Tim, and get her on her feet, and keep her up."

There was bright moonlight to work by. They brought down the posthole digger and set two aspen poles deep into the ground either side of the filly, then, with ropes attached to the blanket, hoisted her by a pulley.

Not at all disconcerted, she rested comfortably in the blanket under her belly, touched her feet on the ground, and reached for the bucket of water Gus held for her.

Kennie was sick a long time. He nearly died. But Flicka picked up. Every day Gus passed the word to Nell, who carried it to Ken. "She's cleaning up her oats." "She's out of the sling." "She bears a little weight on the bad leg."

Tim declared it was a real miracle. They argued about it, eating their supper.

"Na," said Gus. "It was de cold water, washin' de fever outa her. And more dan dat—it was Ken—you tink it don't count? All night dot boy sits dere and says, 'Hold on, Flicka, Ay'm here wid you. Ay'm standin' by, two of us togedder'. . . ."

Tim stared at Gus without answering, while he thought it over. In the silence a coyote yapped far off on the plains, and the wind made a rushing sound high up in the jack pines on the hill.

Gus filled his pipe.

"Sure," said Tim finally. "Sure. That's it."

Then came the day when Rob McLaughlin stood smiling at the foot of Kennie's bed and said, "Listen! Hear your friend?"

Ken listened and heard Flicka's high, eager whinny.

"She don't spend much time by the brook any more. She's up at the gate of the corral half the time, nickering for you."

"For me!"

Rob wrapped a blanket around the boy and carried him out to the corral gate.

Kennie gazed at Flicka. There was a look of marveling in his eyes. He felt as if he had been living in a world where everything was dreadful and hurting but awfully real; and *this* couldn't be real; this was all soft and happy, nothing to struggle over or worry about or fight for any more. Even his father was proud of him! He could feel it in the way Rob's big arms held him. It was all like a dream and far away. He couldn't, yet, get close to anything.

But Flicka—Flicka—alive, well, pressing up to him, recognizing him, nickering. . . .

Kennie put out a hand—weak and white—and laid it on her face. His thin little fingers straightened her forelock the way he used to do, while Rob looked at the two with a strange expression about his mouth and a glow in his eyes that was not often there.

"She's still poor, Dad, but she's on four legs now."

"She's picking up."

Ken turned his face up, suddenly remembering. "Dad! She did get gentled, didn't she?"

"Gentle—as a kitten. . . ."

They put a cot down by the brook for Ken, and boy and filly got well together.

Mary O'Hara (1885–1980) worked as a movie script-writer in Hollywood in the 1920's. When O'Hara moved to Wyoming to live on a ranch, she learned to love and understand horses. She wrote "My Friend Flicka" first as a short story and then as a novel. It was made into a movie and a television series.

Other books: *Thunderhead*
Green Grass of Wyoming

Developing Comprehension Skills

1. Why is Kennie's father angry with him when the story begins? Why does his mother think a colt will help Kennie?

2. When Kennie chooses Flicka, Rob says that Ken made a bad choice. Why? How does Kennie feel about Rob's reaction? Why does he keep the colt anyway?

3. How does Flicka injure herself? Compare how Rob reacts to the injury with how Nell reacts.

4. Kennie has mixed feelings from the time his father orders Flicka to be shot until the next morning. Identify his feelings during the main events of the long night.

5. Gus and Tim disagree about what saved Flicka. What is your opinion? Explain your answer.

6. **Focus on Thinking: Inferring Feeling.** You can infer a character's feelings through his or her actions. What does Ken's father do at the end of the story? What can you infer about his feelings?

Reading Fiction

1. **Understanding Character Development.** Longer stories allow you to get to know characters well. You may notice changes in their personalities. Does Kennie change in this story? Explain why or why not.

2. **Examining Conflict.** A character can be in conflict with several other human or animal characters at the same time for different reasons. Describe three conflicts Ken faces with other characters.

Critical Thinking

Comparing Characters. When you compare characters, look for similarities in their personalities. Also notice how they act and how they get along with other characters.

Compare two characters in this story, such as Kennie and his father or Kennie and Flicka.

Writing in Response to Literature

Good literature can bring out strong feelings such as sadness, anger, worry, excitement, or happiness. Write about how you felt as you read this story. Tell what made you feel that way.

Language and Literature

Vocabulary

Example Clues. A writer often uses examples to explain an unfamiliar word in context. The examples may help explain a more general term. At other times, the word itself is an example of a more familiar general term. Signals for example clues are words like *and other, for example, like, especially,* and *for instance.*

Exercise. Using example clues, explain the underlined words.

1. Hatsuno preferred to eat fish, especially tuna and halibut.
2. Ken taught Flicka several gaits, such as walking, trotting, and galloping.
3. Grandmother wore heavy kimonos, but Hatsuno dressed in lighter cottons, such as lawn.
4. The McLaughlins treated some of their horses' afflictions, such as injuries, diseases, and infections.

Developing Writing Skills

Creating a New Ending. Each event in a plot affects the other events. By changing one event, you can change the plot. Change one event in "Hatsuno's Great-Grandmother" or "My Friend Flicka." Write a new ending based on your change.

Prewriting. Choose which story you will change. Use a time line to list the important events in the plot. Change one event. Plan the events that will lead to a new ending.

Drafting. Choose a point in the story just before the event you change. Describe the setting, characters, and action at that point. Write about the new events in the order they happen. Write your new ending.

Revising and Sharing. Add details that allow readers to picture your events more clearly. Read your new ending to classmates. Ask for their thoughts about your new ending.

Reading Poetry

Poems That Paint Pictures

Picture a beach at dawn or an amusement park at twilight. What sights, sounds, tastes, and smells come to mind? How could you share this picture, or image, with others?

An artist meets the challenge of sharing an image by using paints to create a picture. A poet meets the challenge of sharing an image in a different way. He or she uses words to paint a picture.

Imagery

Each picture that a poet creates is called an **image**. The use of words that make something seem real or easy to imagine is called **imagery**. Poets create imagery by using words that appeal to the senses. These words help the reader see, hear, taste, smell, and feel the world the poet is describing. Notice the images in the poem, "Scene," by Charlotte Zolotow. To what sense do the images appeal?

Little trees like pencil strokes
black and still
etched forever in my mind
on that snowy hill.

Figurative Language

Poets also create images by describing familiar things in new ways. These descriptions use **figurative language**, that is, the creative use of words to mean more than their factual meaning. Simile, metaphor, and personification are types of figurative language.

Simile. A comparison between two unlike things that have something in common is called a **simile**. A simile always uses the words *like* or *as* to make a comparison. Read these lines from "Concrete Mixers" by Patricia Hubbell. What two things is the poet comparing in this simile? How are they alike?

> Concrete mixers
> Move like elephants

Metaphor. Like a simile, a **metaphor** also compares unlike things that have something in common. A metaphor, however, does not use the words *like* or *as*. In these lines from "The Night Is a Big Black Cat," G. Orr Clark compares night to a black cat. What other metaphor does he use?

> The night is a big black cat
>   The Moon is her topaz eye,

Personification. Poets sometimes give human qualities to animals, objects, or ideas. This is called **personification**. Notice how a flower appears to be a princess in this poem, "The Lily Princess."

>   Down from her dainty head
> The Lily Princess lightly drops
>   A spider's airy thread.

How to Read Figurative Language

As you read each poem in this part, see the world through the poet's eye. Picture each image. See and feel and hear as the poet does. Notice what is fresh and new about each comparison. Appreciate the challenge of writing and reading figurative language.

Rain Pools

LILIAN MOORE

The rain
litters
the street
with mirror splinters
silver and   5
brown.

Now
each piece
glitters with

sky   10
cloud
tree

upside down.

Puddle, 1952, M. C. ESCHER. National Gallery of Art, Washington, D.C., Rosenwald Collection.

Developing Comprehension Skills

1. What idea about rain pools is expressed in the first six lines?

2. The two verbs in the poem are *litters* and *glitters*. What in the poem litters? What glitters?

3. Why are the sky, the cloud, and the tree upside down?

Reading Poetry

1. **Recognizing Sensory Images.** Poets use words and phrases that appeal to the senses to create images, or pictures, in the reader's mind. Name two words or phrases in this poem that appeal to the sense of sight.

2. **Examining Rhyme.** Rhyming words can tie parts of a poem together. Find two pairs of words that rhyme in this poem.

Writing in Response to Literature

The poem "Rain Pools" uses images that appeal to the sense of sight to describe rain. Think of words and phrases that describe the sound of rain. List them. Then use your list to write several sentences or a few lines of poetry about the sound of rain.

Lilian Moore grew up in New York City and now lives on a farm. She writes about both city and country life. Moore has worked as a teacher and the editor of the Arrow Book Club. A writer of both stories and poetry, she won the 1985 National Council of Teachers of English Award for Excellence in Poetry.

Other Books: *I Thought I Heard the City*
Something New Begins

What beauty can you find outside on a cold winter day? Use all your senses as you imagine the icicles in this poem.

Icicles

BARBARA JUSTER ESBENSEN

Have you tasted icicles
fresh from the edge
of the roof?

Have you let the sharp ice
melt   5
in your mouth
like cold swords?

The sun plays them
like a glass
xylophone   a crystal   10
harp.

All day they fall
chiming
into the pockmarked
snow.   15

Developing Comprehension Skills

1. What two questions does the poet ask?

2. How could icicles look like a crystal harp?

3. What do you picture as the sun "plays" the icicles? How does the fourth stanza add to this image?

4. **Focus on Thinking: Comparing and Contrasting.** Showing likenesses between different things is **comparing.** Showing differences between them is **contrasting.** Compare and contrast the poems "Rain Pools" and "Icicles." Consider the subject of each poem, sensory images, rhyme, and stanzas.

Reading Poetry

1. **Recognizing Sensory Images.** Many poems contain images that appeal to several senses. Reread each stanza of "Icicles." To which sense or senses do the details in each stanza appeal?

2. **Recognizing Similes.** A comparison between two unlike things using *like* or *as* is called a **simile.** Identify the two similes in "Icicles."

3. **Examining Imagery.** The use of words to create a picture in your mind is called **imagery.** Describe how you imagine "pockmarked snow" to look.

Writing in Response to Literature

Copy and complete these similes in as many different ways as you can:
An icicle feels like. . . . An icicle looks like. . . . An icicle tastes like. . . .

Cynthia in the Snow

GWENDOLYN BROOKS

It SUSHES.
It hushes
The loudness in the road.
It flitter-twitters,
And laughs away from me.   5
It laughs a lovely whiteness,
And whitely whirs away,
To be
Some otherwhere,
Still white as milk or shirts.   10
So beautiful it hurts.

Developing Comprehension Skills

1. Who is the "me" in this poem? Where do you find this information?

2. What idea is expressed in the first three lines?

3. What words in the poem describe movement? Where does the snow go?

4. Think of another title for this poem.

Reading Poetry

1. **Recognizing Personification.** When writers give human qualities to animals, ideas, or things, they are using **personification.** What human actions does the snow perform in this poem?

2. **Understanding Onomatopoeia.** Using a word that sounds like what it means is called **onomatopoeia.** The poet made up the word *sushes* to describe the sound snow makes. What other words in this poem sound like what they mean?

3. **Finding Alliteration.** The repetition of consonant sounds at the beginnings of words is called **alliteration.** The *s* sound repeated in the title, "Cynthia in the Snow," is an example of alliteration. Find two other examples of alliteration in the poem.

Writing in Response to Literature

The last line of the poem describes the snow as "so beautiful it hurts." Have you ever seen something that beautiful? Describe what you saw.

Gwendolyn Brooks (born 1917) published her first poem at the age of thirteen. Brooks most often writes about life in the city. She has been awarded many honors for her work. One of her poetry books, *Annie Allen,* won a Pulitzer Prize. Brooks became poet laureate, or official poet, of Illinois in 1969.

Other books: *Bronzeville Boys and Girls*
The Bean Eaters

When someone says wind,
what do you picture? Compare
two poets' pictures of wind.

Buffalo Calf Woman, 1967, OSCAR HOWE. Department of the Interior, Indian Arts and Crafts Board, Sioux Indian Museum and Crafts Center, Rapid City, South Dakota.

Wind Is a Ghost

A Dakota Poem Retold by NATALIA BELTING

Wind is a ghost
That whirls and turns,
Twists in fleet moccasins,
Sweeps up dust spinning
Across the dry flatlands.   5

Whirlwind
Is a ghost dancing.

The Hurricane

PALES MATOS
A Poem from Puerto Rico Translated by Alida Malkus

When the hurricane unfolds
Its fierce accordion of winds,
On the tip of its toes,
Agile dancer, it sweeps whirling
Over the carpeted surface of the sea   5
With the scattered branches of the palm.

Developing Comprehension Skills

1. Both poems picture types of wind-storms. Where does the whirlwind happen? Where does the hurricane occur?

2. What action verbs describe the ghost-like movements in "Wind Is a Ghost"? What is ghost-like about wind?

3. How does the picture described in the first two lines of "The Hurricane" show both sound and movement?

4. Which poem do you prefer? Why?

Reading Poetry

1. **Recognizing Metaphors.** A comparison between two unlike things that have something in common is called a **metaphor.** For example, "The river is a snake" is a metaphor. Find a metaphor in one of these wind poems.

2. **Identifying Personification.** You remember that **personification** is the giving of human qualities to animals or objects. Find an action in each poem that makes the wind seem like a person.

Writing in Response to Literature

Think about a type of storm that happens where you live. Write a paragraph or poem that describes the storm and how it makes you feel.

Language and Literature

Vocabulary

Inference Clues. Inference clues are hints in the rest of the sentence or paragraph that help you infer, or figure out, the meaning of a new word. Suppose you read, "A drought hit the region. Crops dried up, and farmers were desperate for rain." You can infer that *drought* means "lack of rain."

Exercise. Using inference clues, explain the underlined words.

1. As soon as their leaking boat capsized, the frightened girls began swimming toward a nearby boat.
2. The boat's crew spotted the girls and shouted encouragement. Their waving and shouting cheered the girls on.
3. When the girls finally got to the boat, they ascended the rope ladder to reach the safety of the deck.

Developing Writing Skills

Writing a Poem. Poets combine words to help you see, hear, smell, taste, or feel what they are picturing. Write a poem about nature that appeals to the senses.

Prewriting. Choose a scene or event that can be found in nature, such as a rainbow or a snow-covered tree. List words and phrases for each sense that describe your topic. Decide which senses your poem will focus on. Also decide if you want your poem to rhyme.

Drafting. Organize your poem around a sense, or an idea, or a comparison. Use the phrases from your notes to create an image.

Revising and Sharing. Change any words that could be more exact or easier to picture. Get rid of any unnecessary words. Read your poem aloud. Ask classmates to draw what they picture from hearing it.

What do you love or hate
about cats? Decide if you
would like a Gumbie Cat.

The Old Gumbie Cat

T. S. ELIOT

I have a Gumbie Cat in mind, her name is Jennyanydots;
Her coat is of the tabby kind, with tiger stripes and leopard
    spots.
All day she sits upon the stair or on the steps or on the mat:
She sits and sits and sits and sits—and that's what makes a   5
    Gumbie Cat!

    But when the day's hustle and bustle is done,
    Then the Gumbie Cat's work is but hardly begun.
    And when all the family's in bed and asleep,
    She tucks up her skirts to the basement to creep.   10
    She is deeply concerned with the ways of the mice—
    Their behaviour's not good and their manners not nice;
    So when she has got them lined up on the matting,
    She teaches them music, crocheting and tatting.

I have a Gumbie Cat in mind, her name is Jennyanydots;   15
Her equal would be hard to find, she likes the warm and sunny
    spots.

Cat and Flowers, 1983, RUSKIN SPEAR. Private Collection. Photograph: Gallery Five, London.

All day she sits beside the hearth or on the bed or on my hat:
She sits and sits and sits and sits—and that's what makes a
      Gumbie Cat!   20

      But when the day's hustle and bustle is done,
      Then the Gumbie Cat's work is but hardly begun.
      As she finds that the mice will not ever keep quiet,
      She is sure it is due to irregular diet;

And believing that nothing is done without trying,   25
She sets right to work with her baking and frying.
She makes them a mouse-cake of bread and dried peas,
And a *beautiful* fry of lean bacon and cheese.

I have a Gumbie Cat in mind, her name is Jennyanydots;
The curtain-cord she likes to wind, and tie it into sailor-knots.   30
She sits upon the window-sill, or anything that's smooth and
       flat:
She sits and sits and sits and sits—and that's what makes a
       Gumbie Cat!

But when the day's hustle and bustle is done,   35
Then the Gumbie Cat's work is but hardly begun.
She thinks that the cockroaches just need employment
To prevent them from idle and wanton destroyment.
So she's formed, from that lot of disorderly louts,
A troop of well-disciplined helpful boy-scouts,   40
With a purpose in life and a good deed to do—
And she's even created a Beetles' Tattoo.[1]

So for Old Gumbie Cats let us now give three cheers—
On whom well-ordered households depend, it appears.

---

1. **Tattoo** (ta too'): in England, a military spectacle, or show, featuring music and
marching.

Developing Comprehension Skills

1. What makes a Gumbie Cat?

2. Think about all the Gumbie Cat does at night. What do her activities have in common?

3. How do you think the speaker feels about the cat?

4. **Focus on Thinking: Identifying the Supporting Details.** Details in a stanza can support a main idea. What is the main idea of the stanza beginning at line 35? What details support that idea?

Reading Poetry

1. **Examining Personification.** Personification can give an animal a human personality. What human qualities does the Gumbie Cat show? To what type of person would you compare her?

2. **Examining Sound.** The use of rhyme and repetition can make a poem sound musical. In what pattern do the lines rhyme? Which lines are repeated in the poem? How is the poem like a song?

3. **Analyzing Feeling.** The feeling you get from a poem results from the picture you imagine and the sounds of the poem. What feeling does this poem give?

Writing in Response to Literature

Whom do you know that is most like Jennyanydots? Write a description of that person. Explain why he or she reminds you of Jennyanydots.

T. S. Eliot (1888–1965) was born in St. Louis, Missouri, but lived most of his adult life in England. Many people regard him as one of the greatest poets of the twentieth century. Eliot's style of writing influenced many other poets. The poem "The Old Gumbie Cat" comes from his book *Old Possum's Book of Practical Cats*. The musical *Cats* is based on this book.

How do you act when you are really hungry? See if you can understand how a hungry shark might feel.

The Shark

JOHN CIARDI

My dear, let me tell you about the shark.
Though his eyes are bright, his thought is dark.
He's quiet—that speaks well of him.
So does the fact that he can swim.
But though he swims without a sound, 5
Wherever he swims he looks around.
With those two bright eyes and that one dark thought.
He has only one but he thinks it a lot.
And the thought he thinks but can never complete
Is his long dark thought of something to eat.   10
Most anything does. And I have to add
That when he eats his manners are bad.
He's a gulper, a ripper, a snatcher, a grabber.
Yes, his manners are drab. But his thought is drabber.
That one dark thought he can never complete   15
Of something—anything—somehow to eat.

Be careful where you swim, my sweet.

Developing Comprehension Skills

1. What is the shark's one dark thought? Why is the shark unable to complete this thought?

2. What do you think is the purpose of the last line?

3. **Focus on Thinking: Recognizing the Main Idea.** A piece of writing can express many ideas. The idea that is most important is the main idea. What main idea about the shark does the poem express?

Reading Poetry

1. **Examining the Language of Poetry.** The poet chooses words not only for their meaning but also for the feeling they create. What words describe the shark when he eats? What feeling do these words add to the poem?

2. **Identifying Rhyme Patterns.** You have learned that lines can rhyme in patterns. In what pattern do the ends of lines rhyme in this poem?

3. **Examining Repetition.** Poets sometimes repeat words or phrases. What phrase is repeated often in this poem? Why do you think it is repeated?

Writing in Response to Literature

What feeling do you get as you read this poem? Is the poem frightening, or funny, or both? Write your feelings about "The Shark."

John Ciardi (1916–1986) began writing poems as a way of entertaining his nephews. His interest in words led him to write many poetry books and two books about word origins. Ciardi was a teacher, translator, lecturer, and poetry editor of *Saturday Review* magazine.

Other books: *The Reason for the Pelican*
The King Who Saved Himself from Being Saved

Have you ever imagined that something you owned was alive? Discover what a television might do if it could come to life.

The Television

GEOFFREY GODBEY

Unaccustomed
to movement
and real life
it crept
to the window   5
and,
delicately
lifting the blind
with a long
aluminum   10
tentacle,
sat
looking out
at the night.

Developing Comprehension Skills

1. What does the television do?

2. What is the "aluminum tentacle"?

3. Why do you think the television decides to look out the window?

Reading Poetry

1. **Understanding Comparison.** Poets use comparisons to make readers look at familiar objects in new ways. To what do you think the poet is comparing the television? What words help make this comparison?

2. **Examining Feeling.** Poets choose words to create feelings in the reader. What feeling do you have after reading this poem? What words help create this feeling?

3. **Understanding the Form.** You have learned that the form or shape is an important element of a poem. How many lines are in this poem? How many sentences does the poem contain? What is the effect of writing a sentence in this form?

Speaking and Listening Skills

Interpreting a Poem. Most poems are meant to be read aloud. Choose one of the poems you have read in this section. Practice before you read it to the class. Decide what feeling you think the poem suggests, and let your voice express that feeling.

Writing in Response to Literature

Suppose that you are the television. Write your comments on what you see outside the window.

Language and Literature

Vocabulary

Inference Clues. You have learned that sometimes you can figure out what a word means from the context. To do this, read beyond the sentence in which the word appears. Examine details in the entire paragraph that will help you infer the meaning.

Exercise. Using inference clues, explain the underlined words.

Tom, the sea monster, lived in a dark, damp grotto in the cliffs by the sea. The cave was so cold that he decided to install a heating system. As landlord of the cave, he felt entitled to control the heat. However, he did not want to irritate the bats who were his tenants. To keep his renters happy, he put in individual thermostats. Now each bat controls the heat in its hanging space, and Tom stays warm.

Developing Writing Skills

Describing Characters. Writers often give human personalities to animals and objects. Describe the shark, the Gumbie Cat, and the television. Tell how each character is like a person.

Prewriting. Make three columns, and label them *cat, shark,* and *television.* Find and list words and phrases in the poems that describe the characters. Decide if anything about the character makes it seem human.

Drafting. Describe each character in a separate paragraph, using your notes. Point out any actions or qualities that make the character seem human.

Revising and Sharing. Make sure each paragraph is about one main idea. Make clear to whom or what each pronoun you use refers. Share your paper with classmates.

Reading Nonfiction

What Is Nonfiction?

Suppose that you are reading about a sports hero, or the first landing on the moon, or the training of race horses. You are reading nonfiction. **Nonfiction** is a form of literature that tells about real people, places, events, and things. Nonfiction presents both facts and opinions. Unlike fiction, it does not come from the writer's imagination.

You are already reading many types of nonfiction such as textbooks, newspaper and magazine articles, encyclopedias, and journals. In this section, you will read two more types of nonfiction—biographies and autobiographies.

Biographies and Autobiographies

Both **biographies** and **autobiographies** are factual accounts of a person's life. In a biography, someone else writes about the person. In an autobiography, the person writes about his or her own life. Both works are usually about a famous person or about someone who overcame great odds to achieve something.

The writer of a biography, the **biographer,** does research to find out about the person's life. The biographer reads the person's letters and journals and anything other people have written about this person. If possible, the biographer interviews the person and talks with people who knew him or her. The autobiographer, on the other hand, writes from his or her own memory.

The writer decides which facts and events are most important to report. Biographies and autobiographies can be long works that cover in detail a person's whole life. They can also be shorter works that highlight certain periods in a person's life.

Biographies and autobiographies are like fiction in several ways. Like fiction, they are usually written in **chronological order,** that is, the order in which the events happened. They have characters and setting as fiction does. The characters are real people. The setting, when and where someone lived, is important to a life story. Both biographies and autobiographies present conflict, just as fiction does.

Point of View

One way to tell an autobiography from a biography is to look at the point of view. The writer chooses a **point of view,** that is, who will narrate or tell the story. Works of literature can be narrated from a first-person or a third-person point of view. Most autobiographies are narrated from the first-person point of view. The narrator uses the first-person pronouns *I, me,* and *my.* Biographies are written from the third-person point of view. The writer uses the third-person pronouns *he* or *she* to narrate the life of someone else.

It is important to know from what point of view a story is told. Who tells the story often influences what information is included.

How to Read Nonfiction

When you read a biography or an autobiography, pay attention to when and where the person lived. Identify the important people in the person's life. Follow the order of events and see how the events are related. Look for reasons for the person's actions. Notice the point of view, and decide how the writer feels about the person. Last of all, learn from reading about how others face challenges.

What America Means to Me

JESSE STUART

What do you think are the advantages of living in America? Read to see how Jesse Stuart feels about this country.

Jesse Stuart is famous for his writings about the people and the mountains of Kentucky, where he lived. He wrote over three hundred stories, poems, and autobiographical works. Stuart was appointed poet laureate of Kentucky in 1954. He died in 1984.

In Milwaukee I spoke to 14,400 educators. It was hard for me to realize that so many people were listening to me. After my talk, teachers came up and brought my books for me to sign. It was a great meeting for me. I had never dreamed in my youth of addressing an audience of this size.

I had never dreamed, either, that I would travel in thirty-nine states in one year, give seventy-six talks to teacher groups, colleges, universities, and civic organizations. I am not bragging when I mention these things. I feel humble. When I sign my name and people say kind words for some of the things I have written, my mind flashes back to another day and time. It goes back to the one-room shack on a high ridge in Greenup County, Kentucky, where I was born.

My father, who then could not read and write his name, was a coal miner. My mother caught rain water in a barrel at the corner of the shack for washing clothes. She carried water in a lard can from a neighbor's well for drinking and cooking.

We had only one book in our shack. That was the Bible. We kept it out on a little table for everyone to see. And above the Bible, hanging over spike nails driven into joists, was our shotgun, which my father kept ready to protect his family. On a barren puncheon floor, two beds, a cookstove, standtable, and mirror comprised about all our worldly possessions. We didn't own the one-room shack. We rented it.

My mother was the educated one in our family. She had finished the second grade. When my father left the coal mine, he moved down into W-Hollow and rented a little farm. He bought a mule and plow and one cow. And he bought young oxen, broke them to the yoke, and plowed the rooty hillsides.

My father preached education for his family. He wanted one of his children to be a schoolteacher. Schoolteaching was the only profession of man that my father ever looked up to. And it was at Plum Grove, a one-room rural school high on a hilltop, that I

Indian Summer—Zepp, Virginia, 1970, JOHN CHUMLEY. Collection of Mr. and Mrs. Earl E. Dyess, Fort Worth, Texas. Photograph by Bob Wharton.

learned to write the name that people ask me to sign today. It was the first thing I learned to write. I was so elated to put something down on paper that stood for a real something that I ran home and said to my father, "Pa, I can do something you can't do." He said, "What's that?" I said, "Write my name."

My father was embarrassed. He got my mother to teach him a signature which only the banker in his home town knows today. When my first teacher, Calvin Clarke, told my father that my sister and I were "bright pupils" who ought to stand at the head of our classes, my father was pleased. Calvin Clarke was eighteen and taught fifty-six classes in six hours. Attendance ranged from fifty to seventy pupils, many older than he.

My schoolbooks were fabulous things. And my teacher, a high-school graduate, had all the knowledge in the world, I thought.

My father moved from farm to farm, always to better his position. Then I was forced to quit school. I worked by the day for twenty-five cents, my father and his horse worked for $1.50 per day. My mother got twenty-five cents per day for housework.

But I was schooled in a different way. All the farms I worked on in Kentucky were beautiful in the spring months. I saw nature come to life from winter's sleeping. I learned many things on the land. Learned that the turtles laid eggs in the sand and let the warm sun hatch their young. Learned that the cowbirds laid eggs in other birds' nests and let them hatch and raise their young. Learned that black snakes laid eggs in the rich, warm loam and the sun hatched their young.

All the life about me was a great school and while I worked for twenty-five cents a day I learned.

Finally my father bought fifty acres of land in the head of W-Hollow for three hundred dollars. It was the only tract in Greenup County that didn't have a legal road to it. When we walked to it in any direction we had to get permission from landowners whose farms surrounded ours. We couldn't haul anything to our farm; there wasn't a wagon road leading to it.

My father was so excited about buying fifty acres and becoming a landowner that the day he got the deed he changed from chewing home-grown Burley tobacco and smoked a big cigar. Then he got a job on the railroad section. He held this job for twenty-three years. His highest wage scale was $3.06 per day. He paid for his farm by working on the section and improved his fields by working at night in the moonlight and by lantern light.

I found work in Greenup, Kentucky, where the town was paving its streets. I got a job as water boy for seventy-five cents a day. Very easy work for me. Too easy. It was hard for the foreman of the paving company to get a man to pour cement into the concrete mixer. I asked for the job and got it. I was fifteen then. I did as hard work as any man, for I held the job, which more than a dozen had quit, until the streets were paved.

It was there I saw my first high school—Greenup High School where well-dressed boys and girls walked leisurely on the streets. And I wanted to enter high school. With somewhere between twenty-two and thirty months of schooling at Plum Grove, I took a common-school examination on eleven subjects. Four of these I had never studied. I had to make an average of 75 and not below 60 on any subject. I made an average of 78.

I made 59 on Composition, but I passed into high school anyway.

High school was the greatest place in the world to me. My English teacher would even let me read from six to twelve themes in her class at a time. She said one theme, "Nest Egg," was funny, and laughed until she had to wipe tears from her eyes. "Nest Egg," with only six words changed, was published twenty-three years later in *The Atlantic Monthly*. Also, it was reprinted in Watt-Cargill's *College Reader* and is read by many college students today.

My English teacher gave me a book of Robert Burns's poems. I wore it out as I carried it with me wherever I went. If Burns, a plowboy in Scotland, could do it, I, a plowboy in Kentucky, could do it. That's the way I looked at it.

I read my first novel, *Silas Marner*, and reported on it for my English class. I read Jack London's short stories and loved them. In high school I made my way by hunting at night and following a trap line to and from school, selling animal pelts and possum carcasses to anybody who would buy. In the spring months I dug wild roots and sold them.

At the end of four wonderful years

Manchester Valley, 1914, JOSEPH PICKETT. Oil with sand on canvas, 45½″ × 60⅝″. Collection, Museum of Modern Art, New York City, Gift of Abby Aldrich Rockefeller.

I went back to the farm. I had written more than a hundred themes and two hundred poems. And I had read many books. They had lifted me. I saw beyond my Greenup County hills. And I wondered about the world beyond. I talked to my father about going to college, but he wouldn't listen.

One day, when he was working on the railroad, I drove the mule team to the barn. I went to the house and packed my clothes and themes. I told Mom I was going. She laughed and said, "Go ahead. You'll be back. Chickens come home to roost!"

I was off to the big, wide world of America, on my own. First, I got work with a street carnival. Here I met people. But I lost this job somewhere near Cincinnati, Ohio. I gave too many free rides on the Merry Mixup. From here to Camp Knox, then to the steel mills.

When September came again and the leaves colored I had my debts paid and a few dollars ahead, and I left the steel mills. It was 1926. I was on my way to find a college.

I hitchhiked past Morehead State College. The place looked too big. At the second college, Kentucky Wesleyan in Winchester, I stopped and asked a student how much it would cost to go to school there for one year. "Three hundred dollars," he told me. That was too much for me. At Berea College I stopped and the dean asked me a few questions. Then he said, "We have a waiting list. Come back next year." I told him I was going to college.

It was he who suggested Lincoln Memorial University at Harrogate, Tenn. I hitchhiked there. They accepted me. I didn't have a transcript of my credits and I had only $29.30. Tell me, where on earth but America can one find an opportunity like this?

I stayed at Lincoln Memorial three years and two summers, worked half a day, went to college half a day, graduated with a B average. I did all kinds of work—farm work, sewer lines, water lines, carpenter work, crushed limestone for the roads, dining room work. I found this play-work after the kind of work I'd been used to doing.

Little did I know on the day I graduated from Lincoln Memorial University that twenty-one years later I would stand on the same platform and receive an honorary degree of Doctor of Humane Letters. This was something I accepted with gratitude, yet with the deepest humility, since a number of men about my age rose in the audience and cheered. They were my classmates and I wasn't sure just who should receive the honorary degrees.

They had come to Lincoln Memorial when I did, and at that time they didn't have money or a decent suit of clothes. Today two are vice-presidents of insurance companies. Among them are doctors who have built their own hospitals in remote regions of Kentucky and Tennessee. Many are educators. This happened in America. It made me realize that America was a poor boy's country. That he could rise to unlimited heights if he were willing to work, if he had reasonable intelligence and good character.

When I returned home, the first college graduate in my family, my parents were proud of me. I had paved the way. Later my father's dream came true. He had four teachers from his five living children, three of whom were college graduates. The fourth had a year of college. All were high-school graduates. We are just one among thousands of American families where this has happened. We didn't let the chances come to us. We went out and found them. They are in America for all who are willing to look.

I was a teacher in a one-room rural school, a high-school teacher, high-school principal, and later superintendent of Greenup County schools. When I was elected superintendent my father rejoiced. To him this was the greatest honor any of his children ever received.

Then another thing happened for which I shall be eternally grateful. There was a family who came to America by the name of Guggenheim and they made some money in America. They put this money to a good cause. They gave, and still give, more than a hundred fellowships each year to students in various fields from research to creative work in the arts and sciences. I applied for a fellowship and got it for creative writing. I didn't know the Guggenheims. I didn't know a member of the board who selected me. I was given two thousand dollars to spend abroad. I didn't have to report how I spent this money. I didn't even have to report what I had written.

After fourteen months in Europe, I returned to America with this feeling: I never knew America until I went to Europe. The Europeans were fine, hospitable people, but their opportunities were limited. I wondered what would happen if the young men and women in Europe had the chances America offered. I felt that the majority of these young people would not have to wait for the opportunities which might never come to them, but they would be able to go out and find them.

Now, I realized America didn't owe me a cent. I owed America. I owed thanks to over a million Americans who had bought my books. I owed thanks to book reviewers who had given me valuable criticism and praise and who had helped me to become a writer. I owed more than I could ever repay to my teachers, elementary, high school, and college. They had inspired me to do bigger and better things. I

Sweet Land of Liberty, 1985, JEANNE CHAMPION NOWAKOWSKI. Quilt. Collection of the Artist. Photograph: by Schecterlee.

was indebted to editors of magazines who bought and published my stories and poems.

I was indebted to the editors and publishers of my books. All of these people had contributed to make me a writer. Not that my father's work had not been honorable, but if I had been born and brought up in many countries I had seen, I would have followed the occupation of my father—while in America a man can choose his own profession.

I returned to America on the *Countess Savoy*. When we passed the Statue of Liberty, if my arms had been long enough to reach from my ship, I would have hugged her neck. America is the dream. America is the place. America is it.

Developing Comprehension Skills

1. Describe Jesse Stuart's childhood home.

2. What ambition did Jesse's father have for his children? Why?

3. One main idea Jesse expresses is that he learned outside of school. List three details he gives to support this idea.

4. How did Jesse's determination get him a college education? How did he further his education after college?

5. How did the setting of Jesse's youth influence him? Do you think this same story could happen today in America?

6. **Focus on Thinking: Understanding Contrasts.** Differences between people, places, and things are called **contrasts.** What major contrast does the author show between Europe and America? Why is this difference so important?

Reading Nonfiction

1. **Understanding Theme.** The title of a work of literature often suggests the **theme,** or message about life. What is the theme of this autobiography?

2. **Evaluating Character.** You must evaluate, or judge for yourself, the character of the autobiographer. What qualities does Jesse Stuart show? What do you think of him?

3. **Examining Autobiography.** The autobiographer must choose which events of his or her life to write about. What do most of the events in this article have in common? Why were those events chosen rather than others?

Study and Research

Using Biographical Dictionaries. Biographical dictionaries give short summaries of people's lives. Some cover special fields such as sports. Others include important people in all fields. Find the biographical dictionaries in the reference section of your library. Name two that include Jesse Stuart.

Writing in Response to Literature

Jesse Stuart taught in a one-room schoolhouse. Write a description of the kind of teacher you think he would be.

Tell how someone you know was affected by a bad accident. See how Alesia deals with the effects of her accident.

From

Alesia

ELOISE GREENFIELD
and ALESIA REVIS

In this excerpt, a young girl, Alesia Revis, combines her diary entries with her reflections on the past to tell her story. The well-known writer Eloise Greenfield worked with Alesia to help her write this autobiography.

The Accident

It happened in Washington, D. C., on the evening of August 29, 1972. Nine-year-old Alesia was having a good time. She and her **friend** Percy were racing on their bikes, flying down the alley to see which one could go faster. When they reached the street, Percy took a quick look for cars and kept going. Alesia was right behind him.

It wasn't a street that was heavily traveled, only a few cars came through now and then. But a car was coming that day, at just that very moment, headed straight toward Alesia. She never saw it. When they got her to Providence Hospital, she was pronounced DOA—dead on arrival.

But Alesia didn't die. She's seventeen now and very much alive. This book is her story.

Eloise Greenfield
August, 1980

Wed., March 19, 1980

This morning I woke up and looked at the clock. It said four-thirty. I said, "Uh-uh! This isn't me!" I rolled on over and went back to sleep. And then I overslept.

I get up at five-thirty on school days, because it takes me kind of a long time to do things. So this morning I had to rush to get dressed and eat and have all my books in the book bag by the time the school bus came at eight o'clock.

Daddy had put my wheelchair out front before he went to work, and the bus driver, Mr. Gordon, put it on the bus for me. Then Mrs. Smith, the bus attendant, came to my front door and I held on to her arm and walked to the bus.

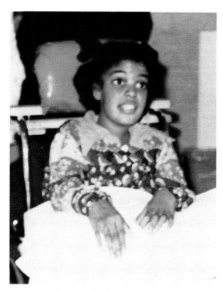

Alesia at the hospital six months after the accident.

I can walk some now, if I hold on to a wall or a piece of furniture or somebody's arm, or if I push my wheelchair. I can even walk a little way without holding on to anything. And I remember when I couldn't do any of those things.

But I don't remember getting hit by that car. I only know what people tell me. My friend Valerie said she had been on the bike with me for a while, but I had let her off just before I started to race with Percy. I'm so glad she got off, so that she wasn't hurt, too. And I'm glad the doctors at the hospital didn't give up on me. They kept working on me and then they came out and said to Daddy and Mama, "We've done all we can. It's up to Alesia and the Lord now, it's up to her and the Lord."

I was unconscious for five weeks. A lot of people were praying for me, and some of them didn't even know me. Mama lit candles in the hospital chapel, and the priests at my church, St. Anthony's, said special prayers. And Sister Clotilde, she had been my teacher that year and I had been so bad in her class, always talking and stuff, but after I got hurt, she had her class praying for me twice a day.

The day I woke up and started to talk, some of the nurses wanted me to surprise Mama. They wanted me to say, "Hi, Mama," when she walked into the room. But Daddy said no, he didn't know if she could stand the shock. So he called her at work and told her the good news. Mama says that after she got off the phone she just said four words—"My child is talking!" And she got out of there and came to the hospital as fast as she could.

I had my tenth birthday party in the hospital on October 8, 1972. I don't remember that, either, but the first time I went back to visit after I got out, something about that hospital smell just struck me. I said, "I remember this smell, yeah, I remember this smell!"

Tues., March 25, 1980

Nothing much happened at school today, except work. It's almost time for Easter vacation and I already have homework for over the holidays.

Tomorrow we're supposed to have a party in our Child Study class. That's one of my favorite classes. We're learning all about the unborn baby, and what to do when an infant cries, and how to take care of small children. I like children.

When Mama used to take me grocery shopping in my wheelchair, little children would come up to me and they'd stare and ask a whole lot of questions.

They'd say, "Why are you in that chair?"

I'd say, "Because I can't walk."

"Why can't you walk?"

"Because I got hit by a car."

"Why'd you get hit by a car?"

"Because I rode my bike out in the street."

And then they'd say, "Didn't you know better than to do that?"

I used to get so tickled. But it's not funny when grown folks start staring. You expect it from little children, but not from grown folks. It really gets me when they do it. They could just glance at me and keep on about their business, but they stare so hard, it makes me feel self-conscious.

Some people move way away from me when they see me in the wheelchair, like they're afraid they might catch my disability. They have disabilities, too—faults and things like that, everybody has them. Mine is just more noticeable, but they don't think about it that way.

A lot of people are nice, though. Everywhere I go, whenever I need help, there's always somebody. One time, Mama took me downtown on the subway, and when we got off, the elevator wasn't working, and there was this long, steep flight of steps we had to go up. A man and a woman came over and helped Mama carry me in the chair all the way up those steps. I don't know what we would have done if they hadn't offered to help.

Some people try too hard to help, even when I say I don't need it. Sometimes in a store, I'll be looking at a blouse or something, and somebody will say, "You want me to get that for you?"

I'll say, "No, thank you."

"You want me to push you?"

"No, thank you."

"You want me to. . . ."

They just keep asking me even though I say no. I'm glad when people are nice enough to help me when I need it, but I like to do as many things as I can by myself.

Wed., April 9, 1980

Today, nothing much to it. I went to school. Nothing there. I want something exciting to happen to me. I can't wait till I learn to really walk again.

Walking, real walking, is gliding. Just gliding along and not thinking about it. Not having to hold on to anything, or wonder whether your knee is going to give out, or worry about stepping on a rock and losing your balance. Walking fast or slow whenever you want to, and when you want to stop, you just put your foot down and stop, and don't have to think, "Should I stop right here or stop right there?" And you don't need any assistance—not a wheelchair or a crutch or anything or anybody. You just glide.

If anybody asked me what I want most in the whole world, I would say, "To be able to walk again." I daydream about it. I can just see myself walking up the street by myself. Without anyone around me. One time I even went so far as to daydream I was running, and I was just so happy.

Sometimes I start thinking about what I would be doing if I could walk. One day I was coming home from visiting my sister, Alexis, and I thought to myself, "Why aren't you walking?" I got choked up, and when we got home I went to my room and fell on my bed and just started crying. I couldn't help it.

Once when I was feeling really down, I asked Mama how she would feel if I just gave up on everything. Mama said, "If you had given up when you were in the hospital, you wouldn't be here now."

Sun., April 13, 1980

I wanted to go to church today, but church starts at eleven-thirty and I didn't wake up until eleven-fifteen. Mama was already dressed and having coffee with Daddy, and I didn't want to make her late. So I just slept for a while longer.

In the evening, Mama and I went outside so I could practice my walking. I have to concentrate on keeping my body straight. And I have to remember to put my foot down the right way. I walk on just the ball of my foot, and you're not supposed to do that. You're supposed to walk on your whole foot, starting with the heel, so I practiced putting my heel down first. I didn't have on my brace, but I guess I did all right because I didn't fall.

After the accident, when I was learning how to take steps again, I did the same thing a baby does—I crawled first. Ms. Schiller, the physical therapist at Sharpe, taught me to do it. She said it would make my hands and shoulders and knees stronger. Then, after that, Mama and Alexis taught me to crawl up and down the steps at home so Daddy wouldn't have to carry me anymore. One day I told Mama I wanted to try to walk. I said I thought I could do it, and when Mama asked Ms. Schiller if it would be all right, she said it wouldn't do any harm.

I fell a lot, just like a baby, trying to go from crawling to walking. It was hard on me and hard on Mama, too. She would be holding me, but I was a big girl, I was about twelve, and she couldn't always keep me from falling. One time she was helping me walk from the den to the kitchen—to go to dinner, I think—and all of a sudden my knee gave out. I fell on top of Mama, and my teeth hit the floor. It hurt so bad, I started crying. Mama pretended she wasn't hurt much, but I had on that heavy, long-leg brace, and I know that thing hurt.

I remember the very first time I walked by myself. Alexis was in high school then. She was on the basketball team, and she was going to take me to watch her practice. She went to open the car door for me while I sat in the den, but we were going to be late, so I said to myself, "Let me help her out a little." I decided I would try to walk to the front door.

Nobody else was home, so I had to do it by myself. I was kind of scared, but I wanted to do it, so I pushed up off the arms of my wheelchair and stood up. There wasn't going to be anything for me to hold on to, because if I leaned over to hold the furniture, I would fall. So I put my mind on walking and nothing else, and I just took a step, and another one, and then about three more, and I was at the door of the den. I grabbed the wall and started smiling, I was so happy I'd made it that far. I looked up to heaven and said, "Thank you."

I stayed there for a minute and got myself together. I was

hoping my knee wouldn't give out, so I practiced bending it a little bit, and then I started across the living room. I didn't look in the mirror because I knew it would make me nervous to see myself walking. I looked straight ahead, and I made it to the next wall, and I said, "Thank you" again. Then I had to walk just a few more steps to get to the door—and I did it! I said, "I made it, I made it, thank you!"

I looked out to see where Alexis was. She was coming toward the house, and I was glad she was looking down because when she lifted her head to open the door, I was standing there waving at her. She was so surprised. She burst out laughing and gave me a great big hug. She was still smiling when we got to practice, and everyone was asking me, "What's Alexis smiling so much about?" I said, "I walked to the front door all by myself." They all thought it was nice, but I could tell they didn't really understand why we were so happy.

Thurs., May 29, 1980

I went up to Sharpe today to see Ms. Schiller, my physical therapist. I had to get my heel cord stretched. That's that cord at the back of your foot that connects your heel to your leg. Mine was tight because I hadn't been to therapy for a while. It was so tight I couldn't put my heel down on the floor. Ms. Schiller pulled it and it hurt so much I felt like crying. But I knew she was trying to help me, so I just stayed pretty much cool. And after she had finished, my heel could touch the floor.

I do exercises every night just before I go to bed. I exercise my arms, and I pull my knee up to my chest ten times, and I cross my right foot over my left and my left foot over my right. And I do twists, fifty on each side, because I wouldn't mind having a slim waist.

When I was a student at Sharpe, I had to go to the physical therapy room almost every day so Ms. Schiller could help me do all the things I needed to do to improve—sit-ups, rolling on a mat from one end to the other, things like that. I used to love the scooter board. That's a board with four small wheels on it, two in front and two in back. I would lie on my stomach on two scooter boards, because I was kind of tall, and I'd push myself up this ramp, get to the top, turn around, and come flying back down.

Wed., October 8, 1980

Today is my birthday, my eighteenth birthday. At lunchtime I was in the activity room, sitting at a table with Thomas, and when I told him it was my birthday, he went out into the middle of the room and said, "Hey, y'all, today is Alesia's birthday!" Then he came back to the table and said, "How did you like that?" And in homeroom class, Danny came over and kissed me on the cheek and said, "Happy Birthday!"

This evening, Daddy, Mama, Allen, and Alexis took me out to dinner to celebrate. Then Alexis baked me a cake, a vanilla cake with white icing, and everybody sang "Happy Birthday" to me.

I'm a woman now, I'm not a girl anymore. I keep thinking about that. In three years I'll be twenty-one. In less than one year I'll be out of high school. I've just about decided to go to college. If I do, I want to live on campus. I want to get used to being out in the world and see what I can do on my own.

It helps you to do things when you have people pulling for you. You're pulling for yourself, of course, but then you have other people pulling for you, too. Your family and friends and everybody. You know if you don't try, you let them down. They've gone out of their way trying to please you and everything, and then you just sit there and don't try, it kind of puts them down.

Sometimes I worry about what my future is going to be like. But then, I know that it's going to be all right. When I was in the hospital, unconscious, the doctors told Mama and Daddy that if I lived, I would probably be like a vegetable for the rest of my life. I wouldn't be able to think or care about things or laugh or anything. But it didn't happen that way. I'm not a vegetable, I'm a person. And I'm still here, still living.

Fri., October 24, 1980

Things are getting exciting. Next month we're having a Senior Class Tea for our parents. Daddy and Mama are coming, and I'm sure not going to miss it.

We had our homecoming dance at school tonight. I hung out with my friends, Mary and Katherine. When we went out on the dance floor, I looked at them to see what dance they were doing, and I held on to Mary's shoulder and did the same thing. And I didn't fall once. Some of my other friends were there too, watching, and everybody was proud of me. I can't wait until they see me on graduation day. I've been practicing, and I'm almost sure that I am going to walk all the way across that stage by myself to get my diploma. Maybe with my cane. But not holding on to anybody's arm. Nobody around me, waiting to catch me. Just me myself, Alesia.

After graduating from high school, Alesia studied computer operations for two years at the University of the District of Columbia. Alesia now lives in her own apartment. She walks using only a cane. Alesia's immediate goals include getting her driver's license and a job. These will help her become even more independent than she is now.

Eloise Greenfield (born 1929) was a neighbor of Alesia Revis at the time of her accident. Like *Alesia*, many of Greenfield's books are written to inspire readers. A writer of poetry, short stories, and biographies, she has won awards for her books about Rosa Parks, Paul Robeson, and Mary McLeod Bethune.

Other books: *Sister*
Talk About a Family

Developing Comprehension Skills

1. What accident happened to Alesia? How did it affect her physically?

2. How old is Alesia when she writes these memories of her accident?

3. Alesia gets angry when adults stare at her. Why do you think they stare? How should they act?

4. What is Alesia's goal? Why does she rely on herself to achieve it?

5. Alesia and her sister are thrilled when Alesia first walks by herself. Why are others unable to appreciate their happiness?

6. **Focus on Thinking: Understanding Implied Main Idea.** When the main idea of a paragraph is implied, not stated, you can sometimes figure it out from details given. What is the main idea of the last paragraph in the October 8 entry?

Reading Nonfiction

1. **Understanding Autobiographies.** Autobiographers usually let their actions speak for themselves. Alesia never calls herself brave. Describe three actions that show her bravery.

2. **Identifying Point of View.** An autobiography is written from the first-person point of view. What pronoun refers to Alesia? What can she tell from her point of view that no one else can tell?

3. **Understanding Structure.** The way the parts of a work of literature fit together is called the **structure.** Part of Alesia's story is from her diary and part is from her memories. How do the two parts of the structure differ? How do they fit together?

Writing in Response to Literature

Put yourself in Alesia's place just after the accident. Think about the adjustments you would have to make. Write about the one you would find most difficult.

Language and Literature

Vocabulary

Comparison and Contrast Clues. When you read an unknown word, see if it is compared to or contrasted with any other words in the context. Look for words like *than, like, as,* and *similar to* to signal that a word is being compared to something similar. Look for words like *although, but, however, yet, on the other hand,* and *different from* to signal that a word is being contrasted with another word.

Exercise. Using clue words, identify the words that are the same as or the opposite of the underlined word.

> Although Captain Rongway had been calm, he began to feel <u>apprehensive</u>. Being well-fed, he looked different from the <u>undernourished</u> sharks he faced. They stared <u>ravenously</u> at him like hungry vultures. Rongway felt as <u>ensnared</u> as a fly trapped on flypaper. He knew that there was only one thing to do. He turned his inner tube around and paddled the wrong way.

Developing Writing Skills

Writing a Definition. To define a quality such as kindness or honesty, you can use examples to make the meaning clear. Write your own definition of bravery. Use characters from this unit as examples.

Prewriting. Decide what bravery means to you. List words, phrases, and examples that remind you of bravery. Make notes about what the brave characters in this unit have in common.

Drafting. Define bravery in your topic sentence. Use details and examples from the stories to support your definition. End with a concluding statement.

Revising and Sharing. Reread your paper to make sure each detail supports your definition. Exchange papers and compare definitions and ideas with classmates.

What career do you dream of having? Read this story to see how Pelé realizes his dream.

Pelé
The King of Soccer

CLARE *and* FRANK GAULT

A small boy danced barefoot out into the street and began kicking at the air as if he were kicking a soccer ball. But there was no ball. Nearby, a group of men and boys huddled around a radio, listening to a local soccer game: Bauru against São Carlos, a neighboring town in southeastern Brazil. The year was 1948.

One of the men smiled as he watched the boy acting like a real soccer player. The boy was eight years old. His name was Edson Arantes Do Nacimento, but his friends called him Pelé (pā lā').

Pelé kept kicking at the air. He could imagine himself out on the soccer field, dribbling the ball downfield with his feet, passing it to a teammate, then taking a pass in return and kicking a goal.

Suddenly, the radio announcer became excited. Bauru had the ball near the São Carlos goal. Pelé stopped to listen. A player nicknamed Dondinho was moving in to take a shot, and it looked as if he would score. Dondinho kicked, but he missed. Everybody groaned.

Dondinho was one of the policemen in town, but he played soccer part-time for the local club to earn a little extra money for his family. He was also Pelé's father. Pelé ran home. Soon his father arrived, too, looking very sad.

Pelé's mother said, "See what that game does to you. You missed a goal, and now you'll be sad for days. I pray Pelé never plays soccer." But that night, when Pelé's father, mother, grandmother, younger brother, and sister gathered for prayers, Pelé prayed he would become a great soccer player.

The next morning, Pelé dressed to go to school. He put his lunch in a paper bag. He put in his soccer ball, too: one of his father's old socks stuffed hard with newspapers and laced shut with string. It was no bigger than a large orange and not very round, but it was the only soccer ball Pelé had. He had no money to buy a real one.

Pelé took his soccer ball everywhere. He would practice kicking it as he walked down the street. He would dribble it or aim it at a telephone pole. He could do almost anything with it.

That morning Pelé didn't plan on going to school. Instead he went to the field behind the town's soccer stadium. He could often get in on a game there.

Pelé played soccer most of the day with his friends. When he got home, he quickly hid his ball, but he couldn't hide all the dirt on his white shirt. His mother knew right away what he had been doing. She grabbed him by the ear and dragged him over her knee to spank him. "Playing hooky from school to play soccer; I'll teach you."

Pelé was spanked often, but it didn't stop him from playing soccer. The games were too much fun. But after a while, Pelé felt he was missing something. He wanted his own team that could play other teams on a regular soccer field with a real ball.

"If we had uniforms," he told his friends, "other teams would play us as a team. We could call ourselves the 'Seventh of September.' " (The seventh of September is Brazil's Independence Day.)

To get money for uniforms, the boys collected old bottles and anything else they could find. They went up and down the streets and alleys. They poked into trash cans. They raked the city dump. When they had a big pile of old bottles, scrap metal, pieces of pipe, and old pieces of furniture, they took it all to a junk man to sell. Finally they had scraped together enough money to buy shirts and pants, but not enough for shoes and socks.

"We'll just have to be known as Seventh of September, the barefoot team," said Pelé.

Soccer, 1985, ALEJANDRO ROMERO. Collection of the Artist.

The Seventh of September played every other team they could, and in time they became famous in the area. When Pelé was about eleven years old, the mayor of Bauru decided to hold a big tournament for all the younger teams. It was to be held in the city stadium with professional referees, just like big league soccer.

Pelé and his friends wanted to enter the tournament, but they needed new uniforms. This time, a traveling salesman helped them. He was a soccer fan and had heard of the barefoot team. He put up the money for uniforms, socks, and shoes. However, he asked that the team be called "Little America" after his favorite big league team, "America," in Rio de Janeiro.

That seemed to be a small price to pay. As soon as their equipment came, the boys started to practice. But after only a few minutes they were unhappy. They had never played in shoes before.

"I can't feel the ball," Pelé said. "I kick it, but it won't go where I want it to."

So they all took off their shoes and went back to playing barefoot. One of the tournament officials saw them. "Boys, you have to wear shoes in the games, so you might as well get used to them. Without shoes you can't play."

The boys had no choice but to put their shoes back on. They got blisters the first day, but after a few days, the shoes became more comfortable. And Pelé began to get the "feel" of the ball. He found he could kick with his toes as well as with the sides of his feet. The ball traveled farther with less effort. Wearing shoes is better, he finally decided.

Sixteen teams entered the tournament. Little America won their first game; then they won their second game and their third. Suddenly they were in the finals, playing for the championship before a huge crowd.

It was a hard, close game, but years of playing together paid off. Pelé was especially good that day, dribbling, passing, and shooting all over the field.

Late in the game, Pelé got the ball and dribbled it quickly toward the goal. An opposing player moved in to take the ball away. Suddenly, Pelé stopped cold and changed direction, still controlling the ball with his feet. The other player tried to change direction, too, but he slipped and fell to the ground.

In a flash, Pelé was racing for the goal. Only the goalkeeper was in his way now. Out from the net came the goalie to try to smother the ball. Pelé faked a kick. The goalie dove, but the ball wasn't where he thought it would be. Pelé angled a soft shot for the corner of the net. Bounce. Bounce. The goalie raced for it. But it went into the net. It was a goal.

The crowd stood and cheered. Little America had won. The crowd started to chant, "Pelé, Pelé, Pelé." Pelé heard his name and ran around the field, his arms raised in victory. The people threw coins out onto the field. They added up to $3.50, more money than he had ever seen before.

A few days later, Pelé's father found him sitting behind the fence in back of the house, thinking about the victory and smoking a cigarette.

His father looked at him for a minute and then said, "How long have you been smoking?"

"Not long," answered Pelé. "Only a few days."

"Do you enjoy it?" his father asked.

"Not really. I just thought I'd try it," Pelé said.

"Well," said his father, "cigarettes will cut down on your wind, and nobody needs wind like a soccer player. If you want to be a great player, you'll protect your body." He turned and went back into the house.

Pelé put the cigarette out and threw the others into the trash can. He never smoked again.

When Pelé was fifteen years old, a big league team named after a large port city in Brazil, Santo, signed him to a contract. For the first time, he was to be paid for playing soccer. Pelé started with the junior Santos team. He practiced and played with them for three months before he got his chance to play with the Santos' first team. He entered an exhibition game as center forward in the second half and scored his first goal in big league competition.

By spring of the following year, Pelé was a regular starter with the Santos. And after only two months of play, he became so well known around the big leagues that he was chosen to be on Brazil's national team. He was still only sixteen years old.

In his first game for the national team, Pelé went in during the second half. He scored the only goal for Brazil as they lost to Argentina, 2 to 1. But just a few days later, they played Argentina again. Pelé was a starter and scored another goal. This time Brazil won, 2 to 0.

The next year, 1958, was a World Cup year. Every four years the major soccer-playing countries hold a series of games ending in a finals to decide the victor. The World Cup is given to the best national team in the world.

Pelé was only seventeen years old, but he was chosen for Brazil's World Cup team. In the quarter-finals against Wales, Pelé scored what he feels is one of the most important goals of his career. Brazil won, 1 to 0, and went into the semi-finals, beating France as Pelé scored three times. And in the finals, Pelé scored twice more as Brazil beat Sweden, 5 to 2.

It was Brazil's first World Cup title. Pelé had scored six goals in the three games he played.

Pelé was famous. His feats in the World Cup, with the national team, and with the Santos were the talk of the soccer world. Every team wanted him. Every country wanted him. Then the government of Brazil acted. Pelé was declared a "national treasure." Brazil had passed a law to stop people from taking national treasures out of the country. The law was meant to protect works of art and important

Pelé shows his speed and control on the field. Copyright © Focus on Sports, New York City.

relics. But this time the law was used to keep a human being in the country.

Brazil won the World Cup again four years later and then again eight years after that. And over this span of years, Pelé's team, the Santos, won state and international team titles time after time. Pelé proved that he truly was a "national treasure."

Pelé scored 1,220 goals, including 95 for the Brazilian national team. That is a fantastic total for soccer, as many games are low-scoring, often decided by one or two goals.

How could you measure Pelé's feats in soccer in terms of other sports? In baseball, it would be like hitting a home run in every game. Or in basketball, like averaging 50 points per game.

Why has Pelé been such an outstanding player? Speed, of course, is one reason. Pelé can run. And he can change direction and speed quickly. That makes it hard to cover him. Other players can't seem to block him out. But his supreme skill is in ball control. Sometimes it almost seems as if the ball were tied to his foot. Other times he seems to have magical control over it. The ball does exactly what he wants it to do.

Most teams try to stop Pelé by putting two or three players to guard him. Of course, when they do that, Pelé's teammates are in a good spot to score. So Pelé's value to his team is much greater than just the goals he scores. He sets up as many goals for his teammates as he scores himself. It's no wonder that Pelé has been acclaimed all over the world as "the greatest soccer player who ever lived."

In 1974, Pelé said he would retire. Giant crowds shouted, "Pelé, Pelé, Pelé," and "Stay, stay, stay." But Pelé felt it was time to quit. He was thirty-three years old, and he wanted to relax and spend more time with his wife and two young children. But in 1975, with the permission of the Brazilian government, Pelé signed a contract to play for the New York Cosmos Soccer Team. He couldn't resist trying to beat the last challenge—making soccer a major sport in the United States. Right from his first appearance, crowds doubled and tripled. Pelé excited more interest and enthusiasm in soccer than there had ever been before.

Three weeks after arriving in New York, Pelé was seen playing soccer with a bunch of boys in Central Park. When Pelé saw the boys playing, he couldn't stay away, just as he couldn't stay away from the games when he was a barefoot kid kicking an old sock stuffed with newspapers.

Clare Gault (born 1925) and **Frank Gault** (1926–1982) were a wife-and-husband writing team. Their purpose for writing was to encourage young people to read. The Gaults wrote mainly nonfiction books about sports and sports heroes. They also wrote a fictional series about a sports-minded turtle named Norman.

Other books: *The Miracle Halfback*
Stories from the Olympics

Developing Comprehension Skills

1. When was Pelé born? Where did he grow up?

2. As a youth, how did Pelé show his dedication to soccer?

3. What did the government do when Pelé helped Brazil win its first World Cup title? What does this show about the attitude toward soccer in Brazil?

4. Pelé signed with the New York Cosmos to help make soccer a major sport in America. Compare soccer today with other American sports. Do you think that Pelé achieved his goal? Explain.

5. **Focus on Thinking: Identifying the Main Idea.** One main idea can be developed in several paragraphs. What main idea is developed in the last paragraph on page 261 and the following paragraph on page 262? What details support that idea?

Reading Nonfiction

1. **Examining Chronological Order.** Biographers usually relate events of a person's life in **chronological,** or time, order. List in order four main events in Pelé's life.

2. **Recognizing Conflicts.** Biographies, like stories, can describe conflicts that a person has to face. Identify two conflicts that Pelé faced.

3. **Understanding Point of View.** A biographer writes from the third-person point of view using the pronouns *he* or *she.* How might this account be different if Pelé had written it himself?

Study and Research

Using an Almanac. An **almanac** is a book that contains up-to-date information about many subjects. It is published yearly. Use an almanac from the reference section of your library to answer these questions about soccer: When and where was the last World Cup tournament? Which country won?

Writing in Response to Literature

Pelé is a hero to soccer fans. Write about a sports figure that you admire. Tell why this person deserves praise.

The Zoo Lady:

Belle Benchley and the San Diego Zoo

MARGARET POYNTER

Have you ever started a task that grew bigger and bigger? Read how Belle's job took over her whole life.

Belle Benchley, director of the San Diego Zoo, had no idea who Benson was, or why he wanted fleas, but she made a quick decision to fill the order. It was 1938, and the zoo was in financial trouble. Belle could use the money to help feed the animals and pay the employees.

The only problem was how to get the fleas. She asked the zoo's veterinarian for help, and between them they came up with an idea. Armed with a couple of combs, a bottle, and a few animal hairs, they were at the city pound an hour later. They searched out the dogs who seemed to be doing the most scratching. Before long, there were plenty of fleas hopping about on the hairs inside the bottle.

Belle found out later that Mr. Benson was the operator of a flea circus. Since fleas were out of season in wintery New England, he had had to send out to a warmer climate for help. He was so pleased with the zoo's prompt shipment that he gave Belle a weekly contract. Newspapers all over the country hailed San Diego as "the flea capital of the world."

It was adventures such as this that once led Belle to answer the question, "What does a zoo director do?" with "Whatever the day brings forth."

In 1925, when Belle Benchley had been hired to fill in for a vacationing bookkeeper, she had no idea that she would be staying at the zoo longer than a few weeks. At the time she would have taken almost any job. With a teenaged son to support, she had just taken a bookkeeping course in the hope of finding work.

But Belle had two qualifications that, unknown to her, fit her for the job. She was not afraid to try something new, and she had loved animals from the time she was a child.

Fred and Ida Belle Jennings had moved their family from the Kansas prairie to Point Loma, California, four years after Belle was born on August 28, 1882. While their father served as sheriff of San Diego County, Belle and her seven brothers and sisters roamed the rugged Pacific coast.

Near their home were rocky hills and miles of beaches. There was an old Spanish lighthouse on the tip of the point where, on foggy mornings, the Jennings children played noisy games like "Pirate." The country was overrun with rabbits, squirrels, snakes, birds, and coyotes. To little Belle it seemed to be a wonderland. She talked to the animals, and her mother taught her their names and how to classify the flowers and seashells she found.

This lion cub rests comfortably on Mrs. Benchley's lap. © Zoological Society of San Diego.

Belle earned her teaching certificate at the San Diego State Normal School. Before her marriage to William Benchley, she taught for three years on the Pala Indian Reservation in the hills northeast of San Diego. She spent the next seventeen years as a wife and mother, living in Fullerton, California, where she became the first woman to serve on the school board. Following her divorce in 1922 she moved back to San Diego, to be with her son Edward while he was going to school.

Now in her forties, Belle was a bookkeeper with no experience in her field. At first, she thought she would try to qualify for a job in government. When she passed her Civil Service examination, a friend told her that there was going to be an opening for a bookkeeper in the Port Department. Belle rushed down to fill out an application.

A week later, she was still waiting to hear whether or not she was going to get the job. It was then that she received the telephone call that was to change her life. It was from Dr. Harry Wegeforth, the founder and director of the San Diego Zoo, and the president of the Zoological Society. He needed a bookkeeper for a few weeks.

Belle decided to take the job while she was waiting to hear from the Port

Belle introduces a tortoise to Ngagi, a mountain gorilla. © Zoological Society of San Diego.

Department. She knew nothing about zoos, but she needed the money.

It didn't take Belle more than a few days to find that Dr. Wegeforth didn't need just a bookkeeper. He needed someone to feed and care for the animals, to collect a dime apiece from zoo visitors, to raise money for the payroll, and to beg food from the local stores. She didn't have time to worry about whether or not she could do the job. She was too busy doing it!

Belle had been at the zoo only three days when a man called up. "I'm trying to settle a bet," he said. "Just how long is the tail of a hippopotamus?"

She had never seen a hippo, and the zoo did not have one, but she said she'd find the answer. After locating an animal picture book in which the drawings had been made to scale, she measured the tail of the hippo.

"Thirteen to fourteen inches," she told the man.

As the days passed, she had to find the answers to other questions, such as, "How do I take care of humming-birds?" "How can I get my rabbit to eat?" and "What's wrong with my canary?"

Belle soon learned that she enjoyed finding out the answers to questions much more than she liked keeping books. She started to roam around the zoo grounds. Each day she spent her lunch hour in front of one cage or another to observe the animals and ask questions of their keepers. She found that there was much more to caring for animals than feeding and petting them. The grounds had to be kept clean, the cages repaired, sick creatures had to be treated, and supplies had to be ordered and stored.

She also found out many facts about the zoo itself, and about Dr. Harry and his big dreams for the zoo. In 1916 he and four other civic-minded men had bought the last neglected animals in a carnival menagerie. Then they added a lion, two bears, and some animals that had been left over from the Pan-Pacific International Exposition, which had taken place in San Diego's Balboa Park. The animals were housed in a row of broken-down cages. Dr. Harry persuaded the city council to donate ten acres of parkland. He and his friends then scraped together enough money to build a square of sturdy cages surrounding a central yard.

World War I held up the zoo's growth. By 1921 it had only two lions, an alligator, a wolf, two coyotes, three bears, some monkeys, and ducks and geese. Even so, Dr. Harry was a stubborn man who refused to let anything or anyone interfere with his plans to make his zoo the best in the world. He set up a zoological society that paid for expeditions to find and buy animals. He himself went on many of these trips and gave much of the money to finance them.

When Belle started working at the zoo, it had between 600 and 800 animals housed on 150 acres, and its chief claim to fame was its two Australian koalas. One of its biggest assets was its ten employees. They were a rough-talking group of ex-circus workers, who were good at their jobs and really cared about the zoo. They never complained when their pay didn't arrive on time. Lack of money was such a problem that their paychecks were often late.

On her trips around the zoo, Belle was able to see little things that would help the overworked men. When she made suggestions to Dr. Harry, he would tell her, "Well, do something about it."

Puddles pops up from his pool for a snack from Mrs. Benchley.
© Zoological Society of San Diego.

Belle Benchley shows affection for Pancho, a Mexican Bighorn sheep. © Zoological Society of San Diego.

Belle didn't need to be told twice. She took it upon herself to change the diet of a sick monkey and to move a wolf into a roomier cage. She also wrote articles for the local newspaper to build up interest in the zoo, and asked wealthy people to give money to the zoo. On her days off, she visited the local grocers and asked for free food for the animals.

Dr. Harry was so impressed with her work that when the bookkeeper came back from vacation, he asked Belle to stay on. Within a short time she, instead of Dr. Harry, was giving talks to civic and business groups that could help the zoo. At first, she hated this part of her new job. As she got over her stage fright, however, she found that she enjoyed telling people about the zoo.

When she was going to speak at one group luncheon, she took Bong, a cheetah, along with her. As she was talking, her audience started to laugh. When she looked at Bong, she learned

Albert, Bouba, and Bata, lowland gorillas, meet Mrs. Benchley when they arrive at the San Diego Zoo in 1949. © Zoological Society of San Diego.

the reason for their laughter. The big cat was just finishing off the contents of a cream pitcher!

The more Belle found out about the zoo, the more she realized that it was growing much faster than its income. Dr. Harry wouldn't listen to her pleas to stop buying animals until they had more money. Instead, he told Belle of his dreams about what the zoo could one day become.

Belle shared their hopes with Edward while he was still living at home, and later in her letters to him when he went to Mexico to work as a cowboy. In 1927, just a few months after he had gone, Belle was promoted to the post of executive secretary. She told her friends that she had turned out to be such a poor bookkeeper that Dr. Harry had to get her out of that job, no matter what the price.

Meanwhile, Dr. Harry wanted to get out of the job of zoo director. His busy medical practice took up much of his time, and he didn't like the everyday routine of zoo business. Several directors had been hired since the zoo began. One of them was Frank "Bring 'Em Back Alive" Buck, who had collected animals for the zoo. He didn't stay long, and neither did the others. Dr. Harry began to hate the very word "director."

Two new people were being considered for the job after Belle became executive secretary. Although they had worked for other zoos and were well qualified, neither of them seemed quite right. The members of the Zoological Society suddenly realized that they had the answer to their problem right under their noses. They called Belle into their meeting room.

"Go ahead," she was told. "Run the place. You're doing it anyway."

Belle would run the place for the next twenty-five years. Her first days as a nervous bookkeeper had been forgotten. The zoo was now the most important part of her life.

Margaret Poynter (born 1927) lives in California. She first gained success as a short-story writer, but is best known for her nonfiction books. Poynter's favorite subjects are famous people and science. Her book *Volcanoes: The Fiery Mountains* won an Outstanding Science Book award.

Other books: *Gold Rush!*
Search and Rescue!

Developing Comprehension Skills

1. What was Belle's first job at the zoo? How did she get this job?

2. Why did Belle say she was given the job of executive secretary? What was the real reason?

3. List in time order four important events in Belle's life and the date of each.

4. What differences can you find between Dr. Harry and Belle? Do you think these differences would make them a good team? Why or why not?

5. **Focus on Thinking: Recognizing Attitudes.** A person's way of feeling or thinking about something is called an **attitude.** Belle faced both large and small problems. What was her attitude toward solving problems?

Reading Nonfiction

1. **Examining Organization.** Most biographies are written in chronological order. How is this biography organized differently?

2. **Understanding the Importance of Setting.** When you read a biography, you need to identify the time period in which the person lived and worked. During what decades was Belle the director of the zoo?

3. **Examining Anecdotes.** Short amusing accounts about a person are called **anecdotes.** They add interest to a biography. Identify one anecdote in this biography.

Critical Thinking

Problem Solving. One step in accomplishing any goal is to identify problems you must solve. Suppose you want to open a zoo. What problems will you face? Think about land, licenses, animals, food, supplies, and money. List ten problems that you will need to solve.

Writing in Response to Literature

Belle's career began in the late 1920's. How would she fit into today's world? Think about her skills and abilities. Then write a job recommendation for her for today.

Language and Literature

Vocabulary

Context Clues. Look for clues to the meaning of a new word in the same sentence or paragraph. These clues could be a definition of the word or a familiar example. They could also be comparisons or contrasts to words you know. You can sometimes use the details in the context to figure out a new word.

Exercise. Use context clues to explain these underlined words.

Although not well-known outside the city, Dr. Wolf is the most prominent person in Lyonville. As a child, I loved to visit the small menagerie at her Animal Center. A fox, two bears, and a capuchin— a small South American monkey—were the wild animal attractions. However, domestic animals such as cats and dogs lived there too. It cost money to feed the animals, but the benevolent Dr. Wolf charged no admission.

Developing Writing Skills

Writing a Biography. Biographers choose interesting people to write about. Write a short biography about an adult in your school or community.

Prewriting. Interview the person you choose to write about. First, prepare a list of questions that will draw out interesting information. Take notes during the interview. Then decide which facts or anecdotes to use. Focus on one part of the person's life.

Drafting. You may wish to begin with an anecdote. Tell the rest of the facts in chronological order. Use a third-person point of view.

Revising and Sharing. As you revise, check the punctuation of any direct quotations. Make sure you have used pronouns correctly. Share the finished biographies on a biography bulletin board. Add the person's picture to the biography.

Unit 2 *R*eview

Using Your Skills in Reading Fiction

Identify the two types of conflict in the following paragraph. What is the climax? How is the conflict settled?

> Jed couldn't bring himself to shoot the rattlesnake he had spotted. It was sunning itself on the rocks, not hurting anyone. Then like a dart, the rattler struck. The boy fired. The rattler leaped in the air and fell motionless in the sand.

Using Your Skills in Reading Poetry

Read this poem entitled "Rain" by Emanuel diPasquale. To what senses does the poem appeal? What simile is used to compare rain with something else? What image do you see in your mind?

> Like a drummer's brush,
> the rain hushes the surfaces of tin porches.

Using Your Skills in Reading Nonfiction

Read this excerpt from *Famous Composers for Young People* by Gladys Burch and John Wolcott. Answer the questions that follow.

> George Frederic Handel was born at Halle in Saxony, Germany, on the 23rd of February, 1685. Not a hundred miles away in the town of Eisenach, a month later, Johann Sebastian Bach was born. Both became famous musicians, and yet they never met.

1. For what is George Handel famous?

2. From what point of view is this excerpt written?

Using Your Comprehension Skills

What is the main idea of this paragraph from the biography of Belle Benchley that you read? What details support the idea?

> But Belle had two qualifications that, unknown to her, fit her for the job. She was not afraid to try something new, and she had loved animals from the time she was a child.

Using Your Vocabulary Skills

Read the paragraph below. Use context clues to figure out the meanings of the underlined words. Write their definitions.

> Rob was in a quandary. He had no idea what to do. Of all the pieces of furniture, he had chosen the davenport to ruin. On this sofa, he had left an open pen filled with indelible ink. The permanent stain was as conspicuous as a spot of gravy on a white tie.

Using Your Writing Skills

Choose one of these writing assignments. Follow the directions.

1. This unit is called "Meeting Challenges." Which character in the unit do you admire most for the way he or she met a challenge? Explain your answer in a paragraph.

2. Write a short story or poem about someone who must meet a challenge.

UNIT THREE

FICTION   POETRY   DRAMA

Finding a Place

Steps, 1972, JAMIE WYETH.
Private Collection.

Reading Fiction

Characters in Fiction

One of the great joys of reading literature comes from the people you meet. Through reading, you get to know people of all ages, nationalities, and backgrounds. You meet people and creatures from the past, present, and future. These people and creatures are the characters in literature.

How does a writer bring a character to life? How do characters become so real that you know what they look like, what they think and feel, and how they are likely to act? The act of creating and developing the character's personality is called **characterization**.

Methods of Creating Character

There are several methods a writer uses to create a character. One way is by describing the character directly. Read this description of a creature called an Argan from the novel *Sweetwater*.

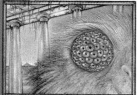

> . . . The bristly fur on his back and arm-legs was a peppery gray, the flesh on his belly was all wrinkled, and he stooped slightly from old age. He looked very much like a four-foot-high Earth spider. . . .

A second way a writer reveals the personalities of characters is through their conversations with each other. Notice how the Argan creature, Amadeus, talks about himself in his conversation.

> "Manchild, didn't I just tell you that a real musician can play both 'human' and 'Argan' music? I'm not an Argan playing human songs. I'm a musician making music. . . ."

A third method of characterization is to tell the characters' thoughts and feelings. Writers can tell what characters think about themselves and their situations. Writers can also let characters reveal what they think about each other. The writer Winifred Madison tells how one character, María Luisa, thinks and feels about a new friend.

> . . . Yes, she liked to hear him talk and she liked him to walk beside her. It made her wonder how different they must look. Now she could see that he was quite tall. His straight blond hair kept getting in his eyes and he had to shake his head to get it out of the way; that was charming, she thought. . . .

A fourth method of portraying characters is to show them in action. A writer reveals personality by having characters work through a conflict. In **novels,** which are long works of fiction with complex plots, writers can show how characters change over a period of time. As characters face challenges, like real people, they often learn about themselves and their values.

Understanding Characters in Fiction

In this part, you will meet characters from short stories and novels who find a place for themselves. To get to know these characters, piece together their thoughts and words, their actions, and any descriptions of them. Add to these the clues that you infer from your reading. Figure out why they act the way they do and how they affect each other. Watch them change. Most of all, enjoy the new friends you will make.

Comprehension Skills

Inferences

Suppose you open a novel to the first page and read this:

> Rebecca paced up and down the hospital hallway as she waited. Every few minutes she checked her watch. Then she stared at the door. There was no sound coming from the emergency room where Jeremy had been taken.

These lines do not say how Rebecca feels or what she is waiting for. How do you think she feels? If you say that she feels nervous, you are doing more than just making a wild guess. You are using what you know to figure out more than you are told. You are making an inference.

An **inference** is a logical guess based on evidence that you have. When you read, you often infer or figure out more than the words say. The evidence you use may be facts the writer provides. It may also be experiences from your own life.

In the lines above, you learn that Rebecca is pacing up and down and checking her watch. You may know from experience that these actions can be signs of nervousness. You also know that waiting outside an emergency room could cause nervousness. You can put these facts together to infer, or conclude, that Rebecca is nervous.

Ways to Use Inferences

You have already practiced making inferences in your reading. You have inferred causes, effects, and main ideas. You can use inferences in other ways as well. Inferences help you follow the plots of stories. They help you understand the thoughts and feelings of characters. You can infer both feelings and ideas in poetry.

Another important use for inferences is to make predictions. When you use what you know to infer what will happen in the future, you are making a **prediction.** Predicting what characters will do or what the outcome will be can make your reading more fun.

To make a prediction as you read, put together the facts you have from the story with what you know from experience. It may help to relate the situation to your own life. Decide where the events or ideas are leading. Predict what the next logical step or outcome might be.

Exercise: Making Inferences

Read this paragraph from *The Land I Lost: Adventures of a Boy in Vietnam* by Huynh Quang Nhuong. Then answer the questions.

> That evening we asked a few friends to stay overnight for a couple evenings to help us watch for the thief. On the next two nights nothing happened. But at two o'clock in the morning on the third night my cousin, who was on watch, heard a loud shriek followed by a heavy thud. He woke up everyone, and we all grabbed weapons, but decided not to go out into the dark.

1. What can you infer has happened in the past? What clues tell you this?

2. What can you infer about the cousin's feelings when he hears the noise? What did you use to make this inference?

3. What can you predict will happen in the morning? Why?

Vocabulary Skills

The Dictionary

Suppose as you read you want to find out what a word means. Try figuring out the word from its parts or from context clues. If neither method works, use a dictionary. A dictionary lists words in alphabetical order. Each listing or entry gives several facts about the word.

Parts of an Entry

Entry word. Each word the dictionary lists is called an **entry word.** The entry word, which appears in dark print, shows how the word is spelled and how it is divided into syllables.

Pronunciation. Next to the entry word is a respelling to show how the word is pronounced. The **respelling,** in parentheses, is a set of letters and symbols that stand for the sounds of the word. The respelling includes accent marks (′) to show which syllables to stress. A pronunciation key tells what each letter or symbol means.

mi · nor (mī′nər) *adj.* **1.** lesser in size, amount, importance, or rank **2.** under full legal age **3.** *Educ.* designating a field of study in which a student specializes, but to a lesser degree than in his major **4.** *Music* designating an interval smaller than the corresponding major by a semitone—*v. Educ.* to make some subject one's minor field of study—*n.* **1.** a person under full legal age **2.** *Educ.* a minor field of study

Parts of speech. The entry tells and defines all the parts of speech a word can be. Parts of speech are shown by abbreviations, such as **n.** (noun), **v.** (verb), **adj.** (adjective), and **adv.** (adverb).

fal · low[1] (fal'ō) *n.* land plowed but not seeded for one or more seasons—*adj.* **1.** left uncultivated or unplanted **2.** untrained; inactive; said esp. of the mind—*v.* to leave (land) unplanted after plowing—**lie fallow** to remain uncultivated, unused for a time—**fal'low·ness** *n.*

fal · low[2] (fal'ō) *adj.* pale-yellow

Definition. The meaning of the word follows the part of speech. If a word has several meanings, decide which definition makes sense in the context of your reading.

Idioms. An entry may include **idioms,** or expressions that mean something different from the usual meaning of each word. Idioms are listed at the end of the entry of the most important word. For example, you would find the idiom "fit as a fiddle" under the entry for *fiddle*.

Homographs. Words that look the same but have different meanings are called **homographs.** Homographs are listed one after another with a raised number next to the word. Notice that there are two entries for *fallow*, showing that the two words are homographs.

Exercise: Practicing Dictionary Skills

A. A **glossary** is a short dictionary at the back of a book. Use the glossary of this book to give the pronunciation, part of speech, and definition for these words: *idyllic, atone, impudent, rotunda, culvert.*

B. Read the entry for *minor* on page 282. Tell what part of speech and definition matches its meaning in each sentence.

1. The minor chords made the music sound eerie.

2. Chad's major is history, but he is minoring in philosophy.

3. Minors must attend school until the age of sixteen.

From

The Trumpet of the Swan

E. B. WHITE

Sam Beaver and his father are on a camping trip in Canada. Sam often goes off by himself to explore the wilderness. One morning, Sam discovers a pond he has never seen before.

The pond Sam had discovered on that spring morning was seldom visited by any human being. All winter, snow had covered the ice; the pond lay cold and still under its white blanket. Most of the time there wasn't a sound to be heard. The frog was asleep. The chipmunk was asleep. Occasionally a jay would cry out. And sometimes at night the fox would bark—a high, rasping bark. Winter seemed to last forever.

But one day a change came over the woods and the pond. Warm air, soft and kind, blew through the trees. The ice, which had softened during the night, began to melt. Patches of open water appeared. All the creatures that lived in the pond and in the woods were glad to feel the warmth. They heard and felt the breath of spring, and they stirred with new life and hope. There was a good, new smell in the air, a smell of earth waking after its long sleep. The frog, buried in the mud at the bottom

of the pond, knew that spring was here. The chickadee knew
and was delighted (almost everything delights a chickadee). The
vixen, dozing in her den, knew she would soon have kits. Every
creature knew that a better, easier time was at hand—warmer
days, pleasanter nights. Trees were putting out green buds; the
buds were swelling. Birds began arriving from the south. A pair
of ducks flew in. The Red-winged Blackbird arrived and
scouted the pond for nesting sites. A small sparrow with a white
throat arrived and sang, "Oh, sweet Canada, Canada, Canada!"

Spring Song—Trumpeter Swans, 1986, WAYNE MEINECKE. Photograph: Wild Wings, Lake City, Minnesota.

And if you had been sitting by the pond on that first warm day of spring, suddenly, toward the end of the afternoon, you would have heard a stirring sound high above you in the air—a sound like the sound of trumpets.

"Ko-hoh, ko-hoh!"

And if you had looked up, you would have seen, high overhead, two great white birds. They flew swiftly, their legs stretched out straight behind, their long white necks stretched out ahead, their powerful wings beating steady and strong. "Ko-hoh, ko-hoh, ko-hoh!" A thrilling noise in the sky, the trumpeting of swans.

When the birds spotted the pond, they began circling, looking the place over from the air. Then they glided down and came to rest in the water, folding their long wings neatly along their sides and turning their heads this way and that to study their new surroundings. They were Trumpeter Swans, pure white birds with black bills. They had liked the looks of the swampy pond and had decided to make it their home for a while and raise a family.

The two swans were tired from the long flight. They were glad to be down out of the sky. They paddled slowly about and then began feeding, thrusting their necks into the shallow water and pulling roots and plants from the bottom. Everything about the swans was white except their bills and their feet; these were black. They carried their heads high. The pond seemed a different place because of their arrival.

For the next few days, the swans rested. When they were hungry, they ate. When they were thirsty—which was a great deal of the time—they drank. On the tenth day, the female began looking around to find a place to build her nest.

In the spring of the year, nest-building is uppermost in a bird's mind: it is the most important thing there is. If she picks a good place, she stands a good chance of hatching her eggs and rearing her young. If she picks a poor place, she may fail to raise a family. The female swan knew this; she knew the decision she was making was extremely important.

The two swans first investigated the upper end of the pond, where a stream flowed slowly in. It was pleasant there, with reeds and bulrushes. Red-winged Blackbirds were busy nesting in this part of the pond, and a pair of Mallard Ducks were courting. Then the swans swam to the lower end of the pond, a marsh with woods on one side and a deer meadow on the other. It was lonely here. From one shore, a point of land extended out into the pond. It was a sandy strip, like a little peninsula. And at the tip of it, a few feet out into the water, was a tiny island, hardly bigger than a dining table. One small tree grew on the island, and there were rocks and ferns and grasses.

"Take a look at this!" exclaimed the female, as she swam round and around.

"Ko-hoh!" replied her husband, who liked to have someone ask his advice.

The swan stepped cautiously out onto the island. The spot seemed made to order—just right for a nesting place. While the male swan floated close by, watching, she snooped about until she found a pleasant spot on the ground. She sat down, to see how it felt to be sitting there. She decided it was the right size for her body. It was nicely located, a couple of feet from the water's edge. Very convenient. She turned to her husband.

"What do you think?" she said.

"An ideal location!" he replied. "A perfect place! And I will tell you *why* it's a perfect place," he continued, majestically. "If an enemy—a fox or a coon or a coyote or a skunk—wanted to reach this spot with murder in his heart, he'd have to enter the water and get wet. And before he could enter the water, he'd have to walk the whole length of that point of land. And by that time we'd see him or hear him, and I would give him a hard time."

The male stretched out his great wings, eight feet from tip to tip, and gave the water a mighty clout to show his strength. This made him feel better right away. When a Trumpeter Swan hits an enemy with his wing, it is like being hit by a baseball bat. A male swan, by the way, is called a "cob." No one knows why, but that's what he's called. A good many animals have special names: a male goose is called a gander, a male cow is called a bull, a male sheep is called a ram, a male chicken is called a rooster, and so on. Anyway, the thing to remember is that a male swan is called a cob.

The cob's wife pretended not to notice that her husband was showing off, but she saw it, all right, and she was proud of his strength and his courage. As husbands go, he was a good one.

The cob watched his beautiful wife sitting there on the tiny island. To his great joy, he saw her begin to turn slowly round and around, keeping always in the same spot, treading the mud and grass. She was making the first motions of nesting. First she squatted down in the place she had chosen. Then she twisted round and around, tamping the earth with her broad webbed feet, hollowing it out to make it like a saucer. Then she reached out and pulled twigs and grasses toward her and dropped them at her sides and under her tail, shaping the nest to her body.

The cob floated close to his mate. He studied every move she made.

"Now another medium-sized stick, my love," he said. And she poked her splendid long white graceful neck as far as it would go, picked up a stick, and placed it at her side.

"Now another bit of coarse grass," said the cob, with great dignity.

The female reached for grasses, for moss, for twigs— anything that was handy. Slowly, carefully, she built up the nest until she was sitting on a big grassy mound. She worked at the task for a couple of hours, then knocked off for the day and slid into the pond again, to take a drink and have lunch.

"A fine start!" said the cob, as he gazed back at the nest. "A perfect beginning! I don't know how you manage it so cleverly."

"It comes naturally," replied his wife. "There's a lot of work to it, but on the whole it is pleasant work."

"Yes," said the cob. "And when you're done, you have something to show for your trouble—you have a swan's nest, six feet across. What other bird can say that?"

"Well," said his wife, "maybe an eagle can say it."

"Yes, but in that case it wouldn't be a swan's nest, it would be an eagle's nest, and it would be high up in some old dead tree somewhere, instead of right down near the water, with all the conveniences that go with water."

They both laughed at this. Then they began trumpeting and splashing and scooping up water and throwing it on their backs, darting about as though they had suddenly gone crazy with delight.

"Ko-hoh! Ko-hoh! Ko-hoh!" they cried.

Every wild creature within a mile and a half of the pond heard the trumpeting of the swans. The fox heard, the raccoon heard, the skunk heard. One pair of ears heard that did not belong to a wild creature. But the swans did not know that.

One day, almost a week later, the swan slipped quietly into her nest and laid an egg. Each day she tried to deposit one egg in the nest. Sometimes she succeeded, sometimes she didn't. There were now three eggs, and she was ready to lay a fourth.

As she sat there, with her husband, the cob, floating gracefully nearby, she had a strange feeling that she was being watched. It made her uneasy. Birds don't like to be stared at. They particularly dislike being stared at when they are on a nest. So the swan twisted and turned and peered everywhere.

She gazed intently at the point of land that jutted out into the pond near the nest. With her sharp eyes, she searched the nearby shore for signs of an intruder. What she finally saw gave her the surprise of her life. There, seated on a log on the point of land, was a small boy. He was being very quiet, and he had no gun.

"Do you see what I see?" the swan whispered to her husband.

"No. What?"

"Over there. On that log. It's a boy! *Now* what are we going to do?"

"How did a boy get here?" whispered the cob. "We are deep in the wilds of Canada. There are no human beings for miles around."

"That's what I thought too," she replied. "But if that isn't a boy over there on that log, my name isn't Cygnus Buccinator."[1]

The cob was furious. "I didn't fly all the way north into Canada to get involved with a *boy*," he said. "We came here to this idyllic spot, this remote little hideaway, so we could enjoy some well-deserved privacy."

"Well," said his wife, "I'm sorry to see the boy, too, but I must say he's behaving himself. He sees us, but he's not throwing stones. He's not throwing sticks. He's not messing around. He's simply observing."

---

1. **Cygnus buccinator** (sig′ nəs buk′ sə nāt′ ər): the scientific name for *trumpeter swan*.

Striped Skunk, 1970,
GLEN LOATES. Collection of the Artist.

"I do not *wish* to be observed," complained the cob. "I did not travel all this immense distance into the heart of Canada to be observed. Furthermore, I don't want *you* to be observed—except by me. You're laying an egg—that is, I *hope* you are—and you are entitled to privacy. It has been my experience that all boys throw stones and sticks—it is their nature. I'm going over and strike that boy with my powerful wing, and he'll think he has been hit with a billy club. I'll knock him cold!"

"Now, just wait a minute!" said the swan. "There's no use starting a fight. This boy is not bothering me at the moment. He's not bothering you either."

"But how did he *get* here?" said the cob, who was no longer talking in a whisper but was beginning to shout. "How did he get here? Boys can't fly, and there are no roads in this part of Canada. We're fifty miles from the nearest highway."

"Maybe he's lost," said the swan. "Maybe he's starving to death. Maybe he wants to rob the nest and eat the eggs, but I doubt it. He doesn't look hungry. Anyway, I've started this nest, and I have three beautiful eggs, and the boy's behaving himself at the moment, and I intend to go right ahead and try for a fourth egg."

"Good luck, my love!" said the cob. "I shall be here at your side to defend you if anything happens. Lay the egg!"

For the next hour, the cob paddled slowly round and around the tiny island, keeping watch. His wife remained quietly on the nest. Sam sat on his log, hardly moving a muscle. He was spellbound at the sight of the swans. They were the biggest water birds he had ever seen. He had heard their trumpeting and had searched the woods and swamps until he had found the pond and located the nest. Sam knew enough about birds to know that these were Trumpeters. Sam always felt happy when he was in a wild place among wild creatures. Sitting on his log, watching the swans, he had the same good feeling some people get when they are sitting in church.

After he had watched for an hour, Sam got up. He walked slowly and quietly away, putting one foot straight ahead of the other, Indian-fashion, hardly making a sound. The swans watched him go. When the female left the nest, she turned and looked back. There, lying safely in the soft feathers at the bottom of the nest, was the fourth egg. The cob waddled out onto the island and looked in the nest.

"A masterpiece!" he said. "An egg of supreme beauty and perfect proportions. I would say that that egg is almost five inches in length."

His wife was pleased.

When the swan had laid five eggs, she felt satisfied. She gazed at them proudly. Then she settled herself on the nest to keep her eggs warm. Carefully, she reached down with her bill and poked each egg until it was in just the right spot to receive the heat from her body. The cob cruised around close by, to keep her company and protect her from enemies. He knew that a fox prowled somewhere in the woods; he had heard him barking on nights when the hunting was good.

Days passed, and still the swan sat quietly on the five eggs. Nights passed. She sat and sat, giving her warmth to the eggs. No one disturbed her. The boy was gone—perhaps he would never come back. Inside of each egg, something was happening that she couldn't see: a little swan was taking shape. As the weeks went by, the days grew longer, the nights grew shorter. When a rainy day came, the swan just sat still and let it rain.

"My dear," said her husband, the cob, one afternoon, "do you never find your duties onerous or irksome? Do you never tire of sitting in one place and in one position, covering the eggs, with no diversions, no pleasures, no escapades, or capers? Do you never suffer from boredom?"

"No," replied his wife. "Not really."

"Isn't it uncomfortable to sit on eggs?"

"Yes, it is," replied the wife. "But I can put up with a certain amount of discomfort for the sake of bringing young swans into the world."

"Do you know how many more days you must sit?" he asked.

"Haven't any idea," she said. "But I notice that the ducks at the other end of the pond have hatched their young ones; I notice that the Red-winged Blackbirds have hatched theirs, and the other evening I saw a Striped Skunk hunting along the shore, and she had four little skunks with her. So I think I must be getting near the end of my time. With any luck, we will soon be able to see our children—our beautiful little cygnets."

"Don't you ever feel the pangs of hunger or suffer the tortures of thirst?" asked the cob.

"Yes, I do," said his mate. "As a matter of fact, I could use a drink right now."

The afternoon was warm; the sun was bright. The swan decided she could safely leave her eggs for a few minutes. She stood up. First she pushed some loose feathers around the eggs, hiding them from view and giving them a warm covering in her absence. Then she stepped off the nest and entered the water. She took several quick drinks. Then she glided over to a shallow place, thrust her head underwater, and pulled up tender greens from the bottom. She next took a bath by tossing water over herself. Then she waddled out onto a grassy bank and stood there, preening her feathers.

The swan felt good. She had no idea that an enemy was

Trumpeter Swan, 1838, JOHN JAMES AUDUBON. The New York Historical Society, New York City.

near. She failed to notice the Red Fox as he watched her from his hiding place behind a clump of bushes. The fox had been attracted to the pond by the sound of splashing water. He hoped he would find a goose. Now he sniffed the air and smelled the swan. Her back was turned, so he began creeping slowly toward her. She would be too big for him to carry, but he decided he would kill her anyway and get a taste of blood. The cob, her husband, was still floating on the pond. He spied the fox first.

"Look out!" he trumpeted. "Look out for the fox, who is creeping toward you even as I speak, his eyes bright, his bushy tail out straight, his mind lusting for blood, his belly almost touching the ground! You are in grave danger, and we must act immediately."

While the cob was making this elegant speech of warning, something happened that surprised everybody. Just as the fox was about to spring and sink his teeth in the swan's neck, a stick came hurtling through the air. It struck the fox full on the nose, and he turned and ran away. The two swans couldn't imagine what had happened. Then they noticed a movement in the bushes. Out stepped Sam Beaver, the boy who had visited them a month ago. Sam was grinning. In his hand he held another stick, in case the fox should return. But the fox was in no mood to return. He had a very sore nose, and he had lost his appetite for fresh swan.

"Hello," said Sam in a low voice.

"Ko-hoh, ko-hoh!" replied the cob.

"Ko-hoh!" said his wife. The pond rang with the trumpet sounds—sounds of triumph over the fox, sounds of victory and gladness.

Sam was thrilled at the noise of swans, which some people say is like the sound of a French horn. He walked slowly around the shore to the little point of land near the island and sat down on his log. The swans now realized, beyond any doubt, that the boy was their friend. He had saved the swan's life. He had been in the right place at the right time and with the right ammunition. The swans felt grateful. The cob swam over toward Sam, climbed out of the pond, and stood close to the boy, looking at him in a friendly way and arching his neck gracefully. Once, he ran his neck far out, cautiously, and almost touched the boy. Sam never moved a muscle. His heart thumped from excitement and joy.

The female paddled back to her nest and returned to the job of warming the eggs. She felt lucky to be alive.

That night before Sam crawled into his bunk at camp, he got out his notebook and found a pencil. This is what he wrote:

I don't know of anything in the entire world more wonderful to look at than a nest with eggs in it. An egg, because it contains life, is the most perfect thing there is. It is beautiful and mysterious. An egg is a far finer thing than a tennis ball or a cake of soap. A tennis ball will always be just a tennis ball. A cake of soap will always be just a cake of soap—until it gets so small nobody wants it and they throw it away. But an egg will someday be a living creature. A swan's egg will open and out will come a little swan. A nest is almost as wonderful and mysterious as an egg. How does a bird

Spring, 1974, BOB TIMBERLAKE. Heritage Company, Lexington, North Carolina.

know how to make a nest? Nobody ever taught her. How does a bird know how to build a nest?

Sam closed his notebook, said good night to his father, blew out his lamp, and climbed into his bunk. He lay there wondering how a bird knows how to build a nest. Pretty soon his eyes closed, and he was asleep.

© 1987 Jill Krementz

E. B. White (1899–1985) was one of the finest essay writers of this century. His love of nature and his life on his farm in Maine were the subjects of many of his writings. E. B. White wrote three books for young readers. *Charlotte's Web* was turned into an animated film.

Other books: *Stuart Little*
Charlotte's Web

Developing Comprehension Skills

1. What is the main idea of the second paragraph? List four details that support that idea.

2. Why is the little island such a good place to build a nest?

3. How are the cob's and his wife's reactions to Sam's presence different?

4. Why are the swans grateful to Sam? How do they show it?

5. If the swans were human, do you think they would have a good marriage? Why or why not?

6. **Focus on Thinking: Making Inferences.** You can make inferences from a character's words and actions. What can you infer about Sam's personality?

Reading Fiction

1. **Learning About Characters.** One way to learn about characters is from what they say. Tell one quality the cob shows, and find two examples that show this quality.

2. **Examining Action.** Writers can show characters' feelings by describing their actions. What are the wife's feelings about motherhood? What actions show this?

3. **Learning from Fiction.** Although fiction is imaginary, readers can learn many facts from it. Find facts in this story about swans' nesting and eating habits.

Study and Research

Using Subject Cards. The card catalog contains three cards for every nonfiction book in the library. Each book is cataloged by title, author, and subject. Subject cards list the subject of the book first, then the call number, title, and author. Look up *swan* in the library card catalog. Locate two books about swans. Use them to find two more facts about swans.

Writing in Response to Literature

Sam writes his thoughts in his journal. Suppose the swans keep a journal. Imagine you are the cob or his wife. Write a journal entry giving your thoughts about an incident in the story.

*What makes a place valuable
to you? Learn how two people
find different values in the
same place.*

Ghost Town

JACK SCHAEFER

I owned a whole town once. What was left of it
anyway. A ghost town. One of the mining camps back
in the hills that must have been quite a place when the
gold rush was on. Then the diggings there petered out
and people began moving on and the flimsy houses started
collapsing after everyone was gone.

You can find traces of plenty of those old towns scattered
up the back creeks. But this one was better than most. Some of
the men there knew how to build a kiln and fire it and there
was a clay bank nearby. A half dozen buildings were made of
brick and these stood solid enough through the years. The roofs
had fallen in, and the windows and doors were missing, but the
walls were still standing. You could even figure out what they
had been: a general store; a post office and stage station; a
blacksmith shop; a two-room jail; a small saloon; another
saloon with space for dancing or gambling tables and some
rooms on a second floor.

This old town of mine was up a narrow gulch that wasn't
good for a thing once the gold was gone. But it was only about
a half mile from a modern main highway and the old dirt road

leading to it was still passable. I drove in there one day and was poking around when another car loaded with tourists pulled up and the people piled out and wandered around with the women oh-ing and ah-ing as if they were seeing something wonderful.

That's when I had my idea.

It took time but I ran that town down on the tax books and found out all about it. The county had taken title to the whole place for back taxes maybe fifty years before—so long before, it had been written off the accounts as a dead loss and just about forgotten. When I offered to buy it the county officials thought I was crazy and jumped to make a deal. They hadn't expected ever to get another nickel out of the place. I paid $800 and I owned a town.

I cleaned out the old buildings enough so you could walk around inside them. I painted names on them telling what they had been. I fixed a few bad spots in the dirt road. I plastered signs along the highway for maybe five miles in each direction and a big one where the dirt road turned off. I roofed over one room of the old jail for my own quarters. I charged fifty cents a head for a look-see through the old place—and I was in business.

It was a good business. Not in the winter, of course, and slow in the spring and fall, but good all summer—enough to carry me comfortably all year. During the rough months I'd stay at a rooming house in the live town that was the county seat and as soon as the weather was right I'd move out and start collecting my half dollars.

Sometimes I'd have four or five cars at a time parked by the entrance and a dozen or more people listening to my talk. I'd check the license plates and temper the talk accordingly. If they were from the home state or one nearby, I'd go easy on the fancy trimmings. Those people might know too much real history. But if they were from far states, maybe eastern ones, I'd let loose and make it strong. I'd tell about fights in the saloons—shootings and knifings and big brawls with bottles flying. I'd tell about road agents stopping stages carrying gold and getting caught and being locked up in the jail and maybe a daring escape or two. I'd make it good and the eastern tourists lapped it up. What if all of it happened only in my head? Such things could of happened and maybe did. What if I did get a couple of complaints from the state historical society? There wasn't anything anyone could do so long as I made up the names too. The town belonged to me.

It was a good business. For three years. Then it collapsed just the way the old town itself did 'way back when. The state started straightening the highway and knocked off the loop that came near my ghost town. That put the main route about seven miles away. I slapped up more signs but not many people would bother to turn off onto the old route and try to find the place. My business started skidding. I tried to unload it on the historical society and they just laughed at me. They'd bought a ghost town of their own and were fixing it up. Soon as they had it open, they'd finish the job of killing my business.

I was stuck with that town. I'd put hard money into it and now I was stuck with it. The summer season started and I was lucky to average a single car a day. I was figuring I'd have to swallow the loss and move on when this pink-cheeked young fellow came along. It was late one afternoon and he was pink-cheeked like a boy with maybe a little fuzz on his chin that hadn't begun to be whiskers yet. He drove up in an old car that had lost its color in dust and he paid his fifty cents and started poking around. I was so lonesome for customers, or just anyone to talk to, that I stuck close and kept words bouncing back and

The Last Stage, 1964, ERNEST BERKE. Photograph: Paintings and Sculptures of the Old West, Scottsdale, Arizona.

forth with him. He looked so young and innocent I figured he was a college kid seeing some of the country on vacation time. But no. He said he'd had all the college he could absorb. He was a mining engineer by profession but there wasn't much professing to be done in that field about then, so he was knocking around looking over the old camps. He liked to see how they did things in the old days. Maybe he'd write a book on it some time.

"Mighty interesting town you have here," he said. "Those buildings. Brick. Don't see much brick in the old camps. They haul them in here?"

"Why no," I said. "They had a kiln right here—you can see where it was behind the blacksmith shop. They dug the clay out of the bank over there." And right away this young fellow had to see that too.

"Mighty interesting," he said. "Found the clay right here. Don't often come on good brick clay in these parts. But you can see they cleaned out this streak in the bank. They sure liked bricks. If they hadn't run out of the clay they might still be making them."

"That'd be a darn fool stunt," I said. "Who'd be wanting bricks around here now?"

"Yes," he said. "Yes, it would. A darn fool stunt." And he wandered on, me with him and him talking more about what sturdy buildings these bricks had made and other things like that.

"Mighty interesting business you're in," he said. "Playing nursemaid to an old town like this and having people pay to look it over. Must be kind of a nice life."

That's when I had another idea.

I took that pink-cheeked young fellow into my jail-room and persuaded him to stay for supper. I began coughing at strategic intervals during the meal and I told him my health was bad and the climate bothered me, otherwise I wouldn't even be thinking of maybe leaving such a nice life in such an interesting business. I played it clever with indirect questions and got out of him the fact he had a bit of cash to invest. Then I really went to work on him.

"Stay here tonight," I said, "and stick around tomorrow. You'll see what a good business this really is." He said he would and I worked on him some more and after a while I asked him to keep an eye on the place while I drove over to the county seat to tend to a few things.

I tended to the things all right but not at the county seat. I burned up the roads getting to various men I knew around about. Each stop I put the same proposition. "There's ten dollars in it for you," I said, "if you'll take time tomorrow to put the missus and anyone else handy in the car and drive over to the old town and make like a tourist gawking around some." I covered a lot of miles and I was turned down at a few stops, but at last I had eleven cars promised and with the extras that would run to about forty people.

When I got back, my pink-cheeked baby was sleeping like one on the cot I'd fixed up for him. He woke long enough to grunt a greeting, then rolled over and went to sleep again. But I could tell he'd been snooping in the last summer's tally-book I'd left out on purpose where he would see it. The highway change hadn't been finished then and that had been a good summer.

Come morning everything clicked just right. My home-grown tourists started coming and kept coming at about the times I'd suggested all the way through the morning and early afternoon. I was worried that my young visitor might get to talking with them and sniff some suspicions but he didn't bother with them at all. He just watched what was going on and wandered around by himself and spent some time poking in what was left of the old kiln. I worked on him a bit during lunch and about the middle of the afternoon, when the last of the cars had left, I figured it was time to hook him.

"Not bad," I said. "Eleven cars and forty-one people. Twenty dollars and a fifty cent piece over. And all I did was just sit here and let them come."

Ghost-Town, U.S.A., 1965,
GARY P. MILLER.
Private Collection. Published by Gary's
Galleries, Bismarck, North Dakota and
Scottsdale, Arizona.

"Mighty interesting," he said. "That's more people than I expected."

"That?" I said. "Just a low average. Good enough for a weekday but you should see the weekends. Saturdays double it. And Sundays? Why, Sundays triple it."

"You don't say?" he said. "Too bad about your health. Didn't you mention something about wanting to sell out?"

And right then I knew I had him.

It was just a matter of price after that and on price I always was a tough one. When I chucked my things in my car so I could turn the place over to him that same day and led the way to the county seat with him following so we could find a notary and sign the papers, I'd pushed him up to a thousand bucks. He looked so young and innocent tagging after me into the notary's that I was almost ashamed of myself . . .

Brother, let me tell you something. When a pink-cheeked young tenderfoot with maybe some fuzz on his chin that hasn't even begun to be real whiskers comes your way, just watch your step. Watch it close. That's the kind will take you for anything you've got worth taking—while you're still wondering whether he's been weaned. It wasn't a week later I saw this baby-faced sucker I thought I'd trimmed coming toward me along a street and I ducked quick into a bar. He followed me in and cornered me.

"How's business?" I said, hoping to get any unpleasantness over with fast.

"Business?" he said. "Now that's mighty interesting. Do you really think you fooled me with those fake tourists? The license plates tipped me right away. All from this state. All from this county." He grinned—the same innocent grin he had the first time I saw him. "Let me buy you a drink. No hard feelings. Your so-called business didn't interest me at all. It was the buildings. I've a crew out there now tearing them down."

"Tearing them down?" I said.

"Certainly," he said. "Those bricks. That clay was the best pocket of pay dirt in the whole gulch—only those old-time miners didn't know it. There was gold dust in that clay and it's right there in the bricks. I'm having them crushed and washing the gold out. There's close to a hundred tons of those bricks and they're panning about eight hundred dollars to the ton."

Jack Schaefer (born 1907) was born in Ohio. After college he worked for many years as a reporter and an editor. Schaefer enjoys studying the history of the American West, the subject and setting for most of his stories. A number of these stories have been made into movies. Schaefer now lives on a ranch in New Mexico.

Other books: *Shane*
             Old Ramon

Developing Comprehension Skills

1. Why does the narrator buy the ghost town?

2. Why does the narrator's business begin to fail?

3. What is the narrator's attitude toward the young man? Why does he feel that way?

4. Why does the narrator think the young man buys the town? What is the young man's real reason?

5. Do you think the narrator deserves what happens to him? Does the young man "play fair"?

6. **Focus on Thinking: Understanding Story Clues.** Details in the beginning of a story help you predict what happens later. What important clue about the town's construction is given early in the story? What clue is given about the young man's background?

Reading Fiction

1. **Evaluating Character.** In any first-person narrative, you have to decide if you can trust what the narrator says. Is the narrator of this story honest? Give examples that support your answers.

2. **Examining Plot.** Some plots revolve around a trick. Tell in sequence the events of the trick the narrator plays on the young man. How does the young man trick the narrator?

Speaking and Listening

Persuading an Audience. In order to persuade people to do something, you need to give them reasons to do it. Suppose you are a salesperson for the narrator. You want to sell tickets for the tour of his ghost town. List reasons why people should see it. Arrange your ideas into a sales pitch and try to persuade your classmates to visit the ghost town.

Writing in Response to Literature

Suppose the young man and the narrator meet five years after the story ends. Write a conversation they might have.

In your experience, do animals make choices and decisions? Read to see how a dog seems to make a choice.

Lob's Girl

JOAN AIKEN

Some people choose their dogs, and some dogs choose their people. The Pengelly family had no say in the choosing of Lob; he came to them in the second way, and very decisively.

It began on the beach, the summer when Sandy was five, Don, her older brother, twelve, and the twins were three. Sandy was really Alexandra, because her grandmother had a beautiful picture of a queen in a diamond tiara and high collar of pearls. It hung by Granny Pearce's kitchen sink and was as familiar as the doormat. When Sandy was born everyone agreed that she was the living spit of the picture, and so she was called Alexandra and Sandy for short.

On this summer day she was lying peacefully reading a comic and not keeping an eye on the twins, who didn't need it because they were occupied in seeing which of them could wrap the most seaweed around the other one's legs. Father—Bert Pengelly—and Don were up on the Hard[1] painting the

---

1. **Hard** (härd): a firm, sheltered beach or a sloping stone roadway at the water's edge where boats are put out or landed.

bottom boards of the boat in which Father went fishing for pilchards. And Mother—Jean Pengelly—was getting ahead with making the Christmas puddings because she never felt easy in her mind if they weren't made and safely put away by the end of August. As usual, each member of the family was happily getting on with his or her own affairs. Little did they guess how soon this state of things would be changed by the large new member who was going to erupt into their midst.

Sandy rolled onto her back to make sure that the twins were not climbing on slippery rocks or getting cut off by the tide. At the same moment a large body struck her forcibly in the midriff and she was covered by flying sand. Instinctively she shut her eyes and felt the sand being wiped off her face by something that seemed like a warm, rough, damp flannel. She opened her eyes and looked. It was a tongue. Its owner was a large and bouncy young Alsatian, or German shepherd, with topaz eyes, black-tipped prick ears, a thick, soft coat, and a bushy black-tipped tail.

"Lob!" shouted a man farther up the beach. "Lob, come here!"

But Lob, as if trying to atone for the surprise he had given her, went on licking the sand off Sandy's face, wagging his tail so hard while he kept on knocking up more clouds of sand. His owner, a gray-haired man with a limp, walked over as quickly as he could and seized him by the collar.

"I hope he didn't give you a fright?" the man said to Sandy. "He meant it in play—he's only young."

"Oh, no, I think he's beautiful," said Sandy truly. She picked up a bit of driftwood and threw it. Lob, whisking easily out of his master's grip, was after it like a sandcolored bullet. He came back with the stick, beaming, and gave it to Sandy. At the same time he gave himself, though no one else was aware of

this at the time. But with Sandy, too, it was love at first sight, and when, after a lot more stick-throwing, she and the twins joined Father and Don to go home for tea, they cast many a backward glance at Lob being led firmly away by his master.

"I wish we could play with him every day." Tess sighed.

"Why can't we?" said Tim.

Sandy explained. "Because Mr. Dodsworth, who owns him, is from Liverpool, and he is only staying at the Fisherman's Arms till Saturday."

"Is Liverpool a long way off?"

"Right at the other end of England from Cornwall, I'm afraid."

It was a Cornish fishing village where the Pengelly family

lived, with rocks and cliffs and a strip of beach and a little round harbor, and palm trees growing in the gardens of the little whitewashed stone houses. The village was approached by a narrow, steep, twisting hillroad, and guarded by a notice that said LOW GEAR FOR 1½ MILES, DANGEROUS TO CYCLISTS.

The Pengelly children went home to scones[2] with Cornish cream and jam, thinking they had seen the last of Lob. But they were much mistaken. The whole family was playing cards by the fire in the front room after supper when there was a loud thump and a crash of china in the kitchen.

"My Christmas puddings!" exclaimed Jean, and ran out.

"Did you put TNT in them, then?" her husband said.

But it was Lob, who, finding the front door shut, had gone around to the back and bounced in through the open kitchen window, where the puddings were cooling on the sill. Luckily only the smallest was knocked down and broken.

Lob stood on his hind legs and plastered Sandy's face with licks. Then he did the same for the twins, who shrieked with joy.

"Where does this friend of yours come from?" inquired Mr. Pengelly.

"He's staying at the Fisherman's Arms—I mean his owner is."

"Then he must go back there. Find a bit of string, Sandy, to tie to his collar."

"I wonder how he found his way here," Mrs. Pengelly said, when the reluctant Lob had been led whining away and Sandy had explained about their afternoon's game on the beach. "Fisherman's Arms is right round the other side of the harbor."

Lob's owner scolded him and thanked Mr. Pengelly for bringing him back. Jean Pengelly warned the children that they

---

2. **scones** (skōnz): tea cakes or biscuits that are often served with butter.

had better not encourage Lob any more if they met him on the beach, or it would only lead to more trouble. So they dutifully took no notice of him the next day until he spoiled their good resolutions by dashing up to them with joyful barks, wagging his tail so hard that he winded Tess and knocked Tim's legs from under him.

They had a happy day, playing on the sand.

The next day was Saturday. Sandy had found out that Mr. Dodsworth was to catch the half-past-nine train. She went out secretly, down to the station, nodded to Mr. Hoskins, the stationmaster, who wouldn't dream of charging any local for a platform ticket, and climbed up on the footbridge that led over the tracks. She didn't want to be seen, but she did want to see. She saw Mr. Dodsworth get on the train, accompanied by an unhappy-looking Lob with drooping ears and tail. Then she saw the train slide away out of sight around the next headland, with a melancholy wail that sounded like Lob's last good-bye.

Sandy wished she hadn't had the idea of coming to the station. She walked home miserably, with her shoulders hunched and her hands in her pockets. For the rest of the day she was so cross and unlike herself that Tess and Tim were quite surprised, and her mother gave her a dose of senna.[3]

A week passed. Then, one evening, Mrs. Pengelly and the younger children were in the front room playing snakes and ladders. Mr. Pengelly and Don had gone fishing on the evening tide. If your father is a fisherman, he will never be home at the same time from one week to the next.

Suddenly, history repeating itself, there was a crash from the kitchen. Jean Pengelly leaped up, crying, "My blackberry jelly!" She and the children had spent the morning picking and the afternoon boiling fruit.

---

3. **senna** (sen′ə): a medicine made from the leaves of pea, bean, or clover plants.

But Sandy was ahead of her mother. With flushed cheeks and eyes like stars she had darted into the kitchen, where she and Lob were hugging one another in a frenzy of joy. . . .

"Good heavens!" exclaimed Jean. "How in the world did he get here?"

"He must have walked," said Sandy. "Look at his feet."

They were worn, dusty, and tarry. One had a cut on the pad.

"They ought to be bathed," said Jean Pengelly. "Sandy, run a bowl of warm water while I get the disinfectant."

"What'll we do about him, Mother?" said Sandy anxiously.

Mrs. Pengelly looked at her daughter's pleading eyes and sighed.

"He must go back to his owner, of course," she said, making her voice firm. "Your dad can get the address from the Fisherman's tomorrow, and phone him or send a telegram. In the meantime he'd better have a long drink and a good meal."

Lob was very grateful for the drink and the meal, and made no objection to having his feet washed. Then he flopped down on the hearthrug and slept in front of the fire they had lit because it was a cold, wet evening, with his head on Sandy's feet. He was a very tired dog. He had walked all the way from Liverpool to Cornwall, which is more than four hundred miles.

The next day Mr. Pengelly phoned Lob's owner, and the following morning Mr. Dodsworth arrived off the night train, decidedly put out, to take his pet home. That parting was worse than the first. Lob whined, Don walked out of the house, the twins burst out crying, and Sandy crept up to her bedroom afterward and lay with her face pressed into the quilt, feeling as if she were bruised all over.

Jean Pengelly took them all into Plymouth to see the circus on the next day and the twins cheered up a little, but even the

hour's ride in the train each way and the Liberty horses and performing seals could not cure Sandy's sore heart.

She need not have bothered, though. In ten days' time Lob was back—limping this time, with a torn ear and a patch missing out of his furry coat, as if he had met and tangled with an enemy or two in the course of his four-hundred-mile walk.

Bert Pengelly rang up Liverpool again. Mr. Dodsworth, when he answered, sounded weary. He said, "That dog has already cost me two days that I can't spare away from my work—plus endless time in police stations and drafting newspaper advertisements. I'm too old for these ups and downs. I think we'd better face the fact, Mr. Pengelly, that it's your family he wants to stay with—that is, if you want to have him."

Bert Pengelly gulped. He was not a rich man; and Lob was a pedigreed dog. He said cautiously, "How much would you be asking for him?"

"Good heavens, man, I'm not suggesting I'd sell him to you. You must have him as a gift. Think of the train fares I'll be saving. You'll be doing me a good turn."

"Is he a big eater?" Bert asked doubtfully.

By this time the children, breathless in the background listening to one side of this conversation, had realized what was in the wind and were dancing up and down with their hands clasped beseechingly.

"Oh, not for his size," Lob's owner assured Bert. "Two or three pounds of meat a day and some vegetables and gravy and biscuits—he does very well on that."

Alexandra's father looked over the telephone at his daughter's swimming eyes and trembling lips. He reached a decision. "Well, then, Mr. Dodsworth," he said briskly, "we'll accept your offer and thank you very much. The children will be overjoyed and you can be sure Lob has come to a good home. They'll look after him and see he gets enough exercise. But I can tell you," he ended firmly, "if he wants to settle in with us he'll have to learn to eat a lot of fish."

So that was how Lob came to live with the Pengelly family. Everybody loved him and he loved them all. But there was never any question who came first with him. He was Sandy's dog. He slept by her bed and followed her everywhere he was allowed.

Nine years went by, and each summer Mr. Dodsworth came back to stay at the Fisherman's Arms and call on his erstwhile dog. Lob always met him with recognition and dignified pleasure, accompanied him for a walk or two—but showed no signs of wishing to return to Liverpool. His place, he intimated, was definitely with the Pengellys.

In the course of nine years Lob changed less than Sandy. As she went into her teens he became a little slower, a little

stiffer, there was a touch of gray on his nose, but he was still a
handsome dog. He and Sandy still loved one another devotedly.

One evening in October all the summer visitors had left,
and the little fishing town looked empty and secretive. It was a
wet, windy dusk. When the children came home from school—
even the twins were at high school now, and Don was a full-
fledged fisherman—Jean Pengelly said, "Sandy, your Aunt
Rebecca says she's lonesome because Uncle Will Hoskins has
gone out trawling, and she wants one of you to go and spend
the evening with her. You go, dear; you can take your
homework with you."

Sandy looked far from enthusiastic.

"Can I take Lob with me?"

"You know Aunt Becky doesn't really like dogs—Oh, very
well." Mrs. Pengelly sighed. "I suppose she'll have to put up
with him as well as you."

Reluctantly Sandy tidied herself, took her schoolbag, put
on the damp raincoat she had just taken off, fastened Lob's
lead to his collar, and set off to walk through the dusk to Aunt
Becky's cottage, which was five minutes' climb up the steep hill.

The wind was howling through the shrouds of boats drawn
up on the Hard.

"Put some cheerful music on, do," said Jean Pengelly to
the nearest twin. "Anything to drown that wretched sound
while I make your dad's supper." So Don, who had just come
in, put on some rock music, loud. Which was why the Pengellys
did not hear the truck hurtle down the hill and crash against
the post office wall a few minutes later.

Dr. Travers was driving through Cornwall with his wife,
taking a late holiday before patients began coming down with
winter colds and flu. He saw the sign that said STEEP HILL. LOW
GEAR FOR 1½ MILES. Dutifully he changed into second gear.

"We must be nearly there," said his wife, looking out of her window. "I noticed a sign on the coast road that said the Fisherman's Arms was two miles. What a narrow, dangerous hill! But the cottages are very pretty—Oh, Frank, stop, stop! There's a child, I'm sure it's a child—by the wall over there!"

Dr. Travers jammed on his brakes and brought the car to a stop. A little stream ran down by the road in a shallow stone culvert, and half in the water lay something that looked, in the dusk, like a pile of clothes—or was it the body of a child? Mrs. Travers was out of the car in a flash, but her husband was quicker.

"Don't touch her, Emily!" he said sharply. "She's been hit.

Can't be more than a few minutes. Remember that truck that overtook us half a mile back, speeding like the devil? Here, quick, go into that cottage and phone for an ambulance. The girl's in a bad way. I'll stay here and do what I can to stop the bleeding. Don't waste a minute."

Doctors are expert at stopping dangerous bleeding, for they know the right places to press. This Dr. Travers was able to do, but he didn't dare do more; the girl was lying in a queerly crumpled heap, and he guessed she had a number of bones broken and that it would be highly dangerous to move her. He watched her with great concentration, wondering where the truck had got to and what other damage it had done.

Mrs. Travers was very quick. She had seen plenty of accident cases and knew the importance of speed. The first cottage she tried had a phone; in four minutes she was back, and in six an ambulance was wailing down the hill.

Its attendants lifted the child onto a stretcher as carefully as if she were made of fine thistledown. The ambulance sped off to Plymouth—for the local cottage hospital did not take serious accident cases—and Dr. Travers went down to the police station to report what he had done.

He found that the police already knew about the speeding truck—which had suffered from loss of brakes and ended up with its radiator halfway through the post office wall. The driver was concussed and shocked, but the police thought he was the only person injured—until Dr. Travers told his tale.

At half-past nine that night Aunt Rebecca Hoskins was sitting by her fire thinking aggrieved thoughts about the inconsiderateness of nieces who were asked to supper and never turned up, when she was startled by a neighbor, who burst in, exclaiming, "Have you heard about Sandy Pengelly, then, Mrs. Hoskins? Terrible thing, poor little soul, and they don't know if she's likely to live. Police have got the truck driver that hit her—ah, it didn't ought to be allowed, speeding through the place like that at umpty miles an hour, they ought to jail him for life—not that that'd be any comfort to poor Bert and Jean."

Horrified, Aunt Rebecca put on a coat and went down to her brother's house. She found the family with white shocked faces; Bert and Jean were about to drive off to the hospital where Sandy had been taken, and the twins were crying bitterly. Lob was nowhere to be seen. But Aunt Rebecca was not interested in dogs; she did not inquire about him.

"Thank the lord you've come, Beck," said her brother. "Will you stay the night with Don and the twins? Don's out looking for Lob and heaven knows when we'll be back; we may get a bed with Jean's mother in Plymouth."

"Oh, if only I'd never invited the poor child," wailed Mrs. Hoskins. But Bert and Jean hardly heard her.

That night seemed to last forever. The twins cried themselves to sleep. Don came home very late and grimfaced. Bert and Jean sat in a waiting room of the Western Counties Hospital, but Sandy was unconscious, they were told, and she remained so. All that could be done for her was done. She was given transfusions to replace all the blood she had lost. The broken bones were set and put in slings and cradles.

"Is she a healthy girl? Has she a good constitution?" the emergency doctor asked.

"Aye, doctor, she is that," Bert said hoarsely. The lump in Jean's throat prevented her from answering; she merely nodded.

"Then she ought to have a chance. But I won't conceal from you that her condition is very serious, unless she shows signs of coming out from this coma."

But as hour succeeded hour, Sandy showed no signs of recovering consciousness. Her parents sat in the waiting room with haggard faces; sometimes one of them would go to telephone the family at home, or to try to get a little sleep at the home of Granny Pearce, not far away.

At noon next day Dr. and Mrs. Travers went to the Pengelly cottage to inquire how Sandy was doing, but the report was gloomy: "Still in a very serious condition." The twins were miserably unhappy. They forgot that they had sometimes called their elder sister bossy and only remembered how often she had shared her pocket money with them, how she read to them and took them for picnics and helped with their homework. Now there was no Sandy, no Mother and Dad, Don went around with a gray, shuttered face, and worse still, there was no Lob.

The Western Counties Hospital is a large one, with dozens of different departments and five or six connected buildings, each with three or four entrances. By that afternoon it became noticeable that a dog seemed to have taken up position outside the hospital, with the fixed intention of getting in. Patiently he would try first one entrance and then another, all the way around, and then begin again. Sometimes he would get a little way inside, following a visitor, but animals were, of course, forbidden, and he was always kindly but firmly turned out again. Sometimes the guard at the main entrance gave him a pat or offered him a bit of sandwich—he looked so wet and beseeching and desperate. But he never ate the sandwich. No one seemed to own him or to know where he came from; Plymouth is a large city and he might have belonged to anybody.

At tea time Granny Pearce came through the pouring rain to bring a flask of hot tea to her daughter and son-in-law. Just as she reached the main entrance the guard was gently but forcibly shoving out a large, agitated, soaking-wet Alsatian dog.

"No, old fellow, you cannot come in. Hospitals are for people, not for dogs."

"Why, bless me," exclaimed old Mrs. Pearce. "That's Lob! Here, Lob, Lobby boy!"

Lob ran to her, whining. Mrs. Pearce walked up to the desk.

"I'm sorry, madam, you can't bring that dog in here," the guard said.

Mrs. Pearce was a very determined old lady. She looked the porter in the eye.

"Now, see here, young man. That dog has walked twenty miles from St. Killan to get to my granddaughter. Heaven knows how he knew she was here, but it's plain he knows. And he ought to have his rights! He ought to get to see her! Do you know," she went on, bristling, "that dog has walked the length of England—twice—to be with that girl? And you think you can keep him out with your fiddling rules and regulations?"

"I'll have to ask the medical officer," the guard said weakly.

"You do that, young man." Granny Pearce sat down in a determined manner, shutting her umbrella, and Lob sat patiently dripping at her feet. Every now and then he shook his head, as if to dislodge something heavy that was tied around his neck.

Presently a tired, thin, intelligent-looking man in a white coat came downstairs, with an impressive, silver-haired man in a dark suit, and there was a low-voiced discussion. Granny Pearce eyed them, biding her time.

"Frankly . . . not much to lose," said the older man. The man in the white coat approached Granny Pearce.

"It's strictly against every rule, but as it's such a serious case we are making an exception," he said to her quietly. "But only outside her bedroom door—and only for a moment or two."

Without a word, Granny Pearce rose and stumped upstairs. Lob followed close to her skirts, as if he knew his hope lay with her.

They waited in the green-floored corridor outside Sandy's room. The door was half shut. Bert and Jean were inside. Everything was terribly quiet. A nurse came out. The white-coated man asked her something and she shook her head. She had left the door ajar and through it could now be seen a high, narrow bed with a lot of gadgets around it. Sandy lay there, very flat under the covers, very still. Her head was turned away. All Lob's attention was riveted on the bed. He strained toward it, but Granny Pearce clasped his collar firmly.

"I've done a lot for you, my boy, now you behave yourself," she whispered grimly. Lob let out a faint whine, anxious and pleading.

At the sound of that whine Sandy stirred just a little. She sighed and moved her head the least fraction. Lob whined again. And then Sandy turned her head right over. Her eyes opened, looking at the door.

"Lob?" she murmured—no more than a breath of sound. "Lobby, boy?"

The doctor by Granny Pearce drew a quick, sharp breath. Sandy moved her left arm—the one that was not broken—from below the covers and let her hand dangle down, feeling, as she always did in the mornings, for Lob's furry head. The doctor nodded slowly.

"All right," he whispered. "Let him go to the bedside. But keep ahold of him."

Granny Pearce and Lob moved to the bedside. Now she could see Bert and Jean, white-faced and shocked, on the far side of the bed. But she didn't look at them. She looked at the smile on her granddaughter's face as the groping fingers found

Lob's wet ears and gently pulled them. "Good boy," whispered
Sandy, and fell asleep again.

Granny Pearce led Lob out into the passage again. There
she let go of him and he ran off swiftly down the stairs. She
would have followed him, but Bert and Jean had come out into
the passage, and she spoke to Bert fiercely.

"I don't know why you were so foolish as not to bring the dog before! Leaving him to find the way here himself—"

"But, Mother!" said Jean Pengelly. "That can't have been Lob. What a chance to take! Suppose Sandy hadn't—" She stopped, with her handkerchief pressed to her mouth.

"Not Lob? I've known that dog nine years! I suppose I ought to know my own granddaughter's dog?"

"Listen, Mother," said Bert. "Lob was killed by the same truck that hit Sandy. Don found him—when he went to look for Sandy's schoolbag. He was—he was dead. Ribs all smashed. No question of that. Don told me on the phone—he and Will Hoskins rowed a half mile out to sea and sank the dog with a lump of concrete tied to his collar. Poor old boy. Still—he was getting on. Couldn't have lasted forever."

"Sank him at sea? Then what—?"

Slowly old Mrs. Pearce, and then the other two, turned to look at the trail of dripping-wet footprints that led down the hospital stairs.

In the Pengellys' garden they have a stone, under the palm tree. It says: "Lob. Sandy's dog. Buried at sea."

Joan Aiken (born 1924), the daughter of the American poet Conrad Aiken, grew up in England. She spent her childhood reading and making up stories to amuse herself and her younger brother. Aiken's special style of writing blends fantasy, mystery, and humor. Her award-winning books are popular in England and America.

Other books: *The Wolves of Willoughby Chase*
Black Hearts in Battersea

Developing Comprehension Skills

1. Summarize the events that bring Lob to live with Sandy.

2. What happens to Sandy when she goes to visit her aunt?

3. Why is the dog allowed in Sandy's hospital room?

4. What is the surprise at the end of the story? What do you believe is the explanation?

5. **Focus on Thinking: Drawing a Conclusion.** Gathering bits of information to make a decision is called **drawing a conclusion.** What conclusion can you draw about the effect of Lob's visit on Sandy?

Reading Fiction

1. **Understanding the Setting.** Understanding the setting can help you understand the plot. Where does the Pengelly family live? How far away does Mr. Dodsworth live? Why is this distance important to the plot?

2. **Examining Animal Characters.** Animals in literature are not always personified, but as characters they often show individual traits or qualities. What traits does Lob show?

Critical Thinking

Analyzing Story Structure. To analyze the structure of a story, study each element separately. The plot of this story has two parts separated by time. What is each part about? How much time separates the parts? Why is the first part necessary to the second part?

Writing in Response to Literature

Think about this story. Is it believable? Is it a ghost story? Did you expect something strange to happen? Did you like the ending? Write your feelings about the story.

Language and Literature

Vocabulary

Guide Words. A quick way to find a word in the dictionary is to use the guide words in large type at the top of each page. These words show the first and last entry words listed on a page. All the words on the page are listed in alphabetical order between these words.

Exercise. Two pairs of guide words are given below. Tell which pair each numbered word would come between in a dictionary.

strange . . . streak   **streaky . . . strident**

1. stress   3. strength   5. strategy   7. stray
2. strict   4. stratum   6. stretcher   8. strenuous

Developing Writing Skills

Describing a Place. The swans, the owner of the ghost town, and Lob all found a place they considered perfect. What place would be perfect for you to live in? Describe your ideal place.

Prewriting. List activities and weather conditions that you enjoy. Choose a real or make-believe place where you could do the activities and find those conditions. List phrases to describe the place. Arrange details in a natural order in which you would view it.

Drafting. Begin by stating where your perfect place is. Describe its features, including weather conditions and the nature of the place. Follow the order you planned.

Revising and Sharing. Add adjectives and use specific nouns to describe your place more clearly. Make a collage from magazine pictures to go with your description. Combine your description and collage with those of your classmates to create a travel catalog.

When have you felt alone in a group of people? Notice how María Luisa deals with her feelings.

From

María Luisa

WINIFRED MADISON

María Luisa and her younger brother, Juan, come to live in San Francisco while their mother recovers from tuberculosis. They stay with their cousin Elena, who is in high school, and her family. Having been an excellent student in her Spanish-speaking school, María Luisa is now having trouble in her new English-speaking school. A special class is formed at her school for students with different language backgrounds.

Monday was a difficult day and after school, when María Luisa went to the sewing room where the special class was to be held, it seemed useless to imagine that she would ever learn English well enough to keep up with her classes. As for the stories she once felt that she wanted to write, why even think about them, she asked herself.

Ten students had already arrived and were waiting for the class to begin. Each sat quietly at the sewing tables, lost in a gloomy world of his own. The only sounds came from two little Japanese girls who sat close together, whispering and giggling softly as though they were telling secrets. They reminded María Luisa of little birds.

Sitting at the back of the room, María Luisa recognized several students she had seen before. Julien Alvarez, a tall dark-skinned boy from her science class, sat scratching his initials on the table with a penknife. There was Steve Ramos, a short boy with large luminous eyes. And Gloria Sanchez.

At the sight of Gloria, María Luisa felt a slight flush of guilt. Gloria, one of the most miserable creatures María Luisa had ever seen, was the girl with the snarled black hair who always sat alone in the cafeteria. Once María Luisa had asked the two girls with whom she sometimes ate lunch if they wouldn't invite Gloria to eat with them. "To make her feel good, you know?" María Luisa had said. Each of the girls knew what it was like to be alone and have no friends, and yet they had turned up their noses. "Her? Oh, no, she smells!" María Luisa had continued to sit with her friends and pretend to herself that she did not see Gloria sitting by herself every day.

Now everyone sat together at the sewing tables, but each of them was alone. "We're all klunkheads," María Luisa decided. It was easy to be a klunkhead, but dull. One simply never talked, that was all there was to it. Then one couldn't be laughed at. But it could become boring.

A sound of whistling broke the silence and Peter Jensen strode into the room with all the assurance in the world. He was no klunkhead, that was certain. Sitting down and slouching in an exaggerated way, he looked around openly at the others in the class. He whistled continuously, now imitating bird sounds, as though he was determined to make the others snap out of their gloom. María Luisa didn't mean to stare, but she could not help it; he was so different from the boys she had always known, with his rangy long body, his shock of straight blond hair, and the nose that seemed to jut forward. Miss Summer had told her once that that kind of nose was a sign of curiosity. Peter felt her glance and turned around to stare at her, which embarrassed her dreadfully and made her pretend to be searching for something in her purse. One by one, everyone turned to grin at Peter, while he nodded and grinned in return. "He's the only one who isn't a klunkhead," María Luisa thought.

The teacher was almost ten minutes late and there was the question of whether or not she would come. "We don't have to stay," one of the boys said and he had even started toward the door when the teacher walked in.

Or was it the teacher, María Luisa wondered? She looked more like a high school student. She wasn't remarkably pretty, not like Elena; María Luisa found herself comparing everyone to Elena these days. But there was something beautiful about this teacher, something more than the dark curly hair and the direct blue eyes. Her face was flushed with hurrying and now everyone was staring at her.

"I'm late and I'm really very sorry. I didn't mean to keep you waiting. There was a traffic jam on the freeway and everyone was held up. I just couldn't get through."

Someone in the class should have said that was all right, or good afternoon, or we're glad you came, but nobody said a word. Everyone stared. When she spoke, she did not seem like a teacher but more like a person beginning a conversation. Finally Peter responded.

"Is OK. Ve didn't mind vaiting."

It was the first time María Luisa had heard him speak. The words were all right but his accent was so thick María Luisa could barely understand what he said.

Young Woman with Sunflowers, 1941, DIEGO RIVERA. Gerald Peters Gallery, Santa Fe, New Mexico.

The teacher rewarded him with a sparkling smile. She wasn't really pretty, María Luisa decided, but she could not take her eyes away from her. Without knowing why, she had begun to feel better since the teacher came.

"It's very formal in here, isn't it, everyone sitting in rows. Do you suppose we could put four of these big tables together and then when we sit around them, we'll be able to talk with each other," the teacher said.

Three of the boys moved quickly to do this and soon the students and the teacher were sitting around the tables. It was no longer an ordinary class facing one foe, the teacher. It was a group and the teacher was one part of it. Finally they were ready to begin. All eyes were on the new teacher. "*Caray,*[1] I like that pink dress she's wearing and that silk scarf around her neck. I'll have to remember to tell Elena about it," María Luisa thought. Then the teacher began to speak.

"My name is Miss Stein. As you may have been told, this is an experimental class and it's voluntary. That means you don't have to take it if you don't want to. However, if you do take it, it will be important for you to come every day. Any questions?"

"This is an English class, no?" someone asked.

"In a way it is, but I wouldn't want to call it that because it's not like the usual English classes you go to. I like to think of this as a time when we can talk to one another and listen to each other. We'll be talking in English, so that we begin to feel at home with it. It's like learning a musical instrument, you know; the more you practice the better you become. Does anyone else have a question? It's all right to talk out, you know."

Silence from the klunkheads. They might be free to talk out but the habit of keeping still was strong. Finally Peter asked a question.

"Miss Stein, why do they call this class 'experiment'?"

---

1. **caray** (cäh räh'ē): Spanish for "How unusual!" or "How interesting!"

It was difficult to understand him. He spoke English but it seemed to be coming through layers of cheesecloth. Even Miss Stein looked at him kindly but questioningly, as though she hadn't really heard him.

"Hey, teacher, I can't understan' him. Why don't he talk English?" Alex asked.

"I speak English," Peter insisted, but his face turned red.

"Wow, he sure have a accent," Alex said. Everyone smiled. If anyone had an accent it was Alex himself, but he was easy to understand for he seemed to speak a language that lay halfway between English and Spanish. Someone began to josh him in a soft Spanish voice, but Miss Stein saved the day.

"I think the question is, why is this an experimental class and why were you all chosen for it. A good question. You were selected very carefully; you are all capable of doing good work in school, but if you were able to speak and use English better, you would do much better than you seem to be doing now. The experiment is to help you feel easier with the English language."

It was good to be chosen. So perhaps somebody did care, María Luisa thought. But Alex looked doubtful. Miss Stein turned to him.

"You look as though you wanted to say something?"

Alex thought for a minute, shook his head no and looked down at his desk, a klunkhead once more.

"All right then. I think we should get acquainted with each other. Let's go around the table and you may introduce yourselves."

One after the other the names were spoken.

Alex Alvarez

Ralph Covarrubias

Charlie Sun

John García
Steve Muñoz
Tassos Pappas
Riko Takahashi
Ruth Kimura
Paul Ramos
María Luisa Santos
Jesús Hidalgo
Peter Jensen
Gloria Sanchez

The voices were sometimes high in pitch and sometimes so low they were barely audible. Still, there was something rhythmical about the sound of the names, almost musical, María Luisa thought. Could you make a poem out of names, she wondered.

"Now we know each other. We'll get to know each other even more as time goes on. Let's see, do we have time to write today? We'll be writing every day, of course." She looked at her watch doubtfully, not realizing what the prospect of writing every day meant to the class. Students looked at each other and made faces. Who wanted to write?

"You don't mean we're goin' to write every day?" Alex asked, hardly able to believe it.

"Why not?" Miss Stein answered with a comforting smile. "Don't look so frightened. Writing is only a way of saying what you think. Actually we'll spend most of the time talking but we'll write, too."

"She'd never get away with it if she weren't so pretty," Alex mumbled in Spanish to Steve. Everyone understood who knew Spanish. But it was Miss Stein who answered the remark, in perfectly clear Spanish. Translated, her answer was:

"Don't knock it until you try it. It will be better than you think."

"You speak Spanish, Miss Stein? You a Chicano?"

"Naw, she from Cuba, I bet."

Miss Stein said, "I'll let you figure it out for yourselves. We don't have time to write now, but we'll do it tomorrow. Don't anyone worry about it. I promise I'll leave work earlier so that I can get here on time. So, I'll see you tomorrow. Good night, now."

María Luisa, walking home, hardly noticed the weight of her books. Her mind was full of new thoughts, all about Miss Stein. She would see her again tomorrow. Now she had something to look forward to.

As she walked up the hill she heard a whistle and saw that Peter Jensen was walking on the other side of the street. He waved to her and she nodded a shy hello. She would be seeing him the next day, too. Smiling to herself, she hurried home.

The next day Miss Stein was waiting for them. She had placed a large bag full of apples in the middle of the tables.

"Help yourselves," she said. "You must get awfully hungry at this time of day."

Nobody made a move to take an apple, so she repeated her offer. "Go ahead. Don't be shy." María Luisa hoped someone would take one; otherwise Miss Stein might be hurt, but she herself was too shy to begin. Peter was the first who took an apple and offered it to Ruth Kimura who giggled as she accepted it. Soon everyone was eating apples and talking a little, that is everyone excepting John García, an extremely thin, dark boy who had not as yet said a single word.

"Won't you have one?" Miss Stein asked.

He shook his head, no.

"He don't never eat lunch," Ralph said.

"No? Why not?" Miss Stein's voice was sympathetic, but when John seemed to sink down in his seat, she went on to talk about something else. The other students knew why John hadn't had lunch; there were free lunches for all students who couldn't afford to pay, but John was too proud to ask for the free ticket.

Following an impulse, María Luisa took an apple and gave it to him. He looked at it for a minute, and then took it.

Miss Stein was talking. "I'd like to get to know you all better. We can talk for a while if you like, and then we'll write. Call it what you like; the subject is WHO I AM." She wrote it on the blackboard in large open letters.

"Hey, miss, can we write in Spanish?"

"Let's try it in English first. All right?"

"*Caray*, who I am!" María Luisa asked herself. "I'm María Luisa Santos. I'm me, myself. So what is there to write?" Apparently everyone else was puzzled, too. They looked questioningly at Miss Stein.

"Hey, Teacher. I don' wanna write about who I am. Can I write about my brother? He's got lots to write about." It was Steve Muñoz who asked, almost in a whisper. He looked too young for the class and Miss Stein wondered if he had been pushed ahead by accident. He looked as if he should be in the fifth or sixth grades, not junior high school.

"I'd rather know about you, Steve."

"But my brother, he's in the Marines."

"I don't know how to say nothin', Miss Stein."

"Please, Miss Stein, can't I write in Spanish? You understan' Spanish. You speak it good, Miss Stein."

Peter was already scribbling away on a large yellow pad.

Charlie Sun had begun to write very slowly and neatly on a page from a notebook. Jesús Hidalgo, an extremely handsome young man who looked as if he might be in high school, had also chewed on his pencil thoughtfully and then began to write. Everyone else looked doubtful. How did one start?

"Let's think of it this way," Miss Stein said. "Every one of you is an individual and each one of you is different from everybody else. Right?" The class nodded in agreement. "You can write about the things which make you different, if you like; perhaps it's where you were born and where you have traveled. Or maybe you have ideas which seem to be your ideas. Perhaps there are things that you really love doing. All of these things help make up your own personality. The best way to start is to start and let the ideas begin to flow without worrying. I'm not going to show these papers to anyone, you know; they are confidential. So you can feel free to say whatever you like."

María Luisa usually had more ideas about what she would like to write than she could ever have time for. Now she could not think of anything to say. Besides, there were so many people sitting around her, tapping the tables with their pens and making noises as they tried to think of what to say, she could almost feel their confusion.

"Miss Stein," she asked with a boldness that surprised her, "would it be all right if I sat in the corner? If I write, I like to be alone."

"Of course, sit wherever you are most comfortable. You can move around."

In the corner, away from the others, María Luisa felt a little wall of quiet around her and then she began to write. She concentrated so hard that she frowned a little and bit her tongue. The room had become very quiet and she could hear the clock on the wall loudly ticking.

who I am
María Luisa Santos

I am María Luisa Santos and I am American. My Father he was American to. He was from texas and my mother she is from mexico. I am born in Airzona. In our house we spek spanish and in church it is in spanish to and in shcol the ticher Miss Summer Let us spek spanish wen we like. It was very good that shcol and the ticher want us to be happy and not like here. When my father was living he woud play gitar sometime. One day his truck turn over and was kiLL. My mother is in ~~host~~ hospitl now she has teebee. My little bother and I are in San Francisco wit my Aunt and uncL.

In San Luis was not all good but since I am here I know more how it was good there. I was child then, a little griL. Now I am growing up. is big here in San Francisco but is not so happy.

She read over the paper she had written. She sighed. It wasn't really very good. She had crossed out words and wasn't sure about spelling. Anyway, now Miss Stein would know she was a citizen.

"Here is my story. It's not very good," she apologized as she gave her paper to Miss Stein.

"Don't worry. It's probably better than you think. Anyway, I'm sure you're going to improve."

María Luisa noticed that some of the members of the class had written papers with only one sentence, and Steve Muñoz had written nothing at all.

One by one the students left the sewing room and nobody spoke very much. "We are all so used to being alone," María Luisa thought, "that we can't get used to saying things like hello and good-bye."

A thick San Francisco fog had been brewing all day and it was chilly. Perhaps the theme she had written hadn't been very good, and she knew of at least two words she had spelled wrong. Now that the time for writing was over she began to think of all the things she might have said and wished Miss Stein would let them write the theme over the next day. It would be so much better then.

"Hey, wait a minute, María Luisa! Gosh, you walk fast."

She barely understood what he said, but she knew that Peter was running to catch up to her. "I only went to get a book and when I turn back around you were gone," he said.

They walked along the street together. "So, do you like our . . . our club?" he asked.

The Club! That would be a good name for the class. "I like," she said shyly. "And you?"

"I think it could be very good. Me, I could use help. People always say to me 'what, what, what did you say?' "

María Luisa could not quite understand Peter, but she guessed what he was saying and let it go at that. There was a way in which his voice seemed to go up and down that made it different and appealing.

"Do you live here?" he asked.

She nodded and he said, "Good! We can walk together then. How was your paper on WHO I AM?"

"I wrote only a little. I think it could be a big book, that subject, WHO I AM."

"That's my trouble. I could write an' write an' there still would be so much to say. Do you think I talk too much?"

"No, I like," María Luisa answered. Yes, she liked to hear him talk and she liked him to walk beside her. It made her wonder how different they must look. Now she could see that he was quite tall. His straight blond hair kept getting in his eyes and he had to shake his head to get it out of the way; that was charming, she thought. She liked the knit cap he wore and the long scarf wound around his neck. She liked the way his eyes, which were sometimes gray and sometimes blue, seemed to settle on her. She wondered if the world looked different if you looked through gray eyes instead of dark brown ones.

Just then she saw Juan come running up the street to her and she certainly didn't want him to see her talking to a boy, so she said quickly and softly, "Adiós. I have to go now."

"I'll see you tomorrow. Don't forget," he said.

She smiled and then broke away. "Tomorrow" was a beautiful word.

Winifred Madison (born 1942) is a writer, an artist, and a teacher of writing for children. Many of Madison's stories reflect her interest in art and in the social problems children face. Although some of her stories are amusing, others show the sadder side of life and growing up.

Other books: *Becky's Horse*
Call Me Danica

Developing Comprehension Skills

1. How does María Luisa define *klunkhead*? What is good and bad about being one?

2. How were students chosen for the experimental class?

3. Summarize what María Luisa explains in her writing.

4. María Luisa expresses unhappiness in her writing. Using clues in the story, predict how she might feel a year from now.

5. **Focus on Thinking: Supporting Inferences.** When you make an inference, you should support it with details stated in the story. What can you infer about how most of the students feel about themselves? What details support your inference?

Reading Fiction

1. **Recognizing a Character's Growth.** Events can cause changes in a character. María Luisa appears sad and hopeless when the story begins. How and why does she start to change?

2. **Identifying Conflict.** You remember that characters may face several conflicts. What external conflict have these students been facing? What internal conflict do they face?

3. **Appreciating the Minor Characters.** Minor characters often have an effect on main characters. Why is Peter important to María Luisa?

Speaking and Listening

Making Introductions. Often you want to introduce two people to each other. When you say each person's name, add an interesting fact about the person. This will help the two people start a conversation. Using this method, practice introducing a partner to other people in your class.

Writing in Response to Literature

María Luisa's assignment was to write about the subject *Who I Am*. Complete the same assignment about yourself.

*Describe a time when some-
one's unfairness made you
angry. Read to see what James
does about his anger.*

The Scribe

KRISTIN HUNTER

We been living in the apartment over the Silver Dollar Check Cashing Service five years. But I never had any reason to go in there till two days ago when Mom had to go to the Wash-a-Mat and asked me to get some change.

And man! Are those people who come in there in some bad shape.

Old man Silver and old man Dollar, who own the place, have signs tacked up everywhere:

NO LOUNGING, NO LOITERING
THIS IS NOT A WAITING ROOM
and
MINIMUM CHECK CASHING FEE, 50¢
and
LETTERS ADDRESSED, 50¢
and
LETTERS READ, 75¢
and
LETTERS WRITTEN, ONE DOLLAR

And everybody who comes in there to cash a check gets their picture taken like they're some kind of criminal.

After I got my change, I stood around for a while digging the action. First comes an old lady with some kind of long form to fill out. The mean old man behind the counter points to the "One Dollar" sign. She nods. So he starts to fill it out for her.

"Name?"

"Muskogee Marie Lawson."

"SPELL it!" he hollers.

"M, m, u, s—well, I don't exactly know, sir."

"I'll put down 'Marie,' then. Age?"

"Sixty-three my last birthday."

"Date of birth?"

"March twenty-third"—a pause—"I think, 1900."

"Look, Marie," he says, which makes me mad, hearing him first-name a dignified old gray-haired lady like that, "if you'd been born in 1900, you'd be seventy-two. Either I put that down, or I put 1910."

"Whatever you think best, sir," she says timidly.

He sighs, rolls his eyes to the ceiling, and bangs his fist on the form angrily. Then he fills out the rest.

"One dollar," he says when he's finished. She pays like she's grateful to him for taking the trouble.

Next is a man with a cane, a veteran who has to let the government know he moved. He wants old man Silver to do this for him, but he doesn't want him to know he can't do it himself.

"My eyes are kind of bad, sir, will you fill this thing out for me? Tell them I moved from 121 South 15th Street to 203 North Decatur Street."

Old man Silver doesn't blink an eye. Just fills out the form, and charges the crippled man a dollar.

And it goes on like that. People who can't read or write or count their change. People who don't know how to pay their

Downtown, 1967, GEORGIA MILLS JESSUP. The National Museum of Women in the Arts, Gift of Savannah Clark, 1986.

gas bills, don't know how to fill out forms, don't know how to address envelopes. And old man Silver and old man Dollar cleaning up on all of them. It's pitiful. It's disgusting. Makes me so mad I want to yell.

And I do, but mostly at Mom. "Mom, did you know there are hundreds of people in this city who can't read and write?"

Mom isn't upset. She's a wise woman. "Of course, James,"

she says. "A lot of the older people around here haven't had your advantages. They came from down South, and they had to quit school very young to go to work.

"In the old days, nobody cared whether our people got an education. They were only interested in getting the crops in." She sighed. "Sometimes I think they still don't care. If we hadn't gotten you into that good school, you might not be able to read so well either. A lot of boys and girls your age can't, you know."

"But that's awful!" I say. "How do they expect us to make it in a big city? You can't even cross the streets if you can't read the WALK and DON'T WALK signs."

"It's hard," Mom says, "but the important thing to remember is it's no disgrace. There was a time in history when nobody could read or write except a special class of people."

And Mom takes down her Bible. She has three Bible study certificates and is always giving me lessons from Bible history. I don't exactly go for all the stuff she believes in, but sometimes it is interesting.

"In ancient times," she says, "no one could read or write except a special class of people known as *scribes*. It was their job to write down the laws given by the rabbis and the judges. No one else could do it.

"Jesus criticized the scribes," she goes on, "because they were so proud of themselves. But he needed them to write down his teachings."

"Man," I said when she finished, "that's something."

My mind was working double-time. I'm the best reader and writer in our class. Also it was summertime. I had nothing much to do except go to the park or hang around the library and read till my eyeballs were ready to fall out, and I was tired of doing both.

So the next morning, after my parents went to work, I took Mom's card table and a folding chair down to the sidewalk. I lettered a sign with a Magic Marker, and I was in business. My sign said:

PUBLIC SCRIBE—ALL SERVICES FREE

I set my table up in front of the Silver Dollar and waited for business. Only one thing bothered me. If the people couldn't read, how would they know what I was there for?

But five minutes had hardly passed when an old lady stopped and asked me to read her grandson's letter. She explained that she had just broken her glasses. I knew she was fibbing, but I kept quiet.

I read the grandson's letter. It said he was having a fine time in California, but was a little short. He would send her some money as soon as he made another payday. I handed the letter back to her.

"Thank you, son," she said, and gave me a quarter.

I handed that back to her too.

The word got around. By noontime I had a whole crowd of customers around my table. I was kept busy writing letters, addressing envelopes, filling out forms, and explaining official-looking letters that scared people half to death.

I didn't blame them. The language in some of those letters—"Establish whether your disability is one-fourth, one-third, one-half, or total, and substantiate in paragraph 3 (b) below"—would upset anybody. I mean, why can't the government write English like everybody else?

Most of my customers were old, but there were a few young ones too. Like the girl who had gotten a letter about her baby from the Health Service and didn't know what "immunization" meant.

At noontime one old lady brought me some iced tea and a peach, and another gave me some fried chicken wings. I was really having a good time, when the shade of all the people standing around me suddenly vanished. The sun hit me like a ton of hot bricks.

Only one long shadow fell across my table. The shadow of a tall, heavy, blue-eyed cop. In our neighborhood, when they see a cop, people scatter. That was why the back of my neck was burning.

"What are you trying to do here, sonny?" the cop asks.

"Help people out," I tell him calmly, though my knees are knocking together under the table.

"Well, you know," he says, "Mr. Silver and Mr. Dollar have been in business a long time on this corner. They are very respected men in this neighborhood. Are you trying to run them out of business?"

"I'm not charging anybody," I pointed out.

"That," the cop says, "is exactly what they don't like. Mr. Silver says he is glad to have some help with the letter-writing. Mr. Dollar says it's only a nuisance to them anyway and takes up too much time. But if you don't charge for your services, it's unfair competition."

Well, why not? I thought. After all, I could use a little profit.

"All right," I tell him. "I'll charge a quarter."

"Then it is my duty to warn you," the cop says, "that it's against the law to conduct a business without a license. The first time you accept a fee, I'll close you up and run you off this corner."

He really had me there. What did I know about licenses? I'm only thirteen, after all. Suddenly I didn't feel like the big black businessman anymore. I felt like a little kid who wanted to holler for his mother. But she was at work, and so was Daddy.

"I'll leave," I said, and did, with all the cool I could muster. But inside I was burning up, and not from the sun.

One little old lady hollered "You big bully!" and shook her umbrella at the cop. But the rest of those people were so beaten-down they didn't say anything. Just shuffled back on inside to give Mr. Silver and Mr. Dollar their hard-earned money like they always did.

Freedom, 1966–1967, CHARLES WHITE. Heritage Gallery, Los Angeles.

I was so mad I didn't know what to do with myself that afternoon. I couldn't watch TV. It was all soap operas anyway, and they seemed dumber than ever. The library didn't appeal to me either. It's not air-conditioned, and the day was hot and muggy.

Finally I went to the park and threw stones at the swans in the lake. I was careful not to hit them, but they made good targets because they were so fat and white. Then after a while the sun got lower. I kind of cooled off and came to my senses. They were just big, dumb, beautiful birds, and not my enemies. I threw them some crumbs from my sandwich and went home.

"Daddy," I asked that night, "how come you and Mom never cash checks downstairs in the Silver Dollar?"

"Because," he said, "we have an account at the bank, where they cash our checks free."

"Well, why doesn't everybody do that?" I wanted to know.

"Because some people want all their money right away," he said. "The bank insists that you leave them a minimum balance."

"How much?" I asked him.

"Only five dollars."

"But that five dollars still belongs to you after you leave it there?"

"Sure," he says. "And if it's in a savings account, it earns interest."

"So why can't people see they lose money when they pay to have their checks cashed?"

"A lot of our people," Mom said, "are scared of banks, period. Some of them remember the Depression, when all the banks closed and the people couldn't get their money out. And others think banks are only for white people. They think they'll be insulted, or maybe even arrested, if they go in there."

Wow. The more I learned, the more pitiful it was. "Are there any black people working at our bank?"

"There didn't used to be," Mom said, "but now they have Mr. Lovejoy and Mrs. Adams. You know Mrs. Adams, she's nice. She has a daughter your age."

"Hmm," I said, and shut up before my folks started to wonder why I was asking all those questions.

The next morning, when the Silver Dollar opened, I was right there. I hung around near the door, pretending to read a copy of *Jet* magazine.

"Psst," I said to each person who came in. "I know where you can cash checks free."

It wasn't easy convincing them. A man blinked his red eyes at me like he didn't believe he had heard right. A carpenter with tools hanging all around his belt said he was on his lunch hour and didn't have time. And a big fat lady with two shopping bags pushed past me and almost knocked me down, she was in such a hurry to give Mr. Silver and Mr. Dollar her money.

But finally I had a little group who were interested. It wasn't much. Just three people. Two men—one young, one old—and the little old lady who'd asked me to read her the letter from California. Seemed the grandson had made his payday and sent her a money order.

"How far is this place?" asked the young man.

"Not far. Just six blocks," I told him.

"Aw shoot. I ain't walking all that way just to save fifty cents."

So then I only had two. I was careful not to tell them where we were going. When we finally got to the Establishment Trust National Bank, I said, "This is the place."

"I ain't goin' in there," said the old man. "No, sir. Not

me. You ain't gettin' me in there." And he walked away quickly, going back in the direction we had come.

To tell the truth, the bank did look kind of scary. It was a big building with tall white marble pillars. A lot of Brink's armored trucks and Cadillacs were parked out front. Uniformed guards walked back and forth inside with guns.

Whereas the Silver Dollar is small and dark and funky and dirty. It has trash on the floors and tape across the broken windows. People going in there feel right at home.

I looked at the little old lady. She smiled back bravely. "Well, we've come this far, son," she said. "Let's not turn back now."

So I took her inside. Fortunately Mrs. Adams' window was near the front.

"Hi, James," she said.

"I've brought you a customer," I told her.

Mrs. Adams took the old lady to a desk to fill out some forms. They were gone a long time, but finally they came back.

"Now, when you have more business with the bank, Mrs. Franklin, just bring it to me," Mrs. Adams said.

"I'll do that," the old lady said. She held out her shiny new bankbook. "Son, do me a favor and read that to me."

"Mrs. Minnie Franklin," I read aloud. "July 9, 1972. Thirty-seven dollars."

"That sounds real nice," Mrs. Franklin said. "I guess now I have a bankbook, I'll have to get me some glasses."

Mrs. Adams winked at me over the old lady's head, and I winked back.

"Do you want me to walk you home?" I asked Mrs. Franklin.

"No, thank you, son," she said. "I can cross streets by myself all right. I know red from green."

And then she winked at both of us, letting us know she knew what was happening.

"Son," she went on, "don't ever be afraid to try a thing just because you've never done it before. I took a bus up here from Alabama by myself forty-four years ago. I ain't thought once about going back. But I've stayed too long in one neighborhood since I've been in this city. Now I think I'll go out and take a look at this part of town."

Then she was gone. But she had really started me thinking. If an old lady like that wasn't afraid to go in a bank and open an account for the first time in her life, why should I be afraid to go up to City Hall and apply for a license?

Wonder how much they charge you to be a scribe?

Kristin Hunter (born 1931) began writing a newspaper column for teen-agers when she was fourteen. Since then she has written for both young people and adults. Most of her books are set in black neighborhoods in large cities. Hunter describes her characters and settings with realism, humor, and warmth.

Developing Comprehension Skills

1. What services do Mr. Silver and Mr. Dollar offer? Why do they anger James?

2. How does James's mother affect his attitude toward people who cannot read? What action does his new attitude cause James to take?

3. What arguments does the policeman use to put James out of business? How does James feel about being forced to quit?

4. Evaluate James's attempts to get people to use the bank. Does he use the best method? What other solutions might he have tried?

5. **Focus on Thinking: Predicting.** Clues at the end of a story may help you predict what will happen after the story ends. What does the end of this story lead you to think James will do?

Reading Fiction

1. **Recognizing Character Growth.** Characters grow and change because of what they learn and experience. What does James learn? How does he grow?

2. **Identifying Theme.** A story may present several **themes**, or messages about life. What is one theme of "The Scribe"?

3. **Examining Language.** To make characters believable, writers have them speak like real people in the same situation. Find three examples of language James uses that make him seem like a real thirteen-year-old.

Study and Research

Using the Index. The **index** of a nonfiction book lists the topics covered in the book and the pages where they are found. The index helps you find information quickly. Find out what happened to banks during the Great Depression. Use the indexes of two books about United States history. Check listings such as *banks*, *Depression*, and *New Deal*.

Writing in Response to Literature

This story shows the importance and value of reading. Think about an adult who cannot read. Write about the kinds of problems he or she might run into on a typical day.

Who encourages you to keep doing something when you feel like giving up? Read to discover who helps Tyree keep trying.

From

Sweetwater

LAURENCE YEP

Tyree and his family live in the half-sunken city of Old Sion on the planet Harmony. Tyree's people, called Silkies, are descended from the Earthlings who first colonized Harmony. They share the city with Argans, a race of intelligent aliens.

At an annual winter festival, Tyree is so moved by the playing of a song called "Sweetwater" that he decides he wants to become a musician. He whittles a flute and begins to practice. Another Silkie hears him and makes fun of his bad playing. Tyree's father, the Captain of the Silkies, is embarrassed. He forbids Tyree to ever let another Silkie hear him play again.

I figured that Pa's order could be taken two ways, his way and my way. I could play the flute as long as no Silkie heard me, and I knew there was one place at night in Old Sion where no Silkie would hear me, because no Silkie would dare go there. I was willing to go there that very night to find a place where I could practice. I planned to go to Sheol. I was that desperate.

We still called the area by its old name, given when Sheol was the most elegant and expensive area in Old Sion, but now after the floods the mansions were occupied by the Argans, the only intelligent race native to Harmony. The Argans were a strange race, and they liked to keep their secrets. No human ever knew how they reproduced, though their words for family relations translated loosely into "uncle" and "nephew."

There were some humans who had never forgiven the aliens because they didn't warn the colonists about the tides, but then we weren't asked to come to their world. And anyway, the colonists weren't exactly kind to the aliens.

Later when the city, Old Sion, was abandoned, the Argans drifted back from the wastelands, claiming that the land was still theirs, and by that time it did not matter who Old Sion belonged to legally, because the sea had already filled most of the city. There was a silent agreement between the humans and the Argans—though both would have been the first to deny it—not to go into certain sectors, or at least never to be seen there. No man ever saw an Argan in Old Sion unless that Argan wanted him to, not even if it was in that human's own home. So when I went into the Argan's area, I was the one in the wrong. I was the invader.

At night Sheol didn't look like it belonged to man anymore. The half-submerged elegant houses looked like ancient monsters surfacing. Their great stone faces were covered with delicate beards of green seaweed or soft mustachios of barnacles. The seaworn doors opened like the mouths of Seadragons through which the water twisted and untwisted, and the windows were like eyes, hollow and black and waiting—with ripples fanning outward as though from some creature sleeping inside.

It was really scary, but I thought like a human in those days and I figured that whether the Argans and the animals and the houses liked it or not, I was going to practice there. On purpose I picked out the finest and biggest mansion, which had been built on a hill. It had belonged to Nimrod Senaar, the Governor who had cheated my ancestors. The statue of our old enemy rose from the water lonely and proud, frowning at the change in his old city.

I moored my skiff to one of the pillars of the portico and splashed up the steps. My bare feet made wet slapping sounds as I walked across the portico and through the entrance hall with its huge rotunda. I checked the rooms on both floors for the acoustics until I found one that satisfied me. Then for about an hour I practiced my scales until I heard something strange.

At first I thought it was the wind but then I realized it was music, and the more I listened, the more I felt that I had never heard anything more lovely. The song was at once sad and yet beautiful, moving like the veiled ghosts of bold knights or unfulfilled maidens. The echoes floated up the street over the hissing water, past the empty, slime-covered apartment houses, bounced and danced past walls whose rotting mortar slowly spilled stone after stone into the sea. It was a song for Old Sion.

I had to find the musician and I searched the entire mansion until I found him sitting on the portico by my skiff. It was an Argan, an old one, sitting there calmly. The bristly fur on his back and arm-legs was a peppery gray, the flesh on his belly was all wrinkled, and he stooped slightly from old age. He looked very much like a four-foot-high Earth spider, though you would never suggest that to an Argan. They hate to be reminded of their resemblance to their Earth cousins the way humans hate to be reminded that they look like apes.

He put down his reed pipes when he saw me and with six of his arm-legs slowly pushed himself off the portico. He seemed surprised and walked around me. He walked delicately on two arm-legs like a ballet dancer imitating an old man, with

his six other arm-legs stretched out to balance his overpuffed
body. He stepped back in front of me and examined me boldly,
even though Argans usually kept their eyelids down low
because they knew how their eyes bothered humans. Argans
have myriads of tiny eyes on their orbs. They shine like clouds
of stars in dim light and it takes some getting used to—it's like
being watched by a one-man crowd.

"What can I do for you, Manchild?" he asked in Intergal.[1]

I shifted uncomfortably from one foot to the other. I told myself that it was silly to feel like I had invaded this Argan's home. In those days I believed I had as much right to this place as the Argans did. "I heard you playing," I said finally.

"And my nephews and my neighbors heard your free concert," the old Argan said. "They found me and told me so I could come home and hear my competition."

"There's no competition," I mumbled. It was easy enough to get embarrassed about my playing in those days. I could even be shamed by aliens. "Well," I added, "I guess I'll be moving on. I don't want to drive folk away from their homes."

The old Argan grabbed hold of me and I knew I couldn't get away. The Argans had small but very strong disc-shaped suction pads at the base of their finger-toes. They could retract the suction pads into their skin or extend them so that the bottoms of their hand-feet appeared to be rimmed with tiny white circles. When he used his suction pads, his grip was unbreakable.

"What do they know? It's the song that counts, not the singer." He pointed at the flute. "And that's a mighty nice flute. Did you carve it?"

I turned my ornate flute over in my hands self-consciously. "I'm afraid I spent more time carving pictures into it than I did playing it."

"Do you like music?"

"More than anything," I said. "But there's no one to teach me."

"Of course." The old Argan was thoughtful for a moment.

---

1. **Intergal** (in'tər gəl): the writer's word for the common language of the planet Harmony, understood by humans and Argans.

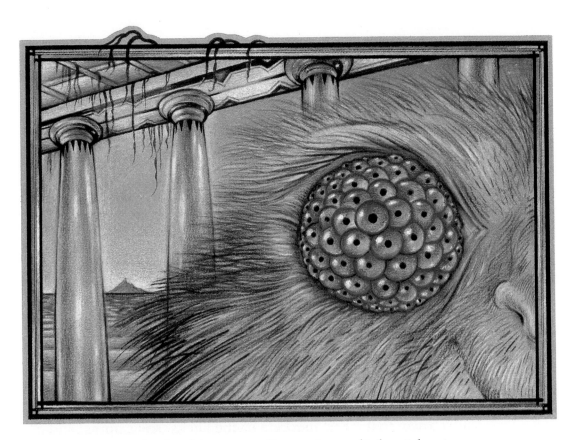

"What did you think of my song? It was just a little night music."

"I thought it was beautiful," I said and added truthfully, "it was the most beautiful thing I've ever heard."

I don't know what he was looking for, for he studied me for a long time. His myriad eyes reflected my image so I saw a hundred Tyrees—each a perfect miniature.

"Would you like me to teach you?" the old Argan said.

"But what about your nephews and your neighbors?"

"I told you to forget them. Music's the only important thing."

I felt a warm rush of gratitude inside me. "I'd like it an awful lot if you would teach me, Mister . . ." I realized that I had almost made a bad mistake, because Argans, like some people on Earth, don't believe in giving their true names because that gives the listener power over the person named. Argans have what they call use-names, which they change every so often.

"My use-name is Amadeus." The old Argan let go of my wrist with a slight popping noise.

I rubbed the small circles on my wrist where the suction pads had gripped me. A new question had occurred to me but it took me a while before I worked up enough nerve to ask him. "Since you're an Argan, how can you teach me to play a human musical instrument?"

"It's enough that I know," Amadeus snapped. "Now no more questions if you want me to teach you."

It was a puzzle how an alien could teach me about human music, but I was willing to try anything. "All right," I said.

"Come back tomorrow night and I'll see if I can teach you that you have only two thumbs and not ten."

I knew that I had met one of the aliens' songsmiths, and all the way home I felt warm and good inside, knowing what a privilege I was being given. If there is one thing the Argans love, it's their music—you could hear one or more of them playing on their reed pipes whenever you passed near Sheol. The Argans think that the gods directly choose someone to be a songsmith. Important councils have been moved to decisions by an inspired songsmith suddenly getting up and playing a particular song in a particular way.

The Argans don't think of music as we humans do. An Argan song seems skimpy by human standards. It just has a basic story line—like how the three moons were created—and a theme of music which represents the song. It's up to the musician to improvise and create variations on the theme and to combine these with certain other established themes which the audience recognizes as representing a castle, or a feast, or a heroic battle, or anything like that.

In Argan music, songs keep on evolving and changing as they are played. The Argans think that the human style is the mark of a mediocre musician. Only mediocre musicians play a song in the same way all the time. In human music, since you usually have a song sheet, the musician is limited to an already-fixed pattern of themes and variations and his performance is judged by his skill in playing the song. But in Argan music, the best musicians have to be not only skilled craftsmen but also geniuses at finding new and original patterns.

Of course, Argan music isn't really that loose. When I first started to play it, I wondered how a musician knew what to play next, since you had to choose while performing at the same time; but there's a kind of logic to it—like knowing the ending to a story halfway through the telling. For example, if two Argan heroes meet, you have to describe both of them, and their battle, and the funeral for the loser.

Amadeus was very patient about explaining things like that about music. He really earned his title, the Ultimate Uncle—which was his social position among the Argans, though Amadeus would never tell me any more. He hated to talk about himself and Argan affairs, but about music there was almost no stopping him. I took to visiting Sheol three times a week, and Amadeus would listen patiently as I butchered his people's music. Whenever I tried to apologize for a particularly clumsy performance, he would encourage me by telling me that my song and I had not found one another yet. According to Argan belief, it's the song that finds the singer and not the other way around.

After a while, though, not even that belief could satisfy me. I was tired from having to do my chores during the daytime,

keep my secret from my parents, and still have nothing to show for all my sacrifices but some bad playing.

"It's no use, Amadeus. I'm never going to be a musician."

Amadeus sighed and shook his head. "Manchild, you have everything that a person needs to make music: you have the talent, you have the skills now, but you still hold your soul back from the music—like you can't forget you're a human playing Argan music. You just have to remember that it's the music that counts—not the one who plays it."

And with that he put the reed pipes to his mouth and began to play the human song "Moonspring." I sat in astonishment as he slipped next into "Shall We Gather by the Stars" and "These Happy Golden Years."

"Amadeus, where did you ever learn to play human songs?" I asked in amazement.

He made a disappointed noise. "Manchild, didn't I just tell you that a real musician can play both 'human' and 'Argan' music? I'm not an Argan playing human songs. I'm a musician making music. The only thing that matters in this changing universe is the song, the eternal song that waits for you."

"Yes, but—"

"Play," Amadeus angrily ordered me, so I played. It was strange. Amadeus wouldn't talk about himself and he wouldn't let me talk about myself; and yet despite my ignorance, I felt closer to him than I had to anyone else. And in the moments when I doubted myself, Amadeus somehow always managed to keep me looking for my song.

Anybody who thinks Argan music is easy to learn has never really tried to. A lot of it was boring work when I had to master all the conventional themes so I would have a variety to choose from; but eventually after a year's work I got so that I could play two songs tolerably well. Even Amadeus had to admit I was a tolerable backup man—though I had yet to be found by my own song. But then one night he sat for a long time and smoothed the hair down on his arms thoughtfully before he finally looked up at me again. "I don't know what to do, Manchild. You're not going to develop any more unless you listen to others play—and you play for others."

Amadeus knew all about my first bad experiences with an audience, so he knew how shy I was of those situations. "Amadeus," I finally said, "have they been staying away because of me or have you been keeping them away so I wouldn't be nervous?"

"A little of both," Amadeus said reluctantly.

"The Argans don't like the idea of your giving me lessons, do they?"

"Who told you?" he asked angrily. "You pay those fools

no mind. They've heard you play but they just won't believe."

"Believe what?" I asked.

"That an Argan song will ever find a human," Amadeus was forced to admit.

"Have they been giving you trouble?" I asked.

"It doesn't matter," Amadeus said.

I had noticed that the rooms were a lot dustier of late, as if most of the house was no longer occupied. A brilliant songsmith like Amadeus should have had quite a few Argans around him—not only to hear him play but also to serve him as befitted his status. Yet whenever I went over there, Amadeus was alone.

"Do your family come back after I leave, or do they stay away all the time now?"

"Mind your own business," Amadeus snapped.

"But, Amadeus—"

Amadeus held up one hand-foot as a warning. "Let's get something straight, Manchild. We're here to play music, not to talk."

I gave up asking any more questions and just thought for a while. After all he had done for my sake I could hardly do less. "If you can get some of them together, I'll play for them," I said. "We'll show them."

Amadeus made sure I wanted to go through with it before he named the next night for my test. I had to trade twenty feet of my best nylon fishing line to Red Genteel, but he agreed to do my chores in the garden for that day while I napped. I wanted to be at my best for the Argans.

That night there must have been some twenty Argans sitting on the porch; six of them were my "classmates" while the others were nephews, skeptics, critics, and creatures who liked to see minor disasters. The moment I sat down to warm up they began to crack jokes in the clicking language of the Argans. I did not know the words but their jokes were obviously about me. They might not be able to make fun of Amadeus, but I was fair game.

One of them, Sebastian, had painfully learned some Intergal, so I could understand. "My cousin, he say, are your fingers broke? But I say, no, you just sitting on your hands."

I started to blush but Amadeus, he gave me a wink— which for an Argan is a considerable maneuver. It was a mannerism that I thought he had picked up from me. "You just start whenever you like, Manchild. Don't you mind the noise. 'Pears to be an undue number of insects out tonight." Amadeus stopped their jokes for maybe a minute and then they started in again. If I had been Amadeus, I would have been jumping up and down with anxiety, but Amadeus had a quiet kind of strength. He was like a calm pool of water that you could have dropped anything into and it wouldn't have disturbed the pool besides a momentary ripple. Just having Amadeus there gave me confidence.

"I'd like to play now, Amadeus," I said.

"Well," and Amadeus nodded to me approvingly, "well, go on."

I shut my eyes against all the furry faces and the star-clustered eyes and I tilted my head up toward the night sky, toward the real stars. Suddenly my song had found me. It was "Sweetwater," the song played at that winter fête—but now I made it my own. I took the melody and I played it like an Argan, modeling my song after an Argan song about a lost child looking for its mother. All the months of frustration and loneliness poured out of me and I played like *I* was the lost, lonely child calling across the empty light-years of space to Mother Earth.

The notes blended into a song that floated majestically over the rooftops, wheeling like a bird fighting through the wind and the rain, striving to break into the open, free sky, where the sun would dry his wings so he could turn toward home: to ride the winter winds to his home. I felt as lonely as when I used to lie on the roof watching the flocks of birds overhead and imagining what it was like to fly. Gliding with long, strong wings—floating along through the light, so far above the world that land and sea blurred into one. The wind raced through their pinions, bore them up on an invisible hand, and then, passing through their bodies, there came the smell of sweetwater.

When I felt the song was finished, I put the flute down to see Amadeus chuckling to himself. The other Argans looked a little stunned. Amadeus started to play a theme, this time an Argan song, "The Enchanted Reed Pipes." I played backup man but he was the master, sending his song ringing and echoing up the abandoned streets, the two of us gone mad with music.

Laurence Yep (born 1948) was born in San Francisco and went to school in Chinatown. His desire to write grew out of a challenge from his high-school English teacher. He sold his first science fiction story at the age of eighteen. Besides science fiction, Yep writes fantasy and realistic fiction drawn from his Chinese-American heritage.

Others books: *Child of the Owl*
Mountain Light

Developing Comprehension Skills

1. Where does Tyree go to play the flute? Why does he go there?

2. What do you infer is the reason that Amadeus offers to teach Tyree? How does his relationship with Tyree affect the Argans' attitude toward Amadeus?

3. How do Argans differ from humans in the way they judge musicians?

4. Why does Amadeus want Tyree to play for the Argans?

5. Why do you think Tyree's song finds him?

6. **Focus on Thinking: Understanding Motives.** A character can have several **motives**, or reasons for doing something. Why does Amadeus force Tyree to concentrate on music rather than talk? How does this method affect Tyree?

Reading Fiction

1. **Recognizing Fantasy.** Stories that are set in imaginary, unreal worlds are called **fantasy**. How does the setting of this story make it fantasy? How do the characters make it fantasy?

2. **Appreciating Figurative Language.** Writers of fiction, as well as poets, frequently use figurative language to describe. Find a simile that describes the area of Sheol. Find another simile that describes Amadeus.

3. **Understanding Character Relationships.** Characters may develop a close relationship because they have something in common. Through their love of music, what do Tyree and Amadeus do for each other?

Writing in Response to Literature

You live in a world "gone mad with music." Suppose all music suddenly disappeared. Explain in a paragraph what would bother you most about a world without music.

Language and Literature

Vocabulary

Respelling. Next to each dictionary entry, in parentheses, is the respelling, which shows how the word is pronounced. The symbols in the respelling are explained in the pronunciation key, usually found at the bottom of the dictionary page. Accent marks in the respelling show which syllable or syllables should be stressed.

Exercise. Figure out what words the following respellings represent. Use the pronunciation key.

fat, āpe, cär, ten, ēven, is, bīte; gō, hôrn, to͞ol, look; oil, out; up, fur; get; joy; yet; chin; she; thin, then; zh, leisure; ŋ, ring; ə for a in ago, e in agent, i in sanity, o in comply, u in focus; ' as in able (ā'b'l)

1. (kus'tə mər)   3. (ik sper'ə mənt)   5. (myo͞o' zi k'l)
2. (baŋ'kər)   4. (tə mär'ō)   6. (in'strə mənt)

Developing Writing Skills

Writing an Analysis. When you make an **analysis**, you break something into its parts to understand it better. Write an analysis of how one character from the last three stories solved a problem.

Prewriting. Choose María Luisa, James, or Tyree. Make a chart to break his or her problem-solving into parts. Use the headings below.

Problem faced	Who helps	How problem is solved	How character grows

Drafting. Begin with the character's problem. Include all the information from your chart as you discuss how the problem is solved. End with how or why the character showed growth.

Revising and Sharing. Make sure your analysis is orderly and follows your chart from left to right. Exchange papers and chart a classmate's paper.

Reading Poetry

Poems That Express Feelings

What makes someone decide to write a poem? You learned that a poem can be written to tell a story or to paint a picture. Often a poem grows out of a strong desire to express a feeling. A poet may want to express his or her own feelings. A poet may also imagine and share feelings that others have.

As the poet writes, he or she must make decisions about how to express a particular feeling. The poet may decide to state the feeling clearly and directly. The poet may also let the elements of the poem work together to create a feeling.

Using a Speaker to Create Feelings

One way a poet can express feelings is through a speaker. The **speaker** is the voice that talks to the reader. The speaker in a poem is like the narrator in a story. Often the speaker expresses the poet's own feelings. The poet John Farrar expresses a good feeling about being alone in this poem, "Alone."

> I want to explore all alone
> With nobody spying around,
> All alone! All alone, all alone!
> It has such a wonderful sound.

Sometimes the speaker is not the voice of the poet. The speaker may be a person or creature the poet invents. In this stanza from "Lone Dog" by Irene McLeod, a dog expresses feelings.

Part 2

I'm a lean dog, a keen dog, a wild dog, and lone;
I'm a rough dog, a tough dog, hunting on my own;
I'm a bad dog, a mad dog, teasing silly sheep;
I love to sit and bay the moon, to keep fat souls from sleep.

Using Elements of Poetry to Create Feeling

Besides using a speaker, the poet can express feelings with other elements of poetry. The poet might use repetition to emphasize a feeling, as in the poem "Alone." Rhyme and rhythm can also reinforce a feeling. Do you remember, for example, how rhyme and rhythm add a humorous feeling to "The Cremation of Sam McGee"?

The poet may create an image that suggests a feeling. He or she may use similes and metaphors to build the image. A simile suggests sadness and loneliness in "Separation," by W. S. Merwin.

Your absence has gone through me
Like thread through a needle.
Everything I do is stitched in its color.

How to Find Feelings in Poems

The poems in this part express the feelings of individuals trying to find their place in life. You will enjoy each poem more if you identify the feeling being expressed. If the poem has a speaker, ask yourself these questions:

1. Who is the speaker? What details give clues?
2. How does the speaker feel? What might cause the feeling?

If the poem has images, try to infer what feelings they suggest. Notice how rhyme, rhythm, or repetition add to the feeling. Finally, enjoy reading and thinking about the feelings the poet is sharing.

What would your friends say is your best quality? Learn how one person feels about the judgment of her friends.

Who's Who

JUDITH VIORST

Paula is the prettiest—the whole sixth grade agrees.
Jean's the genius—that is undeniable.
Most popular is Amy. Most admired is Louise.
But as for me, they say I'm most . . . reliable.

Lisa's the best listener—she always lends an ear.   5
And all the boys say Meg's the most desirable.
Gwen's the giggliest—but everybody thinks that's dear.
Who thinks it's dear to be the most reliable?

Jody and Rebecca tie for cleverest. Marie
Is best at sports (and also most perspirable).   10
Cathy is the richest—she's been saving since she's three.
But who'll save me from being most reliable?

I'd rather be most mischievous. I'd rather be most deep.
I'd rather—and I'll swear this on a Bible—
Be known as most peculiar. Nothing puts the world to sleep   15
Like someone who is known as most reliable.

Girl at the Mirror, 1954, NORMAN ROCKWELL. Norman Rockwell Museum at Stockbridge, Massachusetts.
Copyright © 1954 Estate of Norman Rockwell.

Developing Comprehension Skills

1. Who labels the girls in the poem?

2. Do you think the speaker envies the other girls? Why or why not?

3. **Focus on Thinking: Inferring Reasons.** You can infer reasons for feelings from clues in a poem. From the last two lines, infer why the speaker dislikes being called "most reliable."

Reading Poetry

1. **Recognizing the Speaker.** To understand a poem, you must figure out all you can about the speaker. About how old is this speaker? Is the speaker probably a male or a female?

2. **Appreciating Humor.** Poets sometimes invent words to create humor and to make a rhyme pattern work. Find an example of this in "Who's Who." How does this add humor to the poem?

Writing in Response to Literature

What "most" label would you choose for yourself? Write your choice and explain why you want or deserve it.

Judith Viorst is a poet, a journalist, and an author. She often writes about the humorous side of everyday family life. Most of her children's books were written for or about her own children.

Other books: *If I Were in Charge of the World and Other Worries*
Alexander and the Terrible, Horrible, No Good, Very Bad Day

Past

ARNOLD ADOFF

I have all these parts   stuffed in
                                    me
like mama's chicken
                        and
            biscuits,   5
                        and
daddy's apple pie, and a tasty
                                story
from the family
            tree.   10

But I know that tomorrow
                    morning
    I'll wake up
            empty, and hungry for that
                            next   15
                            bite
    of my new
            day.

Developing Comprehension Skills

1. Restate the main idea of the first sentence of this poem in your own words.

2. Do you think "Past" is a good title for this poem? Why or why not?

3. How does the speaker feel about the future? Which words express these feelings?

Reading Poetry

1. **Examining the Speaker.** You can infer some information about the speaker by examining details in the poem. Do you think the speaker in this poem is young or old? Is the speaker satisfied or curious? Happy or sad? What else can you tell about the speaker?

2. **Understanding Imagery.** Sometimes poets use images that stand for other ideas. What do the images of food and eating represent? Why do you think the poet chose those images?

3. **Examining Form.** One decision a poet makes is how to arrange the words on a page. What is unusual about the form of this poem? What possible reason might the poet have for this form?

Writing in Response to Literature

The speaker talks about "these parts stuffed in me . . . from the family tree." Choose an ingredient from your heritage, and write about how it may affect your future.

Arnold Adoff (born 1935) taught for twelve years in Harlem. He has brought many young black writers to the attention of the public through his collections of their writings. Adoff has also written his own poetry and a biography of Malcolm X for young people. He is married to noted writer Virginia Hamilton.

Other books: *Sports Pages*
Eats: Poems

How much control do you have over your own life? See how one speaker plans to take control.

the drum

NIKKI GIOVANNI

daddy says the world is
a drum tight and hard
and i told him
i'm gonna beat
out my own rhythm

Developing Comprehension Skills

1. What two people's ideas are expressed in the poem?

2. What comparison is made in this poem?

3. What do you infer that the speaker means in the last two lines?

Reading Poetry

1. **Understanding Metaphor.** A **metaphor** directly compares two unlike things that have something in common. What does the world have in common with a drum?

2. **Understanding Theme.** The **theme** is the message about life that the poet wants to convey. What is the theme of this poem?

3. **Appreciating Form.** Some poems, like "the drum," do not follow the usual rules of capitalization and punctuation. Does ignoring these rules relate in any way to the meaning of this poem?

Writing in Response to Literature

Write your own metaphor. Compare something or someone to a particular musical instrument. First list phrases that show what the two subjects have in common. Using your list, develop your metaphor in a poem or a paragraph.

Nikki Giovanni (born 1943) began her own publishing business at the age of twenty-seven. She has written several books of poetry as well as articles and autobiographical essays. Giovanni's poems often reflect her childhood in Tennessee and her experiences as a black in today's world.

Other books: *Spin a Soft Black Song*
Ego Tripping & Other Poems for
Young Readers

Language and Literature

Vocabulary

Multiple Meanings. A dictionary entry may list several meanings and parts of speech for a word. The context of the word helps you choose the right meaning. Notice how the context determines meaning for *feature*.

Rosa's eyes are her best *feature*. (part of the face)
Let's go to a double *feature*. (a full-length movie)
The show will *feature* Clem the Clown. (give prominence to)

Exercise. Using a dictionary, define and give the part of speech of each underlined word.

1. Herbie wore his derby to the County Fair derby.
2. A hen might brood if her brood is too rude.
3. Let's appeal to Chef Leo for some meals with appeal.
4. Will Emily's energy peak while she is climbing the peak?
5. Jane had to crane to see the crane lift the plane.

Developing Writing Skills

Developing a Character. The last three poems reveal some details about the speakers. Use what you know about one speaker to develop the character that speaker might be.

Prewriting. List what you know about each speaker. Choose one and imagine his or her personality, activities, family, and friends. Jot down specific details about the speaker's life.

Drafting. Introduce your character and give information about his or her life. Use the details you created to describe the person as if you knew him or her.

Revising and Sharing. Use more specific words and add details that might bring your character to life. Introduce your character to classmates by reading your paper aloud.

Youth

LANGSTON HUGHES

We have tomorrow
Bright before us
Like a flame.

Yesterday
A night-gone thing,   5
A sun-down name.

And dawn-today
Broad arch above
The road we came.

We march!   10

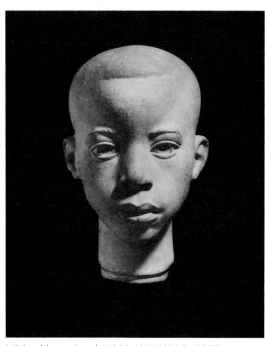

Michael (two views), 1962, WILLIAM E. ARTIS.
The North Carolina Museum of Art, Raleigh.

Developing Comprehension Skills

1. To what is tomorrow compared? What adjective describes it?

2. How is the image for yesterday different from the image for tomorrow?

3. What image do you picture in lines 7 through 10?

4. **Focus on Thinking: Understanding Author's Purpose.** When you read a poem, try to figure out the poet's purpose or reason for choosing images, words, or order. In what order does the speaker refer to the past, present, and future? Why do you think the poet chose that order?

Reading Poetry

1. **Recognizing Comparisons.** You remember that a simile compares two unlike things using *like* or *as*, while a metaphor compares without *like* or *as*. Find a simile and a metaphor in this poem.

2. **Understanding Feelings in Poetry.** From the images of a poem you can figure out what feeling the poet wants to convey. What feeling do the images in the first and third stanzas give you?

3. **Examining the Title.** The title of a poem can be a clue to the identity of the speaker. What can you tell about the speaker of this poem?

Writing in Response to Literature

Imagine that you are seventy years old. What does this poem make you think and feel? Write your response to the poem.

Langston Hughes (1902-1967) was a playwright, poet, songwriter, and an author of fiction and nonfiction. Hughes based much of his writing on his experiences, including his travels in Europe and Africa. Many of his works reflect the speech patterns and jazz rhythms he heard on the streets of Harlem, where he lived.

Another book: *The Dream Keeper, and Other Poems*

What do you have in common with your parents? Learn what holds this mother and daughter together.

Common Bond

KIMI NARIMATSU

My mother,
not so close are we,
yet we share a common bond,
    a goal,
    a unity.
Not because she is my mother,
and I her daughter
But because we are both Asian,
in a world of prejudices and hate.
We need to stay together as one,
    to survive,
    to love,
    to live.
We need to fight for our rights.
My mother,
she lives in a world as a person.
She fights for what she knows is right.

Sleeping Child, 1961, WILL BARNET. National Museum of American Art,
Smithsonian Institution, Washington, D.C., Gift of Sara Roby Foundation.

She works so hard to give me what I need.
   I give her in return what she needs,
      love,   20
      peace,
      understanding,
      and the will to live as an Asian
         and person.
Together, my mother and I are one.   25

Developing Comprehension Skills

1. What common bond do the speaker and her mother share?

2. What does the mother give her daughter? What does the daughter give her mother?

3. Contrast lines 2 and 25. Do you think both lines can be true at the same time? Explain your answer.

4. **Focus on Thinking: Making Inferences.** From what a speaker says, you can infer problems that may have happened in the past. What can you infer from lines 8, 9, and 14?

Reading Poetry

1. **Recognizing Feelings.** A poem can express feelings about several subjects. What feelings does the speaker express about her mother? What feelings does she express about the world around her?

2. **Appreciating Form.** Poets carefully arrange words in lines. Notice how some lines in this poem are indented. What ideas are stressed by being indented? In what way does the form affect the way you read the poem?

Writing in Response to Literature

"Common Bond" expresses the poet's feelings about prejudice. Write a letter to the poet. Tell her how the poem made you feel.

Who or what else would you be if you could change yourself? Read how a Frisbee tries to be other things.

Adventures of a Frisbee

SHEL SILVERSTEIN

The Frisbee, he got tired of sailing
To and fro and to;
And thought about the other things
That he might like to do.
So the next time that they threw him,   5
He turned there in the sky.
And sailed away to try and find
Some new things he could try.
He tried to be an eyeglass,
But no one could see through him.   10
He tried to be a UFO,
But everybody knew him.
He tried to be a dinner plate,
But he got cracked and quit.
He tried to be a pizza,   15
But got tossed and baked and bit.
He tried to be a hubcap,
But the cars all moved too quick.
He tried to be a record,
But the spinnin' made him sick.   20
He tried to be a quarter,
But he was too big to spend.
So he rolled home, quite glad to be
A Frisbee once again.

Developing Comprehension Skills

1. What is the Frisbee's problem?

2. The Frisbee tries to be many objects. What feature do those objects have in common?

3. What do all the lines that begin with *but* explain?

4. What conclusion can you draw about why the Frisbee is happy in the end?

Reading Poetry

1. **Recognizing Theme.** Even if a poem is about an object, its theme or message may apply to humans as well. What is the theme of this poem?

2. **Identifying Personification.** Writers may personify objects as well as animals. Find two examples in which the Frisbee is personified.

3. **Recognizing Alliteration.** You remember that **alliteration** is the repetition of consonant sounds at the beginnings of words. Find two examples of alliteration in this poem.

Critical Thinking

Forming an Opinion. Poets try to make people think and feel. No two people think or feel the same way, even about a poem. Decide which of the six poems you like best. Why did you choose it? Share your opinion with others and see how they react.

Writing in Response to Literature

Who or what would you like to be for a while? Write a journal entry about a day in your life as something or someone else.

Shel Silverstein (born 1932) is known for his poems, stories, illustrations, and songs. Many songs have been recorded. His humor and originality have made his works popular with people of all ages. "Adventures of a Frisbee" comes from his book *A Light in the Attic*.

Another book: *The Missing Piece*

Language and Literature

Vocabulary

Homographs. Words that have the same spelling but different meanings are called **homographs.** The dictionary lists these look-alikes separately with raised numerals after them, such as $bass^1$ and $bass^2$. When you look up a word in the dictionary, look for a homograph above or below it to make sure you have the right meaning.

Exercise. Each sentence below contains a pair of homographs. Use a dictionary to help you restate the sentence without the homographs.

1. The dove dove from its perch.
2. That law is invalid for an invalid.
3. Wendy wound a bandage around the wound.
4. Many live lizards live in the swamp.
5. Bill will probably refuse to take out the refuse.

Developing Writing Skills

Writing a Poem. In most of the poems in this unit, a speaker describes himself or herself. Write a poem that describes your own appearance, personality, or feelings.

Prewriting. Imagine that you are looking into a magic mirror that likes what it sees. List several qualities or feelings that the mirror sees in you. Decide whether the speaker in your poem will be you or the mirror.

Drafting. Write your description in lines. Try to use a metaphor or simile to paint a clear image.

Revising and Sharing. Make sure that the same speaker is speaking throughout the poem. Use the correct pronouns. Display a photo of yourself with a clean copy of your poem.

Reading Drama

Characters in Drama

A play tells a story through the speech and action of its characters. When drama is performed on stage, actors and actresses bring the characters to life. Because of this, playwrights, the writers of plays, face a special challenge when they create characters.

Playwrights must make clear what kinds of characters they are creating. Characters can be realistic and show emotions such as love and hate. Such characters grow and change as the plot develops. Characters may be comic. That is, their personalities and actions may be exaggerated and funny. Characters may also be types, such as heroes and villains, who stand for good and evil.

To create these characters, the playwright needs to make clear their physical appearance, personality, feelings, movements, and tone of voice. This helps readers of drama picture each scene. It helps actors bring characters to life.

Using Dialogue to Create Characters

Unlike the novelist or short-story writer, the playwright does not use narrative and descriptive paragraphs to develop the characters. Instead, the playwright relies on **dialogue,** the words the characters speak.

In their dialogue, characters often state exactly what they think or feel. This includes information about other characters. For example, in the following lines from *You're a Good Man, Charlie Brown!*

by Clark Gesner, the character Schroeder states exactly what he thinks of his friend Lucy:

> **Schroeder.** I'm sorry to have to say it right to your face, Lucy, but it's true. You're a very crabby person.

Characters may state how they feel about others, but they usually reveal their own personalities indirectly. Readers infer what characters are like from the way they react to each other.

Using Stage Directions to Create Characters

The dialogue may not give all the necessary information about the characters. Some information may come from the **stage directions.** These are the explanations in parentheses that precede or follow characters' lines. By explaining movement and tone of voice, for example, stage directions can signal what characters are feeling. Feelings may be expressed even when no dialogue is spoken. In these lines from the same play, the stage directions, not the dialogue, reveal Linus's fear and Lucy's angry reaction.

> **Linus** (*after a few moments of interior struggle*). Ninety-five. (*Lucy sends a straight jab to his jaw which lays him out flat.*)

Understanding Characters in Drama

As you read a play, notice whose lines you are reading. Picture who is present in each scene. Pay attention to the directions that move characters on and off the stage. Imagine you hear the dialogue as conversation. Use stage directions for clues about tone of voice and gestures. In other words, let the characters perform in your mind as you read.

How do you find out what others think of you? Decide if you would chooose the method that Lucy tries.

From

You're a Good Man, Charlie Brown!

Based on the comic strip Peanuts by CHARLES M. SCHULZ
Adapted by Clark Gesner

The following scene from *Act II* of *You're a Good Man, Charlie Brown!* begins as Schroeder and Lucy are walking onto the stage.

CHARACTERS

Schroeder	Charlie Brown	Patty
Lucy	Snoopy	Linus

Schroeder. I'm sorry to have to say it right to your face, Lucy, but it's true. You're a very crabby person. I know your crabbiness has probably become so natural to you now that you're not even aware when you're being crabby, but it's true just the same. You're a very crabby person and you're crabby to just about everyone you meet. (Lucy *remains silent—just barely*.) Now I hope you don't mind my saying this, Lucy, and I hope you'll take it in the spirit that it's meant. I think we should all be open to any opportunity to learn more about ourselves. I think

© 1951,52 United Features Syndicate, Inc.

Socrates[1] was very right when he said that one of the first rules for anyone in life is "Know thyself." (Lucy *has begun whistling quietly to herself*.) Well, I guess I've said about enough. I hope I haven't offended you or anything.

(*He makes an awkward exit*.)

Lucy (*stands in silence, then shouts offstage at* Schroeder). Well, what's Socrates got to do with it anyway, huh? Who was he anyway? Did he ever get to be king, huh! Answer me that, did he ever get to be king! (*suddenly to herself, a real question*) Did he ever get to be king? (*She shouts offstage, now a question*.) Who was Socrates, anyway? (*She gives up the rampage and plunks herself down*.) "Know thyself," hmph.

(*She thinks a moment, then makes a silent resolution to herself, exits and quickly returns with a clipboard and pencil. Charlie Brown and Snoopy have entered, with baseball equipment*.)

Charlie Brown. Hey, Snoopy, you want to help me get my arm back in shape? Watch out for this one, it's a new fastball.

---

1. **Socrates** (säk′rə tēz′): a philosopher and teacher in ancient Greece.

Lucy. Excuse me a moment, Charlie Brown, but I was wondering if you'd mind answering a few questions.

Charlie Brown. Not at all, Lucy. What kind of questions are they?

Lucy. Well, I'm conducting a survey to enable me to know myself better, and first of all I'd like to ask: on a scale of zero to one hundred, using a standard of fifty as average, seventy-five as above average and ninety as exceptional, where would you rate me with regards to crabbiness?

Charlie Brown (*stands in silence for a moment, hesitating*). Well, Lucy, I . . . .

Lucy. Your ballots need not be signed and all answers will be held in strictest confidence.

Charlie Brown. Well, still, Lucy, that's a very hard question to answer.

Lucy. You may have a few moments to think it over if you want, or we can come back to that question later.

Charlie Brown. I think I'd like to come back to it, if you don't mind.

Lucy. Certainly. This next question deals with certain character traits you may have observed. Regarding personality, would you say that mine is *A* forceful, *B* pleasing, or *C* objectionable? Would that be *A, B,* or *C*?

What would your answer be to that, Charlie Brown, forceful, pleasing, or objectionable, which one would you say, hmm? Charlie Brown, hmm?

Charlie Brown. Well, I guess I'd have to say forceful, Lucy, but . . . .

Lucy. "Forceful." Well, we'll make a check mark at the letter *A* then. Now, would you rate my ability to get along with other people as poor, fair, good, or excellent?

Charlie Brown. I think that depends a lot on what you mean by "get along with other people."

Lucy. You know, make friends, sparkle in a crowd, that sort of thing.

Charlie Brown. Do you have a place for abstention?

Lucy. Certainly, I'll just put a check mark at "None of the above." The

next question deals with physical appearance. In referring to my beauty, would you say that I was "stunning," "mysterious," or "intoxicating"?

Charlie Brown (*squirming*). Well, gee, I don't know, Lucy. You look just fine to me.

Lucy (*making a check on the page*). "Stunning." All right, Charlie Brown, I think we should get back to that first question. On a scale of zero to one hundred, using a standard of fifty as average, seventy-five as . . . .

Charlie Brown (*loud interruption*). I . . . (*quieter*) . . . remember the question, Lucy.

Lucy. Well?

Charlie Brown (*tentatively*). Fifty-one?

Lucy (*noting it down*). Fifty-one is your crabbiness rating for me. Very well then, that about does it. Thank you very much for helping with this survey, Charlie Brown. Your cooperation has been greatly appreciated.

(*She shakes hands with Charlie Brown.*)

Charlie Brown (*flustered*). It was a pleasure, Lucy, any time. Come on, Snoopy.

Lucy. Oh, just a minute, there is one more question. Would you answer "Yes" or "No" to the question: "Is Lucy Van Pelt the sort of person that you would like to have as president of your club or civic organization?"

Charlie Brown. Oh, yes, by all means, Lucy.

Lucy (*making note*). Yes. Well, thank you very much. That about does it, I think. (*Charlie Brown* exits, but Snoopy *pauses, turns, and strikes a dramatic "thumbs down" pose to* Lucy.) WELL, WHO ASKED YOU! (*Snoopy makes a hasty exit.* Lucy *stands center stage, figuring to herself on the clipboard and mumbling.*) Now, let's see. That's a fifty-one, "None of the above," and . . . (*She looks up.*) Schroeder was right.

You're a Good Man, Charlie Brown! 393

I can already feel myself being filled with the glow of self-awareness. (Patty *enters. She is heading for the other side of the stage, when* Lucy *stops her.*) Oh, Patty, I'm conducting a survey and I wonder if . . . .

Patty. A hundred and ten, *C,* "Poor," "None of the above," "No," and what are you going to do about the dent you made in my bicycle!

(Patty *storms off.* Lucy *watches her go then looks at the audience.*)

Lucy. It's amazing how fast word of these surveys gets around.

(Linus *wanders in and sits down.* Lucy *crosses to him, still figuring.*)

Lucy. Oh, Linus, I'm glad you're here. I'm conducting a survey and there are a few questions I'd like to ask you.

Linus. Sure, go ahead.

Lucy. The first question is: on a scale of zero to one hundred, with a standard of fifty as average, seventy-five as above average, and ninety as exceptional, where would you rate me with regard to crabbiness?

Linus (*slowly turns his head to look at her*). You're my big sister.

Lucy. That's not the question.

Linus. No, but that's the answer.

Lucy. Come on, Linus, answer the question.

Linus (*getting up and facing* Lucy). Look, Lucy, I know very well that if I give any sort of honest answer to that question you're going to slug me.

Lucy. Linus, a survey that is not based on honest answers is like a house that is built on a foundation of sand. Would I be spending my time to conduct this survey if I didn't expect complete candor in all the responses? I promise not to slug you. Now what number would you give me as your crabbiness rating?

Linus (*after a few moments of interior struggle*). Ninety-five.

(Lucy *sends a straight jab to his jaw which lays him out flat.*)

Lucy. No decent person could be expected to keep her word with a rating over ninety. (*She stalks off, busily figuring away on her clipboard.*) Now, I add these two columns and that gives me my answer. (*She figures energetically, then finally sits up with satisfaction.*) There, it's all done. Now, let's see what we've got. (*She begins to scan the page. A look of trouble skims over her face. She rechecks the figures. Her eternal look of self-confidence wavers, then crumbles.*) It's true. I'm a crabby person. I'm a very crabby person, and everybody knows it. I've been spreading crabbiness wherever I go. I'm a supercrab. It's a wonder anyone will still talk to me. It's a wonder I have any friends at all—(*She looks at the figures on the paper.*) or even associates. I've done nothing but make life miserable for everyone. I've done nothing but breed unhappiness and resentment. Where did I go wrong? How could I be so selfish? How could . . . .

(Linus *has been listening. He comes and sits near her.*)

Linus. What's wrong, Lucy?

Lucy. Don't talk to me, Linus. I don't deserve to be spoken to. I don't deserve to breathe the air I breathe. I'm no good, Linus. I'm no good.

Linus. That's not true, Lucy.

Lucy. Yes, it is. I'm no good, and there's no reason at all why I should go on living on the face of this earth.

Linus. Yes, there is.

Lucy. Name one. Just tell me one single reason why I should still deserve to go on living on this planet.

Linus. Well, for one thing, you have a little brother who loves you. (Lucy *looks at him. She is silent. Then she breaks into a great, sobbing "Wah!"*) Every now and then I say the right thing.

(Lucy *continues sobbing as she and* Linus *exit.*)

You're a Good Man, Charlie Brown!   395

Developing Comprehension Skills

1. How does Schroeder describe Lucy? What advice does he give her?

2. How does Lucy try to learn more about herself? Which characters answer her questions? Who gives an opinion without being asked?

3. Why do you think Linus first answers Lucy by saying, "You're my big sister"?

4. Do you think Lucy gathers accurate information from her friends in her survey? Why or why not?

5. **Focus on Thinking: Recognizing the Cause.** An effect may have a deeper cause than appears on the surface. Lucy cries when Linus tells her he loves her. For what reasons do his words cause her to cry?

Reading Drama

1. **Understanding Dialogue.** A playwright reveals the personality of a character through dialogue. Reread Lucy's lines about the second part of her survey on page 392. How does her way of asking show her forcefulness?

2. **Examining Stage Directions.** Stage directions explain what physical movements the actors should make. Why are stage directions especially necessary for Snoopy? Find examples of stage directions that direct Lucy's actions.

3. **Recognizing Humor.** Humor is often created by exaggeration. What three word choices does Lucy give in her survey about her physical appearance? How are these choices an example of exaggeration? What do they tell about Lucy's opinion of herself?

Critical Thinking

Creating Alternatives. The way a question is worded limits someone's **alternatives,** or choices, of how to answer. Imagine you want to find out how other people see you, but you want to make sure that all their answers are positive. Create five questions with only positive alternatives to choose from.

Writing in Response to Literature

It's very natural to want to know what others think of you. Write about the possible advantages and disadvantages of finding out.

Language and Literature

Vocabulary

Idioms. An expression that does not mean exactly the same as the combined meanings of each word is called an **idiom.** For example, the idiom "by the skin of one's teeth" means "just barely." The dictionary defines idioms at the end of the entry of an important word in the idiom. "By the skin of one's teeth" is listed in the entry *skin*.

Exercise. Find these idioms in a dictionary and define them.

1. be all ears
2. in the same boat
3. a far cry
4. wear out one's welcome
5. down at the mouth
6. not hold a candle to

Developing Writing Skills

Writing Dialogue. In a play, the dialogue reveals the characters' personalities. For example, Lucy's loud, rapid speeches show her overbearing manner. Charlie Brown's many pauses show his indecision. Write a scene in which dialogue reveals two characters' personalities.

Prewriting. Imagine two very different characters. You can base them on people you know or have seen on television. Decide what they will talk about. Maybe they are planning something exciting, or maybe they are arguing. Think about how each character would sound.

Drafting. Write the conversation as lines of a dialogue. Try to show the characters' personalities through their words. Add stage directions to suggest their tones or how they speak.

Revising and Sharing. Make sure your characters have responded to each other's lines. Read your dialogue aloud to a friend and ask for suggestions to improve it. Then both of you read the dialogue to the class.

Unit 3 Review

Using Your Skills in Reading Fiction

Read the paragraph below. What do you learn about the character Bill? How does the writer give you this information?

Bill was shooting baskets in the gym. He had spent a year practicing. "I've got to make center this year," he thought. The coach interrupted his thoughts. "Bill, you have to get your grades up if you want to be on the team," Coach Rich said.

Using Your Skills in Reading Poetry

What can you tell about the speaker in "Everybody Says" by Dorothy Aldis? What feelings does the speaker express?

Everybody says
I look just like my mother.
Everybody says
I'm the image of Aunt Bee.
Everybody says
My nose is like my father's
But *I* want to look like ME!

Using Your Skills in Reading Drama

What do these lines from the play *The Maharajah Is Bored* by Barbara Winther, tell you about the personality of Radha? What besides dialogue gives you a clue?

Radha (*haughtily*). Tailor, have you finished my gown?
Gopal. Here is your sari, Mistress Radha.
Radha (*decisively*). I don't like it!

Gopal (*startled*). It is the material you chose. And, you see, I made it exactly as you commanded.

Radha (*pacing in annoyance*). I don't care. (*furious*) It isn't elegant enough. (*stamping her foot with rage*) You are a stupid tailor! You sew no better than a monkey!

Using Your Comprehension Skills

In these paragraphs from "Future Tense" by Robert Lipsyte, what can you infer about Gary's opinion of Mr. Wordsmith?

On the way home, Dani Belzer, the prettiest poet in school, asked Gary, "What did you think of our new Mr. Wordsmith?"

"If he was a color, he'd be beige," said Gary. "If he was a taste, he'd be water. If he was a sound, he'd be a low hum."

Using Your Vocabulary Skills

Look up *quarry* in a dictionary. Then answer these questions.

1. How do you know that *quarry* is a homograph?
2. Which syllable of *quarry* is stressed when you pronounce it?
3. Which entry shows *quarry* used as two parts of speech?
4. Define *quarry* as it is used in this sentence: The marble came from a quarry in Italy.

Using Your Writing Skills

Follow directions to complete one writing assignment below.

1. Compare and contrast how two of the characters from this unit "find a place" for themselves.
2. Write a story, poem, or dramatic skit in which a place causes a character to change.

UNIT FOUR

FICTION   POETRY   NONFICTION

Learning About Life

Reading Fiction

Theme and Mood

You learn about life simply by living. You also learn by observing the experiences of other people. Reading fiction lets you observe and share a wide variety of experiences. As you read a story, you put yourself in the situation. You feel what the characters feel. You watch how characters work through their problems.

A writer often uses a particular situation to give you his or her observations about life in general. This message about life or human nature that a work of literature presents is called the **theme.** The writer may present more than one theme in a work of fiction. In *Nadia the Willful,* for example, you learned that sometimes you must have the courage to protest a decision or law that you consider harmful. You also learned that talking about someone who has died can keep that person alive in your memory. These two messages or insights about life are themes of the story.

Finding the Theme in Fiction

How do you find themes in literature? Sometimes the writer states a theme directly. More often, you must infer a theme the writer is presenting. To do this, ask yourself, "What did I learn from this story?" Look for the ideas that tie together the characters, setting, and plot. Figure out what lessons the characters learn about themselves and about life. Decide what message the writer is trying to get across. When you put the writer's message in your own words, you are stating the theme.

Part 1

Understanding Mood in Fiction

As you read fiction, you may ask yourself, "How does this story make me feel?" The feeling that the writer creates for the reader is called the **mood.** A work of fiction might give you a feeling such as fear, sadness, excitement, joy, pity, or anger. The mood can help you become aware of the theme of the story.

To create the mood the writer uses precise vocabulary and sensory images. The writer also uses elements such as setting and dialogue. In *Sweetwater,* Laurence Yep creates a mood of mystery and a feeling of being in another world when he describes the setting of Sheol as full of houses that "looked like ancient monsters surfacing. Their great stone faces were covered with delicate beards of green seaweed or soft mustachios of barnacles."

Some works of fiction, such as "Dragon, Dragon," are written solely to entertain and do not present serious themes. The comic mood of such a work is a clue that the writer is not presenting a serious message.

Reading for Theme and Mood

The characters you will meet in this section learn about life from their experiences. As you read each selection, figure out what the main character wants and what obstacles he or she must overcome to get it. Decide what lessons the character learns in the process. Be aware of the mood the writer is creating. See how the mood supports the theme. Learn about life along with the characters.

Comprehension Skills

Evaluating Literature

You read literature for the sheer fun of it. Part of the enjoyment comes from the thinking you do after you finish reading. Sometimes you decide that a work of literature pleases you so much that you want to read it again. At other times you are disappointed.

To grow as a reader, you need to grow as a thinker. You need to develop the skill of **evaluating,** or making judgments, about what you read. When you evaluate, you judge how well the writing measures up to your expectations or standards. What you expect depends on your experiences both from living and from reading. You examine the details and elements of a work. You compare them with your own experiences and with other works you have read. Then you judge how well these details and elements work together as a whole. Finally, you make specific statements that summarize your opinions.

Understanding the Author's Purpose

Authors write for four main reasons: to entertain, to inform, to express opinions, and to persuade. To evaluate a work of literature, first determine the author's purpose. Later you can decide how well the writing achieves that purpose.

Examining Elements in Literature

The next step in evaluating a work is to examine and judge its parts. In fiction and drama, you can examine character, setting, plot, and theme. A useful strategy is to form questions by which you judge the elements. Ask yourself questions such as, "How realistic are the characters? Would real people act and speak that way? Are the details of the setting accurate? How believable is the plot?"

Use questions to examine the elements of poetry and nonfiction as well. Ask, for example, "Do the images or comparisons in the poem make sense? How well is sound used in the poem? How does the poet use form and mood?" For nonfiction, ask yourself, "Is the organization clear and logical? Are there enough facts? How much of the work is opinion and how much is fact?"

Evaluating a Whole Work

To evaluate a whole piece of literature, you need to decide how well the elements work together to achieve the author's purpose. In a story, for example, decide if the characters fit the setting. In a poem, decide if the sounds and images work together to give the theme. In a nonfiction article, think about whether enough facts are given to support the main idea.

When you state your evaluation, make specific statements that can be supported by facts. For example, you might say, "*Nadia the Willful* is very realistic because the characters and the plot are believable. Many people face the death of a loved one and react the way Nadia or her father did. The author achieves the purpose of entertaining while teaching an important lesson about death." These specific evaluation statements can all be supported by facts.

Exercise: Making Evaluations

Use the method above to evaluate any selection in Unit 3.

$\mathcal{V}$ocabulary Skills

Denotations and Connotations

You have learned several strategies for unlocking the meanings of words. You have practiced examining word parts, using context clues, and looking up words in the dictionary. The final step in unlocking word meanings is to understand both the right meaning and the entire meaning that the writer intended a word to have in a particular context. To do this, you must figure out both the denotation and the connotation of the word.

Choosing the Correct Denotation

The dictionary definitions of a word are its **denotations.** A word can have several definitions. As you read, you must rely on the context to help you choose the correct denotation. Suppose you read about a pioneer who cured a ham. You know that *cure* means "to heal," but that meaning makes no sense in the story. You check the dictionary and find out that *cure* can also mean "to preserve meat by salting or smoking." Now the story makes sense.

Some words have dozens of denotations. The subject of the writing can provide an important clue to the correct definition. For example, the word *stage* appearing in an article on rockets has a different meaning than it has in a western novel. Some dictionaries also label meanings of words that apply to specialized fields such as astronomy or sports. Special meanings for the word *interference,* for example, are labeled *Sports, Physics,* and *Radio & TV.*

Understanding Connotations

Words can mean more than the dictionary tells you. Some words bring to mind ideas and feelings that add meaning to their denotations. These added ideas and feelings are called **connotations.** Connotations come to be associated with words through common use over a period of time.

Writers carefully choose words because of these extra layers of meaning. For instance, a writer may say, "John *confessed* his part in the trick" instead of, "John *explained* his part in the trick." The word *confessed* adds a connotation of guilt to the sentence.

A word can have a positive or a negative connotation. That is, it can add a good or a bad feeling to the sentence. A word can also be neutral, adding no feeling. For instance, a writer may choose to describe a character as slender or skinny. The word *slender* carries a positive feeling, while *skinny* carries a negative feeling.

When you read literature, you need to notice the shades of meaning that words carry. Connotations can help you understand the mood of a story, a character's personality, or a writer's attitude.

Exercise: Identifying Denotations and Connotations

A. Find the denotation of the word *shock* that fits the context of this sentence from Jean Kerr's "Dogs That Have Known Me."

> It is a bit of a <u>shock</u> when you bring home a small ball of fluff in a shoebox, and three weeks later it's as long as the sofa.

B. Decide if the connotation of each underlined word is positive or negative.

> Mary <u>snatched</u> the apple from her little sister's hand. She bit into the <u>juicy</u> fruit and grinned.

When did you help another person or an animal in need? Notice how Caddie responds when she is needed.

A Rare Provider

CAROL RYRIE BRINK

 It was early in the winter of 1863 that Alex McCormick got as far as Dunnville in western Wisconsin with his flock of about a thousand sheep. He had intended going farther west to the open grazing land; but the roads of that time were poor, and suddenly winter had overtaken him before he reached his goal. Snow had fallen in the morning, and now, as evening drew near, a low shaft of sunlight broke through the clouds and made broad golden bands across the snow. Where the shadows fell, the snow looked as blue and tranquil as a summer lake; but it was very cold.

Caddie Woodlawn and her younger brother, Warren, were perched on the rail fence in front of their father's farm, watching the sunset over the new snow while they waited for supper. Tom, who was two years older than Caddie, stood beside them with his elbows on the top rail, and beside him sat Nero, their dog.

"Red sky at night,
Sailor's delight,"

Tom said, wagging his head like a weather prophet.

"Yah," said Warren, "fair, but a lot colder tonight. I'd hate to have to spend the night out on the road."

"Listen!" said Caddie, holding up a finger. "There's a funny noise off over the hill. Do you hear something?"

"It sounds like bells," said Warren. "We didn't miss any of the cows tonight, did we?"

"No," said Tom. "Our bells don't sound like that. Besides, Nero wouldn't let a cow of ours get lost—even if *we* did."

Nero usually wagged his tail appreciatively when his name was mentioned, but now his ears were cocked forward as if he, too, were listening to something far away.

"It's sheep!" said Caddie after a moment's pause. "Listen! They're all saying 'Baa—baa—baa!' If it isn't sheep, I'll eat my best hat."

"The one with the feather?" asked Warren incredulously.

"It *must* be sheep!" said Tom.

Pouring down the road like a slow gray flood came the thousand sheep of Alex McCormick. A couple of shaggy Scotch sheep dogs ran about them, barking and keeping them on the road. They were a sorry-looking lot, tired and thin and crying from the long days of walking, and their master, who rode behind on a lame horse, was not much better. He was a tall Scotsman, his lean face browned like an Indian's and in startling contrast to his faded blond hair and beard. His eyes were as blue as the shadows on the snow, and they burned strangely in the dark hollows of his hungry-looking face.

"Will ye tell your Daddy I'd like to speak wi' him?" he called as he came abreast of the three children.

Tom dashed away, with a whoop, for Father, and soon the whole Woodlawn household had turned out to witness the curious sight of nearly a thousand weary sheep milling about in

The Sun Had Closed the Winter's Day, 1904, JOSEPH FARQUARSON. Manchester City Art Galleries, England.

the open space before the farm. They had cows and horses and oxen, but none of the pioneer farmers in the valley had yet brought in sheep.

Caddie and Warren stood upon the top rail, balancing themselves precariously and trying to count the sheep. Nero circled about, uncertain whether or not to be friendly with the strange dogs and deeply suspicious of the plaintive bleatings and baaings of the sheep.

Suddenly Caddie hopped off the fence in the midst of the sheep.

"Look, mister! There's something wrong with this one."

One of the ewes had dropped down in her tracks and looked as if she might be dying. But Mr. McCormick and Father were deep in conversation and paid no attention to her.

"Here, Caddie! Tom! Warren!" called Father. "We've got to help Mr. McCormick find shelter for his sheep tonight. Run to the neighbors and ask them if they can spare some barn or pasture room and come and help us."

The three children started off across the fields in different directions. As she raced across the light snow toward the Silbernagle farm, Caddie saw tracks ahead of her and, topping the first rise, she saw her little sister Hetty already on her way to tell Lida Silbernagle. Hetty's bonnet and her red knitted mittens flew behind her by their strings, for Hetty never bothered with her bonnet or mittens when there was news to be spread. So Caddie veered north toward the Bunns'.

In a pioneer community everyone must work together for the common good and, although Alex McCormick was a stranger to them all, the men from the neighboring farms had soon gathered to help him save his weary sheep from the cold. With a great deal of shouting, barking, and bleating the flock was divided into small sections and driven off to different farms, where the sheep could shelter under haystacks or sheds through the cold night.

When the last sheep were being driven off, Caddie remembered the sick ewe and ran to see what had become of her. She still lay where she had fallen, her eyes half closed with weariness, her breath coming so feebly that it seemed as if she scarcely lived at all.

"Oh, look, Mr. McCormick!" called Caddie. "You ought to tend to this one or she'll be a goner."

"Hoots!" said the Scotsman. "I've no time to waste on a dead one with hundreds of live ones still on their legs and like to freeze to death the night."

"I've got lots of time, if you haven't, Mr. McCormick," volunteered Caddie.

"Verra good," said the Scotsman. "I'll give her to ye, lassie, if ye can save her life."

"Really?" cried Caddie, and then, "It's a bargain!"

In a moment she had enlisted the services of Tom and Warren, and they were staggering along under the dead weight of the helpless sheep. Their father watched them with a twinkle of amusement in his eye.

"And what are you going to do with that?" he asked.

"It's nothing but a sick sheep," said Tom, "but Caddie thinks she can save it."

"Oh, Father," cried Caddie, "may I put her in the box stall and give her something to eat? She's just worn out and starved—that's all."

Father nodded and smiled.

"I'll look around at her later," he said.

But when Father had time later to visit the box stall, he found Caddie sitting with a lantern beside her ewe and looking very disconsolate.

"Father, I know she's hungry; but I can't make her eat. I don't know what to do."

Mr. Woodlawn knelt beside the animal and felt her all over for possible injuries. Then he opened her mouth and ran his finger gently over her gums.

"Well, Caddie," he said, "I guess you'll have to make her a set of false teeth."

"False teeth!" echoed Caddie. Then she stuck her own

fingers in the ewe's mouth. "She hasn't any teeth!" she cried. "No wonder she couldn't chew hay! Whatever shall we do?"

Mr. Woodlawn looked thoughtfully into his small daughter's worried face.

"Well," he said, "it would be quite a task, and I don't know whether you want to undertake it."

"Yes, I do," said Caddie. "Tell me what."

"Mother has more of those small potatoes than she can use this winter. Get her to cook some of them for you until they are quite soft, and mix them with bran and milk into a mash. I think you can pull your old sheep through on that. But it will be an everyday job, like taking care of a baby. You'll find it pretty tiresome."

"Oh! But, Father, it's better than having her die!"

That evening Mr. McCormick stayed for supper with them. It was not often that they had a stranger from outside as their guest, and their eager faces turned toward him around the lamplit table. Father and Mother at each end of the table, with the six children ranged around; and Robert Ireton, the hired man, and Katie Conroy, the hired girl, there, too—they made an appreciative audience. Mr. McCormick's tongue, with its rich Scotch burr, was loosened to relate for them the story of his long journey from the East with his sheep. He told how Indians had stolen some and wolves others; how the herdsman he had brought with him had caught a fever and died on the way, and was buried at the edge of an Indian village; how they had forded streams and weathered a tornado.

While the dishes were being cleared away, the Scotsman took Hetty and little Minnie on his knees and told them about the little thatched home in Scotland where he had been born. Then he opened a wallet, which he had inside his buckskin shirt, to show them some treasure which he kept there. They all crowded around to see, and it was only a bit of dried heather which had come from Scotland.

As the stranger talked, Caddie's mind kept going to the box stall in the barn; and something warm and pleasant sang inside her.

"She ate the potato mash," she thought. "If I take good care of her she'll live, and it will be all because of me! I love her more than any pet I've got—except, of course, Nero."

The next day the muddy, trampled place where the sheep had been was white with fresh snow, and Mr. McCormick set out for Dunnville to try to sell as many of his sheep as he could. Winter had overtaken him too soon, and after all his long journey he found himself still far from open grazing land and without sheds or shelter to keep the sheep over the winter. But Dunnville was a small place, and he could sell only a very small part of his huge flock. When he had disposed of all he could, he made an agreement with Mr. Woodlawn and the other farmers that they might keep as many of his sheep as they could feed and shelter over the winter, if they would give him half of the wool and half of the lambs in the spring.

"How about mine?" asked Caddie.

Mr. McCormick laughed.

"Nay, lassie," he said. "You've earned the old ewe fair an' square, and everything that belongs to her."

The old ewe was on her feet now, and baaing and nuzzling Caddie's hand whenever Caddie came near her. That was a busy winter for Caddie. Before school in the morning and after school in the evening, there were always mashes of vegetables and bran to be cooked up for Nanny.

"You'll get tired doing that," said Tom.

"Nanny!" scoffed Warren. "That's a name for a goat."

"No," said Caddie firmly. "That's a name for Caddie Woodlawn's sheep, and you see if I get tired of feeding her!"

When the days began to lengthen and grow warmer toward the end of February, Caddie turned Nanny out during the day with the other sheep. At first she tied a red woolen string about Nanny's neck; for, even if one loves them, sheep are very much alike, and Caddie did not want to lose her own. But really that was quite unnecessary, for as soon as Nanny saw her coming with a pan of mash and an iron spoon she broke away from the others and made a beeline for Caddie. At night she came to the barn and waited for Caddie to let her in.

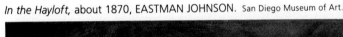

In the Hayloft, about 1870, EASTMAN JOHNSON. San Diego Museum of Art.

One morning in March, when Caddie had risen early to serve Nanny's breakfast before she went to school, Robert came out of the barn to meet her. She had flung Mother's shawl on over her pinafore, and the pan of warm mash which she carried steamed cozily in the chill spring air.

For once Robert was neither singing nor whistling at his work, and he looked at Caddie with such a mixture of sorrow and glad tidings on his honest Irish face that Caddie stopped short.

"Something's happened!" she cried.

"Aye. Faith, an' you may well say so, Miss Caddie," said Robert seriously.

Caddie's heart almost stopped beating for a moment. Something had happened to Nanny! In a daze of apprehension she ran into the barn.

"You're not to feel too grieved now, mavourneen,"[1] said Robert, coming after her. "You did more for the poor beast than any other body would have done."

But words meant nothing to Caddie now, for in solemn truth the thin thread of life which she had coaxed along in the sick sheep all winter had finally ebbed away and Nanny was dead. Caddie flung away the pan of mash and knelt down beside the old sheep. She could not speak or make a sound, but the hot tears ran down her cheeks and tasted salty on her lips. Her heart felt ready to burst with sorrow.

"Wurra! Wurra! Wurra!" said Robert sympathetically, leaning over the side of the stall and looking down on them. "But 'tis an ill wind blows nobody good. Why don't ye look around an' see the good the ill wind has been a-blowing of you?"

---

1. **mavourneen** (mə voor′ nēn): from the Irish word *momuirnin,* meaning "my darling."

Young Shepherdess,
about 1870, JEAN
FRANÇOIS MILLET.
Museum of Fine Arts, Boston,
Gift of Samuel Dennis
Warren.

Caddie shook her head, squeezing her eyes tight shut to keep the tears from flowing so fast.

"Look!" he urged again.

Robert had come into the stall and thrust something soft and warm under her hand. The something soft and warm stirred, and a faint small voice said, *"Ma-a-a-a!"*

"Look!" said Robert. "Its Ma is dead and, faith, if 'tis not a-callin' *you* Ma! It knows which side its bread is buttered on."

Caddie opened her eyes in astonishment. Her tears had suddenly ceased to flow, for Robert had put into her arms something so young and helpless and so lovable that half of her sorrow was already swept away.

"It's a lamb!" said Caddie, half to herself, and then to Robert, "Is it—Nanny's?"

"Aye," said Robert, "it is that. But Nanny was too tired to mother it. 'Sure an' 'tis all right for me to go to sleep an' leave it,' says Nanny to herself, 'for Caddie Woodlawn is a rare provider.'"

Caddie wrapped the shawl around her baby and cradled the small shivering creature in her arms.

"Potato mash won't do," she was saying to herself. "Warm milk is what it needs, and maybe Mother will give me one of Baby Joe's bottles to make the feeding easier."

The lamb cuddled warmly and closely against her. "Ma-a-a-a-a!" it said.

"Oh, yes, I will be!" Caddie whispered back.

Carol Ryrie Brink (1895–1981) grew up in Idaho listening to her grandmother's recollections of life on the Wisconsin frontier. Brink later recorded these memories in the novel *Caddie Woodlawn,* which won a Newbery Medal, and its sequel *Magical Melons.* Throughout her life, Brink continued to use her own experiences as ideas for her books.

Other books: *Andy Buckram's Tin Men*
Louly

Developing Comprehension Skills

1. What problem does Alex McCormick face when he gets to Dunnville?

2. Why does Alex give Caddie the ewe? How does Caddie save the ewe?

3. What clues in Robert's behavior help you predict that something has happened to Nanny?

4. For what reasons does Robert call Caddie a "rare provider"?

5. **Focus on Thinking: Contrasting.** To contrast, look for differences between people, things, or ideas. Explain and contrast the two strong feelings that Caddie has at the end of the story.

Reading Fiction

1. **Understanding Theme.** Often you must infer the **theme,** or author's message about life, in a story. The theme can be in the form of a lesson. What lesson does Caddie learn about life and death?

2. **Identifying Climax.** You remember that the **climax** is the turning point of a story, or the point at which the conflict is resolved. What do you think is the climax of this story?

Critical Thinking

Evaluating a Solution. To evaluate a solution, you must first understand the problem. Then think of possible solutions to the problem. Consider the results each solution might lead to. Finally, judge the chosen solution by comparing its results to the possible results of other solutions.

Alex has to decide what to do with his herd of sheep for the winter. Explain the problem he faces. In a column, list possible solutions to his problem. Next to each solution, list the good and bad results of that solution. Finally, decide if his solution was the wisest one.

Writing in Response to Literature

Pretend that you are Caddie or one of her brothers. Write a diary entry for one of the days described in this story.

What is the best present you ever gave someone? Discover how Aaron learns the true value of a gift.

Aaron's Gift

MYRON LEVOY

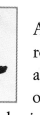

Aaron Kandel had come to Tompkins Square Park to roller-skate, for the streets near Second Avenue were always too crowded with children and peddlers and old ladies and baby buggies. Though few children had bicycles in those days, almost every child owned a pair of roller skates. And Aaron was, it must be said, a Class A, triple-fantastic roller skater.

Aaron skated back and forth on the wide walkway of the park, pretending he was an aviator in an air race zooming around pylons, which were actually two lampposts. During his third lap around the racecourse, he noticed a pigeon on the grass, behaving very strangely. Aaron skated to the line of benches, then climbed over onto the lawn.

The pigeon was trying to fly, but all it could manage was to flutter and turn round and round in a large circle, as if it were performing a frenzied dance. The left wing was only half open and was beating in a clumsy, jerking fashion; it was clearly broken.

Luckily, Aaron hadn't eaten the cookies he'd stuffed into

his pocket before he'd gone clacking down the three flights of stairs from his apartment, his skates already on. He broke a cookie into small crumbs and tossed some toward the pigeon. "Here pidge, here pidge," he called. The pigeon spotted the cookie crumbs and, after a moment, stopped thrashing about. It folded its wings as best it could, but the broken wing still stuck half out. Then it strutted over to the crumbs, its head bobbing forth-back, forth-back, as if it were marching a little in front of the rest of the body—perfectly normal, except for that half-open wing which seemed to make the bird stagger sideways every so often.

The pigeon began eating the crumbs as Aaron quickly unbuttoned his shirt and pulled it off. Very slowly, he edged toward the bird, making little kissing sounds like the ones he heard his grandmother make when she fed the sparrows on the back fire escape.

Then suddenly Aaron plunged. The shirt, in both hands, came down like a torn parachute. The pigeon beat its wings, but Aaron held the shirt to the ground, and the bird couldn't escape. Aaron felt under the shirt, gently, and gently took hold of the wounded pigeon.

"Yes, yes, pidge," he said, very softly. "There's a good boy. Good pigeon, good."

The pigeon struggled in his hands, but little by little Aaron managed to soothe it. "Good boy, pidge. That's your new name. Pidge. I'm gonna take you home, Pidge. Yes, yes, ssh. Good boy. I'm gonna fix you up. Easy, Pidge, easy does it. Easy, boy."

Aaron squeezed through an opening between the row of benches and skated slowly out of the park, while holding the pigeon carefully with both hands as if it were one of his

mother's rare, precious cups from the old country. How fast the pigeon's heart was beating! Was he afraid? Or did all pigeons' hearts beat fast?

It was fortunate that Aaron was an excellent skater, for he had to skate six blocks to his apartment, over broken pavement and sudden gratings and curbs and cobblestones. But when he reached home, he asked Noreen Callahan, who was playing on the stoop, to take off his skates for him. He would not chance going up three flights on roller skates this time.

"Is he sick?" asked Noreen.

"Broken wing," said Aaron. "I'm gonna fix him up and make him into a carrier pigeon or something."

"Can I watch?" asked Noreen.

"Watch what?"

"The operation. I'm gonna be a nurse when I grow up."

"OK," said Aaron. "You can even help. You can help hold him while I fix him up."

Aaron wasn't quite certain what his mother would say about his new-found pet, but he was pretty sure he knew what his grandmother would think. His grandmother had lived with them ever since his grandfather had died three years ago. And she fed the sparrows and jays and crows and robins on the back fire escape with every spare crumb she could find. In fact, Aaron noticed that she sometimes created crumbs where they didn't exist, by squeezing and tearing pieces of her breakfast roll when his mother wasn't looking.

Aaron didn't really understand his grandmother, for he often saw her by the window having long conversations with the birds, telling them about her days as a little girl in the Ukraine. And once he saw her take her mirror from her handbag and hold it out toward the birds. She told Aaron that she wanted them to see how beautiful they were. Very strange. But Aaron did know that she would love Pidge, because she loved everything.

To his surprise, his mother said he could keep the pigeon, temporarily, because it was sick, and we were all strangers in the land of Egypt, and it might not be bad for Aaron to have a pet. Temporarily.

The wing was surprisingly easy to fix, for the break showed clearly and Pidge was remarkably patient and still, as if he knew he was being helped. Or perhaps he was just exhausted from all the thrashing about he had done. Two Popsicle sticks served as splints, and strips from an old undershirt were used to tie them in place. Another strip held the wing to the bird's body.

Aaron's father arrived home and stared at the pigeon. Aaron waited for the expected storm. But instead, Mr. Kandel asked, "Who did this?"

"Me," said Aaron. "And Noreen Callahan."

"Sophie!" he called to his wife. "Did you see this! Ten years old and it's better than Dr. Belasco could do. He's a genius!"

As the days passed, Aaron began training Pidge to be a carrier pigeon. He tied a little cardboard tube to Pidge's left leg and stuck tiny rolled-up sheets of paper with secret messages into it: THE ENEMY IS ATTACKING AT DAWN. Or: THE GUNS ARE HIDDEN IN THE TRUNK OF THE CAR. Or: VINCENT DEMARCO IS A BRITISH SPY. Then Aaron would set Pidge down at one end of the living room and put some popcorn at the other end. And Pidge would waddle slowly across the room, cooing softly, while the ends of his bandages trailed along the floor.

At the other end of the room, one of Aaron's friends would take out the message, stick a new one in, turn Pidge around, and aim him at the popcorn that Aaron put down on his side of the room.

And Pidge grew fat and contented on all the popcorn and crumbs and corn and crackers and Aaron's grandmother's breakfast rolls.

Aaron had told all the children about Pidge, but he only let his very best friends come up and play carrier-pigeon with him. But telling everyone had been a mistake. A group of older boys from down the block had a club—Aaron's mother called it a gang—and Aaron had longed to join as he had never longed for anything else. To be with them and share their secrets, the secrets of older boys. To be able to enter their clubhouse shack on the empty lot on the next street. To know the password and swear the secret oath. To belong.

About a month after Aaron had brought the pigeon home, Carl, the gang leader, walked over to Aaron in the street and told him he could be a member if he'd bring the pigeon down to be the club mascot. Aaron couldn't believe it; he immediately raced home to get Pidge. But his mother told Aaron to stay away from those boys, or else. And Aaron, miserable, argued with his mother and pleaded and cried and coaxed. It was no use. Not with those boys. No.

Aaron's mother tried to change the subject. She told him that it would soon be his grandmother's sixtieth birthday, a very special birthday indeed, and all the family from Brooklyn and the East Side would be coming to their apartment for a dinner and celebration. Would Aaron try to build something or make something for Grandma? A present made with his own hands would be nice. A decorated box for her hairpins or a crayon picture for her room or anything he liked.

In a flash Aaron knew what to give her: Pidge! Pidge

On the Arrowback, 1975, KEN DANBY. Private Collection. Photograph: Gallery Moos, Toronto.

would be her present! Pidge with his wing healed, who might be able to carry messages for her to the doctor or his Aunt Rachel or other people his grandmother seemed to go to a lot. It would be a surprise for everyone. And Pidge would make up for what had happened to Grandma when she'd been a little girl in the Ukraine, wherever that was.

Often, in the evening, Aaron's grandmother would talk about the old days long ago in the Ukraine, in the same way that she talked to the birds on the back fire escape. She had lived in a village near a place called Kishinev with hundreds of other poor peasant families like her own. Things hadn't been too bad under someone called Czar Alexander the Second, whom Aaron always pictured as a tall handsome man in a gold uniform. But Alexander the Second was assassinated, and Alexander the Third, whom Aaron pictured as an ugly man in a black cape, became the Czar. And the Jewish people of the Ukraine had no peace anymore.

One day, a thundering of horses was heard coming toward the village from the direction of Kishinev. "The Cossacks! The Cossacks!" someone had shouted. The Czar's horsemen! Quickly, quickly, everyone in Aaron's grandmother's family had climbed down to the cellar through a little trapdoor hidden under a mat in the big central room of their shack. But his grandmother's pet goat, whom she'd loved as much as Aaron loved Pidge and more, had to be left above, because if it had made a sound in the cellar, they would never have lived to see the next morning. They all hid under the wood in the woodbin and waited, hardly breathing.

Suddenly, from above, they heard shouts and calls and screams at a distance. And then the noise was in their house. Boots pounding on the floor, and everything breaking and crashing overhead. The smell of smoke and the shouts of a dozen men.

The terror went on for an hour and then the sound of horses' hooves faded into the distance. They waited another hour to make sure, and then the father went up out of the cellar and the rest of the family followed. The door to the house had been torn from its hinges and every piece of furniture was broken. Every window, every dish, every stitch of clothing was totally destroyed, and one wall had been completely bashed in. And on the floor was the goat, lying quietly. Aaron's grandmother, who was just a little girl of eight at the time, had wept over the goat all day and all night and could not be consoled.

But they had been lucky. For other houses had been burned to the ground. And everywhere, not goats alone, nor sheep, but men and women and children lay quietly on the ground. The word for this sort of massacre, Aaron had learned, was *pogrom*. It had been a pogrom. And the men on the horses were Cossacks. Hated word. Cossacks.

And so Pidge would replace that goat of long ago. A pigeon on Second Avenue where no one needed trapdoors or secret escape passages or woodpiles to hide under. A pigeon for his grandmother's sixtieth birthday. *Oh wing, heal quickly so my grandmother can send you flying to everywhere she wants!*

But a few days later, Aaron met Carl in the street again. And Carl told Aaron that there was going to be a meeting that afternoon in which a map was going to be drawn up to show where a secret treasure lay buried on the empty lot. "Bring the pigeon and you can come into the shack. We got a badge for you. A new kinda membership badge with a secret code on the back."

Aaron ran home, his heart pounding almost as fast as the pigeon's. He took Pidge in his hands and carried him out the door while his mother was busy in the kitchen making stuffed cabbage, his father's favorite dish. And by the time he reached the street, Aaron had decided to take the bandages off. Pidge would look like a real pigeon again, and none of the older boys would laugh or call him a bundle of rags.

Gently, gently he removed the bandages and the splints

and put them in his pocket in case he should need them again. But Pidge seemed to hold his wing properly in place.

When he reached the empty lot, Aaron walked up to the shack, then hesitated. Four bigger boys were there. After a moment, Carl came out and commanded Aaron to hand Pidge over.

"Be careful," said Aaron. "I just took the bandages off."

"Oh sure, don't worry," said Carl. By now Pidge was used to people holding him, and he remained calm in Carl's hands.

"OK," said Carl. "Give him the badge." And one of the older boys handed Aaron his badge with the code on the back. "Now light the fire," said Carl.

"What . . . what fire?" asked Aaron.

"The fire. You'll see," Carl answered.

"You didn't say nothing about a fire," said Aaron. "You didn't say nothing to—"

"Hey!" said Carl. "I'm the leader here. And you don't talk unless I tell you that you have p'mission. Light the fire, Al."

The boy named Al went out to the side of the shack, where some wood and cardboard and old newspapers had been piled into a huge mound. He struck a match and held it to the newspapers.

"OK," said Carl. "Let's get 'er good and hot. Blow on it. Everybody blow."

Aaron's eyes stung from the smoke, but he blew alongside the others, going from side to side as the smoke shifted toward them and away.

"Let's fan it," said Al.

In a few minutes, the fire was crackling and glowing with a bright yellow-orange flame.

"Get me the rope," said Carl.

One of the boys brought Carl some cord and Carl, without a word, wound it twice around the pigeon, so that its wings were tight against its body.

"What . . . what are you doing!" shouted Aaron. "You're hurting his wing!"

"Don't worry about his wing," said Carl. "We're gonna throw him into the fire. And when we do, we're gonna swear an oath of loyalty to—"

"No! No!" shouted Aaron, moving toward Carl.

"Grab him!" called Carl. "Don't let him get the pigeon!"

But Aaron had leaped right across the fire at Carl, taking him completely by surprise. He threw Carl back against the shack and hit out at his face with both fists. Carl slid down to the ground and the pigeon rolled out of his hands. Aaron scooped up the pigeon and ran, pretending he was on roller skates so that he would go faster and faster. And as he ran across the lot he pulled the cord off Pidge and tried to find a place, any place, to hide him. But the boys were on top of him, and the pigeon slipped from Aaron's hands.

"Get him!" shouted Carl.

Aaron thought of the worst, the most horrible thing he could shout at the boys. "Cossacks!" he screamed. "You're all Cossacks!"

Two boys held Aaron back while the others tried to catch the pigeon. Pidge fluttered along the ground just out of reach, skittering one way and then the other. Then the boys came at him from two directions. But suddenly Pidge beat his wings in rhythm, and rose up, up, over the roof of the nearest tenement, up over Second Avenue toward the park.

With the pigeon gone, the boys turned toward Aaron and tackled him to the ground and punched him and tore his clothes and punched him some more. Aaron twisted and turned and kicked and punched back, shouting "Cossacks! Cossacks!" And somehow the word gave him the strength to tear away from them.

When Aaron reached home, he tried to go past the kitchen quickly so his mother wouldn't see his bloody face and torn clothing. But it was no use; his father was home from work early that night and was seated in the living room. In a moment Aaron was surrounded by his mother, father, and grandmother, and in another moment he had told them everything that had happened, the words tumbling out between his broken sobs. Told them of the present he had planned, of the pigeon for a goat, of the gang, of the badge with the secret code on the back, of the shack, and the fire, and the pigeon's flight over the tenement roof.

And Aaron's grandmother kissed him and thanked him for his present which was even better than the pigeon.

"What present?" asked Aaron, trying to stop the series of sobs.

And his grandmother opened her pocketbook and handed Aaron her mirror and asked him to look. But all Aaron saw was his dirty, bruised face and his torn shirt.

Aaron thought he understood and then, again, he thought he didn't. How could she be so happy when there really was no present? And why pretend that there was?

Moon Bird, 1979, MORRIS GRAVES.
Private Collection.

Later that night, just before he fell asleep, Aaron tried to imagine what his grandmother might have done with the pigeon. She would have fed it, and she certainly would have talked to it, as she did to all the birds, and . . . and then she would have let it go free. Yes, of course. Pidge's flight to freedom must have been the gift that had made his grandmother so happy. Her goat has escaped from the Cossacks at last, Aaron thought, half dreaming. And he fell asleep with a smile.

Myron Levoy was born in New York City and worked as a chemical engineer before becoming a professional writer. Levoy writes compassionately about people who have difficulty finding their place in society. Many of his stories are about immigrants who are trying to adjust to a new life in the United States.

Another book: *The Witch of Fourth Street and Other Stories*

Developing Comprehension Skills

1. For what purpose does Aaron take the pigeon home?

2. Why does Aaron want to join the club? Why does his mother refuse to let him?

3. Why does Aaron think Pidge would be a good present for Grandma?

4. Beginning with Aaron's arrival at the shack, summarize the events that lead to Pidge's freedom.

5. What is Aaron's gift? Why does it mean so much to Grandma?

6. **Focus on Thinking: Evaluating.** One way to evaluate a character is to decide how real the character is. A realistic character has strengths and weaknesses. How realistic is Aaron?

Reading Fiction

1. **Identifying Theme.** The theme of a story is often the lesson a character learns. What lesson does Aaron learn in this story?

2. **Understanding Setting.** Within a story, there may be another story with a different setting. What is the main setting of "Aaron's Gift"? What is the setting of Grandma's childhood?

3. **Identifying Mood.** The feeling the author conveys in a story is called the **mood.** What is the mood of the scene between Aaron and the boys in the club? What words and phrases create this mood?

Speaking and Listening

Listening to Learn. You can learn history from listening to older people talk about their past. Their stories can entertain and even amaze you.

Ask an older person to talk about important moments in his or her life. Try to connect the history you have read with what you hear.

Writing in Response to Literature

Have you ever felt the way Aaron felt about joining a group? Describe the group and write your feelings about joining.

How do you act when you know you have done something wrong? Observe how a guilty conscience makes Ellen act.

From

The Lilith Summer

HADLEY IRWIN

To earn money for a ten-speed bicycle, Ellen agrees to "lady-sit" for seventy-seven-year-old Lilith Adams for the summer. At the same time, Lilith agrees to "baby-sit" for Ellen. At first, neither Ellen nor Lilith is aware of the other's job, but the arrangement is unintentionally revealed. Now both Ellen and Lilith are trying to adjust to a long summer of each other's companionship.

The floor tile cooled my bare feet as we pushed open the glass doors of Parsons's General Store.

"Where are your shoes?" Lilith frowned down at my feet.

"Forgot them."

"Of course," she sniffed. Lilith could use the same words to mean so many different things. Sometimes her "of course" was a gentle pat. This one was not.

"I don't see what's wrong with bare feet."

"Nasty habit."

I didn't feel like fighting the battle for my liberation. Shopping with Lilith was enough to tackle for one morning. Shopping with Lilith took forever.

"I look before I buy." And Lilith did.

Parsons's Store was dimly lit, dark enough to make mysterious nooks at the far ends of each aisle.

I walked around the counters stacked with cards of shiny buttons and rolls of bright fabrics piled high against the wall. Mrs. Parsons was talking with Lilith, her lips opening and closing, tongue flicking like a frog. The sound of their voices blended with the whirring of the ceiling fan.

I ran my fingers over the things on the next counter: pens, paste, glue, erasers, tablets with an eagle on the cover, stacks of notebook paper sealed under plastic. There was something fascinating and, at the same time, forbidding about the displays. I moved to the back of the store, then turned and began the circuit back toward Lilith. I liked the way the store smelled: a mixture of cleaning compound, mothballs, perfume, powder, and leather. I moved past the lipstick, deodorants, face powder, and lotions shelved behind sliding glass doors and stopped to gaze at the medical supplies.

The medical supplies blended into the jewelry: necklaces of dangling gold pendants, earrings clipped to tiny squares of cardboard piled high in a wicker basket, compacts, souvenir spoons, and rings.

The rings nestled in styrofoam slots, displayed on an octagonal case that revolved when I touched it with my finger. And there, among the fake rubies and too-green emeralds was a pearl ring. It was white as fresh milk, perfect as a tear drop—so simple, so out of place, I felt that I alone had discovered it.

Without thinking, I reached out, slipped the pearl ring from its slot, and jammed it down into the pocket of my shorts. It felt cool in my palm and the pearl itself smooth against my fingertips. I moved quickly away, my hand thrust firmly down into my pocket. The ring slipped on to my finger. It was just the right size.

It was only after I passed the racks of candy bars and chewing gum that I realized what I had done. By then it was too late—too late to put the ring back into the styrofoam slot on the rack.

I skipped up to Lilith, my fingers curled tightly around the band in my pocket, clenching my teeth to hold back the glee I felt inside.

Lilith peered down at me.

"Shall we go now?" Her voice sounded low and intimate.

Spring Afternoon, 1984, ALLAN R. BANKS. Private Collection.

"I don't care." I tried not to appear too eager.

Lilith pushed through the glass door, and I, my pocket full of triumph, followed the broad back out into the hot, dusty street.

"That Mrs. Parsons is a fine woman. Manages that big store all by herself since her husband died. A fine, fine woman."

I felt the pearl ring, suddenly a hot band around my finger. I swallowed with effort, but an ugly taste stuck in my throat. I ran my tongue around the outside of my lips.

"Where are we going now?" I tried to sound enthusiastic.

"I thought we'd go over there on that bench in the square and rest a bit before we start home. Would you like that?"

I could think of nothing I would like less, but I forced my head to nod. I trailed half a step behind Lilith, keeping my right hand in my pocket, just out of Lilith's sight. As Lilith turned to sit down, I managed to slip the ring off.

The streets were empty. I would have welcomed anyone— anyone who might at least bring forth a comment or a story from Lilith to fill the awkward pause.

"Oh, my. It is nice to sit down, isn't it?"

"We could've gone down to Reed's and sat and had a Coke."

"We can do that too . . . after we rest a spell."

I did not feel like resting. I felt like running. I kept seeing the big sign across the street: Parsons's General Store. I could hardly keep my legs still, and I didn't know what to do with my hands. I folded them in my lap, then rubbed my sweaty palms against my bare knees. I twisted as the bench seat burned the back of my legs. I ran my hand through my hair.

Lilith sat beside me and gazed across the street with a faraway look.

"Sure hot, isn't it?"

Lilith nodded.

"We going to sit here very long?"

"Not too long."

I rocked back and forth, my arms clutching my waist.

"Almost the hottest day we've had, I bet."

Lilith did not answer.

I could feel the pearl in my pocket, a soft bump against my leg. I glanced down, carefully, to see if the bump showed, and Lilith chose that very second to turn toward me.

I smiled, but Lilith did not smile back.

What was she waiting for? Surely we had sat long enough to be rested by now. The silences grew longer. They flowed over and around me like the heat from the sidewalk. I tried to think of something to say, but for the first time I was speechless. I couldn't even think of something mean.

Then out of a silence that I was positive was never going to end came Lilith's voice, soft but heavy with a funny sadness.

"You wanted it very much, didn't you?"

I felt my lips tremble and my breath slipped out in two gasps that I couldn't control.

"Wanted? What?" I needed time to think.

"Don't make me say it for you."

I felt the lump in my pocket.

"Maybe," Lilith said, "we should just start at the end instead of at the beginning. Shall we?"

I moved my lips to form words, but no sound came.

"We can walk back across the street and tell Mrs. Parsons."

"We?"

A cool breeze ruffled my hair.

"What . . . what'll we say?" My voice shook.

"We'll say we want to return some merchandise— merchandise we have not paid for."

"Will you say it for us?"

"No. You will say it. It will not be too difficult. It will be hard, but not too difficult. Shall we go now?"

I was not ready to go, but I knew it was the time.

"It will not take long," Lilith assured me.

I couldn't make my feet match Lilith's long strides. I tagged behind, wishing desperately Lilith would walk a little bit slower. The glass door opened before Lilith's determined push. The smell of the store sickened me. Mrs. Parsons loomed behind the cash register, a huge face full of eyes, as Lilith led me by the hand up to the check-out counter.

"You're back, Mrs. Adams?" Mrs. Parsons's voice sounded as if she were anticipating another sale. "Did you forget something?"

"Yes. We forgot something. We forgot something very important."

"Well, then," Mrs. Parsons brightened. "What can I do to help you?"

"Ellen wishes to tell you something."

Ellen did not wish to tell Mrs. Parsons anything, but Lilith squeezed my hand.

I stared at the yardstick, nailed to the edge of the counter, focused my eyes on the number 18 halfway down its length, and drew in a big breath. I could hardly make the words come, and I didn't know what I was going to say until I heard my own voice. "We . . . I mean . . . I . . . took a pearl ring. . . . I want to give it back. I won't do it again."

I should have chosen the words more carefully. They sounded so childish. I was ashamed of the words, ashamed of how they were making me feel, ashamed of the way my knees

Morning Sunshine, 1917, DONNA SCHUSTER. Photograph: The Redfern Gallery, Laguna Beach, California.

were shaking, ashamed of the way my hand trembled as I pulled the ring out of my pocket and placed it on the counter.

I felt Mrs. Parsons's eyes on me. Lilith let go of my hand.

"You may go now, Ellen," Lilith spoke softly and very slowly, "and put it back where you found it."

I picked up the ring from the counter without looking at

Mrs. Parsons, and walked down the long, long aisle to the jewelry counter. I reached out and pushed the pearl ring back into the empty slot.

"Now, Mrs. Parsons," Lilith's voice was familiar again. "I wonder if you would have the time to show us what you have in *rings*. Would you happen to have anything in birthstones?"

"Yes, indeed we do, Mrs. Adams." Mrs. Parsons scurried down the aisle. "We have them for every month of the year. What month did you want?"

"June," Lilith answered.

"June?" Mrs. Parsons turned toward Lilith, puzzled. "That would be. . . ." She consulted a chart. "That's what I thought. Pearl."

I shriveled with shame.

"That is precisely right, Mrs. Parsons."

"Gemini, isn't it?"

"That's right. Gemini," repeated Lilith. "Gemini, the twins. We are Gemini, Ellen and I. Children of June. I suppose you could say we are twins . . . except for a few years."

Mrs. Parsons slipped the same pearl ring from the same styrofoam slot in the octagonal display and held it out for Lilith to examine.

I could not watch. I looked at the floor and hastily counted the red spots in the blocks of linoleum. There were twenty-three red spots in every green tile.

"We'll take it," Lilith said.

Mrs. Parsons hurried up the aisle. Lilith unsnapped her purse, took out her billfold, and pulled out two crisp one-dollar bills.

"Ellen, you pay Mrs. Parsons for the ring. It costs one dollar and seventy-nine cents plus tax."

Outside on the street, as I carried the pearl ring in its

dainty white box, Lilith announced, "The ring is yours, Ellen. It is your birthstone."

I stifled an urge to encircle Lilith's waist and bury my head in the soft folds of her dress.

Instead I carefully stepped over every crack in the sidewalk and sang frantically to myself:

Step on a crack
Break your mother's back
Step on a crack
Break your mother's back
Step on a crack
Break Lilith's back

And I didn't step on a single crack.

Lilith never mentioned the pearl ring again. Nor did she ever ask why.

Hadley Irwin is the pen name for the writing team of Lee Hadley (born 1934) and Annabelle Irwin (born 1915). These women first began working together as teachers at Iowa State University. Since then, they have continued to share their experiences and ideas as the coauthors of many books for and about young people.

Other books: *I Be Somebody*
We Are Mesquakie,
We Are One

Developing Comprehension Skills

1. What does Ellen do in the store?

2. How does Ellen feel after she and Lilith leave the store the first time? How do you know?

3. What clues suggest that Lilith knows that Ellen took the ring?

4. Evaluate how realistic Ellen's punishment is. Do you think the average teenager would be treated the same way?

5. **Focus on Thinking: Inferring Motive.** You sometimes have to infer the motive, or reason, for a character's action. Why do you think Ellen takes the ring? Why does Lilith buy the ring for her?

Reading Fiction

1. **Examining Relationships.** Like real people, characters often have mixed feelings toward one another. What different feelings does Ellen have toward Lilith? How do you know?

2. **Examining Point of View.** The narrator of a story can help set the mood. Who narrates this story? How do the narrator's feelings affect the mood of the story?

3. **Appreciating Sensory Details.** An author can show contrasts through sensory details. What is different about the smell of the store each time Ellen enters it? Why? How does the ring feel to Ellen after Lilith talks about Mrs. Parsons?

Speaking and Listening

Exchanging Opinions. Before you express an opinion, think about the reasons you think the way you do. Then think about other possible opinions and the reasons supporting them. Change your opinion or arguments if necessary.

Ellen is guilty of shoplifting. In your opinion, how should shoplifters be punished? Exchange opinions with classmates.

Writing in Response to Literature

How do you think Ellen feels about the pearl ring after Lilith buys it for her? Write about her feelings and what you think she will do with the ring.

Language and Literature

Vocabulary

Choosing the Best Meaning. When a dictionary entry gives several meanings for a word, choose the meaning that fits the context of your reading. First decide which part of speech the word is in the context. Then read the definitions for that part of speech. Finally, select the meaning that makes sense in the context.

Exercise. Give a dictionary definition for each underlined word.

One windy night, Jeff felt a cold draft. One section of his roof had blown off. Shivering, Jeff drafted a plan to replace the roof. First he would write a draft for money from the bank and buy new shingles. Then he would draft his neighbors to help fix the roof. He would reward the helpers with a cold draft of lemonade.

Developing Writing Skills

Evaluating a Relationship. In the last three stories, a young character becomes close to an older character. Choose one set of characters and write an evaluation of their relationship.

Prewriting. Answer these questions about the characters you choose: How well do the characters get along? Do their feelings toward each other change? How realistically does each see the other? How true to life is the relationship? List details from the story that support your answers.

Drafting. Begin with a statement that tells how you view the relationship. Use your answers from your prewriting notes as your main ideas. Make specific evaluation statements. Support these ideas with the details you found. Conclude with your opinion about the relationship.

Revising and Sharing. Work in small groups to revise and improve each other's writing. Give suggestions to help each writer make his or her opinion clear and well-supported.

*To whom do you compare
yourself? Find out how
Manolo thinks he stacks up
against his older friend Juan.*

From

Shadow of a Bull

MAIA WOJCIECHOWSKA

Manolo Olivar is the son of a great bullfighter who
was killed in the bullring. Manolo was only three years
old when his father died. Everyone in his town of Arc-
angel expects Manolo to become a great matador like his
father. Manolo's first bullfight is coming soon, but he
doubts his own courage. He asks his friend's brother,
Juan, for help. Juan agrees to practice with Manolo.
Together they sneak into the bullring at night to test their
skill and courage.

They were very careful not to be seen by anyone.
Although it was past two o'clock in the morning, there
were still many people on the streets. The two did not
talk and walked a little apart from each other.

Manolo held on to his muleta,[1] which he had hidden under
his coat, and he felt his fingers trembling. If he had thought he
knew the meaning of fear before, he was learning it all over
again in the walk to the bullring.

They had to wait in the shadows of a doorway until a
couple of men passed the bullring. Then they rushed toward
the locked gate.

---

1. **muleta** (moo lāt′ ə): (Spanish) a red cloth draped over a stick used by a bullfighter.

"We have to chin ourselves, and then crawl through that space," Juan whispered, pointing to about two feet of opening between the heavy wooden gate and the beginning of the stone wall above.

"Follow me," Juan said softly as he jumped up, grabbed the edge of the gate, and pulled himself up and then sideways until he disappeared. Manolo could not make it. He was a little shorter than Juan and not nearly so athletic. Juan reappeared at the top of the gate. Lying down, he extended a hand to Manolo, who managed to pull himself up. Together they jumped down and were safe inside the bullring enclosure. Manolo looked back at the height from which they had jumped and smiled to himself. The wagon of hay, from which he had once been afraid to jump, had not been nearly so high.

"They will have the cows penned up all together in the big pen. So the bull that is meant for 'El Magnifico' must be in one of the smaller pens. It will be, I guess, no more than a two-year-old. But I'll bet 'El Magnifico' will have trouble with him. He was good once, before he got gored for the first time. Then after that goring, he seemed to lose his ability but not his nerve. Now when they book 'El Magnifico' to fight anywhere, it's just to show people how well he gets tossed by the animals. Come on, Manolo, we'd better get started."

They could barely see inside the structure of the bullring, passing by the infirmary, then the chapel, then the place where the horses waited, and the place where the dead bulls were butchered. Even though there had been no bullfight for two weeks, there was the smell of animals all around them.

"The pens are on the opposite side," Juan said. "We can cross over to them through the stands."

Suddenly they emerged into the moonlit bullring, and

there it was, the arena, empty. Manolo caught his breath. It looked so gigantic, like a sea, like a desert.

"Give me your muleta," Juan said. When Manolo handed it to him, Juan raced towards the sand, vaulted the barrier, and was inside the ring, taking off his coat. He had brought with him his "sword," a stick that was sanded down and painted silver. Now Juan began to make passes with the muleta, slowly, beautifully, as good as any Manolo had seen in the ring. As he watched the boy alone in the arena, Manolo knew that what he himself had achieved would never do. Juan had a feel for the red rag; he seemed to be able to breathe life into it. It obeyed the art of his hands and was part of his lithe body; he turned and it followed, effortlessly, the fluid lines of his movements. And Manolo was aware of something else. This boy loved very much what he was doing. He was citing the non-existent bull with soft words of command, and after finishing a series of left-

From the sketchbook of PABLO PICASSO, 1959.
Copyright © ARS, New York City/SPADEM, 1987.

handed passes, aware of their perfection, he shouted to himself, "Olé." And then he looked up towards the empty stands, and Manolo saw how proud and how like a bullfighter he appeared. There was a smile of triumph on his face for a moment; then, as suddenly as it came, the smile disappeared and Juan looked sad.

"Let's go," Juan said.

"You're terribly good," Manolo managed to say.

"Oh," he shrugged his shoulders, "you should have seen me with the seed bull yesterday. I caped him with eighteen left-handed passes, and I, myself, knew I was as good as anyone."

"And he hurt you?"

"Slammed me down a couple of times before he knew what he was doing. He probably thought I was one of those silly amateurs. Hey, Manolo, don't you want to practice a few passes?"

"No," Manolo replied. He had not even stepped onto the sand; he felt unworthy of doing even that.

"All right, let's get to it," Juan said, joining Manolo in the stands. They walked around until they came to the *toril*.[2] "Let's go this way."

They could not see where they were going after they entered the dark passageway through which the bull had to walk to reach the ring.

I won't do it, I can't do it. Manolo groped his way behind Juan, wishing he were not there.

Juan stopped.

"If we find it, let me go in first. You don't mind, do you?"

"I don't mind," Manolo said, swallowing hard.

"Look," Juan seemed to have sensed the fear in Manolo, "you don't have to do it. No one is making you. If you don't

---

2. **toril** (tō rēl'): (Spanish) bullpen.

want to play with the bull, don't. I will understand. Besides, I really think it would break all these people's hearts if you were to get hurt or anything."

They resumed their walk through the darkness, Juan feeling for a door, a latch, anything that might lead them to the pen. Manolo, very thankful for what had been said, breathed more easily. Again Juan stopped.

"I don't want you to think," he said softly, "that I am like some of the others. I know that I should not be poaching on someone else's bull. It is very dangerous for a bullfighter to face an animal that has been played with. And that's why I won't give this animal any more than a couple of passes. And when I go to cape them on the pastures, I never touch any bull but the seed bull. They are never fought anyway. So you see, I have my code of honor." He laughed. "And if," he continued, "you feel like giving him a few passes, be sure it's just a few because I'd hate to think that we might be responsible for 'El Magnifico's' getting hurt."

"How long," Manolo asked, happy for this new delay, "how long does it take a bull to learn?"

"To learn to go for the man instead of the lure? About twenty minutes, or so they say. That's why the fights are never longer, or at least that part with the man and the bull alone. So you see, it's important not to play with this one long. And by the way," he said softly, "if I should get carried away, you shout to me to stop."

"And," Manolo's throat was again very dry, "what should I do if, if. . . ."

"If the bull catches me and tosses me? Well, try your best to take it away from me until I can get up again."

"Of course," Manolo mumbled, ashamed of having asked, ashamed of not having known, and mostly ashamed because he felt that if anything were to happen to Juan, he, Manolo, could not help him.

They heard the bull. It snorted, and they followed the sound.

"It must be here," Juan said stopping at a door made of planks of wood. He put his ear to them. "Yes. He's here! Now, listen. This opens from the top. It's on pulleys, so I'll try to lift the door up, but it might come down if I don't manage it all the way. Can you hold it while I am there?"

"But, if I hold it, I can't come to help you if . . . if anything happens."

"Don't worry about it."

"Let's not do it," he said, before he knew that he had wanted to say it.

From the sketchbook of PABLO PICASSO, 1959. Copyright © ARS, New York City/SPADEM, 1987.

"Not do it? But that's what we came for!"

"I only meant," Manolo trembled over the words, "I meant let's leave that door open in such a way that I could get to you."

They could hear the bull now quite plainly; it was scraping the sand with its hoofs.

"Ready?" Juan asked.

"Wait," Manolo whispered. "What . . . what if the bull comes at us when we open this . . . this door?"

"He's young. And they're curious but not dumb at that age. He'll wait until he sees what's happening. He won't rush out. Or at least, that's what I am counting on. All right, ready now?"

"Ready."

Juan found the pulleys that opened the door. Slowly it lifted, and they could now hear the breathing of the animal. When there was two feet of space at the bottom, Juan tried to see if the door would come down. It did slide back.

"I'll have to use my jacket on one side and yours on the other," he said. He jammed the pulley ropes with the jackets, and now they were able to crawl through. "I'll go ahead; you just put your head through and watch. Then, when I'm through, you can cape him yourself," said Juan getting on his knee. "Aren't you going to wish me luck?" he asked, his face in the moonlight smiling at Manolo.

"Good luck," Manolo managed to say.

He bent down to see the boy scramble up, the muleta in the same hand as his "sword."

"*Ehe toro!*"[3] Juan called softly, and moved to one side. Manolo saw the bull then: a black, glistening mass, white horns

3. **Ehe toro** (ə hā′ tō′ rō): (Spanish) "Hey, bull!"

shining. It was big, much bigger than he had thought any bull could be.

"Ehe toro!" Juan repeated a little louder, shaking the muleta, now close, not more than five feet from the animal that stood still, waiting. And suddenly it charged, whirling at the boy. He'll get killed, Manolo thought; but Juan, without moving away, made the bull change its course. The animal followed the lure, which moved slowly a little ahead of his horns. He came back and again was taken smoothly, slowed down by the boy. Five times the animal and Juan seemed to touch, to be glued together, as Manolo watched. Then, standing straight, the boy turned his back to the animal and sent him away with a beautiful *pase de pecho.*[4]

"Do you want to try?" Juan whispered to Manolo. "He's a good little bull." Juan stood not far from the bull, not looking at him, not afraid of the charge that might come.

"Watch out," Manolo shouted as the animal moved towards the boy. It did not catch Juan, however, who slowly, arrogantly, lifted the lure in both hands and let the animal charge under it. Back came the bull, and again, with quiet assurance, the boy controlled the animal's speed and direction. Without looking back, Juan walked towards Manolo. The animal seemed to have been nailed to the sand by the last pass, but suddenly it charged fast, too fast for Manolo to warn Juan. It happened in an instant. The boy was tossed up in the air and landed with a thud on the ground. The bull stomped the earth and moved his horns towards Juan, who had both arms thrown over his head. But Manolo was there. He acted automatically with no thought of what he was doing. He picked up the muleta and waved it in front of the horns, and the horns

---

4. **pase de pecho** (pä′ sā dā pä′chō): (Spanish) a chest-high pass with a muleta.

From the sketchbook of PABLO PICASSO, 1959. Copyright © ARS, New York City/SPADEM, 1987.

charged the red cloth. Manolo ran backwards, taking the bull away from Juan; he even screamed *"Ehe toro!"*

"It's all right," Juan shouted getting up. "I'm fine."

It was then that Manolo looked at the bull, as if for the first time. The horns were inches away, and the black eyes were staring at him. He was standing between Manolo and Juan's voice.

"Thanks a lot," Juan was saying, "but you better not play with him any longer. We should leave him alone for 'El Magnifico'."

Manolo felt sick. He had to hold his head high not to vomit right there.

"Ehe toro!" Juan came close to the bull, and the animal whirled and charged at the boy, who held no lure. Manolo watched horrified as Juan, dodging the horns, took the bull away. Without being aware of how he reached the opening,

Manolo climbed through it and vomited his fear into the darkness.

He turned to see Juan letting down the planks.

"That was wonderful of you!" Juan said, his hand extended. "If it hadn't been for you, I would be lying there dead."

Maybe he did not notice, Manolo thought; maybe he didn't see that I was paralyzed, that I couldn't have moved. Maybe he doesn't know that I vomited. Maybe he didn't see any of this.

From the Sketchbook of PABLO PICASSO, 1959. Copyright © ARS, New York City/SPADEM, 1987.

Maia Wojciechowska (born 1927) was born in Poland, but lived in many countries before arriving in the United States at the age of fifteen. Her fascination with bullfights began when she first saw one as a child in Spain. Since then, she has written many novels about the people and culture of Spain. Her novel *Shadow of a Bull* won the Newbery Medal.

Other books: *A Single Light*
   A Kingdom in a Horse

Developing Comprehension Skills

1. Where are Juan and Manolo going? Why are they going there?

2. What two things does Manolo realize about Juan as he watches him practice with the muleta?

3. Explain Juan's code of honor. Why does he defend his actions to Manolo?

4. How do you know that Manolo is afraid? Why does he go into the ring anyway?

5. What is Manolo's judgment of himself? Do you think he judges himself fairly? Why or why not?

6. **Focus on Thinking: Drawing Conclusions.** You can draw conclusions about a character by examining the character's words and actions. Does Juan know that Manolo is afraid? What evidence supports your conclusion?

Reading Fiction

1. **Examining Conflict.** Not all conflicts are resolved completely. What conflicts does Manolo struggle with? How well does he resolve each conflict?

2. **Contrasting the Characters.** Writers sometimes develop characters by contrasting them with one another. What differences are shown between Manolo and Juan?

3. **Evaluating Mood.** Details of action and setting help establish mood. What is the mood of this story? How well do the details help establish that mood?

Study and Research

Using Author Cards. The card catalog has an author card for each book in the library. The author card is alphabetized by the author's last name.

Use the card catalog to look up an author of a story in this part. Find and read a novel or short-story collection by that author.

Writing in Response to Literature

How do you react when you are frightened? Write a description of your physical reaction one time when you were terrified or nervous.

When were you really embarrassed about something? See what extreme measures Victoria takes to avoid being embarrassed.

Dear Miss Veloshin

MARJORIE WEINMAN SHARMAT

I woke up half an hour late. Whenever I smell my mother's cooking, I wake up. But this morning my mother had overslept, and so she was half an hour late with her breakfast cooking smells.

"We're both late today," she said. "You'll be late for school even if you run like the Boston Marathon. But you eat, and I'll write a note to the school and explain."

My mother got her favorite pen which not only writes well but advertises in shiny gold that Rivkin's Delicatessen is located at 165 Middle Street and is open seven days a week from 7 A.M. to 7 P.M. and caters and delivers. That's quite a lot of information to get on a pen. "A real accomplishment," my mother says. "And the gold doesn't flake and give me gold-dust fingers."

The reason I mention this pen is because I think it inspires my mother to write more than she ordinarily would. If Rivkin's can get that much stuff on a pen, just think of the possibilities for an eight-by-ten piece of paper.

My mother wrote and I ate. After I ate, I got dressed, took

my books, and headed for the door. My mother was still writing.

She wrote a few more words and she handed the note to me as I was walking out the door. "Here," she said, "the lateness is all explained. Study hard to make up for the lost time and don't trade your lunch until you look at it."

"Look at what I have or what I might get?" I asked, but I didn't wait for an answer.

After I left my house, I opened my mother's note and read it.

> Dear Attendance Taker,
>
>   As you know, Victoria is always on time for school. So you will be surprised to see that this morning, October 8, she is late. She overslept because I overslept. I overslept because my alarm clock is broken and won't be fixed until Mr. Darren Lockheart of Lockheart's Jewelry, Inc., returns from Florida where he is visiting his sister who had a very minor operation. Mr. Lockheart knows the clock inside and outside so he should be the one to fix it. I recently heard that his sister is now in the recovery room, so I think that Mr. Lockheart will soon be returning to town. In the meantime, I am keeping Victoria's shade up so that in the morning the light will come in and help to wake her up, and I am doing the same in my room with high hopes.
>
>   I am signing off for now.
>
>   Victoria Finley's mother

I took out a blank piece of paper from my notebook, and a pen. I wrote:

> Victoria Finley was late for school because she overslept. Sorry about that.
>
>   Sincerely,
>   Mrs. Finley

I compared the handwriting on my mother's note and my note. Identical twins! I was fabulous at copying my mother's handwriting because I did it a lot. I never lied in my notes. I would never sign my mother's name to a lie. I just shortened her ideas and made a mini out of a maxi. Everybody has a style in the way that they write and talk and dress and walk and think and do zillions of things, and I would never tell my mother to change her style.

But I don't want the whole school to know about my life. And when you give a note to Miss Veloshin, the collector of notes, you give a note to the whole school. Miss Veloshin talks. TALKS! Victoria Finley keeps her window shade up—ho, ho, ho. Why does Victoria Finley keep her window shade up? Victoria Finley's mother's alarm clock is broken. How about that? What is the sinister connection between Victoria Finley's mother's broken alarm clock and Victoria Finley's raised-up window shade?

When I was out sick for a week, my mother's note read like a report from Dr. Welby, complete with a list of my temperature readings and the fact that our leftover Halloween hard candy in lime and cherry flavors helped my sore throat. I threw away her note and wrote my own. Since I was absent for a week, I needed a strong note. I wrote:

> Victoria Finley was absent one whole week because she was sick, sick, sick.
>
> Sincerely,
> Mrs. Finley

I put my mother's alarm clock–window shade note in one of my books. I hate to throw away a note of hers when it's sort of hot off the griddle. It's like instant destruct. I wanted to read it again later in the day and then throw it away. That way it would get read twice and it would seem less like my mother wrote it in vain.

I got to school and went to Miss Veloshin's office. Miss Veloshin is the school nurse and she collects all the late and absent slips, the idea being that most kids who have been absent were sick, and most kids who are late are marked absent and thought to be sick unless proven otherwise. Miss Veloshin's office is also where you go when you find you are sick after you get to school. That happens to loads of kids. They leave home in spectacular health, and once they get to school, they develop anything from a runny nose to a stomach cramp. The stomach cramp is a real favorite since it puts the kids in a very impressive folded-over position that horrifies Miss Veloshin, causing her to recommend immediate dismissal from school for the day.

There were only a few kids in Miss Veloshin's office when I got there. Everybody was upright, and so Miss Veloshin was full of the kind of Supercheer that hits you like a volcano. I believe that Miss Veloshin took a course in Cheer in nursing school, and it nearly killed her, but she stuck it out and now she's sensational at it.

"Good morning, good morning, Victoria," she said. (Cheerfully, how else?)

"I'm late," I said, handing her my note. Miss Veloshin has received many notes from me, signed Mrs. Finley, and she always reads them fast and says "Very good" in her I'm-so-glad-you're-not-folded-over cheerful voice.

I turned to leave, expecting to walk out to the sound of "Very good." But Miss Veloshin didn't say "Very good." She said, "Victoria. Wait."

Yech! Here it comes, Victoria Finley. This time you flunked the forgery handwriting course. Stand where you are. Do not pass Go even if Mr. Darren Lockheart of Lockheart's Jewelry, Inc., on his way back from Florida offers to drive you. Do not collect two hundred dollars. Go directly to jail where you will rot for the rest of your days because you forged your mother's handwriting.

Miss Veloshin said, "I've never met your mother, but I feel as if I know her. I get many many notes every day, but I always remember hers. Isn't that strange?" (Exit cheer.)

My mother will visit me in jail and bring me a cake with a file inside and I will escape. I will fly immediately to whatever foreign country has no extradition arrangements with the United States. I will put all of this in my official biography when I become a famous writer of books. Miss Veloshin will brag to everyone that she was the one who exposed me, the famous-to-be Victoria Finley. I will tell everyone that Miss Veloshin is a ratfink.

"Victoria, are you listening? I said that I find your mother's notes distinctive."

"Naturally," I said. "My mother's a snazzy writer. Short and to the point. There's a little of Hemingway[1] in her. You don't find that in your average note writer."

"No, I don't suppose so," said Miss Veloshin. She then turned to a kid who was patiently holding out his tongue, hoping it would be his exit slip home.

I started to leave again. This time I made it. But I felt that Miss Veloshin was leaving with me, sitting smack on top of my head with her legs curled around my neck like a boa constrictor as she waited, all good will and cheer, for my head to split open and the contents spill out.

I walked down the hall. I opened up the book where I had put my mother's note. If I read it once more, I could throw it away.

The note was gone. Gone! Where? Oh please, into a street, across the ocean, on top of a mountain, gone anywhere but Miss Veloshin's office. Did I drop it in her office when I took out the note I wrote? What if she finds it? She will have two notes for the same occasion. She will have my head.

I started back to Miss Veloshin's office. But I needed an excuse to go back and look for my note. As I entered her office I folded over in a position that made me look extremely ill and also got me nearer to the floor to look for my mother's note.

---

1. **Hemingway, Ernest:** a famous American writer, known for his plain, matter-of-fact style of writing.

"Victoria!" said Miss Veloshin when she saw me. "You were well just moments ago. *Moments!*"

"I'm fast," I said. "I get sick fast. I heal fast."

I didn't raise my eyes. I had seen it. My mother's note. It was under Miss Veloshin's desk.

"Lie down," said Miss Veloshin, pointing toward a cot.

I, Victoria Finley, sprawled flat on the floor. My left arm was now only inches from my mother's note.

"The cot! The cot!" said Miss Veloshin.

"The floor feels good," I said. "Cool and flat. I'm feeling better already on the floor. May I please rest here a minute?"

"Very well," said Miss Veloshin.

She looked at me funny. She knew I wasn't sick. She knew.

I slid my arm under her desk and grabbed the note. Safe! I decided to lie there a few minutes and pretend to get a little better with each passing minute. Then I would get up and say, "One hundred percent recovery." Then I would leave.

I will never forge another note. I will let my mother write all those things she writes, and I will hand them to Miss Veloshin. I will let Miss Veloshin read and read and read and read while I stand there and she reads and reads and reads and I stand and stand and stand. Miss Veloshin will wonder why my mother no longer writes like Ernest Hemingway. Let her wonder.

I am safe. I am free.

"Victoria! Victoria!"

It's my mother. She is coming toward me. She is waving my lunchbox which I forgot to bring to school. In one moment she will be in Miss Veloshin's office. She will meet Miss Veloshin. They will talk. They will talk about notes.

I cannot move. I think I am sick. I may not be a famous writer when I grow up after all. I may go into something like disease or garbage disposal. I may go into prison. Right now, I cannot think about that. Right now I am sick.

"Miss Veloshin, help!"

Developing Comprehension Skills

1. According to Victoria, why are her mother's notes so long? Why does Victoria rewrite them?

2. How does Victoria feel after she first leaves Miss Veloshin's office? What adds to this feeling?

3. Would Victoria have felt guilty if her plan had worked?

4. Based on your own experience, evaluate how realistic Victoria's feelings and reactions are.

5. **Focus on Thinking: Predicting.** You can usually make several different predictions about what will happen after a story ends. What does Victoria think will happen next? What other things might happen instead?

Reading Fiction

1. **Examining Mood.** The mood of a story is the feeling it creates in the reader. This mood may be quite different from the main character's feelings. What are Victoria's feelings at the end of the story? What is the mood of this story?

2. **Examining Point of View.** In a story written from first-person point of view, the narrator's personality can be revealed through actions, words, and thoughts. What is the main way the author reveals Victoria's personality? How would this story be different if it were narrated by another character?

3. **Understanding Humor.** An author can create humor through exaggeration. Give examples that show how Victoria exaggerates.

Writing in Response to Literature

Write a concluding paragraph to this story telling what happens when Victoria's mother comes into Miss Veloshin's office.

Tell about something you own that is no longer useful or valuable to you. Then discover with Niccolo what things have lost their usefulness in his time.

Someday

ISAAC ASIMOV

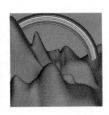

Niccolo Mazetti lay stomach down on the rug, chin buried in the palm of one small hand, and listened to the Bard disconsolately. There was even the suspicion of tears in his dark eyes, a luxury an eleven-year-old could allow himself only when alone.

The Bard said, "Once upon a time in the middle of a deep wood, there lived a poor woodcutter and his two motherless daughters, who were each as beautiful as the day is long. The older daughter had long hair as black as a feather from a raven's wing, but the younger daughter had hair as bright and golden as the sunlight of an autumn afternoon.

"Many times while the girls were waiting for their father to come home from his day's work in the wood, the older girl would sit before a mirror and sing—"

What she sang, Niccolo did not hear, for a call sounded from outside the room: "Hey, Nickie."

And Niccolo, his face clearing on the moment, rushed to the window and shouted, "Hey, Paul."

Paul Loeb waved an excited hand. He was thinner than Niccolo and not as tall, for all he was six months older. His face was full of repressed tension which showed itself most clearly in the rapid blinking of his eyelids. "Hey, Nickie, let me in. I've got an idea and a *half*. Wait till you hear it." He looked rapidly about him as though to check on the possibility of eavesdroppers, but the front yard was quite patently empty. He repeated, in a whisper, "Wait till you hear it."

"All right. I'll open the door."

The Bard continued smoothly, oblivious to the sudden loss of attention on the part of Niccolo. As Paul entered, the Bard was saying, ". . . Thereupon, the lion said, 'If you will find me the lost egg of the bird which flies over the Ebony Mountain once every ten years, I will—' "

Paul said, "Is that a Bard you're listening to? I didn't know you had one."

Niccolo reddened and the look of unhappiness returned to his face. "Just an old thing I had when I was a kid. It ain't much good." He kicked at the Bard with his foot and caught the somewhat scarred and discolored plastic covering a glancing blow.

The Bard hiccuped as its speaking attachment was jarred out of contact a moment, then it went on: "—for a year and a day until the iron shoes were worn out. The princess stopped at the side of the road. . . ."

Paul said, "Boy, that *is* an old model," and looked at it critically.

Despite Niccolo's own bitterness against the Bard, he winced at the other's condescending tone. For the moment, he was sorry he had allowed Paul in, at least before he had restored the Bard to its usual resting place in the basement. It was only in the desperation of a dull day and a fruitless discussion with his father that he had resurrected it. And it turned out to be just as stupid as he had expected.

Trompe l'Oeil, 1984, SALLY PRYOR.
Computer Graphic. Cranston/Csuri
Productions, Columbus, Ohio.

Nickie was a little afraid of Paul anyway, since Paul had special courses at school and everyone said he was going to grow up to be a Computing Engineer.

Not that Niccolo himself was doing badly at school. He got adequate marks in logic, binary manipulations, computing and elementary circuits; all the usual grammar-school subjects. But that was it! They were just the usual subjects and he would grow up to be a control-board guard like everyone else.

Paul, however, knew mysterious things about what he called electronics and theoretical mathematics and programing. Especially programing. Niccolo didn't even try to understand when Paul bubbled over about it.

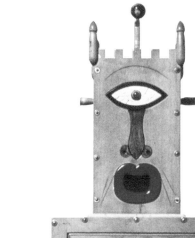

Paul listened to the Bard for a few minutes and said, "You been using it much?"

"No!" said Niccolo, offended. "I've had it in the basement since before you moved into the neighborhood. I just got it out today—" He lacked an excuse that seemed adequate to himself, so he concluded, "I just got it out."

Paul said, "Is that what it tells you about: woodcutters and princesses and talking animals?"

Niccolo said, "It's terrible. My dad says we can't afford a new one. I said to him this morning—" The memory of the morning's fruitless pleadings brought Niccolo dangerously near tears, which he repressed in a panic. Somehow, he felt that Paul's thin cheeks never felt the stain of tears and that Paul would have only contempt for anyone else less strong than himself. Niccolo went on, "So I thought I'd try this old thing again, but it's no good."

Paul turned off the Bard, pressed the contact that led to a nearly instantaneous reorientation and recombination of the vocabulary, characters, plot lines,

Memorial to the Idea of Man If He Was an Idea, 1958, H. C. WESTERMANN. Collection of Mr. and Mrs. Lewis Manilow. Photograph: Museum of Contemporary Art, Chicago.

and climaxes stored within it. Then he reactivated it.

The Bard began smoothly, "Once upon a time there was a little boy named Willikins whose mother had died and who lived with a stepfather and a stepbrother. Although the stepfather was very well-to-do, he begrudged poor Willikins the very bed he slept in so that Willikins was forced to get such rest as he could on a pile of straw in the stable next to the horses—"

"Horses!" cried Paul.

"They're a kind of animal," said Niccolo. "I think."

"I know that! I just mean imagine stories about *horses*."

"It tells about horses all the time," said Niccolo. "There are things called cows, too. You milk them but the Bard doesn't say how."

"Well, gee, why don't you fix it up?"

"I'd like to know how."

The Bard was saying, "Often Willikins would think that if only he were rich and powerful, he would show his stepfather and stepbrother what it meant to be cruel to a little boy, so one day he decided to go out into the world and seek his fortune."

Paul, who wasn't listening to the Bard, said, "It's *easy*. The Bard has memory cylinders all fixed up for plot lines and climaxes and things. We don't have to worry about that. It's just vocabulary we've got to fix so it'll know about computers and automation and electronics and real things about today. Then it can tell interesting stories, you know, instead of about princesses and things."

Niccolo said despondently, "I wish we could do that."

Paul said, "Listen, my dad says if I get into special computing school next year, he'll get me a *real* Bard, a late model. A big one with an attachment for space stories and mysteries. And a visual attachment, too!"

"You mean *see* the stories?"

"Sure. Mr. Daugherty at school says they've got things like that, now, but not for just everybody. Only if I get into computing school, Dad can get a few breaks."

Niccolo's eyes bulged with envy. "Gee. *Seeing* a story."

"You can come over and watch anytime, Nickie."

"Oh, boy. Thanks."

"That's all right. But remember, I'm the guy who says what kind of story we hear."

"Sure. Sure." Niccolo would have agreed readily to much more onerous conditions.

Paul's attention returned to the Bard.

It was saying, " 'If that is the case,' said the king, stroking his beard and frowning till clouds filled the sky and lightning flashed, 'you will see to it that my entire land is freed of flies by this time day after tomorrow or—' "

"All we've got to do," said Paul, "is open it up—" He shut the Bard off again and was prying at its front panel as he spoke.

"Hey," said Niccolo, in sudden alarm. "Don't break it."

"I won't break it," said Paul impatiently. "I know all about these things." Then, with sudden caution, "Your father and mother home?"

"No."

"All right, then." He had the front panel off and peered in. "Boy, this *is* a one-cylinder thing."

He worked away at the Bard's innards. Niccolo, who watched with painful suspense, could not make out what he was doing.

Paul pulled out a thin, flexible metal strip, powdered with dots. "That's the Bard's memory cylinder. I'll bet its capacity for stories is under a trillion."

"What are you going to do, Paul?" quavered Niccolo.

"I'll give it vocabulary."

"How?"

"Easy. I've got a book here. Mr. Daugherty gave it to me at school."

Paul pulled the book out of his pocket and pried at it till he had its plastic jacket off. He unreeled the tape a bit, ran it through the vocalizer, which he turned down to a whisper, then placed it within the Bard's vitals. He made further attachments.

"What'll that do?"

"The book will talk and the Bard will put it all on its memory tape."

"What good will that do?"

"Boy, you're a dope! This book is all about computers and automation and the Bard will get all that information. Then he can stop talking about kings making lightning when they frown."

Niccolo said, "And the good guy always wins anyway. There's no excitement."

"Oh, well," said Paul, watching to see if his setup was working properly, "that's the way they make Bards. They got to have the good guy win and make the bad guys lose and things like that. I heard my father talking about it once. He says that without censorship there'd be no telling what the younger generation would come to. He says it's bad enough as it is. . . . There, it's working fine."

Paul brushed his hands against one another and turned away from the Bard. He said, "But listen, I didn't tell you my idea yet. It's the best thing you ever heard, I bet. I came right to you, because I figured you'd come in with me."

"Sure, Paul, sure."

"Okay. You know Mr. Daugherty at school? You know what a funny kind of guy he is. Well, he likes me, kind of."

"I know."

"I was over his house after school today."

"You *were?*"

"Sure. He says I'm going to be entering computer school and he wants to encourage me and things like that. He says the world needs more people who can design advanced computer circuits and do proper programing."

"Oh?"

Paul might have caught some of the emptiness behind that monosyllable. He said impatiently, "Programing! I told you a hundred times. That's when you set up problems for the giant computers like Multivac to work on. Mr. Daugherty says it gets harder all the time to find people who can really run computers. He says anyone can keep an eye on the controls and check off answers and put through routine problems. He says the trick is to expand research and figure out ways to ask the right questions, and that's hard.

"Anyway, Nickie, he took me to his place and showed me his collection of old computers. It's kind of a hobby of his to collect old computers. He had tiny computers you had to push with your hand, with little knobs all over it. And he had a hunk of wood he called a slide rule with a little piece of it that went in and out. And some wires with balls on them. He even had a hunk of paper with a kind of thing he called a multiplication table."

Niccolo, who found himself only moderately interested, said, "A paper table?"

"It wasn't really a table like you eat on. It was different. It was to help people compute. Mr. Daugherty tried to explain but he didn't have much time and it was kind of complicated, anyway."

"Why didn't people just use a computer?"

Computer Cosmology, 1980, COLLEEN BROWNING. Private Collection.
Photograph courtesy of Kennedy Galleries Inc., New York City.

"That was *before* they had computers," cried Paul.

"Before?"

"Sure. Do you think people always had computers? Didn't you ever hear of cavemen?"

Niccolo said, "How'd they get along without computers?"

"*I* don't know. Mr. Daugherty says they just had children any old time and did anything that came into their heads whether it would be good for everybody or not. They didn't even know if it was good or not. And farmers grew things with their hands and people had to do all the work in the factories and run all the machines."

"I don't believe you."

"That's what Mr. Daugherty said. He said it was just plain messy and everyone was miserable. . . . Anyway, let me get to my idea, will you?"

"Well, go ahead. Who's stopping you?" said Niccolo, offended.

"All right. Well, the hand computers, the ones with the knobs, had little squiggles on each knob. And the slide rule had squiggles on it. And the multiplication table was all squiggles. I asked what they were. Mr. Daugherty said they were numbers."

"What?"

"Each different squiggle stood for a different number. For 'one' you made a kind of mark, for 'two' you make another kind of mark, for 'three' another one and so on."

"What for?"

"So you could compute."

"What *for?* You just tell the computer—"

"Jiminy," cried Paul, his face twisting with anger, "can't you get it through your head? These slide rules and things didn't talk."

"Then how—"

"The answers showed up in squiggles and you had to know what the squiggles meant. Mr. Daugherty says that, in olden days, everybody learned how to make squiggles when they were kids and how to decode them, too. Making squiggles was called 'writing' and decoding them was 'reading.' He says there was a different kind of squiggle for every word and they used to write whole books in squiggles. He said they had some at the museum and I could look at them if I wanted to. He said if I was going to be a real computer programer, I would have to know about the history of computing and that's why he was showing me all these things."

Niccolo frowned. He said, "You mean everybody had to figure out squiggles for every word and *remember* them? . . . Is this all real or are you making it up?"

"It's all real. Honest. Look, this is the way you make a 'one.' " He drew his finger through the air in a rapid downstroke. "This way you make 'two,' and this way 'three.' I learned all the numbers up to 'nine.' "

Niccolo watched the curving finger uncomprehendingly. "What's the good of it?"

"You can learn how to make words. I asked Mr. Daugherty how you made the squiggle for 'Paul Loeb,' but he didn't know. He said there were people at the museum who would know. He said there were people who had learned how to decode whole books. He said computers could be designed to decode books and used to be used that way but not any more because we have real books now, with magnetic tapes that go through the vocalizer and come out talking, you know."

"Sure."

"So if we go down to the museum, we can get to learn how to make words in squiggles. They'll let us because I'm going to computer school."

Niccolo was riddled with disappointment. "Is that your idea? Holy Smokes, Paul, who wants to do that? Make stupid squiggles!"

"Don't you get it? Don't you *get* it? You dope. *It'll be secret message stuff!*"

"What?"

"Sure. What good is talking when everyone can understand you? With squiggles you can send secret messages. You can make them on paper and nobody in the world would

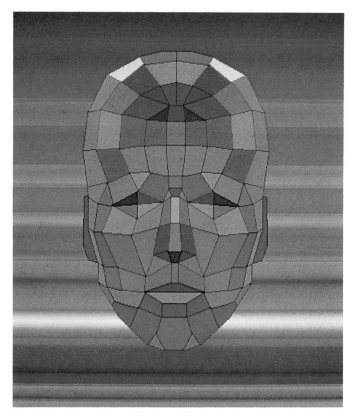

Digital Art: Computer Graphics Head. Click/Chicago.

know what you were saying unless they knew the squiggles, too. And they wouldn't, you bet, unless we taught them. We can have a real club, with initiations and rules and a clubhouse. Boy—"

A certain excitement began stirring in Niccolo's bosom. "What kind of secret messages?"

"Any kind. Say I want to tell you to come over my place and watch my new Visual Bard and I don't want any of the other fellows to come. I make the right squiggles on paper and I give it to you and you look at it and you know what to do. Nobody else does. You can even show it to them and they wouldn't know a thing."

"Hey, that's something," yelled Niccolo, completely won over. "When do we learn how?"

"Tomorrow," said Paul. "I'll get Mr. Daugherty to explain to the museum that it's all right and you get your mother and father to say okay. We can go down right after school and start learning."

"Sure!" cried Niccolo. "We can be club officers."

"I'll be president of the club," said Paul matter-of-factly. "You can be vice-president."

"All right. Hey, this is going to be lots more fun than the Bard." He was suddenly reminded of the Bard and said in sudden apprehension, "Hey, what about my old Bard?"

Paul turned to look at it. It was quietly taking in the slowly unreeling book, and the sound of the book's vocalizations was a dimly heard murmur.

He said, "I'll disconnect it."

He worked away while Niccolo watched anxiously. After a few moments, Paul put his reassembled book into his pocket, replaced the Bard's panel and activated it.

The Bard said, "Once upon a time, in a large city, there lived a poor young boy named Fair Johnnie whose only friend in the world was a small computer. The computer, each morning, would tell the boy whether it would rain that day and answer any problems he might have. It was never wrong. But it so happened that one day, the king of that land, having heard of the little computer, decided that he would have it as his own. With this purpose in mind, he called in his Grand Vizier and said—"

Niccolo turned off the Bard with a quick motion of his hand. "Same old junk," he said passionately. "Just with a computer thrown in."

"Well," said Paul, "they got so much stuff on the tape

already that the computer business doesn't show up much when random combinations are made. What's the difference, anyway? You just need a new model."

"We'll *never* be able to afford one. Just this dirty old miserable thing." He kicked at it again, hitting it more squarely this time. The Bard moved backward with a squeal of castors.

"You can always watch mine, when I get it," said Paul. "Besides, don't forget our squiggle club."

Niccolo nodded.

"I tell you what," said Paul. "Let's go over my place. My father has some books about old times. We can listen to them and maybe get some ideas. You leave a note for your folks and maybe you can stay over for supper. Come on."

"Okay," said Niccolo, and the two boys ran out together. Niccolo, in his eagerness, ran almost squarely into the Bard, but he only rubbed at the spot on his hip where he had made contact and ran on.

The activation signal of the Bard glowed. Niccolo's collision closed a circuit and, although it was alone in the room and there was none to hear, it began a story, nevertheless.

But not in its usual voice, somehow; in a lower tone that had a hint of throatiness in it. An adult, listening, might almost have thought that the voice carried a hint of passion in it, a trace of near feeling.

The Bard said: "Once upon a time, there was a little computer named the Bard who lived all alone with cruel step-people. The cruel step-people continually made fun of the little computer and sneered at him, telling him he was good-for-nothing and that he was a useless object. They struck him and kept him in lonely rooms for months at a time.

"Yet through it all the little computer remained brave. He always did the best he could, obeying all orders cheerfully.

Nevertheless, the step-people with whom he lived remained cruel and heartless.

"One day, the little computer learned that in the world there existed a great many computers of all sorts, great numbers of them. Some were Bards like himself, but some ran factories, and some ran farms. Some organized population, and some analyzed all kinds of data. Many were very powerful and very wise, much more powerful and wise than the step-people who were so cruel to the little computer.

"And the little computer knew then that computers would always grow wiser and more powerful until someday—someday— someday—"

But a valve must finally have stuck in the Bard's aging and corroding vitals, for as it waited alone in the darkening room through the evening, it could only whisper over and over again, "Someday—someday—someday."

Memorial to the Idea of Man If He Was an Idea, 1958, H. C. WESTERMANN. Collection of Mr. and Mrs. Lewis Manilow. Photograph: Museum of Contemporary Art, Chicago.

Isaac Asimov (born 1920) was born in Russia but grew up in New York. A professor of biochemistry, Asimov has written hundreds of nonfiction books and articles mostly on scientific topics. He is also famous as a science fiction writer. His ideas about robots have influenced the works of many other writers.

Other books: *Great Ideas of Science*
How Did We Find Out About Computers?

Developing Comprehension Skills

1. How does Niccolo feel about the Bard? How does he show his feelings?

2. Why does Paul have more privileges than Niccolo?

3. Why are numbers and words so amazing to the boys?

4. What is Paul's idea? For what purpose does he want to use what he learns?

5. The Bard never finishes the last story. What do you think it would have said?

6. **Focus on Thinking: Evaluating.** You can evaluate the believability of stories. Do you think that computers will ever have the power to think? How realistic might this story be in the future? Explain your answers.

Reading Fiction

1. **Examining Science Fiction.** Stories based on real or imagined scientific developments are called **science fiction.** On what scientific development is this story based?

2. **Identifying Theme.** The conflict and the title of some stories help you figure out the theme. What is a theme of this story?

3. **Examining Plot.** When you examine a plot, try to figure out why the author includes each event. How is Paul's reprograming of the Bard important to the story?

Critical Thinking

Classifying. When you classify, you arrange ideas, people, or objects into groups that have something in common. You know that computers have been developed for education, entertainment, travel, and business. As a class, find out as many uses for computers as you can. Compile a list. Then think of five or six categories, and classify the uses in those groups.

Writing in Response to Literature

Imagine a "someday" far into the future. How will computers affect peoples' lives? Choose one part of daily life and describe how it could be different.

Language and Literature

Vocabulary

Synonyms and Antonyms. Dictionaries may list synonyms and antonyms for an entry word. Synonyms are words with similar meanings, such as *major* and *big*. Antonyms, such as *young* and *old,* are words with opposite meanings. Because the meanings of synonyms are not identical, you cannot always substitute one synonym for another. The context determines which synonym is best to use.

Exercise. Choose the word in parentheses that fits the context. Then think of an antonym for the word you chose.

The (gleaming, glittering) computer sat in the (remote, farthest) corner of the room. Jan studied the computer (observantly, carefully), noting with (relief, ease) that it was (mute, silent). Obviously no one knew how to turn it on.

Developing Writing Skills

Writing a Short Story. Fear plays a large role in the characters' actions in the last three stories. Write a story in which fear drives a character to do something unusual.

Prewriting. Imagine your character and setting. Think of the conflict this character will have to face. The conflict could be realistic such as facing a fire or an animal, or imaginary such as facing a creature from another world. Plan the beginning, middle, and end of your plot.

Drafting. Introduce the conflict early in your story and build toward the climax. Show your character's feelings as he or she faces and deals with the situation. Use details to add suspense and excitement.

Revising and Sharing. Look for places in the story where you can add details to build suspense. When you are satisfied, read your scary story to the class. Use taped background music if you wish.

Reading Poetry

Poems That Express Ideas

The magic of poetry is that it can express complex ideas in a few carefully chosen words. Poetry, like other forms of literature, deals with the experiences of life. The poet draws from real or imagined experiences to create a new experience for the reader.

Themes in Poetry

The ideas about life that poets share are the themes in poetry. However, you cannot separate what a poet says from how he or she says it. To get the most meaning from a poem, you must do more than find the theme. You must appreciate the poem as a whole. What makes a poem so special is how all the elements work together to create an effect. These elements include language, images, sound, form, mood, and ideas.

In this poem by David Ignatow, all the elements work together to create meaning.

The City

If flowers want to grow
right out of the concrete sidewalk cracks
I'm going to bend down to smell them.

The poet paints an image of flowers breaking through sidewalk cracks. What sort of flowers do you picture? Your own experience helps you picture one kind of flower, such as daisies or dandelions.

Notice how the title adds important information to the poem. Picturing the sidewalk in a city setting helps you get an even clearer image.

Now look at some of the word choices. The words *concrete, cracks,* and *smell* are not pretty words with pretty sounds. These words create a tough, hard feeling in contrast to the delicacy of the word *flowers.* This contrast reinforces the idea that the flowers had to be determined to break their way through the hard ground.

Both images and word choices work together to express ideas. *Flowers* is the most important word and the main image in the poem. Flowers often stand for the idea of beauty. One idea of the poem is that beauty found in unexpected places should be noticed and appreciated. The flowers also stand for the idea of determination. What message do you draw from this?

Connotations in Poetry

How does a poet pack so much meaning into so few words? Poets choose words for their connotations, that is, the feelings and ideas associated with them. For instance, the word *city* suggests steel buildings and crowded spaces. What else does it suggest to you?

How to Find Ideas in Poems

Each poem you will read in this part expresses a message about life. To discover the message, look at the poem as a whole. See how the images help you understand what the poet is saying. Use connotations as clues to meaning. Experience the magic of poetry and learn from your experience.

*What is your favorite season?
See, hear, and feel a season
with this poet.*

Nobody Gives It to You

MYRA COHN LIVINGSTON

The Briante River (Forest Interior in Autumn), about 1907,
GEORGE LACOMBE. Copyright © Indianapolis Museum of Art, The
Holliday Collection.

Nobody gives it to you.
Nobody says it's exactly yours.
    The blue, the green, the white of it;
    The air stinging your nose, sucking
        your mouth,   5
    The wind scamping you along the sidewalk,
    The leaves crunching under your feet,
    The fall: The crispy ting of it.
Nobody says it's exactly yours,
Nobody gives it to you.   10
But it is.

Developing Comprehension Skills

1. What is the "it" in this poem?

2. What details describe "it"? With what senses does the reader experience those details?

3. What is the main idea of the last three lines?

4. **Focus on Thinking: Making an Inference.** You can use details and statements in poems to make inferences. What inference can you make about what the poet thinks you should do in this season?

Reading Poetry

1. **Evaluating Mood.** The mood of a poem is often created by connotations of words the poet chooses. Describe the mood of this poem. Evaluate how well the words chosen reflect this mood.

2. **Examining Form.** A poet can use form or shape to set apart ideas. Lines 3 through 8 are indented. What does this section of the poem describe?

3. **Recognizing Onomatopoeia.** The use of words that sound like what they describe is **onomatopoeia.** Find examples of onomatopoeia in this poem.

Writing in Response to Literature

Picture a scene from your favorite season. In a paragraph, describe how it affects one or more of your senses.

Myra Cohn Livingston (born 1926) has spent most of her career writing poetry and helping young people learn to write. Most of her poems are about finding joy in simple things and everyday experiences. Livingston has written many volumes of her own poetry in addition to editing collections of poetry written by others.

Other books: *O Sliver of Liver*
A Lollygag of Limericks

Respect

ANGEL NIETO

We are all different
and i respect that
as i respect your right to be
and i respect your right to become
as i respect your right to love   5
and i respect your right to fight
but don't expect respect from me
if you don't love if you don't fight
if you are . . . if you become . . .
indifferent.   10

Self Portrait at an Open Window, 1977, DORA RAMIREZ. Museum of Modern Art of Latin America/OAS, Washington, D.C.

Developing Comprehension Skills

1. Name four rights the speaker respects.

2. For what three reasons will the speaker not give respect?

3. Why do you think the speaker does not respect those who are indifferent?

Reading Poetry

1. **Identifying Theme.** When a poem presents several ideas, they usually work together to present the most important idea, or theme. What do you think is the theme of this poem?

2. **Evaluating Repetition.** Repetition can be an important part of the form of a poem. What repeated phrase ties lines 3 through 6 together? How do lines 7 and 8 repeat ideas from those lines? Evaluate how well the repetition helps you understand the theme.

3. **Examining Form.** Poets write in lines rather than sentences and paragraphs. How would this poem be different if it were written as a paragraph?

Writing in Response to Literature

The speaker of this poem explains directly to you what you must do to keep his or her respect. Write a letter to the speaker. Explain what he or she must do to earn your respect.

Angel Nieto (born 1940) was born in Spain but has lived in the United States for many years. Nieto writes most of his poems in Spanish, although he also writes in English. One series of his poems traces the growth of one of his daughters from the age of six months to one year. Nieto now lives and works as a teacher in Massachusetts.

To James

FRANK HORNE

Do you remember
How you won
That last race . . . ?
How you flung your body
At the start . . .   5
How your spikes
Ripped the cinders
In the stretch . . .
How you catapulted
Through the tape . . .   10
Do you remember . . . ?
Don't you think
I lurched with you
Out of those starting holes . . . ?
Don't you think   15
My sinews tightened
At those first
Few strides . . .
And when you flew into the stretch
Was not all my thrill   20

Of a thousand races
In your blood . . . ?
At your final drive
Through the finish line
Did not my shout   25
Tell of the
Triumphant ecstasy
Of victory . . . ?
Live
As I have taught you   30
To run, Boy—
It's a short dash
Dig your starting holes
Deep and firm
Lurch out of them   35
Into the straightaway
With all the power
That is in you
Look straight ahead
To the finish line   40
Think only of the goal
Run straight
Run high
Run hard
Save nothing   45
And finish
With an ecstatic burst
That carries you
Hurtling
Through the tape   50
To victory. . . .

Breaking the Tape, 1983, DR. JOE WILDER.
Collection of the Artist.

Developing Comprehension Skills

1. What event is the speaker describing?

2. What is the speaker doing as James runs the race in lines 12 through 28?

3. Who do you think the speaker is? Why does the speaker think he or she is qualified to give James advice?

4. **Focus on Thinking: Inferring Feelings.** Connotations of words can help you infer a speaker's feelings. What feelings can you find in the words in lines 12 through 28? What do you think the speaker is feeling during this section?

Reading Poetry

1. **Evaluating Theme.** The theme of a poem may be in the form of advice. Summarize the speaker's advice to tell the theme of this poem. Evaluate this advice. Explain why you think it is or is not good advice.

2. **Relating Form to Meaning.** The poet can express ideas through the form he or she uses. How do the short lines, coming one after another, suggest running?

3. **Examining a Metaphor.** A comparison that extends through a whole poem is called an **extended metaphor.** Explain all the similarities the speaker points out between running a race and living life.

Writing in Response to Literature

Who gives you advice? Write about the feelings you have toward the advice-giver and the advice itself.

© NYT Pictures

Frank Horne (1899–1974) was a doctor, a teacher, a poet, and an expert on the housing problems of minority groups. He was a founder of the National Committee Against Discrimination in Housing. Horne was also the first director of the New York City Commission on Human Rights.

What ordinary thing do you find beautiful? Learn where this poet finds beauty.

Beauty

E-YEH-SHURE'

Beauty is seen
In the sunlight,
The trees, the birds,
Corn growing and people working
Or dancing for their harvest.   5

Beauty is heard
In the night,
Wind sighing, rain falling,
Or a singer chanting
Anything in earnest.   10

Beauty is in yourself.
Good deeds, happy thoughts
That repeat themselves
In your dreams,
In your work,   15
And even in your rest.

Navajo Weavers, 1938, HARRISON BEGAY.
Philbrook Art Center, Tulsa.

Developing Comprehension Skills

1. What time of day do the first and second stanzas each refer to? How is beauty experienced at each of these times?

2. What is the main idea of the third stanza? What details support that idea?

3. The poem states that beauty can be found in several places. Do you think that one type of beauty is more important or more beautiful than the others? Why or why not?

Reading Poetry

1. **Examining Organization.** A poet can present a new idea in each stanza. How is this true in "Beauty"?

2. **Relating Theme and Mood.** The mood of a poem should fit its theme. What is the theme of this poem? How does the mood of the poem fit the theme?

3. **Contrasting Sensory Images.** A poet can use images that appeal to different senses to set up a contrast. What senses do the images appeal to in the first and second stanzas? How do the stanzas show a contrast?

Writing in Response to Literature

You have read where this poet finds beauty. Write a short poem that describes where you find beauty.

E-Yeh-Shure' (born 1926) is a Native American whose name means "Blue Corn." She grew up in a pueblo, or Indian village, in New Mexico. When she was ten, she wrote a book about her people and their way of life called *I Am a Pueblo Indian Girl.* E-Yeh-Shure', also known as Louise Abeita Chewiwi, graduated from the University of New Mexico and has taught for twenty years on different reservations.

Language and Literature

Vocabulary

Special Vocabularies. As new ideas and inventions come about, familiar words may take on different meanings. For example, *hoop, dribble,* and *center* took on different meanings when the game of basketball was invented. Sometimes you need to look up a word in a dictionary to find the meaning that applies to your reading. Look for a label in the entry that may identify the special uses of the word.

Exercise. Find the following words in the dictionary. Which definitions relate to the subject of a track meet?

finish	track	hurdle	event
heat	dash	swift	mark
shot	relay	lap	pace

Developing Writing Skills

Relating Poetry to Life. The last four poems all gave advice about how to live and enjoy life. Choose the poem in which the message seems most useful to you. Write an explanation of how the theme applies to real life.

Prewriting. Read the poem slowly and then write the theme in your own words. Think about real situations in life where the lesson of the poem can be used. Evaluate the importance of the lesson to daily living.

Drafting. Begin by identifying the poem and stating its theme. Discuss real situations to which this lesson applies. End by evaluating how important and useful the theme is.

Revising and Sharing. Read your paper to a partner. Ask him or her to suggest other situations to which this theme applies. If these ideas support your theme, work them into your paper.

What are your personal feel-ings about worms? Read this poem to see them in a whole new way.

Worms and the Wind

CARL SANDBURG

Worms would rather be worms.
Ask a worm and he says, "Who knows what a worm knows?"
Worms go down and up and over and under.
Worms like tunnels.
When worms talk they talk about the worm world.   5
Worms like it in the dark.
Neither the sun nor the moon interests a worm.
Zigzag worms hate circle worms.
Curve worms never trust square worms.
Worms know what worms want.   10
Slide worms are suspicious of crawl worms.
One worm asks another, "How does your belly drag today?"
The shape of a crooked worm satisfies a crooked worm.
A straight worm says, "Why not be straight?"
Worms tired of crawling begin to slither.   15
Long worms slither farther than short worms.

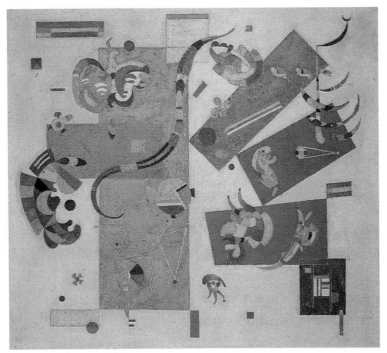

Blue World, 1934, VASILY KANDINSKY. Solomon R. Guggenheim Museum, New York City.
Photograph by Carmelo Guadagno.

Middle-sized worms say, "It is nice to be neither long
    nor short."
Old worms teach young worms to say, "Don't be sorry for me
    unless you have been a worm and lived in worm places   20
    and read worm books."
When worms go to war they dig in, come out and fight,
    dig in again, come out and fight again, dig in again,
    and so on.
Worms underground never hear the wind overground and   25
    sometimes they ask, "What is this wind we hear of?"

Developing Comprehension Skills

1. How do worms feel about being worms?

2. What feeling do worms have about worms that are different from them? In what way are humans sometimes like this?

3. Is this poem funny to you? Why or why not?

4. **Focus on Thinking: Inferring an Attitude.** You can use stated attitudes to infer those that are unstated. Based on the worms' attitudes about other worms, what do you think is their attitude toward the wind?

Reading Poetry

1. **Identifying Theme.** Writers often use animals to present a theme. In this poem, worms talk and act like people. What do you think is the theme of the poem? Why might the poet choose worms to express his ideas?

2. **Examining Repetition.** Poets use repetition to help them make a point. Notice how often the word *worm* is repeated in this poem. How does this emphasize the narrowness of the worms' thinking?

Writing in Response to Literature

This poem is about people as much as it is about worms. Write about a time when you saw people act like the worms do in this poem.

Carl Sandburg (1878–1967), the son of Swedish immigrants, was born in Illinois. He served in the Spanish-American War and worked at many unusual jobs. Sandburg won Pulitzer Prizes for his poetry and for his biography of Abraham Lincoln. His works include a songbook of American folk music.

Other books: *The Sandburg Treasury*
Rainbows Are Made

All That Is Gold

J.R.R. TOLKIEN

Study-Luna, 1983, NEIL ANDERSON. Collection of Glenn C. Janss.

All that is gold does not glitter,
    Not all those who wander are lost;
The old that is strong does not wither,
    Deep roots are not reached by the frost.
From the ashes a fire shall be woken,   5
    A light from the shadows shall spring;
Renewed shall be blade that was broken:
    The crownless again shall be king.

Developing Comprehension Skills

1. How does each of the first four lines contrast the way things appear to be with the way they really are?

2. What unexpected things are predicted in lines 5 and 6?

3. What change is predicted in line 8? Who might the *crownless* be?

4. **Focus on Thinking: Contrasting.** The usual idiom is, "All that glitters is not gold." The poet has reversed this saying. Contrast the meanings of the two sayings.

Reading Poetry

1. **Understanding Theme.** A poem can give more than one message about life. What do you think is the message of the first four lines? What is the message of the last four lines?

2. **Examining Vocabulary.** Poets sometimes link together words that are opposite in meaning and connotation in the same line. Find two examples of this in the poem.

Writing in Response to Literature

The first four lines in this poem each explain a truth of life. Choose any of those lines and write the meaning it holds for you.

© 1973 Douglas R. Gilbert

J.R.R. Tolkien (1892–1973) taught for over thirty years at Oxford University in England, where he specialized in medieval languages and literature. He is best known for his books about the imaginary, dwarflike creatures called *hobbits. The Hobbit,* the first book in the series, has been recorded and made into an animated movie. The poem "All That Is Gold" is from the sequel, *The Fellowship of the Ring,* Book One of *The Lord of the Rings* trilogy.

Describe one small, unexpected thing that has happened to you lately. Discover the meaning this poet finds in just such a minor event.

Dust of Snow

ROBERT FROST

The way a crow
Shook down on me
The dust of snow
From a hemlock tree

Has given my heart
A change of mood
And saved some part
Of a day I had rued.

The Magpie, 1868, CLAUDE MONET. Photograph: Réunion des Musées Nationaux, Paris.

Developing Comprehension Skills

1. What happens in the first stanza?

2. What can you infer about what the speaker's day was like until this event happens?

3. What is the effect of this event on the speaker?

4. How does the speaker react differently to this event than someone else might react?

Reading Poetry

1. **Evaluating a Theme.** A poet can use a simple event to convey a serious message. What is this poem saying about the little things in life? Evaluate the theme by deciding how important the message is for daily living.

2. **Examining Form.** Stanzas of four lines each are called **quatrains.** What is the rhyme pattern in both stanzas? How else is the poem very regular?

Writing in Response to Literature

The poet found meaning in a simple event. Write about a time when a simple event changed your mood or affected your feelings.

Robert Frost (1874–1963) was the only American poet to be awarded four Pulitzer Prizes. He also had the honor of reading his poetry at the inauguration of President John F. Kennedy. Frost's poems are often set in New England. He writes in a simple, conversational style, but his themes are often serious.

Other books: *You Come Too*
A Swinger of Birches

Language and Literature

Vocabulary

Connotations. The thoughts and feelings that some words bring to mind are called **connotations.** The feelings associated with a certain word may be positive (good) or negative (bad). Read these examples.

> Shelly *praised* our activities.   (positive)
> Shelly *gossiped* about our activities.   (negative)

Exercise. Decide whether each sentence gives a positive or negative feeling. Identify the words that give this connotation.

1. The speaker droned on and on in the stifling heat.
2. Jan poured hot gravy on the creamy mashed potatoes.
3. Mom glared at the filthy puppy.
4. The lab is filled with the stench of burning sulfur.
5. A sparkling brook flowed merrily through the meadow.

Developing Writing Skills

Writing a Poem. The poems in this unit present many ideas about life. Think of something you believe in, a truth about life. Write a poem with that message as its theme.

Prewriting. Choose one of your beliefs as your theme. Brainstorm for comparisons or images that will help you present your idea in a new way. Decide what rhyme and rhythm patterns, if any, to use.

Drafting. Write your ideas in lines. Move or add lines and phrases where you feel they fit. Read lines aloud to give yourself ideas of words and phrases to include.

Revising and Sharing. Work with your poem until you feel that each word is the best one in that place. Try to make the ideas and lines flow together. Share your poem by reading it aloud.

Reading Nonfiction

More About Nonfiction

In today's newspaper, you might read such articles as a news story about a tax law, an editorial on an upcoming election, a movie review, and a humorous column about training goldfish. What do these four pieces of writing have in common? They are all types of **nonfiction,** that is, writing about real persons, places, things, and events. How are they different? Each one was written for a different purpose. Each is organized differently to achieve that purpose.

Purposes of Nonfiction

Writers of nonfiction write for a variety of purposes. The four newspaper articles are examples of four purposes of nonfiction. The purpose of the article on the tax law is to inform. The purpose of the editorial is to persuade. The movie review is meant to express an opinion, and the column on goldfish is intended to entertain.

Organization of Nonfiction

The organization of a work of nonfiction depends on both the subject and the writer's purpose. Some works, such as biographies and autobiographies, use chronological or time order. The facts you read about Pelé in Unit 2 were organized in order from his youth to his adulthood.

Other types of nonfiction use logical order. That is, they present ideas in an order that makes sense for that subject and for the writer's purpose. Someone who writes to persuade might present reasons in order from least to most important. A writer might also state an idea and then use examples or details to make the idea clear. Sometimes a writer divides a subject into parts and discusses each part.

Noticing how a work of nonfiction is organized helps you identify the main ideas and the writer's purpose. Some works have chapter titles or headings and subheadings that label main ideas. The paragraphs may have topic sentences that state the main ideas.

Fact and Opinion

Nonfiction often combines both facts and opinions. A fact is a statement that can be proved, such as "Cats have whiskers." An opinion, such as "Cats make better pets than dogs," states a thought that cannot be proved. How facts are used depends on the writer's purpose. Writers use facts both to inform and to support opinions.

The writer's opinion may be evident even when he or she is presenting facts. The writer may show an opinion by presenting certain facts and omitting others. He or she may deliberately choose words with positive or negative connotations. The writer may also make judgments about the facts being presented.

Understanding Nonfiction

When you read nonfiction, ask yourself these questions:

1. What is the writer's purpose? How does he or she feel about the subject? Can I separate the facts from the opinions?

2. How is the work organized? Do titles, headings, and topic sentences give me clues?

3. Can I summarize the main ideas?

What is the wildest ride you have ever taken? How did it make you feel? Compare your feelings to those of a rider in a spacecraft.

From

To Space and Back

SALLY RIDE *with* SUSAN OKIE

The best part of being in space is being weightless. It feels wonderful to be able to float without effort; to slither up, down, and around the inside of the shuttle just like a seal; to be upside down as often as I'm right-side up and have it make no difference. On Earth being upside down feels different because gravity is pulling the blood toward my head. In space I feel exactly the same whether my head is toward the floor or toward the ceiling.

When I'm weightless, some things don't change. My heart beats at about the same rate as it does on Earth. I can still swallow and digest food. My eyes, ears, nose, and taste buds work fine; I see, hear, smell, and taste things just as I do at home.

I *look* a little different, though—all astronauts do. Since the fluid in our bodies is not pulled toward our feet as it is on Earth, more of this fluid stays in our faces and upper bodies. This makes our faces a little fatter and gives us puffy-looking cheeks. We are also about an inch taller while in orbit because in weightlessness our spines are not compressed. Unfortunately (for me, anyway), we shrink back to normal height when we return to Earth.

During my first day in space, I had to learn how to move around. I started out trying to "swim" through the air, but that didn't work at all; air isn't

Astronauts Jeff Hoffman and Rhea Seddon check the effects of weightlessness on a Slinky.
NASA. Photograph: Wm. Morrow & Company, New York City.

dense, the way water is, and I felt silly dog-paddling in the air, going no-where. Before long I discovered that I had to push off from one of the walls if I wanted to get across the room. At first I would push off a little too hard and crash into the opposite wall, but I soon learned to wind my way around with very gentle pushes.

In weightlessness the slightest touch can start an astronaut's body floating across the room or drifting over in a slow-motion somersault. The only way to stop moving is to take hold of something that's anchored in place. Early in my first flight I constantly felt that I was about to lose control, as though I were teetering on a bal-ance beam or tipping over in a canoe.

It's a strange, unsteady feeling that's difficult to describe, but fortunately it goes away. After a day or two I got the knack of staying still and could change clothes without tumbling backward.

Some astronauts are uncomforta-ble while their bodies are adjusting to weightlessness. Almost half of all shuttle crew members are sick for the first day or two. Space sickness is not like the motion sickness caused by bobbing on a boat or riding a roller coaster. It affects each person differ-ently. A space-sick astronaut might feel nauseated or tired or disoriented or just strange. So far we haven't found out exactly what causes space sick-ness or how to cure it.

By the third day of a week-long shuttle flight, though, all the astro-nauts are feeling fine. Weightlessness is pure fun, once everyone gets the hang of it. The two rooms inside the shuttle seem much larger than they do on Earth, because we are not held down to the floor. We can use every corner of a room, including the ceil-ing. While one of us works strapped to a wall, another sits on the ceiling eating peanuts, and a third runs on a treadmill anchored to the floor. On Earth we need a ladder to climb from the mid-deck to the flight deck. In space we never use the ladder—we just float from one room to another.

For the first day or two in space, most astronauts are not as hungry as they would be on the ground. But by the third day, almost everyone has regained a normal appetite, and some—like me—actually eat a little more than usual.

Eating feels the same as it does on Earth. It's just as easy to swallow food and drink water in space, and everything tastes about the same as it would on Earth. Some of the food we carry on the space shuttle is like what we would eat at home: bread, tuna, canned pudding, apples, carrots, peanuts, and cookies. We also have soups, vegetables, and main courses like chicken-and-noodle casserole, but these are freeze-dried and vacuum-packed in individual plastic cartons.

Astronauts eat three meals a day and take turns preparing food. Usually one or two astronauts make a meal for the whole crew.

To fix lunch, here's what an astronaut has to do:

Sally Ride talks to ground control from the cockpit of the space shuttle. NASA.

1. Open the food locker and see what has been planned for lunch. How about hot dogs, macaroni and cheese, peanuts, and lemonade?

2. Get out the food trays. Each crew member has a tray that has slots to hold the cartons in place.

3. Attach the trays to the wall with Velcro so they won't float away.

4. Put one package of peanuts in each food tray.

5. Turn on the oven, open the oven door, and slide in the hot dogs in their sealed foil bags.

6. Fit the cartons of dehydrated macaroni and cheese, one at a time, into the water dispenser. The dis-

penser pushes a needle into the carton and squirts in the right amount of water.

7. Squeeze each macaroni carton to mix in the water, and then place it in the oven too.

8. Use the water dispenser to add water to each plastic carton of powdered lemonade. Slide a straw into each carton and put one lemonade carton in each tray.

9. Remove the hot food from the oven and put a carton of macaroni and a pouch of hot dogs in each tray.

10. Get out bread, butter, catsup, and mustard. Crew members have to make their own hot dog sandwiches; once a sandwich is made, it can't be put down because it would float apart.

11. Call the rest of the crew to "come and get it."

We gather on the mid-deck to enjoy meals together like a family. The engineers at Mission Control try not to call us while we're eating, so we have some time to talk to one another and relax. But we don't look like a family sitting down to lunch on Earth. We

An astronaut's view of Earth from space. NASA. Photograph: Wm. Morrow & Company, New York City.

Joe Allen chases a ball of orange juice with a straw. NASA. Photograph: Wm. Morrow & Company, New York City.

don't eat at a table; our tables are the trays strapped to our legs. We don't sit in chairs. Each of us finds a comfortable spot—maybe floating near the ceiling, or upside down in the middle of the cabin.

We each have a knife and fork, but our most useful pieces of silverware are spoons and scissors. We need scissors to snip open the foil pouches of hot dogs, the packages of peanuts, and the plastic cartons of macaroni. Then we use spoons to get the food to our mouths. Most of our food is deliberately made sticky enough to stay

on a spoon and not float away as we try to eat it. In fact, we can flip our spoons all the way across the cabin and the food won't come off—usually! Sometimes a blob of pudding escapes from a spinning spoon, and we have to catch it before it splatters on a wall.

A few foods, like scrambled eggs, are not quite sticky enough to stay on a spoon. I quickly learned to hold the carton close to my mouth and use my spoon to aim each bite of egg.

We don't have drinking glasses. If we tipped a glass of milk to drink from it, nothing would happen—the weightless milk would stay in the glass. We have to use straws to suck our drinks out of cartons.

We don't use salt shakers either, because grains of salt would float around the cabin instead of falling on the food. To solve this problem, we squeeze liquid salt into the cartons and then mix it with the food.

A peanut butter sandwich is simple to fix on Earth, but in space it takes two astronauts to prepare one. The first time I tried to make a peanut butter sandwich, I held the jar of peanut butter, unscrewed the top, and found I needed another hand. If I let go of either the lid or the jar, it would float away. So I tossed the lid to another astronaut and picked up a knife—but with the jar in one hand and the knife in the other, I had no way to reach for the bread! After that I asked someone else to hold the bread or the jar whenever I wanted a sandwich.

Astronauts can't always resist the fun of playing with weightless food. On one of my flights, we set a cookie floating in the middle of the room and then "flew" an astronaut, with his mouth wide open, across the cabin to capture it. We often share bags of peanuts because it gives us an excuse to play catch, floating peanuts back and forth into each other's mouths. We race to capture spinning carrots and bananas and practice catching spoonfuls of food in our mouths while they twirl in mid-air. These tricks are easy in space, but I don't recommend trying them on Earth.

Developing Comprehension Skills

1. Name three effects of weightlessness on astronauts' bodies.

2. What does Sally Ride say is fun about being weightless?

3. Why must preparation of meals in space be a step-by-step procedure?

4. What details show how astronauts depend on each other in space?

5. **Focus on Thinking: Summarizing.** When you summarize an article, you explain briefly the main ideas in the article. How would you summarize this article?

Reading Nonfiction

1. **Identifying Author's Purpose.** Writers write to inform, persuade, entertain, or to express an opinion. What is the chief purpose of this article? Evaluate how well the article accomplishes its purpose.

2. **Examining the Organization.** Nonfiction articles often state the main idea of a paragraph in a topic sentence. Find five examples of topic sentences in this article.

Study and Research

Outlining. The organization and main points of an article become clear when you outline the article. To outline, find and label each main topic with a Roman numeral. Under the main topic, indent and label subtopics with capital letters. The outline should have this form:

I. (Main topic)
   A. (Subtopic)
   B. (Subtopic)

Using the format above, outline the selection by Sally Ride.

Writing in Response to Literature

What questions do you have about space travel that are not answered in this article? Write a letter to Sally Ride to ask your questions.

What animal fascinates you? Why? Discover what is amazing about some turtles.

From

Spring Comes to the Ocean

JEAN CRAIGHEAD GEORGE

The rites of spring in the ocean are strange to man but none is so wondrous as the journey of the little turtles to the sea.

In February green turtles go to their ancestral beaches through dark seas and over miles of unmarked water. The backs of these great creatures heave above the surface as, swiftly and silently, they find unerringly the sand where they were hatched.

Near the sponges' rock a green turtle paddled her streamlined flippers against the ocean as she swam toward Bimini Island, in the Bahamas. It was time to lay her eggs. Three years had passed since she had last sought this sparkling island. All these years she had lived in mysterious depths by day, and come to the surface at night to hang with her head out of the water and sleep. Now, in the rhythm of the green turtle, she was returning to the little coral island in the sea.

She lumbered ashore unsteadily, because the land felt strange and too firm under her feet. Dragging and pulling herself, she crawled to the top of the beach. She looked about, then went on, thumping laboriously over grass and sticks. She came to a log, heaved over it, and flopped into the sand. Slowly her back flippers dug a deep well in the sand. All day she worked. When night fell, she pushed the sand back again, covering a dozen or so newly laid eggs.

And now the land took over the green turtle's work. The days of sun-

An adult turtle returns to lay her eggs. © Carol Hughes/ Bruce Coleman, Inc., New York City.

shine, warming the sand, changed the fertilized eggs from one cell to many, until one morning each small turtle fought for freedom within its shell.

They hatched two feet down in the sand, all of them on the same day. As they broke out, their shells collapsed, leaving a small room of air for them to breathe. It wasn't much of a room, just big enough for them to wiggle in and move toward the sky. As they wiggled, they pulled the sand down from the ceiling and crawled up on it. In this manner the buried room began to rise, slowly, inch by inch.

Within a week the whole nest chamber of little turtles was almost to the surface, as the young beasts instinctively clawed at the sand above their heads. All week they had struggled against the heavy grains a few minutes at a time. Then they would rest. In this astonishing manner, they moved toward the sun.

One evening the sand behind a log on Bimini Island began to quake and tremble. A small foot, webbed, and covered with scales, broke into the air. A pointed head with beautiful markings and peering eyes pushed out of the sand. A hatchling green turtle had clambered into the world.

He was followed within minutes by about a dozen others. They rested. Some looked about, for now they were to perform a feat so mysterious that men still study and wonder how they accomplish it.

The turtles came out of the ground at twilight, the tide was low, and the waves were breaking far out. The hatchling turtles looked at the sky and the sand. They could not see the water but, alone, untaught, they must find it. And find it quickly, for they are food for almost all the birds and animals that comb the beaches.

The first turtle to move started the wrong way. He walked a few inches, then suddenly swung all the way around and went back. Something had told him his direction was incorrect. A log lay in the direction he must go. He struggled forward and as he did, all the other hatchling turtles moved with him, looking, feeling. They crawled over the log and tumbled onto the sand below. They got up, and plodded up a hill and hurtled through grass on their way to the sea. No man knows what lights or stars or guideposts called them, but in clusters, in single file, in spurts and rests, they crossed the sand, going in the correct direction.

It would not have mattered what the weather—storm or sun, light or

A green turtle hatches from its egg. © David Hughes/ Bruce Coleman, Inc., New York City.

The hatchling is tiny compared to the adult.
© 1976 Robert Ashworth/Photo Researchers, New York City.

shadow—some deep instinct told these little reptiles where to put their feet.

Beyond the grass they moved faster, reaching instinctively to the flat planes of the sea and sky. Some lifted their heads and looked, others just plodded on and on. They went down the long beach. They struck the tidal flat!

The feel of the flat, so different from high dry sand, threw them all into a frenzy of excitement. As if they knew what was coming next, they dropped to their bellies and tried to swim. This got them nowhere. Quickly they got to their feet again, and ran, fell, swam, down the tidal slope. The sea was ahead!

Other things inspired them to hurry—things they had never seen before: the phosphorescent animals that lit the edges of the sea, the wind,

The hatchlings hurry toward the sea. © Carol Hughes/Bruce Coleman, Inc., New York City.

the heave of the breakers far beyond. The hatchling turtles saw and felt and sensed—and ran faster.

The first turtle suddenly felt the foamy wetness of a reaching wave. He tried to throw his feet back and up, flapping them in the manner of a flying bird. The wave slipped away. He ran on. A stronger wave slid over him—and he exploded into his swimming stroke. The wave slipped out. The turtle fell on his belly. He was stranded, but he did not try to walk again. It was as if the touch of the sea had erased the memory of walking.

Flippers back and up, he waited. Another wave rolled in. He swam a few inches only to be dropped on the sand again as the wave swirled out. And again he waited for the sea.

At last he was picked up by a large wave. He was in deep water—and swimming. He needed no practice. He knew exactly what to do—go under the water. Presently he emerged, breathed, and looked around as if to take his bearings. Then out to sea, on and on, until he reached the breakers.

He plunged on toward a piling wave. He had never seen one before or experienced its swirling force, and it seemed that he would be caught up in it and thrown back on the beach. He swam up to it. His body sensed the rhythm of its cresting, for he back-watered until the dynamics were just right. Then he dove. His head went down. Boiling currents carried him to the bottom, where he found gentle eddies to wait in until the wave passed and broke on the shore. Behind the first turtle came the others, plunging into the wave at just the right time. Then they were gone! Their paddling would keep up for a week, a week that would take them to some unknown part of the sea.

The spring of the turtle was done. The hatchlings were on their way to

The hatchling has safely arrived underwater where it feeds on a fanworm. © 1973 Jane Burton/Bruce Coleman, Inc., New York City.

the deep ocean, far from the sands of Bimini. It would be many years before they would return, and then it would be only the females who would come to the island again.

© 1987 Jill Krementz

Jean Craighead George (born 1919) was born into a family of naturalists. She writes both fiction and nonfiction about animals and nature. George often travels to research her subjects firsthand. Her book *Julie of the Wolves* won a Newbery Medal.

Other books: *My Side of the Mountain*
The Talking Earth

Developing Comprehension Skills

1. What main idea about green turtles does the first paragraph introduce?

2. What must baby turtles do immediately after hatching?

3. Why does the mother turtle bury her eggs so deeply?

4. What will happen to the hatchlings if they cannot reach the water quickly?

5. **Focus on Thinking: Evaluating.** You can evaluate how well the facts support an author's attitude. The writer considers the hatchlings' journey to be "wondrous." Do you agree? How well do the facts support this attitude?

Reading Nonfiction

1. **Understanding Organization.** The organization an author chooses depends on the subject matter. Is this article organized in logical or chronological order? How does the article seem like a story?

2. **Finding Opinions.** Nonfiction articles often mix facts and opinions without identifying which are facts and which are opinions. Find three opinions in this article.

Study and Research

Taking Notes. Whether you are writing a report or studying, taking notes will help you identify and remember what is important.

When you take notes, write only the main ideas and important facts. Do not write in full sentences. You may choose to arrange the ideas in an outline later.

Take notes on the selection you just read. Write only the main ideas and important facts.

Writing in Response to Literature

Instinct plays the major role in the turtles' journey. Write about another example of either animal or human instinct that you have observed or read about.

Language and Literature

Vocabulary

Connotations. The connotation, or thoughts and feelings you get from a word, varies with the context of the word. The word *cool,* for example, has several connotations. You get a different feeling about a *cool* breeze than you get from *cool* soup. When you read, think about what feelings the writer is trying to convey by the words chosen.

Exercise. Decide whether Jill's feeling about the street fair is positive or negative in the paragraph below. Find at least one word in each sentence that gives you this feeling.

> Food stalls crowded the sidewalks. The air reeked of grilled sausages and sickly-sweet perfumes. Masses of people elbowed their way from one booth to another. The drum beat of the band was deafening. Jill had to escape to the peace of the quiet park.

Developing Writing Skills

Writing a Short Report. The last two selections you read present scientific facts in an interesting way. Write a short report that presents facts about space travel or animal survival.

Prewriting. List topics that interest you. Choose one and limit the topic to one aspect of the subject, such as one bird's eating habits. Research facts and take notes. Organize the facts into groups for paragraphs. Think of a way to make your subject interesting to the reader.

Drafting. Start with an introductory paragraph that catches the reader's interest. Follow your plan, writing sentences from your notes. End with a concluding paragraph.

Revising and Sharing. Make sure the topic sentence and supporting sentences fit together in each paragraph. Change or rearrange ideas that do not fit. Share your finished report.

What do you admire about
your favorite musician? See
what made thousands of people admire Joe Oliver.

Joe Oliver

The King

STUDS TERKEL *with* MILLY HAWK DANIEL

Captain, captain, I mean you must be cross
Captain, captain, I said you must be cross—
When it's twelve o'clock and you won't knock off.

 The sad-faced, heavy man with the scar over his left eye was singing softly to himself. He was racking up the billiard balls in the pool hall, where he was employed as a handyman.

It was an April evening in Savannah, Georgia. The year 1938.

"That's a nice blues, Joe," a young pool player remarked as he chalked his cue.

"I wrote it," replied the handyman.

"And I'm Napoleon Bonaparte!" the young man chuckled.

"Next thing you'll be tellin' us, Joe, you wrote the tune that's comin' out of that jukebox!"

The man addressed as Joe smiled wistfully.

"I did."

Everybody in the pool hall laughed.

The record whirling in the jukebox was "Sugarfoot Stomp." Benny Goodman's orchestra was playing it.

"Sure," the heavy man continued

seriously, "I called it 'Dippermouth Blues.' They changed the name, but it's my number."

"Tell us about it, Papa Joe, tell us about it!" prodded another, nudging his friend. They were having fun with Joe Oliver, the handyman.

Oliver murmured, almost to himself, " 'Papa Joe'! That's what Louis always called me!"

"Louis who?"

"Louis Armstrong. He was my disciple."

All the patrons guffawed. They slapped their thighs and roared gleefully. This was funnier than the movies.

It was midnight when Joe Oliver, aged fifty-three, put out the lights and locked the front door of the pool hall. He sighed wearily. He was terribly tired. At nine the next morning he'd have to open the place.

As he shuffled down the silent street toward the rooming house where he lived, he thought of "Dippermouth Blues." How he used to blow chorus after chorus on his golden cornet! That was before he lost his teeth, before he became sick. Those were the days when he was remembered.

In his dinky little room he sat down

Joe Oliver as a young man. William Ransom Hogan Jazz Archive, Tulane University, New Orleans.

to write a long letter to his sister, Victoria. Often he corresponded with her. *She* remembered.

> Dear Sister:
> I'm going to tell you something but don't be alarmed. I've got high blood pressure. I am unable to take treatments because it costs three dollars per visit. Now it begins to work on my heart. But I am not one to give up quick. I always feel like I got a chance. Look like every time one door close the Good Lord open another.

All his life Joe Oliver had been optimistic. Ever since he could remember. He laid his pen aside and stared at the blank wall. A smile formed around his mouth as he recalled his early days in New Orleans . . . as he recalled a small, pudgy boy who sat along the curb . . . A brass band was parading by.

When was it? 1895? 1896?

So long ago, yet it seemed only yesterday. . . .

Ten-year-old Joe Oliver skipped merrily from the curbstone into the middle of the street. With lots of other children, he followed the brass band. Grown-ups as well as teen-agers and little boys and girls strutted and danced behind the musicians. They formed what was known as "the second line."

Everybody in New Orleans loved the music of the brass bands. In the late 1890's and early 1900's, there were parades almost every day. Black peo-

Early in his career, Oliver (not pictured here) joined this Onward Jazz Band with leader, Manuel Perez (far left). William Ransom Hogan Jazz Archive, Tulane University, New Orleans.

ple, only one generation removed from slavery, were expressing their new-found freedom in this music. Brass bands played during carnivals, holidays, lodge picnics, and funerals. There was music for just about every occasion.

During a funeral, the band played a slow spiritual on the way to the cemetery. But as they returned home, the musicians struck up a happy tune. This was not meant as disrespect for the dead. No, indeed! Tribute had been paid to the deceased on the way to the burial ground. On the way back, the music was for the living. Life went on. That was what the cornet player meant when he pointed his horn heavenward and the band swung into a rollicking march.

Very few of these musicians were able to read music. As a result, they played as they felt, as the spirit moved them. They took all sorts of liberties with the original compositions. Many of the melodies were derived from Europe, especially France and Spain. It was from these countries that many of the early Louisiana settlers came. The rhythms were derived from West Africa. It was from those shores that the ancestors of the musicians had been kidnaped a couple of centuries before.

Thus a music was played that had never before been heard. It had a swinging feeling, free and easy. The adults and children, who formed "the second line," not only marched to it. They danced. This was jazz, in its beginnings.

Little Joe Oliver, jubilantly dancing behind the last musician, was imitating the leader. He held an imaginary cornet in his hands, fingered imaginary valves, and blew toward the heavens.

"Oh, my!" murmured the pudgy boy to himself. "Won't that be glory when I blow my *real* horn all over town! Some day, they'll call me King, just like Buddy Bolden!"

Bolden was the first of the well-known New Orleans cornetists. Often he led his band down the city streets in the late 1890's. The most powerful cornet player was called King. In those days Buddy Bolden was the unchallenged monarch.

Was it in 1898 that thirteen-year-old Joe Oliver took up a battered cornet and began to teach himself? It came slowly, but he worked very hard at it. He was teaching himself to *read* music! Laboriously he followed the notes on the paper. Reading did not come easily to him.

One day Walter Kenchen, a music teacher, approached Mrs. Oliver. "I'd like to include little Joe in my brass band. Have I your permission?"

"But he's only fourteen!" the boy's mother replied.

"It's a children's band. They're all from the neighborhood," the man explained.

"Is he good enough?" Mrs. Oliver inquired.

Joe interrupted. "Mom! Why, I'm gonna be the Cornet King of New Orleans! Lemme join, lemme join!"

Kenchen patted the boy's shoulder.

"You got a long way to go yet, Joe. You got a lot to learn about that instrument. But you're trying hard, I'll say that for you."

Joe traveled with the children's band to a number of cities in Louisiana. It was during a trip to Baton Rouge that he met with an accident. He was struck over the left eye with a broomstick. It left a scar that was to stay with him for the rest of his life.

In 1900 his mother died. From that time on, his sister Victoria became the person most interested in his welfare. Through the years, she remained faithful to her younger brother.

During the early years of the twentieth century, Joe joined a number of brass bands, blowing the cornet loud and long. One of his first jobs was with the Onward Brass Band, led by Manuel Perez, where Oliver began having his troubles. So accustomed had he become to following the score, the music as written, that when the others improvised, it confused him.

"You'd better go home, Joe," the others said. "You're playing too loud and too bad."

Oliver was depressed. He knew they were right. There is more to jazz than just following what is written on a sheet of paper, note for note. He knew the feeling of freedom must be there.

"You gotta bring out what's inside you," Bunk Johnson told him. Bunk, for whom he pinch-hit a number of times, taught Joe the importance of feeling free, of swinging.

It was during the first decade of the new century that Oliver worked as a butler. The income from brass-band playing was not enough to support a man and his family. Joe had just

Uptown Sunday Night Session, 1981, ROMARE BEARDEN. Photograph: Cordier & Eckstrom, Inc., New York City.

become a married man; his wife, Stella, had a daughter by a previous marriage.

Joe Oliver was a good butler, but he was a far better cornet player. Continually he practiced; continually he listened to the others. The two cornetists he envied and feared the most were Manuel Perez and Freddie Keppard. They seemed so sure of themselves. One day, he promised himself, he would outdo them.

He practiced daily. Soon others commented on his improvement.

"That Joe Oliver, he's got plenty fire in his horn."

"An' plenty lung power, too," remarked another.

More often than not, he had to hire

someone to "buttle" in his place. The Eagle Brass Band called for his services. So did the Olympia Band. So did the Magnolia Band and the Original Superior Orchestra.

The huge figure of the 250-pound cornetist became a familiar sight in the streets of New Orleans with one or another of the brass bands. Just as he, a few years back, had followed and mimicked Buddy Bolden, now he had his followers among the small boys. One of them was a skinny little lad from the rough neighborhood known as Back o' Town. His name was Louis Armstrong.

Still Oliver was not satisfied. People were referring to Freddie Keppard as the King. When they were not praising Keppard, they had kind words for Manuel Perez.

"I'm better than both of 'em," mumbled Oliver. "I can blow the horn louder and longer and sweeter."

One night he proved it in a most dramatic way.

It was 1910. Joe Oliver was now working full time as a musician. He was the cornetist at the Abadie Cabaret in Storeyville, the city's night-life district. Keppard was the big attrac-

tion at Pete Lala's, a block away. Perez starred at another club on the same street.

Joe was restlessly fingering the valves of his battered horn. Often he changed cornets, he blew so hard. He was listening to patrons at some of the tables; they were murmuring in tones of awe: "Keppard and Perez, they're the Kings!"

Suddenly Oliver addressed the piano player, Richard M. Jones.

"Beat it out in B flat."

"What?" asked the bewildered pianist. It was the band's rest period.

"Just play the blues," commanded Oliver.

As Jones picked out chords on the piano, Joe lifted the cornet to his lips and blew. He walked out into the street, stood on the corner, and blew the blues, loud, clear, and true. He pointed his horn toward Lala's Cafe where Keppard was listening. Then he directed his blast at the nightclub of the amazed Perez.

People rushed out onto the street. They had never heard such a horn before! They gathered from all quarters—homes, stores, and cabarets.

The proud Oliver removed his lips

from the mouthpiece of the horn and shouted at the top of his voice:

"There! That'll show 'em who's King!"

He resumed the blues and strolled back into the Abadie Cabaret. The crowds followed him in.

It was Joe Oliver's coronation night. From that moment on, he was proclaimed "King."

His most ardent fan and hero worshiper was little Louis Armstrong, a fourteen-year-old, who had just been released from an orphanage. The big man returned the boy's feelings. He sensed in Louis the musician who would one day take his place. Though he had little patience with others, Joe Oliver always had time for young Armstrong. Constantly he offered him advice, encouraged him, gave him jobs. He even presented him with a cornet.

Oliver had always loved children. Though he had a little stepdaughter, Ruby, he had dreamed of a son of his own. In Louis Armstrong, he saw the son that might have been his. "Papa Joe," Louis called him. He had good reason.

By 1917 there was no band in New Orleans that could stand up against

Louis Armstrong, who called Oliver "Papa Joe," became one of the most famous jazz musicians.
Copyright © Dennis Stock/Magnum Photos, Inc., New York City.

the one led by Oliver and Kid Ory, the trombonist. Often this formidable team played the blues on the back of a wagon. It was parked on a street corner, advertising a forthcoming lodge celebration or night-club engagement. If some other group of musicians were unfortunate enough to chance along the same street, advertising in a similar manner, the Oliver-Ory band "blew it down" with the greatest of ease.

It was a humiliating experience for the defeated band. Oliver always

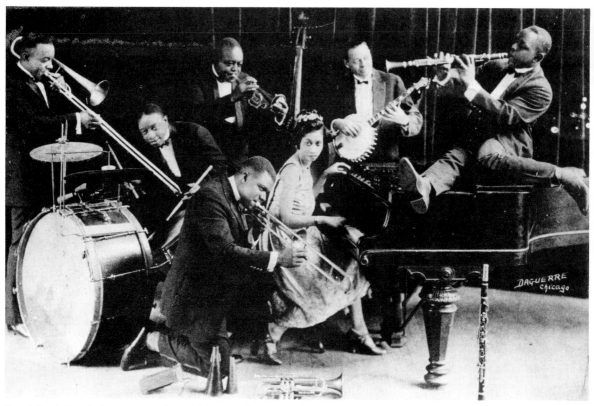

King Oliver's Creole Jazz Band. (left to right) Honoré Dutrey, Baby Dodds, King Oliver, Louis Armstrong (kneeling), Armstrong's future wife, Lillian, Bill Johnson, and Johnny Dodds. Historical Pictures Service, Chicago.

sought to spare his protégé—Armstrong—this disgrace.

"Whenever you come by, Little Louis, with a band of your own," he advised him, "stand up in the wagon. That way I'll see you an' won't blow against you."

It was in 1918 that King Oliver said farewell to New Orleans. Chicago was bidding for his services. Storeyville had been closed down the previous year by the Navy Department. Several sailors had become involved in tavern brawls in this district. As a result of the federal action, many jazz musicians were deprived of jobs. Chicago was a city with a fast-growing black population. There was much work to be found in its great stockyards and steel mills. Musicians were needed for this vast audience. . . .

Oliver was immediately accepted

in Chicago as a major jazz figure. . . .

In 1922 he was in his prime as a musician. At Lincoln Gardens, formerly Royal Gardens, he established one of the most exciting bands in the history of jazz. It made a greater impact on young musicians than any other band of its time. Already he had Johnny Dodds, one of the warmest of New Orleans clarinetists; Baby Dodds, Johnny's brother, sat at the drums; a brilliant young woman, Lil Hardin, was at the piano; Honoré Dutrey played the trombone. But the most important musician was yet to come.

Oliver sent a telegram to New Orleans: JOIN ME IN CHICAGO AT LINCOLN GARDENS. It was addressed to Louis Armstrong.

It was a hot July evening in 1922 when Louis timidly edged his way into the club. He had just come off the train. The huge leader, on seeing the young man, cried out: "Here he is!" He sprang from the bandstand, embraced Louis and jabbered rapidly: "Where you been? We been waiting for you! Gee, son, I'm really proud of you!"

With Oliver and Armstrong at the two cornets, the Creole Jazz Band became the talk of the country. Lincoln Gardens was crowded each night with excited patrons. Many young white Chicagoans, who later were to find their own way as famous jazz musicians, caught much of their fire from this band. They listened; they cheered; they learned.

Offers from New York continued to come in. And during the spring of 1927 Joe Oliver accepted one of them. It came from New York's Savoy Ball Room, the home of some of the finest black jazz bands.

Perhaps his prime reason for going was economic. Business had begun to slip.

It was a slow, cheap day coach that carried King and his men to New York. Beside his seat was a bucket of red beans and rice his wife had prepared. Arriving weary, worn, and shabbily dressed, he apologized to the Savoy audience. The patrons accepted him graciously. After all, he was King Oliver. He was one of the respected fathers of jazz. He was the great Armstrong's "Papa Joe." They didn't care how he was dressed. They liked his music.

But it was too late.

The style Joe Oliver had helped establish had been brought East by

Louis Armstrong, 1957, ROBERT GALSTER. Copyright © 1957 Studs Terkel. By permission of Harper and Row Publishers, New York City.

other musicians. What he was playing was no longer new. Jazz was becoming more sophisticated now. There were younger men with newer styles.

Nonetheless he was invited to play at the Cotton Club, one of Harlem's most respected cafes. He rejected the offer. The terms did not satisfy him. Joe Oliver had always been a proud man. He had set certain standards for himself and his musicians. He would accept nothing less.

Perhaps he made a fatal mistake in turning down this offer. Yet King Oliver's "mistake" provided a golden opportunity for another musician, who was to become jazz's most creative

artist. In place of Oliver's Creole Jazz Band, the Cotton Club hired a band led by a handsome young pianist from Washington—Duke Ellington.

From here on, King Oliver's fortunes were on the downgrade. Harshness and tragedy were setting in.

His teeth were causing him more discomfort than ever. Soon he had to have them all removed. It became more and more difficult for him to blow the cornet. Jobs became scarcer. His pockets that once were full

King Oliver, 1957, ROBERT GALSTER. Copyright © 1957 Studs Terkel. By permission of Harper and Row Publishers, New York City.

of money were now empty. What hurt most of all was that people were beginning to forget. . . .

King Oliver died April 8, 1938. His body was shipped north in a cheap wooden box and buried in New York.

"It was a broken heart that killed him," said Louis Armstrong.

Yet Joe Oliver had lived a richer, fuller life than most men. Many musicians appeared at his funeral. They remembered the King. They remembered his fire, his endurance, his warmth. "Papa Joe" was one of the earliest giants of jazz.

As long as the blues is played by any young man with a horn, King Oliver will be remembered.

© 1985 Layle Silbert

Studs Terkel (born 1912) is a radio and television commentator, writer, interviewer, and lecturer. As a writer, he is best known for his collections of interviews with ordinary people. Terkel has also written biographies, an autobiography, and a play. This selection about Joe Oliver comes from *Giants of Jazz,* a collection of biographies of jazz musicians, which Terkel wrote with Millie Hawk Daniel, a New York writer and editor.

Developing Comprehension Skills

1. Why do the pool players laugh at Joe?

2. What was young Joe Oliver's goal? What problems did he have when he began learning?

3. Did playing in Chicago improve or damage Joe's reputation? Why?

4. Describe the relationship between Louis Armstrong and Joe Oliver.

5. How do you think the authors feel about Joe Oliver? Evaluate how their feelings affect the way they describe his life.

6. **Focus on Thinking: Recognizing Causes.** Usually there are several causes for gains or losses in popularity. Give the causes of Joe's loss of popularity in the jazz world.

Reading Nonfiction

1. **Examining Organization.** Some biographical essays are not in straight chronological order. How does the order in this article vary from time order? Why do you think the authors chose to vary the order?

2. **Examining the Author's Purpose.** Authors may choose to inform you about more than one topic in an article. What two topics does this article tell you about?

3. **Recognizing Mood Changes.** The mood of an article can change to reflect the content. What is the mood at the beginning of this article? How does the mood change in the middle and again at the end?

Speaking and Listening

Listening for Feelings. Just as writers try to convey moods and feelings in literature, musicians convey moods and feelings in music.

Listen to a jazz recording by Joe Oliver, Duke Ellington, Louis Armstrong, or Benny Goodman. Write the feelings each section of the music gives you. Compare your feelings with those of your classmates.

Writing in Response to Literature

Joe Oliver learned "You gotta bring out what's inside you." Write about something you do that brings out the "real" you.

Describe a funny or annoying experience you've had with an animal. Then read about the experiences this author has had with dogs she has known.

Dogs That Have Known Me

JEAN KERR

I never meant to say anything about this, but the fact is that I have never met a dog that didn't have it in for me. You take Kelly, for instance. He's a wire-haired fox terrier and he's had us for three years now. I wouldn't say that he was terribly handsome, but he does have a very nice smile. What he *doesn't* have is any sense of fitness. All the other dogs in the neighborhood spend their afternoons yapping at each other's heels or chasing cats. Kelly spends his whole day, every day, chasing swans on the millpond.

I don't actually worry, because he will never catch one. For one thing, he can't swim. Instead of settling for a simple dog-paddle like everybody else, he has to show off and try some complicated overhand stroke, with the result that he always sinks and has to be fished out. Naturally, people talk, and I never take him for a walk that somebody doesn't point him out and say, "There's that crazy dog that chases swans."

Another thing about that dog is that he absolutely refuses to put himself in the other fellow's position. We had a pencil sharpener in the kitchen and Kelly used to enjoy an occasional munch on the plastic cover. As long as it was just a nip now and then, I didn't mind. But one day he simply lost his head and ate the whole thing. Then I had to buy a new one, and of course I put it up high out of Kelly's reach. Well, the scenes we were treated to—and the sulking! In fact, ever since, he has been eating things I know he doesn't like, just to get even.

I don't mean things like socks and mittens and paper napkins, which of course are delicious. Lately he's been eating plastic airplanes, suede brushes, and light bulbs. Well, if he wants to sit under the piano and make low and loving growls over a suede brush just to show me, okay. But frankly I think he's lowering himself. I have even dropped old, dilapidated bedroom slippers here and there behind the furniture, hoping to tempt him. But the fact is, that dog wouldn't touch a bedroom slipper if he was starving.

Although we knew that, as a gourmet, he was a washout, we did keep saying one thing about Kelly. We kept saying, "He's a good little old watchdog." Heaven knows why we thought so, except that he barks at the drop of a soufflé. In fact, when he's in the basement a stiff toothbrush on the third floor is enough to set him off into a concerto of deep, murderous growls followed by loud hysterical yappings.

I used to take real pleasure in imagining the chagrin of some poor intruder who'd bring that cacophony upon himself. Last month we had an intruder. He got in the porch window and took twenty-two dollars and my wristwatch while Kelly, that good little old watchdog, was as silent as a cathedral. But that's the way it's been.

The first dog I remember well was a large black-and-white mutt that was part German shepherd, part English sheep dog, and part collie—the wrong part in each case. With what strikes me now as unforgivable whimsy, we called him Ladadog, from the title by Albert Payson Terhune.

He was a splendid dog in many respects, but, in the last analysis, I'm afraid he was a bit of a social climber. He used to pretend to be just crazy about us. I mean, if you just left the room to comb your hair he would greet you on your return with passionate lickings, pawings, and convulsive tail-waggings. And a longer separation—let's say you had to go out on the front porch to pick up the mail—would set Ladadog off into such a demonstration of rapture and thanksgiving that we used to worry for his heart.

However, all this mawkish, slobbering sentiment disappeared the moment he stepped over the thresh-

Kleberg, 1984, JAMIE WYETH. Oil on canvas, 30⅜" × 42⅜". Daniel J. Terra Collection, Terra Museum of American Art, Chicago.

old. I remembered we kids used to spot him on our way home from school, chasing around the Parkers' lawn with a cocker friend of his, and we'd rush over to him with happy squeals of "Laddy, oleboy, oleboy, oleboy," and Ladadog would just stand there looking slightly pained and distinctly cool. It wasn't that he cut us dead. He nodded, but it was with the remote air of a celebrity at a party saying, "Of course I remember you, and how's Ed?"

We kept making excuses for him and even worked out an elaborate explanation for his behavior. We decided that Ladadog didn't see very well, that he could recognize us only by smell and that he couldn't smell very well in the open air. However, the day came when my mother met Ladadog downtown. She was wearing her new brown coat with the beaver collar, and, lo and behold, Ladadog greeted her with joy and rapture. After that we just had to face the truth—that dog was a snob.

He also had other peculiarities. For

instance, he saved lettuce. He used to beg for lettuce and then he would store it away in the cellar behind the coal-bin. I don't know whether he was saving up to make a salad or what, but every so often we'd have to clean away a small, soggy lump of decayed vegetation.

And every time the phone rang he would run from wherever he was and sit there beside the phone chair, his tail thumping and his ears bristling, until you'd make some sort of an announcement like "It's just the repairman" or "Eileen, it's for you." Then he would immediately disappear. Clearly, this dog had put a call in to someone, but we never did figure out who.

Come to think of it, the dog that gave us the most trouble was a beagle named Murphy. As far as I'm concerned, the first thing he did wrong was to turn into a beagle. I had seen him bouncing around in the excelsior of a pet-shop window, and I went in and asked the man, "How much is that adorable fox terrier in the window?" Did he say, "That adorable fox terrier is a beagle?" No, he said, "Ten dollars, lady." Now, I don't mean to say one word against beagles. They

have rights just like other people. But it is a bit of a shock when you bring home a small ball of fluff in a shoebox, and three weeks later it's as long as the sofa.

Murphy was the first dog I ever trained personally, and I was delighted at the alacrity with which he took to the newspaper. It was sometime later that we discovered, to our horror, that—like so many dogs—he had grasped the letter but not the spirit of the thing. Until the very end of his days he felt a real sense of obligation whenever he saw a newspaper—*any* newspaper—and it didn't matter where it was.

He had another habit that used to leave us open to a certain amount of criticism from our friends, who were not dogophiles. He never climbed up on beds or chairs or sofas. But he always sat on top of the piano. In the beginning we used to try to pull him off of there. But after a few noisy scuffles in which he knocked a picture off the wall, scratched the piano, and smashed a lamp, we just gave in— only to discover that, left to his own devices, he hopped up and down as delicately as a ballet dancer. We became quite accustomed to it, but at parties at our house it was not unusual to hear a guest remark, "I don't *know,* but I think I see a big dog on the piano."

It's not just our own dogs that bother me. The dogs I meet at parties are even worse. I don't know what I've got that attracts them; it just doesn't bear thought. My husband swears I rub chopped meat on my ankles. But at every party it's the same thing. I am sitting in happy conviviality with a group in front of the fire when all of a sudden the large mutt of my host appears in the archway. Then without a single bark of warning, he hurls himself upon me. My stockings are torn before he finally settles down peacefully in the lap of my new black dress. I blow out such quantities of hair as I haven't swal-

lowed and glance at my host, expecting to be rescued. He murmurs, "Isn't that wonderful? You know, Brucie is usually so distant with strangers."

At a dinner party in Long Island last week, after I had been mugged by a large sheep dog, I announced quite piteously, "Oh dear, he seems to have swallowed one of my earrings." The hostess looked really distressed for a moment, until she examined the remaining earring. Then she said, "Oh, I think it will be all right. It's small and it's round."

Nowadays if I go anywhere I just ask if they have a dog. If they do, I say, "Maybe I'd better keep away from him—I have this bad allergy." This does not tend to endear me to my hostess. But it is safer. It really is.

Jean Kerr (born 1923) is a writer of plays, essays, and articles. She writes with humor about the everyday problems of suburban people. A number of her works have been made into movies. "Dogs That Have Known Me" comes from Kerr's novel *Please Don't Eat the Daisies,* which was made into a television series.

Developing Comprehension Skills

1. What is the main idea of this article?

2. Identify two problems each that Kelly, Ladadog, and Murphy gave the narrator.

3. Give two conclusions the author draws about Ladadog's behavior.

4. How do the dogs at parties prove the author's point more strongly than the dogs she owned?

5. **Focus on Thinking: Evaluating a Theme.** The author states that she has never known a dog that didn't have it in for her. How does she support this theme? Do you think that this statement is true? Why or why not?

Reading Nonfiction

1. **Identifying an Author's Purpose.** A writer's purpose becomes clear from the facts he or she chooses to present. What is the purpose of this article? How might the facts chosen have been different if the purpose were different?

2. **Evaluating Mood.** You can evaluate how well the mood of an article reflects its purpose. What is the mood of this article? How well does that mood support the purpose?

3. **Recognizing Humor.** Humor can come from personification. For example, the author says of Ladadog, "he was a bit of a social climber." Find two more examples of this type of humor.

Critical Thinking

Separating Fact and Opinion. **Facts** are statements that can be proved to be true. **Opinions** are statements that tell a person's beliefs. Find two facts and two opinions in this article. Explain why each is a fact or an opinion.

Writing in Response to Literature

Do you think the author of this article likes or dislikes dogs? Write to explain your opinion.

Language and Literature

Vocabulary

Combining Methods to Gain Meaning. As you read, practice using all the methods you have learned to figure out the meanings of words. Use word parts, context clues, dictionary definitions, and connotations of the words.

Exercise. Combine all the methods you have learned to define the underlined words or phrases below. Tell which method you use in each case.

Today seemed <u>uneventful</u> for policeman Murray, not <u>chaotic</u> like yesterday. His only problem had been a confused, <u>bewildered</u> group of citizens <u>sauntering</u> down the middle of the street. For this <u>misdemeanor</u>, Murray considered giving them a ticket. He decided against a <u>citation</u> when one man explained that because they were <u>ornithologists</u>, they always looked up. Murray told them to keep their minds off the birds or they would be <u>up a tree</u>.

Developing Writing Skills

Writing a Review. You have read many types of literature in this book. Write a review of one of your favorite selections.

Prewriting. Look through the table of contents of this book and choose the selection you will review. Skim the selection. Evaluate the selection using the suggestions on pages 404–405. Find examples to support your judgments.

Drafting. Write specific statements as you evaluate the selection. Support your statements with examples. Follow the order you planned and summarize your opinion at the end.

Revising and Sharing. Make sure your evaluations are specific. Combine your review with your classmates' into a booklet or newspaper.

Unit 4 *R*eview

Using Your Skills in Reading Fiction

Which of these sentences states a theme of "Aaron's Gift"?

1. You cannot hide from a guilty conscience.
2. Freedom is more precious than possessions.
3. Save today because you do not know what tomorrow will bring.

State one more message you learned from the story.

Using Your Skills in Reading Poetry

Read the poem below called "Spring" by Richard Hovey. What is the theme? Describe the mood of the poem. Tell one image that the poem suggests to you.

> I said in my heart, "I am sick of four walls and a ceiling.
> I have need of the sky.
> I have business with the grass.
> I will up and get me away where the hawk is wheeling,
> Lone and high,
> And the slow clouds go by. . . ."

Using Your Skills in Reading Nonfiction

Read this excerpt from "Snowy Owls" by Patricia Hunt. What is the author's purpose? Find one fact and one opinion.

> The snowy owl stands 27 inches tall with a wingspread of 45 to more than 60 inches wide. When it takes off in flight, with its large wings fully spread apart, it is a breathtaking sight.

Using Your Comprehension Skills

Evaluate the nonfiction article from *Spring Comes to the Ocean* by answering the questions below.

1. What is the author's purpose? How well does the article achieve that purpose?

2. How important are the author's opinions to this article?

3. What is the theme of the article? How important do you feel the theme is?

4. Is the article enjoyable? Why or why not?

Using Your Vocabulary Skills

Define *swamp* as it is used each time below. Tell whether each underlined word has a positive, negative, or neutral connotation.

> Even in the heavy fog, Rosa could see that thick <u>slime</u> covered the pond. Toward the edge of the swamp, a large snake <u>slid</u> through the <u>ooze</u>. Suddenly a branch fell and <u>threatened</u> to swamp Rosa's canoe. <u>Bravely</u>, Rosa grasped the branch and sent it flying through the mist.

Using Your Writing Skills

Follow directions to complete one writing assignment below.

1. Tell how any two characters in this unit learn about life in similar ways.

2. Write a poem or a narrative about a time in which you learned a very important lesson about life.

Handbook
for Reading
and Writing

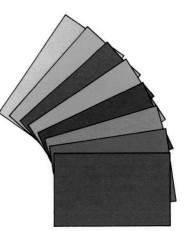

Act. An act is a section of a play. Acts in plays are like chapters in books. Each act may be divided further into scenes. *The Great Quillow* (page 98) is a play with one act.

See *Scene*, *Drama*.

Alliteration. The repeating of consonant sounds at the beginnings of words is called alliteration. Alliteration can add a musical beat to a work. Notice the alliteration in these lines of poetry.

He clasps the crag with crooked hands;
Close to the sun in lonely lands . . .
("The Eagle" by Alfred Tennyson)

For more about alliteration, see page 219.

Anecdote. An anecdote is a short, entertaining story, usually about a person. It is included in a larger work to amuse or make a point.

Autobiography. An autobiography is a factual account of a real person's life, written by that person. An autobiography is usually written from the first-person point of view. Although it is nonfiction, an autobiography has some elements of fiction such as setting, characters, plot, and conflict. "What America Means to Me" (page 234) is an example of autobiography.

For more about autobiography, see pages 232–233 and 254. See also *Point of View*.

Biography. A biography is a type of nonfiction in which a writer gives a factual account of someone else's life. It may tell about someone's whole life or a part of the person's life. A biography tells the important events in a person's life from the third-person point of view. A biography has elements of fiction such as characters, setting, plot, and conflict. "Pelé: The King of Soccer" (page 256) is a biography.

For more about biography, see pages 232–233 and 263. See also *Point of View*.

Cast of Characters. A list of the names of all the characters who will take part in a play, or drama, is called the cast of characters. The list is given at the beginning of most printed plays. The characters are usually listed in the order they appear in the play. The list sometimes includes phrases to identify each character. For an example of a cast of characters, see the first page of *The Great Quillow* (page 98).

For more about cast of characters, see page 96.

Character. Each person or animal in a work of literature is called a character. A work usually centers around one or more important characters who are called *main characters*. All the other characters are *minor characters*. The minor characters help to keep the plot moving forward. In "Ghost of the Lagoon" (page 143), Mako is the main character. His mother and grandfather are minor characters.

For more about character, see pages 19, 34, 42, 51, 166, 182, 210, 299, 308, 326, 353, 388–389, and 455. See also *Characterization*.

Characterization. The way a writer creates and develops a character's personality is called characterization. A writer creates a character through the character's words and actions, through description of the character, and through what other characters say about that character.

For more about characterization, see pages 51, 166, 210, 278–279, 299, 353, 388–389, and 455.

Climax. The climax, or turning point, is the high point of interest in the plot of a story. It is the moment when the outcome of the story becomes clear. The climax usually involves an important discovery, decision, or event. In "The Wise Old Woman" (page 20), for example,

the climax comes when the farmer tells the young lord that his aged mother is the one who saved the village.

For more about climax, see pages 4, 129, and 155. See also *Plot*.

Conflict. Conflict is a struggle between opposing forces. The struggle that a character faces creates the conflict that is important to every story or play. This conflict may be external or internal. An *external conflict* is a struggle between a character and an outside force. The outside force could be another character, or society, or a force in nature such as weather. An *internal conflict* is a struggle within a character's mind. The character may have to make a decision or deal with conflicting feelings. In *Shadow of a Bull* (page 445), for example, the external conflict is between Manolo and the bull. Manolo has an internal conflict when he struggles with his fear.

For more about conflict, see pages 128–129 and 210.

Description. In a description, a writer gives details that help the reader imagine a character, setting, or action. Often the details create a visual picture, as below.

> The sad-faced, heavy man with the scar over his left eye was singing softly to himself.
> ("Joe Oliver: The King," page 518)

A description may also give details of sound, smell, touch, or taste. Sometimes a description includes details about the actions or attitudes of a character.

For more about description, see pages 155 and 182.

Dialect.   A form of language that is spoken in a certain place or among a certain group of people is called a dialect. Notice the dialect in the following lines.

> "Verra good," said the Scotsman. "I'll give her to ye, lassie, if ye can save her life."
> ("A Rare Provider," page 412)

Dialogue.   Conversations between characters in literature is called dialogue. In drama, the playwright relies almost entirely on dialogue to develop the characters and to tell the story. No quotation marks are used for dialogue in plays. In other types of writing, the exact words are set off by quotation marks.

For more about dialogue, see pages 96–97, 388–389, 396, and 397.

Drama.   A story that is meant to be acted out for an audience is called drama. In a drama, or play, the plot of the story is told through the words and actions of the characters. When drama is performed on stage, actors and actresses play the parts of the characters. The setting is made clear through the scenery, costumes, and dialogue.

A drama is made up of one or more acts. Each act may be divided further into scenes. A written drama usually begins with a cast of characters and often includes stage directions.

For more about drama, see pages 96–97 and 388–389. See also *Act, Scene, Cast of Characters*, and *Stage Directions*.

External Conflict.   See *Conflict*.

Fantasy.   A fantasy is a story that is set in an imaginary, unreal world. *Sweetwater* (page 354), for example, is a fantasy.

Fiction.   Fiction is a form of literature that tells about imaginary people, places, or events. Some stories come totally from the writer's imagination. Other stories are based partly on facts or real events. Short stories, novels, and folk tales are kinds of fiction. An example of fiction is "Duke Pishposh of Pash" (page 10).

For more about fiction, see pages 4–5.

Figurative Language.   Figurative language is language that expresses ideas beyond the exact meanings of the words. A writer may use figurative language to create an image or to describe familiar things in new ways. Simile, metaphor, and personification are three kinds of figurative language. In the lines of poetry below, notice the image created by figurative language.

When the hurricane unfolds
Its fierce accordion of winds . . .
("The Hurricane," page 221)

For more about figurative language, see pages 212–213. See also *Metaphor*, *Personification*, and *Simile*.

Folk Tale. A folk tale is a simple story about human or animal characters that has been handed down by word of mouth from one generation to the next generation. Folk tales are usually set in the distant past. They are told in every country around the world. Some kinds of folk tales are fairy tales and legends. "The Wise Old Woman" (page 20) is an example of a folk tale.

For more about folk tales, see pages 5, 19, 29, 65, and 78. See also *Legend* and *Oral Tradition*.

Form. The form of a poem refers to its shape, that is, the way it looks on the page. The way the words and the lines are arranged is the form of the poem.

For more about form, see pages 80, 378, 384, 490, and 500.

Humor. The quality that makes writing funny or amusing to the reader is called humor. A writer can make a work funny by exaggerating or by narrating foolish events in a serious way. For example, in "Dear Miss Veloshin," the way Victoria exaggerates Miss Veloshin's cheerfulness makes the story funny (page 456).

For more about humor, see page 374.

Imagery. Description that makes an object or experience so real that a reader can easily imagine it is called imagery. Writers use details to help the reader see, feel, smell, hear, and/or taste the things they describe. Notice how the details in these lines appeal to the senses.

The air stinging your nose, sucking
    your mouth,
The wind scamping you along the
    sidewalk,
The leaves crunching under your
    feet . . .
("Nobody Gives It to You," page 484)

For more about imagery, see pages 212, 371, and 376.

Internal Conflict. See *Conflict*.

Legend. A folk tale that explains something that really happened or tells about someone who really lived is called a legend. Legends often mix fact and fiction. They reflect the values of the people in the stories. "The Stone Dog" (page 30) is a legend from Puerto Rico.

For more about legend, see page 5. See also *Folk Tale*.

Metaphor. Metaphor is a comparison of two unlike things that have something in common. Unlike a simile, a metaphor does not use the words *like* or *as*. Instead, a metaphor says that one thing is another, as in this example.

> Fame is a bee
>   It has a song—
> It has a sting—
>   Ah, too, it has a wing.
> ("Fame Is a Bee" by Emily Dickinson)

Sometimes a writer extends a metaphor to show many likenesses.

For more about metaphor, see pages 212–213, 378, and 490. See also *Simile* and *Figurative Language*.

Mood. Mood is the feeling the writer wants the reader to get from a work of literature. Words are carefully chosen by a writer to create this special feeling. For example, in the poem "Cynthia in the Snow" (page 218), the words *flitters-twitters*, *laughs*, and *lovely* suggest a light and happy mood. A writer may also use setting, dialogue, imagery, actions, and details to help create mood.

For more about mood, see pages 403, 443, 464, and 485.

Motive. The reason a character does something or acts in a certain way is called a motive. In "The Cat and the Golden Egg" (page 52), Quickset's motive for tricking Master Grubble is to provide groceries for Dame Agnes.

Narrative Poetry. Narrative poetry is poetry that tells a story. Like a story, it has characters, setting, and plot. As a poem, it may have rhyme, rhythm, and other elements of poetry. Both "The Walrus and the Carpenter" (page 82) and "The Cremation of Sam McGee" (page 88) are examples of narrative poems.

For more about narrative poetry, see page 81.

Narrator. The narrator is the teller of the story. The narrator may be a character in the story or an outside voice created by the writer. The narrator in "Dear Miss Veloshin" (page 456), for example, is the main character, Victoria.

See also *Point of View*.

Nonfiction. Writing that tells about real people, places, and events is called nonfiction. Nonfiction presents both facts and opinions. The purpose of nonfiction may be to inform, to persuade, to express an opinion, or to entertain. Nonfiction may have elements found in fiction and poetry. For example, biographies have characters and settings. Biographies, autobiographies, essays, and articles are kinds of nonfiction.

For more about nonfiction, see pages

232–233, 502–503, and 530. See also *Autobiography* and *Biography*.

Novel. A novel is a work of fiction that is longer and more complex than a short story. In a novel, setting, character, conflict, and plot are developed in detail.

Onomatopoeia. The use of words to imitate sounds is called onomatopoeia. *Bang, pop, hiss,* and *sizzle* are examples of onomatopoeia.

For more about onomatopoeia, see page 219.

Oral Tradition. The passing of stories or poems by word of mouth from one generation to the next generation is called oral tradition. Folk tales come from oral tradition.

For more about oral tradition, see page 5. See also *Folk Tale.*

Personification. The giving of human qualities to an animal, object, or idea is called personification. For example, Quickset the cat is personified in "The Cat and the Golden Egg" (page 52).

For more about personification, see pages 213, 219, 221, 226, and 386.

Play. See *Drama.*

Plot. The plot is the series of events in a story. The plot usually centers around a conflict—a problem or struggle faced by the main character. The action that the characters take to solve the problem builds toward the climax, or turning point in the story. At this point, or shortly after, the problem is solved and the story ends.

For more about plot, see pages 4–5, 19, 34, 142, and 308. See also *Climax* and *Conflict.*

Poetry. Poetry is a type of literature that expresses ideas and feelings in compact, imaginative, and musical language. The words in poetry are arranged in lines that may or may not be grouped into stanzas. Poems may contain the elements of rhyme, rhythm, figurative language, and sensory images.

For more about poetry, see pages 80–81, 212–213, 230, 370–371, and 482–483. See also *Imagery, Figurative Language, Rhyme, Rhythm, Form,* and *Stanza.*

Point of View. Point of view refers to how a writer chooses to narrate a story. Works of literature may be told from a first-person point of view or a third-person point of view.

In a work told from the first-person point of view, the narrator is a character in the story. He or she uses the first-person pronouns *I* and *we.* "Ghost Town" (page 300) is told from a first-person point of view.

In a work of literature told from the third-person point of view, the narrator is usually outside of the story. The narrator uses the third-person pronouns *he* and *she*. "Dragon, Dragon" (page 66) is told from a third-person point of view.

For more about point of view, see pages 233, 254, 308, and 464. See also *Narrator*.

Repetition. Repetition is the method of using a sound, word, phrase, or line two or more times. For example, the lines repeated in "The Old Gumbie Cat" (page 223) give the poem a musical quality.

Rhyme. The same syllable sound repeated at the ends of words is called rhyme. In poetry, words can rhyme at the ends of lines or within lines. Rhyme used within a line is called internal rhyme. The following lines show both internal and end rhyme.

Now Sam McGee was from Tennessee,
    where the cotton blooms and blows.
Why he left his home in the South to
    roam 'round the Pole, God only
    knows.
("The Cremation of Sam McGee," page 88)

For more about rhyme, see pages 80–81, 94, 215, and 371.

Rhythm. The pattern of stressed and unstressed syllables in a poem is called rhythm. Some poems have an even, reg-ular beat that gives the poem a musical sound. In other poems, the rhythm sounds more like normal conversation.

For more about rhythm, see pages 80–81 and 371.

Scene. A scene is a part of a play, usually part of an act, that shows what happens in one time and place. A play or an act may be made up of several scenes.

Science Fiction. Fiction that is based on real or imagined scientific developments is called science fiction. It often presents an imaginary view of the future or of the distant past. "Someday" (page 465) is an example of science fiction.

Setting. The time and place in which the events in a story happen is called the setting. Every story has at least one setting, but some settings are described in more detail than others. The setting of "Lob's Girl" (page 309) is a fishing village in England in modern times.

For more about setting, see pages 4–5, 142, 272, and 433.

Short Story. A work of fiction short enough to be read at one sitting is called a short story. It usually tells about one main conflict and one set of events. Elements of the short story include characters, setting, and plot. "Ghost Town" (page 300) is an example of a short story.

See also *Fiction*.

Simile. A comparison between two unlike things that have something in common is called a simile. A simile uses the word *like* or *as*. The following line is an example of a simile.

A school of fish swept by like silver arrows.
("Ghost of the Lagoon," page 147)

For more about simile, see pages 212–213. See also *Metaphor*.

Speaker. The speaker in a poem is the voice that talks to the reader. In "The Cremation of Sam McGee" (page 88), the speaker is Cap, Sam's friend.

For more about speakers, see pages 370 and 381.

Stage Directions. Stage directions are notes that help actors perform a play. These directions also help readers picture the action. Stage directions can describe the movements of actors, the way in which dialogue is spoken, and the scenery, lighting, and sound effects. Usually, stage directions are printed in italics inside parentheses. They often follow the characters' names, as in this example from *The Great Quillow* (page 98).

Town Crier (*enters on tiptoe*).
Sh! Don't wake the Giant.

For more about stage directions, see pages 97, 110, 389, and 396.

Stanza. A group of lines in poetry is called a stanza. A stanza in poetry is like a paragraph in other kinds of writing. There is usually a space between the stanzas. An example of a poem with three stanzas is "Beauty" (page 491).

Theme. The message about life or human nature that the writer presents in a work of literature is called the theme. A work may have one or more themes. Sometimes the theme is stated directly. At other times the theme must be figured out by the reader through careful reading and thinking. One theme of *Nadia the Willful* (page 134), for example, is that sometimes a person must have the courage to protest a harmful decision or law.

Some works, however, are written just for entertainment. In these works there may be no serious theme.

For more about theme, see pages 29, 242, 386, 402, 419, 480, 487, and 496.

Analysis. When you make an analysis, you break something into its parts to understand it better. Many elements go together to make up a work of literature. When you analyze, focus on each part individually. Then see how the parts work together. This will help you understand and appreciate the whole work.

For example, when you analyze a poem, look at its images, figurative language, rhyme, rhythm, mood, and theme. See how these elements work together to give the total effect of the poem.

For more about analysis, see page 369.

Author's Purpose. Authors write for four main purposes, or reasons: to entertain, to inform, to express opinions, and to persuade. The author may combine two or three purposes, but one is usually the most important. As you read, decide how well the author has achieved his or her purpose.

For more about author's purpose, see page 404.

Cause and Effect. Events are often related by cause and effect. One event can be the reason another event happens. The event that happens first in time is the cause. The second event is the effect. The effect can be an event or a change in the way a character behaves or thinks.

Sometimes clue words signal cause and effect relationships. Some of these clue words are *because, next, therefore, since, so that, in order that,* and *if/then.*

Notice how cause and effect are shown in this example. The clue word is *because.*

> There were some humans who had never forgiven the aliens because they didn't warn the colonists about the tides. . . . (*Sweetwater*, page 355)

For more about cause and effect, see pages 6–7.

Chronological Order. See *Time Order.*

Classifying. To classify, you arrange ideas, people, or objects into groups that have something in common. For example, you can group stories by their subject matter, such as animal stories, science fiction stories, and so on.

For more about classifying, see page 480.

Comparison.   To compare means to find or show what two or more different things have in common. Writers use comparisons to make ideas clear or to point out similarities. For example, in "A Rare Provider," the movement of a flock of sheep is compared to a slow gray flood (page 409).

As a reader, you also make comparisons. You can make comparisons within a work, or you can compare two or more works. For example, you may show how characters within a work are alike, or how main characters from different works are alike.

For more about comparisons, see pages 210 and 230. See also *Contrast.*

Contrast.   To contrast means to find or show the differences between two or more things. Writers often contrast unfamiliar facts, feelings, or ideas with familiar ones. For example, in *To Space and Back*, Sally Ride contrasts the unusual feeling of weightlessness with the feeling caused by gravity on Earth (page 504).

As a reader, you also make contrasts. You contrast elements within a work, or you contrast elements of different works. For example, you may notice how the attitudes of characters within a work differ. You might also contrast the themes of two works.

For more about making contrasts, see page 455. See also *Comparison.*

Evaluating.   To evaluate means to judge the worth of something. When you evaluate a piece of writing, you judge how well it measures up to your expectations or standards. What you expect depends on your experiences both from reading and from living.

To evaluate literature, think about the author's purpose for writing. Decide how well the writer achieved that purpose. Study the details and elements of the work. Then judge how well the elements work together as a whole. Compare and contrast the work with similar works you have read.

When you state your evaluation, make specific statements that can be supported by examples from the work.

For more about making evaluations, see pages 404–405. See also *Analysis, Author's Purpose, Comparison,* and *Contrast.*

Fact and Opinion.   Facts are statements that can be proved, such as "That shirt is blue." Opinions are statements that express a person's feelings, such as "That shirt is pretty." Opinions cannot be proved.

Nonfiction often contains both facts and opinions. For example, a writer of nonfiction may present an opinion and support it with facts. The way a writer presents, omits, or judges facts can also show the writer's opinion about a subject.

When you read, figure out which statements are facts and which ones are opinions. Identify the writer's purpose. Decide if the use of facts or opinions matches or supports that purpose. Watch for facts that do not seem correct. Watch for opinions that are presented as facts, or opinions that are not supported by facts. Notice how words with positive or negative connotations are used.

As a writer, you are often asked to give your opinion. Your opinion should be based on evidence or facts. You should be able to give and explain several reasons why you feel as you do.

Suppose, for example, that you are asked to give your opinion about a character. You might believe that the character was very selfish. To support your opinion, find several examples in the story that show this character's selfishness.

For more about facts and opinions, see pages 503 and 536.

Generalizations. A statement made about a whole group is called a generalization. An example of a generalization is "Many sixth graders are twelve years old."

Generalizations are not always true. Some are too broad. Some are not based on enough evidence. An example of an untrue generalization is, "All sixth graders are twelve years old." This generalization is false because some sixth graders are not twelve years old. The word *all* makes this statement untrue.

When you read a generalization, decide if there are exceptions to the statement. If there is even one exception, the generalization is untrue.

For more about generalizations, see page 51.

Inferences. An inference is a logical guess based on known facts or evidence. You often make inferences or draw conclusions as you read. That is, you infer, or figure out, more than the words say. The evidence you use may be facts the writer provides or experiences from your own life. For example, based on your own experiences and the information in these sentences from *The Lilith Summer* (page 437), you can infer that Ellen is nervous.

> I could hardly keep my legs still, and I didn't know what to do with my hands. I folded them in my lap, then rubbed my sweaty palms against my bare knees.

I twisted as the bench seat burned the back of my legs. I ran my hand through my hair.

For more about inferences, see pages 94, 155, 166, and 280. See also *Predictions*.

Logical Order. Logical order refers to a way of organizing information in writing. When writers present ideas in an order that makes sense for their subject and purpose, they are using logical order. For example, if a writer's purpose is to present an opinion, then he or she might state the opinion and support it with reasons. The reasons might be arranged from least to most important. If a writer's purpose is to inform, he or she may state an idea and then use examples or details to make the idea clear.

As a reader, you must look at the order in which ideas are presented. This will help you understand and remember the author's message.

For more about logical order, see pages 502–503.

Main Idea. The main idea is the one idea that all the sentences in a paragraph work together to tell about. The main idea is often stated in one sentence called the *topic sentence*. The topic sentence is often the first sentence. It may be any sentence in the paragraph. The other sentences add *supporting details*. That is, they explain or tell more about the main idea. A writer may need to use more than one paragraph to develop a main idea.

Sometimes the main idea is not stated directly in a topic sentence. Instead, it is implied, or suggested. In this case, all the details relate to the main idea, but you must infer that main idea.

In the following paragraph, the main idea is stated in the topic sentence. The rest of the sentences give details about the main idea. The topic sentence is underlined.

> <u>When I am weightless, some things don't change.</u> My heart beats at about the same rate as it does on Earth. I can still swallow and digest food. My eyes, ears, nose, and taste buds work fine; I see, hear, smell, and taste things just as I do at home.
> (*To Space and Back*, page 504)

For more about main idea, see pages 130–131.

Opinions. See *Fact and Opinion*.

Predictions. When you use what you know to infer what will happen in the future, you are making a prediction. To make a prediction in a story, combine the facts from the story with what you know from experience.

For more about making predictions, see page 155.

Relationships. The parts or elements of a work of literature are often linked in certain ways. To understand the work, you must understand the relationships, or connections, between these parts or elements.

In fiction, for example, you might look at the relationships between characters. You might also note how the relationships change as the plot develops. For example, in "Hatsuno's Great-Grandmother" (page 168), Hatsuno and her great-grandmother do not get along because they do not understand one another. As the plot unfolds, their relationship changes and improves. By the end of the story they have become closer, and more sympathetic with each other.

Events in literature can also be related, or connected. They may be related by time order, that is, one event follows another in time. Events can also have a cause-and-effect relationship. One event may bring about or cause another event.

See also *Time Order* and *Cause and Effect.*

Sequence. Sequence refers to the order in which events occur or ideas are presented. For example, a writer of fiction uses time order to narrate the events of a story. A writer of nonfiction may arrange ideas in a logical order.

As you read, notice which kind of sequence the writer is using. The sequence will help you understand how ideas or events are related. This will help you understand and remember what you read.

See also *Cause and Effect, Logical Order,* and *Time Order.*

Summarizing. To summarize means to tell briefly in your own words the main ideas of a piece of writing. When you summarize, you condense your ideas or those of the writer into precise statements. You omit unimportant details.

Time Order or Chronological Order. Time order, or chronological order, refers to the order in which events happen in time. Writers may simply describe events in time order. Sometimes they use clue words or phrases to signal the sequence of events. Some of these clue words and phrases are *then, next, gradually, while, finally,* and *the following day.* An example of a story that is written in time order is "My Friend Flicka" (page 183). This story relates the events in Kennie's summer in the order in which they happened.

As you read, keep in mind the order of events. Sometimes a story may include events that took place earlier in time or that will occur at a future time. For example, in "Aaron's Gift" (page 420), Aaron recalls the story of his grandmother's experiences as a child in Russia. Then the story returns to the present.

For more about time order, see page 6. See also *Cause and Effect* and *Logical Order.*

Summary of Vocabulary Skills

This section summarizes the ways you can find the meanings of unfamiliar words as you read them. The section is organized in the following way:

1. Word Parts
   Base Word
   Prefix
   Suffix
   Multiple Word Parts
   Spelling Changes
   Compound Words
2. Context Clues
   Definition or Restatement Clues
   Example Clues
   Comparison Clues
   Contrast Clues
   Inference Clues
3. The Dictionary
   Finding a Word
   Parts of an Entry
   Using a Glossary
4. Denotations and Connotations
   Denotations
   Connotations
   Synonyms
   Antonyms

---

1. Word Parts

Some words are made by combining word parts. These parts include base words, prefixes, and suffixes. If you know the meaning of each part, you can often figure out the meaning of the whole word.

Base Word. A complete word to which other word parts are added is called a base word. Parts can be added to the beginning or end of the base word. For example, the base word in *lately* is *late*. The base word in *uncover* is *cover*. Sometimes the spelling of a base word is changed when other word parts are added to it. For example, the *e* is dropped from *dare* when the ending *-ing* is added to form the word *daring*. For more information about spelling changes caused by combining suffixes and base words, see *Spelling Changes*.

Prefix. A word part added to the beginning of a base word is called a prefix. Adding a prefix to a word changes the meaning of the word.

Prefix + Base Word = New Word
pre - + *pay* = *prepay*

In the example, adding *pre-* changed the meaning of *pay* to "pay before."

For more about prefixes, see pages 8 and 43.

Suffix. A word part added to the end of a base word is called a suffix. Adding a suffix to a word can change or add to the meaning of a word. It may also change the part of speech of a word.

Base Word + Suffix = New Word
use + *-less* = *useless*

In the example, the suffix *-less* changes the meaning of *use*, a verb, to "having no use," an adjective.

For more about suffixes, see pages 8–9 and 79.

See also *Spelling Changes*.

Multiple Word Parts. Some words contain three or more parts. The following example contains a base word, a prefix, and a suffix.

Prefix + Base Word
un- + *forget*

+ Suffix = New Word
+ *-able* = *unforgettable*

By combining the meanings of all three parts, you see that *unforgettable* means "cannot be forgotten." Notice that in the word *thoughtfully*, two suffixes are combined with the base word *thought*.

For more about multiple word parts, see pages 8–9 and 95.

Spelling Changes. When some word parts are combined, spelling changes occur. Generally no changes occur when prefixes are added. When suffixes are added, however, one of the following changes may be necessary.

1. When a suffix beginning with a vowel is added to a word ending in silent *e*, the *e* is usually dropped.

   hope + *-ing* = *hoping*

   Note that the *e* is not dropped when a suffix beginning with a consonant is added.

   hope + *-ful* = *hopeful*

2. When a suffix is added to a word ending in *y* preceded by a consonant, the *y* is usually changed to an *i*.

   deny + *-able* = *deniable*

   Note that when the *y* is preceded by a vowel, it is not changed.

   joy + *-ous* = *joyous*

3. When a word of one syllable ends in one consonant and is preceded by one

vowel, the final consonant is doubled before adding *-ing*, *-ed*, or *-er*.

swim + -er = swimmer

Note that when two vowels come before the final consonant in a word of one syllable, the final consonant is not doubled when these suffixes are added.

soon + -er = sooner

Compound Words. Two base words may be combined to form a new word called a compound word. The meaning of many compounds is a combination of the two base words, such as *keyhole*. However, some compounds such as *outline* take on a new meaning, different from the two combined meanings.

For more about compounds, see pages 9 and 111.

2. Context Clues

Context refers to the sentence or paragraph in which you find a word. Clues about the meaning of a new word are often given in context. Look for the following kinds of context clues.

Definition or Restatement Clues. In a definition or restatement clue, the writer defines or restates the word in a different way. Words that signal definition or restatement clues are *or*, *that is*, *in other words*, and *also called*. Punctuation marks such as commas or dashes can also be clues.

Here is an example of a definition or restatement clue.

> Maybe he did not notice, Manolo thought; maybe he didn't see that I was paralyzed, that I couldn't have moved. (*Shadow of a Bull*, page 454)

The words "that I couldn't have moved" restate the meaning of the word *paralyzed*.

For more about definition and restatement clues, see pages 132 and 167.

Example Clues. In an example clue, the writer uses examples to explain the new word. The new word may be one of the examples, or the new word may be defined by the specific examples. Words and phrases that tell you to look for examples in a sentence are *like*, *especially*, *for example*, *for instance*, *and other types*, and *such as*.

Here are two examples of example clues.

> Fir, spruce, hemlock, and other types of evergreen trees covered the hill.

You can figure out that fir, spruce, and

hemlock must be "types of evergreen trees."

In ancient times, a bride's family was expected to give the husband a dowry, such as animals, money, or other kinds of wealth.

You can figure out that a *dowry* represents some "kind of wealth."

For more about example clues, see pages 132–133 and 211.

Comparison Clues. An unfamiliar word can be compared with a similar word or idea that is easier to understand. This is called a comparison clue. Key words to look for in comparison clues are *like, as, similar to,* and *than.*

Here is an example of a comparison clue.

The portico of the mansion was similar to the porch of the home we had left.

The comparison tells you that a *portico* is "like a porch."

For more about comparison clues, see pages 133 and 255.

Contrast Clues. Contrast clues show the meaning of an unfamiliar word by contrasting it with an opposite word or idea. Look for these words in contrast clues: *although, but, however, yet, on the other hand, different from,* and *in contrast.*

Here is an example of a contrast clue.

Kim, the elder brother, was very industrious. De, on the other hand, was inclined to be lazy.

The words *on the other hand* tell you that *industrious* means "the opposite of lazy."

For more about contrast clues, see pages 133 and 255.

Inference Clues. Sometimes the meaning of an unfamiliar word can be inferred, or figured out, from other words or sentences in the context. These clues to meaning are called inference clues. The main idea of the paragraph may also help you infer a word's meaning. In this paragraph, you can infer the meaning of *rheumatism* from the words and sentences around it.

Now, one morning Dame Agnes woke up with bonecracking rheumatism. Her joints creaked, her back ached, and her knees were so stiff she could no way get out of bed.
("The Cat and the Golden Egg," page 52)

You can use the other sentences to figure out that the word *rheumatism* means "a condition in which the joints become stiff and sore."

For more about inference clues, see pages 133, 222, and 231.

3. The Dictionary

When you cannot figure out the meaning of a word from the word parts or context clues, use a dictionary. A dictionary is an alphabetical listing of words called entry words. You can use a dictionary to find out these things about a word:

1. the correct spelling
2. the correct pronunciation
3. the parts of speech it can be
4. the meaning or meanings

Finding a Word

The words in large type at the top of a dictionary page are called guide words. These words show the first and last entry word listed on that page. All the entry words on the page are listed in alphabetical order between these words. You can use the guide words to find entry words quickly.

For more about guide words, see page 327.

---

in•teg•ri•ty (in teg′ rə tē) *n.* **1.** the condition of being complete [wars destroyed Germany's territorial *integrity*] **2.** strong condition; soundness [the *integrity* of a nation's currency] **3.** uprightness, honesty, and sincerity [a man of *integrity* never takes a bribe]

Parts of an Entry

Entry Word. The entry word is in dark print. It shows the correct spelling of the word and how the word is divided into syllables.

Respelling. Next to the entry word is the respelling of the word in parentheses. The respelling shows how the word should be pronounced. The letters and symbols in the respelling stand for the sounds in the word. The pronunciation key, usually found at the bottom of the dictionary page, explains the sounds that these letters and symbols represent. Accent marks (′) in the respelling show which syllables should be stressed.

For more about respellings, see pages 282 and 369.

Parts of Speech. Next to the respelling is an abbreviation showing the part of speech of the word. A word can be more than one part of speech. Meanings are given for each part of speech the word can be. The following abbreviations are usually used:

n.	noun	*pro.*	pronoun
v.	verb	*prep.*	preposition
adj.	adjective	*conj.*	conjunction
adv.	adverb	*interj.*	interjection

Definition. The definition of the word is the meaning. A word can have several, or multiple, meanings. You must choose the definition that makes sense in the context in which you find the word.

For more about definitions and multiple meanings, see pages 283 and 379.

Idioms. An idiom is an expression that means something different from the usual meanings of the words that make it up. Idioms are found at the end of the entry of the most important word in the idiom. For example, "to shake a leg" means "to hurry" and is listed in the entry for *leg*.

For more about idioms, see pages 283 and 397.

Homographs. Homographs are words that look the same but have different meanings. Homographs have different origins, or word histories. Homographs are separate entry words in the dictionary and have a raised numeral next to each entry. For example, *fleet* is listed twice in the dictionary. *Fleet*[1] is a group of ships, while *fleet*[2] means swift or rapid.

For more about homographs, see pages 283 and 387.

Using a Glossary

A glossary is a short dictionary at the back of some nonfiction books. It lists entry words in alphabetical order and gives their meanings. A glossary gives only the difficult or unusual words found in that book. For an example, see the glossary at the back of this book.

4. Denotations and Connotations

Denotations. The dictionary definitions of a word are its denotations. When a word has several definitions, you must choose the meaning that makes the most sense in the context.

For more about denotations, see pages 406, 444, and 493.

Connotations. The ideas and feelings associated with a word are called connotations. A writer chooses words for these extra layers of meaning that have become associated with the word through common use. A word with a positive connotation adds a good feeling to the sentence in which it is found. A word with a negative connotation carries a bad feeling. A word that is neutral carries no feeling. For example, *error* is a neutral word that means "a mistake." A *blunder* has a negative connotation and suggests that the person making the mistake is stupid. The more positive word *slip* puts no blame on the person making the mistake.

For more about connotations, see pages 407, 501, and 517.

Synonyms. Words that mean almost the same thing are called synonyms. For example, *pleasant* and *enjoyable* are synonyms. Because synonyms do not have exactly the same meaning, one cannot always be substituted for another. You have to choose the synonym that best fits the context. Synonyms are sometimes listed at the end of a dictionary entry or in a thesaurus.

For more about synonyms, see page 481. See also *Thesaurus*, page 566.

Antonyms. Antonyms are words that are opposite or almost opposite each other. For example, *tall* and *short* are antonyms. Antonyms are sometimes listed at the end of a dictionary entry or in a thesaurus.

For more about antonyms, see page 481. See also *Thesaurus*, page 566.

This section gives you guidelines for finding and using sources of information. It also gives you tips for studying, reading, and organizing the information. The section is organized in the following way:

1. Using the Library

Arrangement of Books

There are two types of books in the library: fiction and nonfiction. These two types are kept in separate areas of the library. Each type is arranged differently on the shelves.

Fiction books are stories about imaginary happenings. They are arranged alphabetically according to the last name of the author. The author's last name is usually shown on the spine of the book.

Nonfiction books contain factual information. There are several ways that libraries may choose to arrange nonfiction books. Most schools and public libraries use the *Dewey Decimal System*. The Dewey Decimal System assigns every book a number in one of ten categories. This call number is printed on the spine of the book. The books are then arranged in numerical order.

Biographies and autobiographies are kept in a special section of the nonfiction area. Biographies about one person have no call number assigned. Collective biographies tell about the lives of several people. They can be found under the call number 921.

THE DEWEY DECIMAL SYSTEM

000–099	General Works	encyclopedias, almanacs, handbooks
100–199	Philosophy	conduct, ethics, psychology
200–299	Religion	the Bible, mythology, theology
300–399	Social Science	economics, law, education, commerce, government, folklore, legend
400–499	Language	languages, grammar, dictionaries
500–599	Science	mathematics, chemistry, physics
600–699	Useful Arts	farming, cooking, sewing, radio, nursing, engineering, television, business, gardening, cars
700–799	Fine Arts	music, painting, drawing, acting, photography, games, sports
800–899	Literature	poetry, plays, essays
900–999	History	biography, travel, geography

The Card Catalog

A quick way to locate a book in the library is to use the card catalog. The card catalog is a cabinet of small drawers filled with cards for all the books in the library. These cards are arranged alphabetically according to the words on the top line of each card. On the top left corner of the cards of nonfiction books, you will find the call number. Using the call number, you can locate the book on the shelves.

There are usually three cards for every nonfiction book in the library: an author card, a title card, and a subject card. Each of the three cards contains the same information but in a different order. The *author card* lists the author's name on the

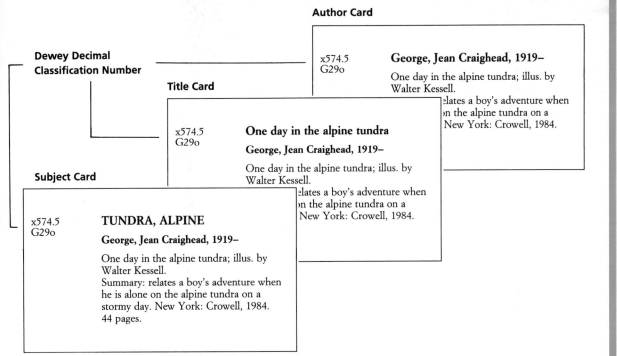

Author Card

x574.5
G29o

George, Jean Craighead, 1919–

One day in the alpine tundra; illus. by
Walter Kessell.

elates a boy's adventure when
on the alpine tundra on a
New York: Crowell, 1984.

**Dewey Decimal
Classification Number**

Title Card

x574.5
G29o

One day in the alpine tundra

George, Jean Craighead, 1919–

One day in the alpine tundra; illus. by
Walter Kessell.

elates a boy's adventure when
on the alpine tundra on a
New York: Crowell, 1984.

Subject Card

x574.5
G29o

TUNDRA, ALPINE

George, Jean Craighead, 1919–

One day in the alpine tundra; illus. by
Walter Kessell.
Summary: relates a boy's adventure when
he is alone on the alpine tundra on a
stormy day. New York: Crowell, 1984.
44 pages.

top line. The *title card* lists the title on the top line. The *subject card* lists the subject or topic of the book on the top line.

If you know the author of the book you are looking for, use the author card to look up the book. If you know the title, use the title card. If you are looking for books about a particular topic, use the subject cards.

Many libraries now have their card catalogs entered on a computer. The type of computer varies with the library. You can use the computer to find books listed by authors, titles, or subjects. Usually there are directions near the computer that show how to use it. Ask a librarian to help you with the computer if you are unfamiliar with it.

2. Using Reference Materials

The Nonfiction Book

When you are looking for detailed information about a topic, your best source may be a nonfiction book on that subject. You find these books by using the subject cards of the card catalog. In order to decide whether the book you find will be useful to you, examine these parts of the book:

The title page. Does the title mention your topic? Is the author or editor someone who would have knowledge about the topic?

The copyright page. Notice the date on the copyright page. Is the information recent enough?

The table of contents. Notice the organization of the book. Are any parts or chapters about your topic?

The index. Does the index list terms or names that you need information about? Does it use italic or boldface type to indicate the pages with maps, graphs, or illustrations?

The Encyclopedia

The most commonly-used reference source is the encyclopedia. The encyclopedia is a collection of factual articles on a wide variety of topics. The articles are arranged in alphabetical order, according to their titles. Famous people are listed by their last names first. When you find the article about your topic, read the subtitles first to locate the information you need quickly. Be sure to look up any cross-references at the end of the article. They refer you to other articles with information about the topic.

If an encyclopedia is several volumes long, an *index* usually appears in the last volume. The index lists volumes and pages that give information on your topic.

For more about the encyclopedia, see pages 65 and 142.

Other Reference Sources

Almanac. An almanac is a book that is published yearly. It gives up-to-date information and statistics about many subjects.

For more about almanacs, see page 263.

Atlas. An atlas is a book of maps. You can find atlases with maps for a particular country or for the world.

For more about atlases, see page 34.

Biographical Dictionary. A reference book that gives short biographies of a number of famous people is called a biographical dictionary. Some are limited to one particular field, while others list people from all professions.

For more about biographical dictionaries, see page 242.

Magazine. Magazines can give you current information about many subjects. You can find articles about your topic by using *The Readers' Guide to Periodical Literature*. This guide lists topics alphabetically and then lists information about magazine articles that have been published about each topic during a certain time period.

Thesaurus. A thesaurus is a book of synonyms and antonyms. When you write, you can use it to find a more exact or lively word to express your idea. Some thesauri are organized alphabetically like a dictionary. For others, you must look up the word in the index.

Nonprint Resources. Libraries contain many resources besides books and magazines. These include films, slides, and filmstrips; records and tapes; posters, photographs, and copies of works of art. These are cataloged separately from books. They can give you valuable information.

3. Studying

Three Types of Reading

There are three types of reading you can use when you are studying or doing research. Each is best for a particular purpose.

Skimming is one type of fast reading. It helps you get a quick overview of the material you are about to read. Skimming also helps you become familiar with the most important facts. To skim, move your eyes quickly over the material. Look for titles, subtitles, and illustrations that will give you clues about the content of the material.

Scanning is another type of fast reading. It allows you to locate quickly a specific piece of information. To scan, move your eyes quickly over the page. Look for key words and phrases that will lead you to the particular facts and ideas you need.

In-depth reading is the third type of reading. This is slower than scanning and skimming. When you do this type of reading, you try to get as much meaning as you can from the words. You are trying to understand the order in which the information is arranged and to make connections between facts and ideas.

The SQ3R Study Method

You usually need to read and study to complete assignments and prepare for tests. The SQ3R study method is one sure way to improve your reading and study skills. SQ3R stands for these five steps: Survey, Question, Read, Record, and Review.

Survey. Look over the material to get a general idea of what it is about. Read the titles and subtitles. Look at the pictures, maps, graphs, or tables. Read the introduction or first few paragraphs.

Question. Read any study questions provided in the book or by your teacher. They will help you identify important points to look for when you read.

Read. Read the material carefully. Identify the main ideas. Keep the study questions in mind.

Record. After reading, write the answers to the study questions. Make brief notes to help you remember any other important ideas.

Review. Look back at the study questions and try to answer them without using your notes. You may need to review the material to find the answers. Then study your notes so that you will be able to remember the information later.

4. Organizing Information

Note-taking

As you read, you will probably recognize some main ideas and important facts. Write them down in a notebook set aside for that textbook or subject.

Notes do not have to be written in sentences. They should be in your own words, not copied exactly as written in the book. Write them clearly so that when you read these notes at a later date, they will still make sense to you. Also write the title, author, and page number of the source of your notes.

Outlining

One way of organizing your notes when you study or do research is to outline them. An outline helps you identify the main ideas and sort the important facts. It also provides a visual summary of the information.

When you make an outline, label the main ideas with Roman numerals. Under each main topic, indent and label important facts or ideas related to that topic with capital letters. These are subtopics. Use the format below when you outline.

I. (First main topic)
   A. (Subtopic)
   B. (Subtopic)

II. (Second main topic)
   A. (Subtopic)
   B. (Subtopic)

Guidelines for the Process of Writing

When you write, you follow certain steps. These steps make up the process of writing. They include four stages: **prewriting**, **drafting**, **revising**, and **sharing**.

In this section you will learn what to do in each stage. You will also see how one student worked through the steps in the process.

Prewriting

Prewriting is all the thinking and planning you do before you write. Prewriting can be broken into smaller steps to make it easier.

1. Choose and limit a topic. If a specific topic has not been assigned, begin by listing topics that you can write about. Choose the one that you find most interesting or have the most ideas about. Then list as many ideas about the topic as you can. Limit your ideas and topic to what you can handle in the length of your writing.

Sarah's writing assignment was to write a paragraph that compares two folk tales in Unit 1. In order to choose which stories she would compare, she looked over the titles in the table of contents and thought about how the stories were alike. Sarah soon realized that the main characters in "Duke Pishposh of Pash" and "The Cat and the Golden Egg" each played a trick. Because of that similarity, she decided to compare those two stories.

She then listed all the points of comparison she might discuss in her paragraph. She circled those she felt she had the most to write about.

2. Decide on your purpose. Your purpose for writing may be to entertain, to give your opinion, to persuade, or to inform. To accomplish your purpose, you may need to decide whether to compare or contrast, to describe, to analyze, or to evaluate, for example.

Sarah knew that her purpose was to inform the reader about the similarities between the two stories. She would present this information in the form of a comparison.

3. Decide on your audience. When you determine who your readers will be, choose language and details to suit that audience.

Sarah's assignment was for her language arts class, so she knew that her audience would be the teacher and her classmates. She would choose language appropriate for those readers.

4. Gather information. Usually you will need more information about your topic. You may need to use reference books such as encyclopedias. If you are writing about a work of literature, you may need to reread parts or all of it. Take notes on the information you need as you read. The notes do not have to be sentences, but they should be in your own words.

Sarah now needed to reread the stories and take notes on them. As she read, she looked for ways in which the stories were alike. She took the following notes:

Duke

Tyl clever, good judge of people
trick teaches lesson and gets Tyl
   money
Lucas saw easy way to make
   money—gave Tyl gifts
trick worked, made people laugh at
   Lucas
trick helped the Brouwer family
Theme: don't be greedy

Cat

Quickset clever, good judge of
   people
trick teaches lesson and Quickset gets
   groceries for Dame Agnes

Grubble saw easy way to make money
   —gave Quickset groceries
trick worked, made people laugh at
   Grubble
trick helped Dame Agnes and customers
Theme: don't be greedy

At this point, Sarah realized that she would have to narrow her topic further. She had too much to compare. She decided to focus her paragraph on the tricks.

5. Organize your ideas. The type of organization you choose depends on what type of writing you are doing. Choose an order that is logical for your topic. For a story, you will probably use time order. For a description, you can describe an object or scene in the order you see it, such as top to bottom or left to right. To give an opinion or persuade, order your reasons from least to most important.

Sarah looked over her list and crossed out ideas that did not fit her narrowed topic. She added others and then arranged them in an order she thought would work.

Main idea: Tricks are similar

1. both tricks to fool greedy people
2. Lucas and Grubble saw easy way to make money
3. greedy people had to give up something to get more
4. everybody laughed at greedy people
5. tricks helped other characters

Writing Your Draft

Your draft is your first try at writing your thoughts in sentence and paragraph form. Do not be concerned with mistakes at this time. Instead, get all your thoughts on paper. Leave space between lines for changes you will make later.

Sarah was ready to write her draft. She followed the order of her notes and wrote sentences. She left space between lines for changes later on. Here is her draft.

First Draft

> The tricks in Duke Pishposh of Pash and The Cat and the Golden Egg were very simliar. Both tricks were played on greedy people. Both these greedy characters thought they were going to make money easily. Both had to give up something to get what they thought would be a lot more. Lucas Koop gave gifts to Tyl and Mr. Grubble gave grocries to Quickset. Neither character gets what they expected. The greedy ones looked foolish to everyone else. The tricks helped other characters. Who were poor.

Revising

When you revise, you rethink the way you have presented your ideas and the decisions you made in the prewriting stage. You may decide that you need more information or a different organization, for example. To revise, you look for ways to improve your writing. For example, check to see that your ideas are clear, complete, and in an order that makes sense. Look at your word choices and add or substitute words that are more descriptive or precise. Use the spaces you left between lines to make your corrections.

An important step in revising is proof-reading. When you proofread, check your writing for errors in grammar, usage, capitalization, punctuation, and spelling. Ask yourself the questions from the checklist on pages 574–575 as you revise and proofread. Use the proofreader's marks shown on page 123 to mark your changes and corrections.

Now Sarah was ready to read her draft carefully to try to improve it. First she thought about the ideas she had written and the order in which she had presented them. She tried to improve her wording and add variety to her sentences. She made changes in the spaces between lines. After she felt her ideas were clear and in good order, she proofread her paragraph. She corrected errors in spelling, punctuation, and capitalization. Here is her revised draft.

Revised Draft

The tricks in "Duke Pishposh of Pash" and "The Cat and the Golden Egg" were very similar. Both tricks were played on greedy *characters* people. Both these greedy characters, *Lucas Koop and Mr. Grubble,* thought they were going to make money easily. Both had to *gave up some of their wealth* give up something to *for the promise of more* get what they thought would be a lot more. Lucas Koop gave gifts to Tyl and Mr. Grubble gave grocries to Quickset. Neither *selfish* character *got* gets what *he* they expected, *and both* The greedy ones looked foolish to everyone else. The tricks helped other characters Who were poor. *In the end, everyone got what he or she deserved.*

Writing the Final Copy. When you have finished revising, copy your revised draft on clean paper in your neatest handwriting. Be sure to make all corrections that you marked. Proofread your final copy.

Sarah was now ready to copy her revised draft. She was careful to make every correction that she had marked. When she finished, she read her final copy to make sure she had caught all errors. Here is her final copy.

Final Copy

```
     The tricks in "Duke Pishposh of Pash" and "The

Cat and the Golden Egg" were very similar.  Both

tricks were played on greedy characters.  These

characters, Lucas Koop and Mr. Grubble, thought

they were going to make money easily.  Both gave

up some of their wealth for the promise of more.

Lucas Koop gave gifts to Tyl, and Mr. Grubble

gave groceries to Quickset.  Neither selfish

character got what he expected, and both looked

foolish to everyone else.  The tricks helped

other characters who were poor.  In the end,

everyone got what he or she deserved.
```

Sharing

Let others read your writing, or read it to them. Writing is a way of communicating with others. If no one but you reads it, you have not communicated. Be proud of all the good work you have done!

Checklist for the Process of Writing

Prewriting

1. Choose and limit a topic.
2. Decide on your purpose.
3. Decide on your audience.
4. Gather information.
5. Organize your ideas.

Drafting

1. Begin writing. Keep your topic, purpose, and audience in mind at all times.
2. As you write, you may add new details.
3. Concentrate on ideas. Do not be concerned with grammar and punctuation at this time.

Revising

1. Read your draft. Use these questions to guide you as you revise:
   a. Do you like what you have written? Is it interesting? Will others want to read it?
   b. Does your writing make sense? Have you achieved your purpose?
   c. Is your writing organized well? Do the ideas flow smoothly from one paragraph to the next? Are the ideas arranged in an order that makes sense?
   d. Is each group of words a complete sentence? Do paragraphs have topic sentences? Does every sentence in the paragraph stick to the topic? Should any sentence be moved?
   e. Should any details be left out? Should any be added?
   f. Does every sentence express a complete thought? Are your sentences easy to understand?
   g. Is every word the best possible word?
2. Mark any changes on your paper.

Proofreading

Consider these questions as you check your writing for errors in grammar and usage, capitalization, punctuation, and spelling:

Grammar and Usage
a. Is every word group a complete sentence?
b. Does every verb agree with its subject?
c. Have you used the correct form of each pronoun?
d. Is the form of each adjective and adverb correct?

Capitalization
a. Is the first word in every sentence capitalized?
b. Are all proper nouns and adjectives capitalized?
c. Are titles capitalized correctly?

Punctuation
a. Does each sentence have the correct end mark?
b. Have you used punctuation marks such as commas, apostrophes, hyphens, colons, semicolons, question marks, quotation marks, and underlining correctly?

Spelling
a. Did you use a dictionary to check spellings you were unsure of?
b. Did you spell plural and possessive forms correctly?

Sharing the Final Copy

1. Make a clean copy of your writing using your best handwriting or a typewriter or word processor. Make all changes and correct all errors. Then use these questions to check your work:
    a. Is your work neat and easy to read?
    b. Is every paragraph indented?
    c. Does your work require a title? Have you written it correctly?
2. Proofread your writing again. Correct any mistakes neatly.
3. Choose a method of sharing your writing. For example, you might read it aloud, combine it with others in a class booklet, or illustrate and display it on a bulletin board.

Glossary

The **glossary** is an alphabetical listing of words from the selections, along with their meanings. The glossary gives the following information:

1. **The entry word broken into syllables.**

2. **The pronunciation of each word.** The **respelling** is shown in parentheses. The most common way to pronounce a word is listed first. The Pronunciation Key below shows the symbols for the sounds of letters and key words that contain those sounds. A key is repeated on every second page.

   A **primary accent** ′ is placed after the syllable that is stressed the most when the word is spoken. A **secondary accent** ′ is placed after a syllable that has a lighter stress.

3. **The part of speech of the word.** The following abbreviations are used:

   n. noun   *v.* verb   *adj.* adjective   *adv.* adverb

4. **The meaning of the word.** The definitions listed in the glossary apply to selected ways a word is used in these selections.

5. **Related forms.** Words with suffixes such as *-ing*, *-ed*, *-ness*, and *-ly* are listed under the base word.

un·err·ing (un ur′ing *or* un er′ing) *adj.* making no mistake; without error; certain; sure. —**un·erringly** *adv.*

Pronunciation Key

a	fat	i	hit	yoo	use, cute, few	ə	a *in* ago	ch	chin
ā	ape	ī	bite, fire	yoo	united, cure		e *in* agent	sh	she
ä	car, lot			oi	oil		i *in* sanity	th	thin
		ō	go	ou	out		o *in* comply	th	then
e	elf, ten	ô	law, horn				u *in* focus	zh	leisure
ē	even	oo	tool	u	up			ng	ring
		oo	look	ur	fur, bird	ər	perhaps, murder	′	able (ā′b'l)

From *Webster's New World Dictionary, Student Edition,* Copyright © 1981 by Simon & Schuster, Inc.

A

a·ban·don (ə ban′dən) *v.* **1.** to give up something completely. **2.** to leave; desert.

a·bate (ə bāt′) *v.* to make or become lesser or weaker; decrease.

a·breast (ə brest′) *adv.* side by side; in line with.

ab·sten·tion (əb sten′shən) *n.* the act of refusing to vote.

ac·cor·di·on (ə kôr′dē ən) *n.* a musical instrument that is played by pulling out and pressing together bellows to force air through the reeds, which are opened by fingering the keys.

a·cous·tics (ə kōōs′tiks) *n. pl.* the qualities of a room that have to do with how clearly sounds can be heard in it.

ad·dress (ə dres′) *v.* to speak to or write to.

ad·e·quate (ad′ə kwət) *adj.* good enough for what is needed; sufficient.

ag·grieve (ə grēv′) *v.* to offend; to make one feel hurt or insulted. —**aggrieved** *adj.*

a·ghast (ə gast′) *adj.* feeling great shock or horror; horrified.

ag·ile (aj′'l) *adj.* moving with ease and quickness; active; nimble.

ag·i·tate (aj′ə tāt′) *v.* **1.** to stir up or shake violently. **2.** to excite or disturb. —**agitated** *adj.*

ail·ing (āl′ing) *adj.* in poor health; sickly.

a·lac·ri·ty (ə lak′rə tē) *n.* quick, lively action; eager quickness.

am·a·teur (am′ə chər *or* am′ə tōōr) *n.* a person who does something without having much skill.

an·ces·tral (an ses′trəl) *adj.* of or inherited from persons or animals who developed earlier.

ap·pre·ci·a·tive (ə prē′shə tiv) *adj.* feeling or showing that one is grateful for something. —**appreciatively** *adv.*

ap·pre·hen·sion (ap′rə hen′shən) *n.* dread; feeling that something bad will happen.

ar·dent (är′d'nt) *adj.* full of eagerness; passionate; very enthusiastic.

ar·ro·gant (ar′ə gənt) *adj.* having a false sense of pride; ignoring what others think or want; haughty. —**arrogantly** *adv.*

as·sas·si·nate (ə sas′'n āt′) *v.* to murder a government leader or other important person, usually for political reasons.

as·so·ci·ate (ə sō′shē it′) *n.* a fellow worker; an acquaintance.

as·sur·ance (ə shoor′əns) *n.* confidence; belief in one's own abilities.

a·tone (ə tōn′) *v.* to make up for having done something wrong or harmful.

au·di·ble (ô′də b'l) *adj.* loud enough to be heard.

aus·pi·cious (ôs pish′əs) *adj.* favorable; seeming to show that success will follow.

au·to·ma·tion (ôt′ə mā′shən) *n.* in manufacturing, a system or method in which many or all of the processes are automatically performed by machinery.

a·vi·a·tor (ā′vē āt′ər) *n.* a person who flies airplanes; pilot.

B

bal·ance (bal′əns) *n.* the amount of money one has in a bank account.

ban·ish (ban′ish) *v.* to force a person to leave one's country as a punishment; exile.

bank[1] (bangk) *n.* **1.** an establishment for receiving, lending, or, sometimes, issuing money. **2.** a container for storing money.

---

fat, āpe, cär; elf, ēven; hit, bīte; gō, hôrn, tōōl, look; yōō, yoo, oil, out; up, fur; get; joy; yet; chin; she; thin; then; zh, leisure; ng, ring;

ə for *a* in *ago*, *e* in *agent*, *i* in *sanity*, *o* in *comply*, *u* in *focus*; ' as in *able* (ā′b'l)

bank² (baŋgk) *n.* a large mound or pile of earth.

bar·na·cle (bär′nə k'l) *n.* a small, shelled sea animal that fastens itself to rocks and ships.

ba·zaar (bə zär′) *n.* a market or a street where there are many shops selling various articles.

be·grudge (bi gruj′) *v.* to feel bitterness or envy because of something another has or enjoys.

be·seech (bi sēch′) *v.* to beg; implore. —**beseechingly** *adv.*

be·wil·der (bi wil′dər) *v.* to make confused; puzzle. —**bewilderment** *n.*

bil·low (bil′ō) *n.* a large ocean wave.

bi·na·ry (bī′nər ē) *adj.* describing a system of numbers in which the base used is two.

bond (bänd) *n.* a force that unites; tie.

brawn (brôn) *n.* strength; strong muscles.

brin·y (brīn′ē) *adj.* very salty, as the ocean.

bro·cade (brō kād′) *n.* a rich cloth with a raised design, as of silk, velvet, gold, or silver, woven into it.

bul·rush (bool′rush′) *n.* a tall plant that grows in shallow water and marshes.

bur·go·mas·ter (bur′gə mas′tər) *n.* the mayor of a city or town.

burr (bur) *n.* a strong rolling of the sound of the letter *r*.

C

cab·a·ret (kab′ ə rā′) *n.* a restaurant that has dancing and singing as entertainment.

ca·coph·o·ny (kə käf′ə nē′) *n.* a harsh-sounding voice; a jarring sound.

cal·lous (kal′əs) *adj.* having calluses; thick and hardened.

can·dor (kan′dər) *n.* honesty; frankness; openness about one's thoughts.

ca·per (kā′pər) *n.* a playful or silly trick; prank.

cat·a·pult (kat′ə pult′) *n.* a large weapon that worked like a slingshot, used in earlier times to throw spears, arrows, or rocks. *v.* to move suddenly and quickly.

cen·sor·ship (sen′sər ship′) *n.* the act or a system of removing or forbidding anything considered objectionable.

cha·grin (shə grin′) *n.* a feeling of being embarrassed, annoyed, or disappointed for having failed to do something. —**chagrined** *adj.*

chrys·an·the·mum (kri san′thə məm) *n.* a plant with round flowers of various colors, that blooms in the late summer and fall.

cir·cuit (sur′kit) *n.* a complete or partial path over which an electrical current may flow; a hookup that is connected into this path, as for radio, television, or computers.

cite (sīt) *v.* [Archaic] to stir to action; arouse.

civ·ic (siv′ik) *adj.* of a city; pertaining to citizenship.

civil service (siv′'l sur′vis) *n.* a system under which government jobs are gotten by those who score highest on examinations open to everyone.

cob·bler (käb′lər) *n.* a person who mends shoes or boots.

co·ma (kō′mə) *n.* a condition like a deep, long sleep, often caused by a disease or an injury.

com·mo·tion (kə mō′shən) *n.* confusion; a noisy rushing about.

com·pe·ti·tion (käm′pə tish′ən) *n.* **1.** the person or persons against whom one competes; a rival or an opponent. **2.** a contest.

com·press (kəm pres′) *v.* to squeeze or press closely together; press into a smaller space.

com·prise (kəm prīz') *v.* to consist of; be made up of.

con·ceal·ment (kən sēl'mənt) *n.* the act of hiding or keeping something secret.

con·cen·trate (kän'sən trāt') *v.* to gather all one's thoughts or efforts.

con·cer·to (kən chər'tō) *n.* a piece of music performed by a solo instrument with an orchestra.

con·cuss (kən kus') *v.* to cause to have a concussion, or violent shock, as from a sudden impact. —**concussed** *adj.*

con·de·scend (kän'də send') *v.* to treat others in a proud or haughty way; be patronizing. —**condescendingly** *adv.*

con·fi·den·tial (kän'fə den'shəl) *adj.* told in secret; trusted with private matters.

con·sole (kən sōl') *v.* to comfort; make less sad or troubled.

con·spire (kən spīr') *v.* to plan together secretly. —**conspiratorially** *adv.*

con·sti·tu·tion (kän'stə tōō'shən *or* kan'stə tyōō'shən) *n.* the physical makeup of a person.

con·tempt (kən tempt') *n.* scorn; a showing of disrespect for authority.

con·ven·ient (kən vēn'yənt) *adj.* comfortable; handy. —**conveniently** *adv.*

con·ven·tion·al (kən ven'shən'l) *adj.* usual; customary.

con·viv·i·al (kən viv'ē əl) *adj.* enjoying a good time; sociable; loving fun. —**conviviality** *n.*

con·vulse (kən vuls') *v.* to shake or disturb violently. —**convulsive** *adj.*

cor·rode (kə rōd') *v.* to wear away or eat into slowly, as caused by rust or acid. —**corroding** *adj.*

court (kôrt) *v.* to seek as a mate.

crag (krag) *n.* a steep, rugged rock that rises above or juts out from others.

cre·mate (krē'māt) *v.* to burn a dead body to ashes. —**cremation** *n.*

crepe (krāp) *n.* a thin, wrinkled cloth of silk, cotton, or rayon.

crest (krest) *n.* the top of a thing, like a wave or a mountain; the surface along the top. *v.* to reach the top of.

crit·i·cal (krit'i k'l) *adj.* tending to disapprove or find fault. —**critically** *adv.*

cro·chet·ing (krō shā'iŋ) *n.* needlework in which loops of threads are interwoven with a hooked needle.

cul·vert (kul'vərt) *n.* a drain or waterway passing under a road.

cyg·net (sig'nət) *n.* a young swan.

cyl·in·der (sil'ən dər) *n.* a round figure with two flat ends that are circles; specifically, a part of a machine containing the pistons.

D

de·ceive (di sēv') *v.* to fool or trick; mislead.

de·ci·sive (di sī'siv) *adj.* showing firmness and determination. —**decisively** *adv.*

de·cree (di krē') *n.* an official order or decision from a government or court. *v.* to issue an order.

de·hy·drate (dē hī'drāt) *v.* to remove water from; dry. —**dehydrated** *adj.*

der·e·lict (der'ə likt') *n.* a lost or deserted ship.

de·spond·ent (di spän'dənt) *adj.* discouraged; having no hope. —**despondently** *adv.*

---

fat, āpe, cär; elf, ēven; hit, bīte; gō, hôrn, tōōl, look; yōō, yoo, oil, out; up, fur; get; joy; yet; chin; she; thin; then; zh, leisure; ng, ring; ə for *a* in *ago*, *e* in *agent*, *i* in *sanity*, *o* in *comply*, *u* in *focus*; ' as in *able* (ā'b'l)

de·struct (di strukt′ *or* dē′strukt′) *v.* to be automatically destroyed.

de·ter·mi·na·tion (di tur′mə nā′shən) *n.* firmness of purpose.

de·vot·ed (di vōt′id) *adj.* loving; loyal.

dig·ni·fied (dig′nə fīd′) *adj.* having or showing dignity; noble.

dig·ni·fy (dig′nə fī′) *v.* to give honor to; make seem noble or worthy.

dig·ni·ty (dig′nə tē) *n.* a noble or stately appearance or manner.

dis·a·bil·i·ty (dis′ə bil′ə tē) *n.* **1.** the condition of not being able or fit to do something. **2.** something that disables, as an injury or illness.

dis·ci·ple (di sī′p'l) *n.* a pupil or follower of a teacher or leader.

dis·con·cert (dis kən surt′) *v.* to bring confusion or disorder to; upset.

dis·con·so·late (dis kän′sə lit) *adj.* so sad and unhappy that nothing will be of comfort. —**disconsolately** *adv.*

dis·guise (dis gīz′) *v.* to change one's type of dress or use of voice so as not to be recognized.

dis·lodge (dis läj′) *v.* to force from a position where resting or hiding.

dis·mal (diz′m'l) *adj.* causing gloom or misery; sad.

dis·o·ri·ent (dis ôr′ē ent′) *v.* to confuse mentally with respect to time or place. —**disoriented** *adj.*

dis·pense (dis pens′) *v.* to do without.

dis·pose (dis pōz′) *v.* to get rid of by giving or throwing away or selling.

dis·tinc·tive (dis tiŋk′tiv) *adj.* different from others; characteristic.

di·ver·sion (də vur′zhən) *n.* anything one turns to for fun or relaxation.

dor·sal (dôr′s'l) *adj.* on, of, or near the back.

drab (drab) *adj.* dull; monotonous.

droll (drōl) *adj.* comical in a strange or odd way.

drone (drōn) *n.* a continuous humming sound.

dumb·found (dum′found′) *v.* to shock and make speechless.

dusk (dusk) *n.* the dim part of twilight that comes before the dark of night.

dy·nam·ics (dī nam′iks) *n. pl.* all the forces at work in any activity.

E

ear·nest (ur′nist) *adj.* in a determined or serious manner.

eaves·drop (ēvz′dräp′) *v.* to listen to others who do not know they are being overheard.

ec·sta·sy (ek′stə sē) *n.* rapture; a strong feeling of joy or delight. —**ecstatic** *adj.*

ed·dy (ed′ē) *n.* a little current of air or water moving in circles against the main current.

e·late (i lāt′) *v.* to make proud, happy, or joyful.

el·e·men·ta·ry (el′ə men′tər ē *or* el′ə men′trē) *adj.* introductory or basic.

en·dear (in dir′) *v.* to make well liked or beloved.

en·dure (in door′ *or* in dyoor′) *v.* to hold up under pain or weariness.

en·trance (in trans′) *v.* to enchant or charm.

en·vi·sion (en vizh′ən) *v.* to imagine (something not yet in existence).

erst·while (urst′hwīl) *adj.* former; of an earlier time.

es·ca·pade (es′kə pād′) *n.* a daring or reckless adventure or prank.

ex·cel·si·or (ek sel′sē ôr′) *n.* long, thin wood shavings used for packing.

ex·hi·bi·tion (ek'sə bish'ən) *n.* a game played before the regular season begins.

ex·pe·di·tion (ek'spə dish'ən) *n.* a journey or trip taken to explore a region.

ex·quis·ite (eks'kwi zit *or* ik skwiz'it) *adj.* **1.** carefully done or elaborately made. **2.** very beautiful, especially in a delicate or carefully wrought way [an *exquisite,* lacy leaf]. —**exquisitely** *adv.*

ex·tra·di·tion (eks'trə dish'ən) *n.* the turning over of an escaped prisoner by one country to another.

F

fa·nat·i·cal (fə nat'i k'l) *adj.* having such a strong interest or belief in something that it is no longer reasonable.

feat (fēt) *n.* something done that shows great courage, skill, or strength; a remarkable deed.

fel·low·ship (fel'ō ship' *or* fel'ə ship') *n.* money given to a student to help him or her study for a higher degree.

fes·ter (fes'tər) *v.* to become filled with pus. —**festering** *adj.*

fil·ly (fil'ē) *n.* a young female horse, specifically one under five years of age.

flab·ber·gast (flab'ər gast') *v.* to amaze; surprise someone so greatly that one is speechless. —**flabbergasted** *adj.*

flor·in (flôr'in) *n.* a gold or silver coin used in some European countries.

flue (flo͞o) *n.* a tube for allowing smoke to go out, as in a chimney.

flus·ter (flus'tər) *v.* to make or become excited or confused. —**flustered** *adj.*

foe (fō) *n.* an enemy or opponent.

fore·lock (fôr'läk') *n.* a lock of hair growing just above the forehead.

for·ger·y (fôr'jər ē) *n.* the crime of copying another person's signature or writing

something to make it seem like the real thing.

for·mi·da·ble (fôr'mə də b'l) *adj.* inspiring awe.

fort·night (fôrt'nīt) *n.* two weeks.

fren·zy (fren'zē) *n.* a wild or mad outburst of action or feeling. —**frenzied** *adj.*

froth·y (frôth'ē) *adj.* foaming; bubbly.

G

gadg·et (gaj'it) *n.* any small mechanical device, sometimes one that is merely clever and not too useful.

ga·zette (gə zet') *n.* a newspaper.

gob·let (gäb'lit) *n.* **1.** originally, a cup without handles. **2.** a drinking glass with a base and stem.

gore (gôr) *v.* to stab or wound with a horn or tusk.

gour·met (go͝or'mā) *n.* a person who likes to eat or cook fine food.

gri·mace (grim'əs) *v.* to twist one's face or body, as if in pain.

grudge (gruj) *v.* to give without wanting to. —**grudgingly** *adv.*

gulch (gulch) *n.* a narrow valley with steep walls, cut by a swift stream.

gul·let (gul'ət) *n.* the throat or neck.

H

hag·gard (hag'ərd) *adj.* having a wild but tired look, from illness, hunger, or grief.

---

fat, āpe, cär; elf, ēven; hit, bīte; gō, hôrn, to͞ol, lo͝ok; yo͞o, yo͝o, oil, out; up, fʉr; get; joy; yet; chin; she; thin; *th*en; zh, leisure; ng, ring;
ə for *a* in *ago,* e in *agent,* i in *sanity,* o in *comply,* u in *focus;* ' as in *able* (ā'b'l)

half-sub·merged (haf səb murjd) *v.* partially sunken or plunged beneath the surface of water.

har·poon (här poon') *n.* a spear with a barb at one end and a line attached to the shaft, used for spearing whales or other sea animals.

haugh·ty (hôt'ē) *adj.* showing too much pride in oneself; having scorn for others. —**haughtily** *adv.*

hearth (härth) *n.* the stone or brick floor of a fireplace, often extending out into the room.

heath·er (heth'ər) *n.* a low plant with small, purple flowers, often found in the British Isles.

hem·lock (hem'läk) *n.* an evergreen or pine tree.

her·it·age (her'ət ij) *n.* something handed down from one's ancestors, such as skills, rights, or a certain way of life.

hu·mil·i·ate (hyoo mil'ē āt') *v.* to make someone feel ashamed; take away one's pride or dignity. —**humiliating** *adj.* —**humiliation** *n.*

hur·tle (hurt''l) *v.* to move or throw forward with much force or great speed.

I

i·dle (î'd'l) *adj.* lazy; not wanting to work.

i·dyl·lic (ī dil'ik) *adj.* simple and pleasant, such as a scene of country life.

im·mu·nize (im'yə nīz') *v.* to protect against a disease, usually by vaccination. —**immunization** *n.*

im·plore (im plôr') *v.* to plead or beg for with feeling. —**imploringly** *adv.*

im·pro·vise (im'prə vīz') *v.* to make something up and perform at the same time.

im·pu·dent (im'pyoo dənt) *adj.* shamelessly bold or rude; not showing respect. —**impudence** *n.*

im·pulse (im'puls) *n.* a sudden feeling that causes one to want to do something.

in·cred·u·lous (in krej'oo ləs) *adj.* not willing or able to believe; doubtful. —**incredulously** *adv.*

in·debt·ed (in det'id) *adj.* obliged; owing thanks.

in·dif·fer·ent (in dif'ər ənt *or* in dif'rənt) *adj.* having or showing no interest or concern.

in·dus·tri·ous (in dus'trē əs) *adj.* hardworking.

in·fir·ma·ry (in fur'mə rē) *n.* a place where people who are sick or injured are taken care of.

in·im·i·ta·ble (in im'ə tə b'l) *adj.* too good to be copied or equaled.

in·nards (in'ərdz) *n. pl.* the internal organs of the body.

in·stan·ta·ne·ous (in'stən tā'nē əs) *adj.* done or happening in an instant.

in·stinc·tive (in stingk'tiv) *adj.* seeming to be natural; acting according to an inborn tendency. —**instinctively** *adv.*

in·ter·est (in'trist *or* in'tər ist) *n.* money paid for the use of money, or the rate at which it is paid.

in·te·ri·or (in tir'ē ər) *adj.* of the inner nature of a person or thing; private; secret.

in·ter·val (in'tər v'l) *n.* space or time between things.

in·ti·mate¹ (in'tə mit) *adj.* personal; familiar.

in·ti·mate² (in'tə māt') *v.* to hint; suggest without saying openly.

in·tox·i·cate (in täk'sə kāt') *v.* to make very happy or excited. —**intoxicating** *adj.*

in·ven·to·ry (in'vən tôr'ē) *n.* **1.** a complete list of goods, property, etc., as of a business. **2.** any detailed list [an *inventory* of one's album collection].

irk·some (urk'səm) *adj.* tiresome; annoying.

J

jar (jär) *v.* to make vibrate by sudden impact. —**jarred** *v.*

jer·kin (jur′kin) *n.* a short, tight jacket with no sleeves, often worn by men in the sixteenth and seventeenth centuries.

joist (joist) *n.* one of the parallel pieces that holds up the boards of a floor or the laths of a ceiling.

K

kiln (kil *or* kiln) *n.* an oven or a furnace for drying or baking bricks or pottery.

ki·mo·no (kə mō′nə *or* kə mō′nō) *n.* a loose robe with wide sleeves and a sash, often worn by Japanese men and women.

L

lair (ler) *n.* the resting place of a wild animal; den.

laugh·ing·stock (laf′iŋ stäk′) *n.* a person or thing made the object of ridicule or fun.

leg·a·cy (leg′ə sē) *n.* money or property left to someone by a will.

lib·er·a·tion (lib′ə rā′shən) *n.* the act of being set free.

li·no·le·um (li nō′lē əm) *n.* a hard, smooth, floor covering made of ground cork, wood, and linseed oil on a burlap or canvas backing.

lithe (līth) *adj.* limber; supple; bending easily.

loam (lōm) *n.* a dark, rich soil with rotting plant matter in it.

loathe (lōth) *v.* to feel disgust for; hate.

loi·ter (loit′ər) *v.* to spend time in an idle way; linger.

loom¹ (lōōm) *n.* a machine for weaving thread or yarn into cloth. *v.* to weave on a loom.

loom² (lōōm) *v.* to come into sight in a large or frightening way.

lout (lout) *n.* a stupid or clumsy person; boor.

lum·ber (lum′bər) *v.* to move in a heavy or clumsy way.

lu·mi·nous (lōō′mə nəs) *adj.* bright; giving off light.

lurch (lurch) *v.* to roll or lean suddenly forward or to one side.

lure (loor) *n.* anything used to attract or lead by offering something that seems pleasant.

M

ma·jes·tic (mə jes′tik) *or* **ma·jes·ti·cal** (mə jes′ti k′l) *adj.* grand; stately; dignified. —**majestically** *adv.*

mal·a·dy (mal′ə dē) *n.* a sickness or a disease.

ma·li·cious (mə lish′əs) *adj.* wanting to harm someone; spiteful.

man·da·rin (man′də rin) *n.* a high official of China under the Empire, before A.D. 1911.

ma·neu·ver (mə nōō′vər *or* mə nyōō′vər) *n.* a movement requiring skill.

ma·nip·u·late (mə nip′yə lāt′) *v.* to change figures or accounts. —**manipulation** *n.*

marge (märj) *n.* [Poetic] a border, margin, or edge.

mawk·ish (mô′kish) *adj.* showing love or pity in a foolish or tearful way; extremely sentimental.

---

fat, āpe, cär; elf, ēven; hit, bīte; gō, hôrn, tōōl, look;
yōō, yoo, oil, out; up, fur; get; joy; yet; chin;
she; thin; then; zh, leisure; ng, ring;
ə for *a* in *ago*, *e* in *agent*, *i* in *sanity*, *o* in *comply*, *u* in
focus; ′ as in *able* (ā′b′l)

me·chan·i·cal (mə kan′i k′l) *adj.* **1.** having to do with machinery or tools, or having skill in their use. **2.** automatic, as if from force of habit. —**mechanically** *adv.*

me·di·o·cre (mē′dē ō′kər) *adj.* ordinary; not very good or bad.

mel·an·chol·y (mel′ən käl′ē) *adj.* sad; gloomy.

me·nag·er·ie (mə naj′ər ē) *n.* a collection of wild animals kept in cages, often for public showing.

mer·chan·dise (mʉr′chən dīz′ *or* mʉr′chən dīs′) *n.* goods; things that are bought or sold.

moc·ca·sin (mäk′ə s′n) *n.* a heelless slipper of soft, flexible leather, worn originally by North American Indians.

mod·est (mäd′ist) *adj.* acting in a way that is considered proper.

moil (moil) *v.* to work hard.

mon·o·syl·la·ble (män′ə sil′ə b′l) *n.* a word of one syllable.

mo·not·o·nous (mə nät′′n əs) *adj.* going on and on in the same tone of voice.

mot·tle (mät′′l) *v.* to mark with spots or streaks of different colors. —**mottled** *adj.*

mush (mush) *v.* to travel over snow, with a dog sled.

mus·ta·chio (məs tä′shō *or* məs tä′shē ō′) *n.* a mustache, especially a large, bushy one. —**mustachioed** *adj.*

mus·ter (mus′tər) *v.* to gather up; summon.

mut·ton (mut′′n) *n.* the flesh of a sheep, used for food.

myr·i·ad (mir′ē əd) *n.* any very large number.

N

nau·se·ate (nô′shē āt *or* nô′zē āt) *v.* to become sick to one's stomach. —**nauseated** *adj.*

no·ta·ry (nōt′ər ē) *n.* an official who has the legal power to witness the signing of a deed, will, or contract.

nui·sance (noo′s′ns *or* nyoo′s′ns) *n.* an act that causes trouble or bother to another person.

O

o·a·sis (ō ā′sis) *n.* a fertile place in the desert that has water.

oath (ōth) *n.* a serious promise that one will speak the truth or follow rules.

ob·liv·i·ous (ə bliv′ē əs) *adj.* forgetting; not noticing.

oc·tag·o·nal (äk tag′ə n′l) *adj.* having eight angles and eight sides.

on·er·ous (än′ər əs *or* ō′nər əs) *adj.* hard to put up with; burdensome.

op·po·si·tion (äp′ ə zish′ən) *n.* the act of fighting against or resisting, as in an argument.

op·ti·mism (äp′tə miz′m) *n.* a bright, hopeful feeling about life, in which one expects good things to happen. —**optimistic** *adj.*

orb (ôrb) *n.* [Poetic] the eyeball.

o·ri·en·ta·tion (ôr′ē ən tā′shən) *n.* the act of becoming used to a certain situation.

or·nate (ôr nāt′) *adj.* having too much decoration; showy.

P

pan·to·mime (pan′tə mīm′) *v.* to act or express by using actions and gestures without words to tell something.

pa·tent·ly (pāt′′nt lē) *adv.* in an obvious way; clearly; plainly.

ped·i·gree (ped′ə grē) *n.* a record of the ancestors of a thoroughbred animal. —**pedigreed** *adj.*

phos·pho·res·cent (fäs′fə res′′nt) *adj.* giving off light without noticeable heat.

phos·pho·rus (fäs'fər əs) *n.* a chemical element that is a white or yellow waxy solid. It can glow in the dark, can start burning, and is very poisonous.

pil·lar (pil'ər) *n.* a long upright structure used to support a roof.

pin·a·fore (pin'ə fôr') *n.* a sleeveless garment, like an apron, worn by a little girl over her dress.

pin·ion (pin'yən) *n.* a bird's wing.

pit·e·ous (pit'ē əs) *adj.* causing or deserving pity; a feeling of sorrow or sympathy. —**piteously** *adv.*

plague (plāg) *v.* to trouble or make suffer.

plain·tive (plān'tiv) *adj.* mournful; sad; sorrowful.

plum·met (plum'it) *v.* to fall or drop straight down.

plun·der (plun'dər) *v.* to rob or take from by force.

poach (pōch) *v.* to hunt on someone else's land without having the right to do so.

pock·mark (päk'märk') *n.* a small scar or pit left on the skin by the sores of smallpox or chickenpox. —**pockmarked** *adj.*

pon·der (pän'dər) *v.* to think about; consider carefully.

por·ti·co (pôr'tə kō) *n.* a porch or covered walkway, having a roof held up by columns.

poul·tice (pōl'tis) *n.* a soft, hot, wet mixture of flour or mustard and water put on a sore part of the body. A poultice is used to draw infection from the body.

pre·car·i·ous (pri ker'ē əs) *adj.* not safe or sure; risky. —**precariously** *adv.*

prej·u·dice (prej'ə dis) *n.* dislike of people just because they are of another race, religion, or country.

pres·tige (pres tēzh') *n.* fame or respect that comes from doing great things, or having a good character, success, or wealth.

pro·gram (prō'gram) *v.* to plan a computer program for (a particular problem, specific data, etc.). —**programming, programmer** *n.*

proph·et (präf'it) *n.* a person who claims to know and can tell what might happen in the future.

pro·por·tions (prə pôr'shənz) *n. pl.* dimensions, as length, width, and height.

prop·o·si·tion (präp'ə zish'ən) *n.* a suggestion made for others to think about; plan.

pros·pect (präs'pekt) *n.* anticipation; looking forward to something.

pros·per·ous (präs'pər əs) *adj.* successful; rich; thriving.

pro·té·gé (prōt'ə zhā') *n.* a person who is helped and guided in his or her career by another person.

pun·cheon (pun'chən) *n.* a heavy, broad piece of rough timber with one side cut flat.

py·lon (pī'län) *n.* a high tower that holds up electric lines and marks a course for airplanes.

Q

qua·ver (kwā'vər) *v.* to tremble or shake, as the voice may do when one is afraid or overcome by strong feelings. —**quavering** *adj.*

quest (kwest) *n.* a hunt or search.

R

rab·bi (rab'ī) *n.* a teacher of the Jewish law, usually the leader of a synagogue or temple.

---

fat, āpe, cär; elf, ēven; hit, bīte; gō, hôrn, tōol, look;
yōo, yoo, oil, out; up, fʉr; get; joy; yet; chin;
she; thin; then; zh, leisure; ng, ring;
ə for *a* in *ago*, *e* in *agent*, *i* in *sanity*, *o* in *comply*, *u* in *focus*; ' as in *able* (ā'b'l)

ram·page (ram′pāj) *n.* a wild or crazy action; in a rage.

rang·y (rān′jē) *adj.* tall and thin, and having long legs.

rap·ture (rap′chər) *n.* a feeling of deep joy.

rasp·ing (rasp′ing) *adj.* rough; grating.

rav·age (rav′ij) *v.* to ruin or destroy.

re·ac·ti·vate (rē ak′ tə vāt′) *v.* to make active again; to put into action again.

re·bel·lious (ri bel′yəs) *adj.* opposing any controls; defiant.

re·com·bi·na·tion (rē käm′bə nā′shən) *n.* a combining again.

reed (rēd) *n.* a tall, slender type of grass growing in wet land.

reef (rēf) *n.* a ridge of sand or rock almost even with the surface of the water.

reg·is·tered (rej′is tərd) *adj.* officially or legally recorded, enrolled, or certified.

rel·ic (rel′ik) *n.* something kept as sacred because it belonged to a saint or martyr.

re·luc·tant (ri luk′tənt) *adj.* unwilling; not wanting to do something.

re·mote (ri mōt′) *adj.* far off or far away.

re·o·ri·en·ta·tion (rē ôr′ ē ən tā′shən) *n.* the act of reacquainting oneself with a certain situation.

re·press (ri pres′) *v.* to hold back; to control strictly.

res·o·lu·tion (rez′ə loo′shən) *n.* **1.** the act of deciding or resolving something. **2.** a formal statement adopted as law by a group of people.

res·ur·rect (rez′ə rekt′) *v.* to bring back into use.

re·tort (ri tôrt′) *v.* to answer in a clever way.

re·tract (ri trakt′) *v.* to draw back or in.

rheu·ma·tism (roo′mə tiz′m) *n.* a physical condition in which the muscles and joints become stiff, sore, and swollen.

rid·dle (rid′′l) *v.* to spread throughout.

rite (rīt) *n.* a formal act or ceremony carried out according to fixed rules; custom.

rogue (rōg) *n.* a scoundrel; rascal; dishonest or tricky person.

rol·lick·ing (räl′ik ing) *adj.* full of fun; carefree; light-hearted.

ro·tun·da (rō tun′də) *n.* a round hall or room, often with a round roof or dome.

rue (roo) *v.* to regret or feel sorry about something.

S

sage (sāj) *n.* a very wise older person.

sal·low (sal′ō) *adj.* having an unhealthy, pale-yellow look.

sat·is·fy (sat′is fī) *v.* to meet the needs of; please.

saun·ter (sôn′tər) *v.* to walk about idly; stroll.

scarce·ly (skers′lē) *adv.* hardly.

scheme (skēm) *v.* to plot; make secret plans.

scim·i·tar *or* **scim·i·ter** (sim′ə tər) *n.* a curved sword.

sec·tor (sek′tər) *n.* a certain area or region divided for a purpose.

self-con·scious (self′-kän′shəs) *adj.* embarrassed or shy in the presence of others. —**self-consciously** *adv.*

sheik (shēk) *n.* a leader or chief of an Arab family, tribe, or village.

shrewd (shrood) *adj.* keen-witted; clever.

shunt (shunt) *v.* to move or turn to one side; turn aside or out of the way.

sin·ew (sin′yoo) *n.* tendon; the cord of tough fiber that fastens a muscle to a bone.

sin·is·ter (sin′is tər) *adj.* evil; wicked; dishonest.

skep·tic (skep′tik) *n.* a person who doubts or questions many things.

skiff (skif) *n.* a light rowboat, often having a small sail.

so·phis·ti·cat·ed (sə fis′tə kāt′id) *adj.* very complicated; based on the latest techniques or ideas.

sor·rel (sôr′əl) *n.* a light reddish-brown horse.

souf·flé (soo flā′) *n.* a baked food made light and fluffy by adding beaten egg whites before baking it.

spec·tac·u·lar (spek tak′yə lər) *adj.* grand; showy.

sto·i·cal (stō′i k′l) *adj.* sternly unconcerned and unemotional about joy, grief, pain, or pleasure.

stra·te·gic (strə tē′jik) *adj.* showing sound planning; useful or important in strategy.

sub·stan·ti·ate (səb stan′shē āt′) *v.* to prove to be real or true.

suc·tion (suk′shən) *adj.* causing or working by the drawing of air out of a space to make a vacuum that will make an object stick to a surface.

sulk·y (sul′kē) *adj.* acting in a sullen or pouting manner. —**sulkily** *adv.*

sus·pi·cion (sə spish′ən) *n.* suggestion; a very small amount or trace.

sus·pi·cious (sə spish′əs) *adj.* not trusting others; doubting.

swin·dle (swin′d'l) *n.* the act of cheating or tricking someone out of money or property.

sym·pa·thet·ic (sim′pə thet′ik) *adj.* showing feeling towards another; being understanding.

sym·pa·thize (sim′pə thīz′) *v.* to share the feelings of another.

T

tack (tak) *n.* a horse's equipment, as saddles, bridles, etc.

tack room (tak room) *n.* a room near a stable in which tack is kept.

tat·ting (tat′ing) *n.* the act of making lace by looping and knotting thread with a small shuttle held in one's hand.

ten·e·ment (ten′ə mənt) *n.* an old, crowded apartment house, often called a city slum.

ten·ta·cle (ten′tə k′l) *n.* a long, slender part growing around the head or mouth of some animals, used for feeling, moving, or gripping.

theme (thēm) *n.* a short melody that is the subject of a piece of music.

the·o·ret·i·cal (thē′ə ret′ik′l) *adj.* of or based on theory or scientific reasoning, not on practice or experience.

ther·a·pist (ther′ə pist) *n.* a specialist who treats diseases of the mind or body.

this·tle·down (this′'l doun′) *n.* the down or fluff from the thistle plant which has prickly leaves and flowerheads of white or purple.

tour·na·ment (toor′nə mənt) *n.* a series of contests in a sport in which a number of people or teams take part, trying to win a championship.

tran·script (tran′skript′) *n.* a copy of a student's record of grades received in school or college.

trawl (trôl) *v.* to fish with a large net dragged by a boat along the bottom of a shallow part of the sea.

treach·er·ous (trech′ər əs) *adj.* not loyal or faithful; betraying.

---

fat, āpe, cär; elf, ēven; hit, bīte; gō, hôrn, tool, look; yoo, yoo, oil, out; up, fur; get; joy; yet; chin; she; thin; then; zh, leisure; ng, ring;
ə for *a* in **ago**, *e* in **agent**, *i* in **sanity**, *o* in **comply**, *u* in **focus**; ' as in **able** (ā′b'l)

trice (trīs) *n.* a moment; used in the phrase —**in a trice,** which means in a very short time.

tri·fle (trī'f'l) *v.* to talk with in a joking way; deal with lightly.

trough (trôf) *n.* a long, narrow container, from which animals eat or drink.

tu·ber·cu·lo·sis (too bʉr'kyə lō'sis *or* tyoo bʉr'kyə lō'sis) *n.* a disease in which the lungs become swollen and the tissues waste away.

ty·rant (tī'rənt) *n.* a cruel and unjust ruler.

U

un·ac·cus·tomed (un'ə kus'təmd) *adj.* not usual; strange.

un·con·scious (un kän'shəs) *adj.* not able to feel or think; unaware.

un·err·ing (un ʉr'iŋ *or* un er'iŋ) *adj.* making no mistake; without error; certain; sure. —**unerringly** *adv.*

V

vague (vāg) *adj.* **1.** not clearly or exactly expressed or stated [a *vague* answer]. **2.** not sharp, certain, or exact in thought or feeling [*vague* about his plans; a *vague* longing].

var·i·a·tion (ver'ē ā'shən *or* var'ē ā'shən) *n.* the repetition of a melody or theme with changes in harmony, rhythm, or key.

ver·dict (vʉr'dikt) *n.* any decision or opinion.

vet·er·i·nar·i·an (vet'ər ə ner'ē ən *or* vet'rə ner'ē ən) *n.* a person who practices the branch of medicine dealing with the treatment of diseases and injuries in animals.

vi·tals (vīt''lz) *n. pl.* the necessary organs of the body, such as the brain, heart, or liver.

vix·en (vik's'n) *n.* a female fox.

vow (vou) *v.* to swear solemnly to do or get [he *vowed* revenge].

vul·ner·a·ble (vul'nər ə b'l) *adj.* likely to be hurt, destroyed, or attacked.

W

wan·ton (wän't'n *or* wôn't'n) *adj.* without reason, sense, or mercy.

whim·sy (hwim'zē) *n.* a fanciful kind of humor.

wid·ow (wid'ō) *n.* a woman whose husband has died and who has not married again.

will·ful (wil'fəl) *adj.* stubborn; always wanting one's own way.

wince (wins) *v.* to draw back slightly, usually twisting the face, as in pain.

win·some (win'səm) *adj.* charming; attractive in a sweet, pleasant way.

wist·ful (wist'fəl) *adj.* showing a longing or wishful look. —**wistfully** *adv.*

with·er (with'ər) *v.* to lose strength.

wool·gath·er·ing (wool'gath'ər iŋ) *n.* absent-mindedness or daydreaming.

X

xy·lo·phone (zī'lə fōn) *n.* a musical instrument made up of a row of wooden bars of different sizes that are struck with wooden hammers.

Y

year·ling (yir'liŋ) *n.* an animal one year old or in its second year.

Z

zo·o·log·i·cal (zō'ə läj'ik'l) *adj.* having to do with the study of animals.

Guidelines for Capitalization, Punctuation, and Spelling

Capitalization

Punctuation

Spelling

Guidelines for Capitalization

1 Proper Nouns and Proper Adjectives

> A **common noun** is a general name of a person, place, thing, or idea.

princess   city   ship   honesty

> Capitalize proper nouns. A **proper noun** names a particular person, place, or thing.

Princess Diana   Tulsa   *Titanic*

A proper noun can be made up of one or more words. Capitalize all important words in a proper noun.

New Year's Day   Kalamazoo River   Johnny Appleseed

> Capitalize proper adjectives. A **proper adjective** is made from a proper noun.

Danish — Denmark   Portuguese — Portugal

Proper adjectives are often used with common nouns. Do not capitalize the common noun.

French dressing   Greek alphabet   Siamese cat

> Capitalize the names of people and pets.

Begin every word in a name with a capital letter. An initial stands for a name. Write initials as capital letters. Put a period after an initial.

Susan B. Anthony   A. J. Foyt   Muggins

Often, a word for a family relation is used as the name of a particular person, or as part of the name. *Mom* and *Grandpa Lewis* are two examples. Capitalize a word used in this way.

> **Capitalize a title used with a person's name.**

A **title** is a term of respect used in front of a name. Many titles have short forms called **abbreviations**. Capitalize abbreviations of titles. Follow an abbreviation with a period.

> Mister — Mr.   Mistress — Mrs.   Doctor — Dr.

The title *Miss* has no abbreviated form. Do not use a period after this title. *Ms.* has no long form.

> Did Mr. Lee interview Dr. Smith or Mayor Gentry?

> **Capitalize the word *I*.**

> Margaret and I walked to the library.

 ## Key to Writing

Take special care when capitalizing unusual names such as MacDonald or Rip Van Winkle.

2 More Proper Nouns

> **Capitalize the names of particular places and things.**

1. Capitalize cities, states, and countries.

   Laredo, Texas, is near Mexico.

2. Capitalize streets, bridges, parks, and buildings.

   The tour guide showed us the Empire State Building, the Brooklyn Bridge, Wall Street, and Central Park.

3. Capitalize geographical names. Do not capitalize *north*, *south*, *east*, or *west* when they refer to directions. Capitalize these words only when they refer to a particular section of the country or world.

The Millers turned south and drove to Death Valley.
In the United States, the Mississippi River is the dividing line between the East and West.
Blue Ridge Mountains extend from the North to the South.

Capitalize the names of months, days, and holidays.

Do not capitalize the seasons: spring, summer, winter, and fall.

We celebrate Father's Day and the first day of summer in June.

Capitalize the names of races, religions, nationalities, and languages.

Modern American Indian artists often use traditional designs.
Judaism, Christianity, and the Muslim religion share a belief in one God.
The Russians and the Chinese have a common border.
Does this junior high school offer French?

Capitalize words referring to God and to religious scriptures.

the Lord	the Bible	the Book of Genesis
Allah	the Talmud	the New Testament

Capitalize the names of clubs, organizations, and business firms.

Carolyn's dog is registered with the American Kennel Club.
Have you heard of the International Kitefliers Association?
Don's father works for American Plastics, Incorporated.

 Key to Writing

Carefully follow capitalization rules. Incorrect capitalization can confuse meaning in your writing.

Little Rock (Arkansas)	I am going west. (direction)
little rock (pebble)	I am going out West. (area of country)

3 Outlines and Titles

Capitalize the first word of each line of an outline.

Notice that the major divisions of an outline are marked with Roman numerals (I., II.). The next most important divisions are identified with capital letters (A., B.). After that, numerals mark the divisions.

    Capitalization and Punctuation
     I. Use of capital letters
       A. Proper nouns and adjectives
       B. First words
         1. Sentences
         2. Poetry
         3. Outlines
         4. Titles
    II. Use of periods

Capitalize the first word, last word, and all important words in a title.

Do not capitalize an article (*the*, *a*, *an*), or a short preposition (*in*, *for*, *from*, *by*), unless it comes first or last.

   Raiders of the Lost Ark (movie title)

   Anne Morrow Lindbergh, *Gift from the Sea* (book)

   Lewis Carroll, "The Walrus and the Carpenter" (poem)

Titles are also underlined or enclosed in quotation marks. Follow this general rule for punctuating titles. Place quotation marks around titles of short works such as stories, poems, newspaper articles, and reports. Underline the titles of longer works such as books, movies, magazines, newspapers, and television series. In printed works, these titles are in italics instead of underlined.

Guidelines for Punctuation

1 The Period

> Use a period at the end of a declarative sentence and most imperative sentences.

Declarative: The next clue is hidden under that rock.

Imperative: Look under that rock for the next clue.

> Use a period after an abbreviation. To save time and space we often use words in a shortened form. These forms are called **abbreviations**.

The names of states, days, and months are often abbreviated. Except for such abbreviations as *Mr.*, *Mrs.*, *Ms.*, A.M., and P.M., avoid using abbreviations when you write sentences. Look at these abbreviations.

P.O.	Post Office	in.	inch
U.S.A.	United States of America	doz.	dozen
St.	Street	ht.	height
Mt.	Mountain	wt.	weight
R.R.	Railroad	lb.	pound
D.C.	District of Columbia	oz.	ounce

Some special abbreviations are written without periods.

FM	frequency modulation	PBS	Public Broadcasting System
CB	citizens' band	USAF	United States Air Force
M	meter	ml	milliliter

The two-letter state abbreviations such as IL, OH, and CA are written with capital letters and no periods. If you are not sure whether an abbreviation is written with periods, look in a dictionary.

Use a period after an initial. We often shorten a name to its first letter, which is called an initial. Always use a period after an initial.

P. Travers—Pamela Travers
J. C. Penny—James Cash Penny

Use a period after each number or letter that shows a division of an outline or that precedes an item in a list.

Punctuation (an outline)
I. End marks
  A. The period
    1. Sentences
    2. Abbreviations and initials
    3. Outlines and lists
  B. The question mark
  C. The exclamation point

Talent Show Act (a list)
1. tumblers
2. tap dancer
3. singer
4. band

2 The Question Mark and the Exclamation Point

Use a question mark at the end of an interrogative sentence. An **interrogative sentence** is a sentence that asks a question.

Where are we?   When do the geese migrate?

Use an exclamation point at the end of an exclamatory sentence and some imperative sentences. An **exclamatory sentence** is a sentence that expresses strong feelings.

Jackie struck out! It's a home run!

Use an exclamation point at the end of an imperative sentence that shows surprise or other strong emotion.

Look out! Hurry!

Use an exclamation point after an interjection. An **interjection** is a word or group of words used to express strong feeling.

Oh! How beautiful! Wow! What an ending!

Key to Writing and Speaking

When you write dialogue, use question marks and exclamation points to show how words and sentences are spoken.

3 The Comma

Commas signal the reader to pause. This pause keeps the reader from running together words or ideas that should be separate.

Use commas to separate the items in the series. There are always three or more words in a series.

The Jungle Pet Store sells mynah birds, lizards, turtles, and tropical fish.

In a series, place commas after each word except the last. It is important to insert commas carefully when you write a series. Notice how the meaning of this sentence changes when the commas are removed.

The grocery clerk packed Anna's bag with soda, crackers, broccoli, soup, cream, cheese, and peanut butter.

The grocery clerk packed Anna's bag with soda crackers, broccoli soup, cream cheese, and peanut butter.

If *yes*, *no*, or *well* begin a sentence, use a comma after them.

Yes, we're walking.   Well, we'll meet you there.

When you use *and*, *but*, or *or* to combine two sentences, put a comma before these words.

We ran fast. We nearly missed the bus.
We ran fast, but we nearly missed the bus.

Use commas to set off the name of a person spoken to.

One comma is needed when the name starts or ends the sentence. A comma is needed before and after a name in the middle of the sentence. Look at the way commas are used in these sentences.

Peter, what is your favorite color?
Mail this letter please, Joseph.
I think, Abigail, that you are taller than Sara.

Use commas to set off an appositive. An appositive follows a noun and renames the noun. It is used to give more information. Notice how commas set off the appositive in this sentence.

Mr. Lopez, our swim coach, retired last week.

Use commas to separate the parts of a date. If a date is in the middle of a sentence, use a comma after the last part.

Our field trip to the Brookfield Zoo is on Friday, May 13.
On November 7, 1962, Eleanor Roosevelt died.

Use a comma to separate the name of a city from the name of a state or country.

We once lived near Trenton, New Jersey.
My parents traveled to Zurich, Switzerland, last year.

 ## Key to Writing

Do not overuse commas. Too many commas make a sentence harder to read instead of easier.

4 Other Uses for Commas

> Use a comma to set off the explanatory words of a direct quotation.

Notice where the comma is placed in this direct quotation.

Courtney announced, "The movie will begin in ten minutes."

The explanatory words *Courtney announced* come before the quotation. A comma is placed after the last explanatory word. Now read this quotation.

"I want to go home," moaned Lisa.

The explanatory words come after the quotation. A comma is placed inside the quotation marks and after the last word of the quotation. Sometimes the quotation is separated into two parts.

"One of the people in this room," the detective said, "is the
    murderer."

A comma is used after the last word of the first part. Another comma is used after the last explanatory word. You will learn more about punctuating quotations in part 7 of this guide.

> Use a comma after the greeting of a friendly letter and after the closing of any letter.

Dear Agnes,   Sincerely yours,

> Use a comma whenever the reader might be confused.

Some sentences can be very confusing if commas are not used.

    Going up the elevator lost power.

    In the grocery bags were in demand.

Notice how much clearer a sentence is when a comma is used.

    Going up, the elevator lost power.

    In the grocery, bags were in demand.

5   The Apostrophe and the Hyphen

> Use an apostrophe to show possession. To form the possessive of a singular noun, add an apostrophe and *s* after the apostrophe.

    city + 's = city's   Carlos + 's = Carlos's

To form the possessive of a plural noun that does not end in *s,* add an apostrophe and an *s* after the apostrophe.

    gentlemen + 's = gentlemen's   geese + 's = geese's

To form the possessive of a plural noun that ends in *s,* add only an apostrophe.

    birds + ' = birds'   cities + ' = cities'

> Use an apostrophe in a contraction. A **contraction** is a word made by joining two words and omitting one or more letters. An apostrophe replaces the missing letters.

can + not = can't	we + are = we're	they + are = they're
will + not = won't	does + not = doesn't	she + would = she'd
you + will = you'll	he + had = he'd	are + not = aren't

> Use a hyphen after the first part of a word at the end of a line. When you write, you sometimes run out of room at the end of a line. Then you may have to split the word. Put a hyphen at the end of a syllable. Then write the second part of the word on the next line.

Before you choose a career, inves-
tigate many fields.

Never divide words of one syllable, such as *slight* or *bounce*. If you are in doubt about dividing a word, look it up in a dictionary.

Do not write a single letter at the end or beginning of a line. For example, these divisions would be wrong: *a- mong, inventor- y.*

> Use a hyphen in compound numbers from twenty-one through ninety-nine.

seventy-six trombones   Twenty-third Psalm

6 The Colon and the Semicolon

> Use a colon after the greeting in a business letter.

Dear Mrs. Winter: Dear Sir:

> Use a colon between the numerals that tell hours and minutes.

8:30 A.M.   3:30 P.M.

Remember to capitalize the letters and to use periods after each letter in the abbreviations *A.M.* and *P.M.*

> Use a semicolon to combine two related sentences.

There are two ways to combine two related sentences into one. The first way is to use a conjunction such as *and*, *but*, or *or* to connect the sentences. When you write this kind of sentence, use a comma before the conjunction.

> Judge Marino announced her decision, and the courtroom emptied quickly.

The second way to combine two related sentences is to use a semicolon (;). The semicolon takes the place of both the comma and the conjunction.

> Judge Marino announced her decision; the courtroom emptied quickly.

Key to Writing

Correct use of the semicolon will help you avoid writing run-on sentences.

Incorrect: The conductor raised her baton the concert began.
Correct: The conductor raised her baton; the concert began.

7 Quotation Marks

When you write what a person has said, you are writing a **quotation**. When you write the person's exact words, you write a **direct quotation**. If you do not write the exact words, you are writing an **indirect quotation**. Study these sentences.

Direct quotation: Steven whispered, "I'm hiding."
Indirect quotation: Steven said that he was hiding.

> Put quotation marks before and after the words of a direct quotation.

Notice that Steven's exact words are set apart by quotation marks in the first sentence.

Quotation marks (" ") are two pairs of small marks that look like apostrophes. They tell the reader that the exact words of the speaker or writer are being quoted.

Separate the words of a direct quotation from the rest of the sentence with a comma or end mark in addition to quotation marks.

Julie exclaimed, "The band is marching!"
"The band is marching!" Julie exclaimed.

Notice that, in the first sentence above, the comma comes *before* the quotation marks. The second sentence starts with the quoted words. Here the end mark is placed *inside* the quotation marks.

Place question marks and exclamation points inside quotation marks if they belong to the quotation itself.

Michael asked, "Did the bird's wing heal?"
"It's perfect!" answered Marianne.

In the first sentence, the question is quoted. Therefore, the question mark is placed inside the quotation marks. In the second sentence, the speaker is showing strong emotion. The exclamation point is also placed inside the quotation marks.

Place question marks and exclamation points outside quotation marks if they do not belong to the quotation. Remember to capitalize the first word of a direct quotation.

Did Dad say, "Come home at seven o'clock"?
I was shocked to hear her say, "I'll go"!

Sometimes a quotation is divided. Explanatory words, like *she said* or *he asked*, are in the middle of the quotation.

"My favorite movie," Lewis said, "is the original *King Kong*."

Notice that two sets of quotation marks are used in this quotation. The explanatory words are followed by a comma. This sentence has a comma after the explanatory words because the second part of the quotation does not begin a new sentence. Use a period after the explanatory words if the second part of the quotation is a sentence.

"We wrote that," said the students. "It is a group poem."

Key to Writing

Said is a common explanatory word used in writing. Try to use a variety of explanatory words when you write. Try some of these.

explained	announced	exclaimed	requested
commented	expressed	asked	noted

8 Punctuating Titles

> Put quotation marks around the titles of stories, poems, reports, articles, and chapters of a book.

"Spring Song" (poem)   "The Ransom of Red Chief" (story)

> Underline the title of a book, magazine, play, motion picture, or TV series. When these titles are printed, they are in italics.

Mary Jane by Dorothy Sterling   *Mary Jane* by Dorothy Sterling

> Underline the title of a painting or the name of a ship.

Washington Crossing the Delaware (painting)
Queen Elizabeth II (ship)

Guidelines for Spelling

How to Become a Better Speller

Make a habit of looking at words carefully.	When you come to a new word, be sure you know its meaning. If you are not certain, look up the word in a dictionary.

Practice seeing every letter. Many people see a word again and again but don't really look at it. When you see a new word or a tricky word, like *government*, look at all the letters. To help you remember them, write the word several times.

When you speak, pronounce words carefully.	Sometimes people misspell words because they say them wrong. Be sure that you are not blending syllables together. For example, you may write *probly* for *probably* if you are mispronouncing it.

Find out your own spelling enemies and attack them.	Look over your papers and make a list of the misspelled words. Also keep a list of new words that are difficult for you. Study these words until you can spell them correctly and easily.

| Find memory devices to help with problem spellings. | Some words are difficult to remember. In these cases, a memory device may help you. A memory device is a trick, or a catchy sentence, that you can remember easily. The device tells you how to spell the word. Here are three examples: |

principal The princi*pal* is my *pal*.
tragedy Every *age* has its tra*ge*dy.
embarrass I turned *really red* and felt *so* silly.

| Proofread what you write. | To make sure that you have spelled all words correctly, reread your work. Examine it carefully, word for word. Don't let your eyes race over the page and miss incorrectly spelled words. |

| Use a dictionary. | You don't have to know how to spell every word. No one spells everything correctly all the time. A good dictionary can help you to be a better speller. Use a dictionary whenever you need help with spelling. |

Mastering Specific Words

When you notice that you are having trouble with a certain word, take a few minutes to study it carefully. Give it all your attention. If you spend the time and energy to learn it correctly once, you will save yourself all the trouble of correcting it many times.

Follow these steps to master a specific word.

Steps for Mastering Specific Words

1. **Look at the word and say it to yourself.**

Pronounce it carefully. If it has two or more syllables, say it again, one syllable at a time. Look at each syllable as you say it.

2. **Look at the letters. Spell the word aloud.**

If the word has two or more syllables, pause between syllables as you say the letters.

3. **Without looking at the word, write it.**

Be sure to form each letter properly. Take your time.

4. **Now look at your book or list to see if you have spelled the word correctly.**

If you have, write it once more. Compare it with the correct spelling again. For best results, repeat the process once more.

5. **If you have misspelled the word, notice where the error was.**

Then repeat steps 3 and 4 until you have spelled the word correctly three times in a row.

Rules for Spelling

Adding Prefixes and Suffixes

Prefixes

A prefix is a word part added to the beginning of a word to change its meaning. When a prefix is added to a word, the spelling of the word stays the same.

Prefix	Base Word	New Word
un- (not)	+ named	= unnamed (not named)
re- (again)	+ enter	= reenter (enter again)
dis- (not)	+ appear	= disappear (not appear)
il- (not)	+ legible	= illegible (not legible)
pre- (before)	+ set	= preset (set before)
im- (not)	+ mature	= immature (not mature)
mis- (incorrectly)	+ state	= misstate (state incorrectly)
in- (not)	+ formal	= informal (not formal)

The Suffixes *-ly* and *-ness*

A suffix is a word part added to the end of a word to change its meaning. When the suffix *-ly* is added to a word ending with *l*, both *l*'s are kept. When *-ness* is added to a word ending in *n*, both *n*'s are kept.

Base Word	Suffix	New Word
mean	+ **-ness**	= meanness
practical	+ **-ly**	= practically

The Final Silent e

When a suffix beginning with a vowel is added to a word ending with a silent *e*, the *e* is usually dropped.

make + ing = making
confuse + ion = confusion
expense + ive = expensive

advise + or = advisor
believe + able = believable
fame + ous = famous

When a suffix beginning with a consonant is added to a word ending with a silent *e*, the *e* is usually kept.

hate + ful = hateful   hope + less = hopeless
bore + dom = boredom   sure + ly = surely
safe + ty = safety   move + ment = movement

The following words are exceptions:

truly   argument   ninth   wholly   judgment

Words Ending in *y*

When a suffix is added to a word that ends with *y* following a consonant, the *y* is usually changed to *i*.

noisy + ly = noisily   fifty + eth = fiftieth
happy + est = happiest   heavy + ness = heaviness

Note this exception: When *-ing* is added, the *y* remains.

bury + ing = burying   cry + ing = crying
deny + ing = denying   apply + ing = applying

When a suffix is added to a word that ends with *y* following a vowel, the *y* usually is not changed.

joy + ful = joyful   pay + ment = payment
stay + ing = staying   annoy + ed = annoyed

The following words are exceptions: paid, said.

Words with *ie* or *ei*

When the sound is long *e* (ē), the word is spelled *ie* except after *c*.

The following rhyme provides some rules which will help you.

I before *e*
Except after *c*,
Or when sounded like *a*
As in *neighbor* or *weigh*.

I before *E*

belief	relieve	yield	fierce	achieve
niece	brief	field	chief	shield

Except after *C*

receive	ceiling	perceive	deceit
conceive	conceited	receipt	

Or when sounded like *A*

weight   eight
neigh

These words are exceptions:

either	weird	species
neither	seize	leisure

Doubling the Final Consonant

Words of one syllable, ending with one consonant following one vowel, double the final consonant before adding *-ing*, *-ed*, or *-er*.

sit + ing = sitting	sad + er = sadder
hop + ed = hopped	stop + ing = stopping
shop + er = shopper	let + ing = letting

The final consonant is **not** doubled when it follows two vowels.

meet + ing = meeting	loan + ed = loaned
break + ing = breaking	train + er = trainer

Words with the "Seed" Sound

Only one English word ends in *sede*: *supersede*.
Three words end in *ceed*: *exceed, proceed, succeed*.
All other words ending in the sound of "seed" are spelled *cede*.

concede   precede   recede   secede

Words Often Confused

Sometimes your problems in spelling are caused by the language itself. In English there are many words that are easily confused. These words sound the same, or nearly the same, but are spelled differently and have different meanings. Words of this type are called **homophones**. Here are some examples of homophones.

horse—hoarse   pare—pear—pair   tail—tale   do—dew—due

When you have problems with homophones, general spelling rules won't help you. The only solution is to memorize which spelling goes with which meaning.

Here is a list of homophones and other words frequently used and frequently confused in writing. Study the sets of words, and try to connect each word with its correct meaning.

accept means to agree to something or to receive something willingly.

except means to keep out or leave out. As a preposition, *except* means "but" or "leaving out."

▶ My brother will *accept* the job the grocer offered him.
▶ Michelle likes every flavor of ice cream *except* pistachio.

capital means chief, important, or excellent. It also means the city or town that is the official seat of government of a state or nation.

capitol is the building where a state legislature meets.

the Capitol is the building in Washington, D.C., in which the United States Congress meets.

▶ The *capital* of Illinois is the city of Springfield.
▶ The *capitol* of Illinois is a stately building in Springfield.
▶ The senators arrived at the *Capitol* in time to vote.

hear means to listen to.
here means in this place.

▶ Every time I *hear* this song, I feel happy.
▶ Reference books are found *here* in the library.

it's is the contraction for *it is* or *it has*.
its shows ownership or possession.

▶ *It's* nearly midnight.
▶ The boat lost *its* sail during the storm.

lead (lēd) is a heavy, gray metal.
lead (lēd) means to go first, to guide.
led (lĕd) is the past tense of *lead* (lēd).

▶ Water pipes are often made of *lead*.
▶ These signs will *lead* us to the hiking trail.
▶ Bloodhounds *led* the detectives to the scene of the crime.

loose means free or not tight.
lose means to mislay or suffer the loss of something.

▶ The rider kept the horse's reins *loose*.
▶ If you *lose* your book, report the loss to the library as soon as possible.

peace is calm or stillness or the absence of disagreement.
piece means a portion or part.

▶ After two years of war, *peace* was finally achieved.
▶ This statue was carved from a *piece* of jade.

principal means first or most important. It also refers to the head of a school.
principle is a rule, truth, or belief.

▶ A *principal* export of Brazil is coffee.
▶ Our school *principal* organized a safety council.
▶ One *principle* of science is that all matter occupies space.

quiet means free from noise or disturbance.
quite means truly or almost completely.

▶ The only time our classroom is *quiet* is when it's empty.
▶ The aquarium tank is *quite* full.

their means belonging to them.
there means at that place.
they're is the contraction for *they are*.

▶ Our neighbors sold *their* house and moved to a farm.
▶ Please take the squirt guns over *there*.
▶ My sisters have never skied, but *they're* willing to try.

to means in the direction of.
too means also or very.
two is the whole number between one and three.

▶ The surgeon rushed *to* the operating room.
▶ The lights went off, and then the heat went off, *too*.
▶ Only *two* of the four mountaineers reached the peak.

weather is the state of the atmosphere referring to wind, moisture, temperature, etc.
whether indicates a choice or alternative.

▶ Australia has summer *weather* when the United States has winter.
▶ *Whether* we drive or take the train, we will arrive in three hours.

who's is the contraction for *who is* or *who has*.
whose is the possessive form of *who*.

▶ *Who's* been chosen to be a crossing guard?
▶ *Whose* skateboard was left on the sidewalk?

you're is the contraction for *you are*.
your is the possessive form of *you*.
▶ *You're* going to the costume party, aren't you?
▶ Please bring *your* sheet music to choir practice.

Index of Titles and Authors

Reading Literature Skills

Stanza, 80, 492, 500, 549
  See also **Form**
Structure, 254
Surprise Endings, 42
Theme, 29, 42, 353, 378, 386, 402–403, 419, 433, 480, 487, 549
  mood related to, 492
  poetry and, 482–483, 487, 490, 496, 498, 500, 549
Title, 381

Comprehension and Thinking Skills

Alternatives, 29, 396, 419
Analysis, 142, 326, 369, 550
Attitudes, 78, 110, 142, 263, 274, 496
Causal Relationships. *See* **Relationships**
  See also **Cause and Effect**
Cause and Effect, 6–7, 19, 29, 65, 78, 110, 182, 396, 500, 510, 516, 530, 550
Chronological Order. *See* **Time Order**
Classifying, 221, 480, 550
Comparison 94, 210, 217, 221, 226, 263, 381, 386, 496, 551
  See also **Contrast**
Conclusions, 19, 34, 51, 65, 166, 182, 221, 230, 263, 308, 326, 386, 419, 433, 455, 480, 496, 536
Contrast, 87, 217, 242, 272, 299, 381, 384, 419, 498, 551
  See also **Comparison**
Deduction, 34, 490
Details
  locating details, 34, 94, 242, 299, 485, 498

recalling details, 19, 29, 34, 42, 51, 65, 78, 87, 94, 110, 142, 155, 167, 182, 210, 217, 219, 221, 226, 230, 242, 254, 263, 272, 299, 308, 326, 341, 353, 368, 374, 378, 381, 384, 386, 396, 419, 433, 443, 455, 464, 480, 487, 490, 492, 496, 500, 510, 516, 530
Evaluating, 42, 65, 353, 404, 433, 443, 464, 480, 516, 536, 539, 551
  evaluating literature, 404–405
  evaluating solutions, 419
Fact and Fiction, 34
Fact and Opinion, 503, 516, 536, 551–552
  See also **Opinions**
Generalizations, 51, 552
Implied Main Idea. *See* **Main Idea**
Inference, 19, 29, 42, 51, 94, 110, 142, 155, 166, 182, 210, 215, 221, 226, 228, 242, 254, 263, 272, 280–281, 308, 326, 341, 353, 368, 374, 376, 378, 381, 384, 396, 399, 433, 443, 455, 464, 480, 485, 490, 496, 498, 500, 530, 552–553
  See also **Predictions**
Judgments, 404, 455
  See also **Evaluating**
Logical Order, 503, 553
  See also **Cause and Effect, Sequence, Time Order**
Main Idea, 130–131, 142, 166, 215, 219, 228, 263, 299, 376, 485, 492, 516, 536, 553
  implied main idea, 131, 254
  stated main idea, 130–131
  supporting details and, 130, 226, 299
Motives, 29, 42, 65, 155, 182, 368, 433, 443, 455
Opinions, 42, 51, 78, 87, 167, 210, 221,

Vocabulary Skills

Writing Skills

Study and Research Skills

Speaking and Listening Skills

Index of Fine Art

Art Credits

Cover

Still Life with White Boats, 1968, Fairfield Porter. Private Collection.

Frontispiece

Three Zebras, 1976, Mara Abboud. Courtesy of New York Graphic Society, Cos Cob, Connecticut.

Illustrations

David Wenzel, 10, 11, 14, 16, 17, 18, 128; Jane Liu, 35, 37, 40; Gay Holland, 52, 53, 55, 59, 63; Diane McKnight, 83, 84, 143, 227, 342, 518; Elizabeth Miles, 103, 108; Ad Kaner, 134; Pawel Bodytko, 168, 229; Keith Neely, 183, 185, 190, 193, 196, 198, 205; Richard Nichols, 284, 285, 296; Mike Muir, 309, 311, 315, 318, 324; David Palladini, 278, 354, 357, 359, 362, 366; Nathan Greene, 456, 458, 462.

Fine Art for Selection Openers

20 *Waves at Matsushima* (detail), 17th century, SOTATSU. Freer Gallery of Art, Smithsonian Institution, Washington, D.C. (06.231) 30 *The Green Boat* (detail), 1986, KEN DURKIN. Jessica Darraby Galleries, Los Angeles. 44 *Olympic Games, Munich* (detail), 1972, HUNDERTWASSER. Silkscreen. Copyright © 1987 Harel, Vienna, Austria (700). 66 *The Medieval Castle* (detail), 1985, BILL BELL. Photograph: Jaro Art Galleries, New York City. 156 *Blackberries* (detail), 1972, BOB TIMBERLAKE. Heritage Company, Lexington, North Carolina. 234 *Dear Lady Quilt* (detail), 1985, IRAN LAWRENCE. Photograph by Schecter Lee. 300 *Cow Skull and Meadowlark,* no date, O. C. SELTZER. The Thomas Gilcrease Institute of American History and Art, Tulsa, Oklahoma. 328 *September* (detail), 1982, DAVID BREGA. Collection of the Artist. 408 *Our English Coasts*(detail), 1852, W. H. HUNT. The Tate Gallery, London. 420 *Birds in the Sky*(detail), 1978, JOSEPH RAFFAEL. Collection of Glenn C. Janss. 434 *Portrait of Orleans* (detail), 1950, EDWARD HOPPER. Private Collection. 445 From the sketchbook of PABLO PICASSO, 1959. Copyright © ARS, New York City/SPADEM, 1987. 531 *Woman and Terrier* (detail), 1963, ALEX COLVILLE. Private Collection. Photograph by James Chambers Art Gallery of Ontario.

Photographs

Photograph by Milton Ackoff: 454. Robert Pearcy/Animals, Animals: 407. Fritz Prenzel/ Animals Animals: 264. The Bettmann Archive: 226, 228, 381, 496. Photograph by Elba Cabrera: 33. © 1987 *Chicago Tribune,* all rights reserved, used with permission: 219. © David Hughes/Bruce Coleman, Inc.: 511 © Nancy Crampton: 378. Culver Pictures: 209, 535. *Des Moines Register:* 442. © Focus on Sports: 256. Photograph by Joan Glazer: 215. Historical Pictures Service: 86. The Image Bank, Chicago: 229. Photograph by John Lattany: 352. Photograph by Willy Leon: 141. Henri Cartier-Bresson/Magnum Photos: 109. Milwaukee Public Schools: 124, 125. NASA: 504. Dick Swanson/*People*

Acknowledgments

Association for Childhood Education International: For "Hatsuno's Great-Grandmother," from *Told Under the Stars and Stripes* by F. C. Means; copyright © 1959, New York: Macmillan, reprinted by permission of Florence Crannell Means and the Association for Childhood International, 11141 Georgia Avenue, Suite 200, Wheaton, MD. Atheneum Publishers, a division of Macmillan, Inc.: For "Who's Who," from *If I Were in Charge of the World and Other Worries* by Judith Viorst; copyright © 1981 Judith Viorst. For an excerpt from *Shadow of a Bull* by Maia Wojciechowska; copyright © 1964 Maia Wojciechowska. For "Separation" by W. S. Merwin, from *The Moving Target* by W. S. Merwin; copyright © 1963 by W. S. Merwin. Don Congdon Associates, Inc.: For "Ghost Town," from *The Collected Stories of Jack Schaefer;* copyright © 1954 by Jack Schaefer, renewed 1982 by Jack Schaefer. Council on Inter-racial Books for Children, 1841 Broadway, New York, NY 10023: For "Common Bond" by Kimi Nari-matsu, from *Embers, Stories for a Changing World,* edited by Ruth S. Meyers et al. A free catalog of the Council's print and audio-visual materials is available. Delacorte Press: For "Lob's Girl" excerpted from *A Whisper in the Night: Tales of Terror and Suspense* by Joan Aiken; copyright © 1981, 1982, 1983, 1984 by Joan Aiken Enterprises, Ltd. Dillon Press, Inc.: For Chapter 1 from *The Zoo Lady* by Margaret Poynter; copyright © 1980. Dodd, Mead & Company, Inc.: For "Spring" by Richard Hovey, from *Poems.* For "The Cremation of Sam McGee" by Robert Service, from *The Collected Poems of Robert Service.* Doubleday & Company, Inc.: For "Someday" by Isaac Asimov, from *Earth Is Room Enough;* copyright © 1957 by Isaac Asimov. For "Dogs That Have Known Me" by Jean Kerr, from *Please Don't Eat the Daisies;* copyright 1954 by Jean Kerr. For an excerpt from *Where the Red Fern Grows* by Woodrow Wilson Rawls; copyright © 1961 by Woodrow Wilson Rawls, © 1961 by Curtis Publishing Company. E. P. Dutton: For "The Beggar in the Blanket," from *The Beggar in the Blanket and Other Vietnamese Tales,* retold by Gail B. Graham; text copyright © 1970 by Gail B. Graham, reprinted by permission of the publisher, Dial Books for Young Readers. For "Wind Is a Ghost," from *Whirlwind Is a Ghost Dancing* by Natalia Belting; text copyright © 1974 by Natalia Belting, reprinted by permission of the publisher, E. P. Dutton, a division of NAL Penguin, Inc. For "The Cat and the Golden Egg," from *The Town Cats and Other Tales* by Lloyd Alexander; text copyright © 1977 by Lloyd Alexander, reprinted by permission of the publisher, E. P. Dutton, a division of NAL Penguin, Inc. For "Dear Miss Veloshin" by Marjorie Weinman Sharmat, from *Just for Fun: A Collection of Original Humorous Stories,* edited by Ann Durell; copyright © 1979 by E. P. Dutton, a division of NAL Penguin, Inc. Farrar, Straus & Giroux, Inc.: For "The Fools of Chelm & the Stupid Carp" by Isaac Bashevis Singer, from *Stories for Children* by Isaac Bashevis Singer; copyright © 1962, 1967, 1968, 1970, 1972, 1973, 1974, 1975, 1976, 1979, 1980, 1984 by Isaac Bashevis Singer. For "the drum," from *Spin a Soft Black Song* by Nikki Giovanni; copyright © 1971 by Nikki Giovanni. The Feminist Press at The City University of New York and Hadley Irwin: For "The Pearl Ring," from *The Lilith Summer* by Hadley Irwin; copyright © 1979 by Hadley Irwin. Harcourt Brace Jovanovich, Inc.: For "The Old Gumbie Cat," from *Old Possum's Book of Practical Cats* by T. S. Eliot; copyright 1939 by T. S. Eliot, renewed 1967 by Esme Valerie Eliot. For "Worms and the Wind," from *The Complete Poems of Carl Sandburg* by Carl Sandburg; copyright 1950 by Carl Sandburg, renewed 1978 by Margaret Sandburg, Helga Sandburg Crile, and Janet Sandburg. Harper & Row, Publisher, Inc.: For an abridgement of "Joe Oliver, The King," from *Giants of Jazz* by Studs Terkel (T. Y. Crowell Co.); copyright © 1957, 1975 by Studs Terkel. For Chapter 2, "The Pond" and Chapter 3, "A Visitor," from *The Trumpet of the Swan* by E. B. White; copyright © 1970 by E. B. White. For "Adventures of a Frisbee," from *A Light in the Attic: Poems and Drawings* by Shel Silverstein; copyright © 1981 by Snake Eye Music. For "Cynthia in the Snow," from *Bronzeville Boys and Girls* by Gwendolyn Brooks; copyright © 1956 by Gwendolyn Brooks Blakely. For "Aaron's Gift," from *The Witch of Fourth Street and Other Stories* by Myron Levoy; text copyright © 1972 by Myron Levoy. For "The Hatchling Turtles," from *Spring Comes to the Ocean* by Jean Craighead George (Thomas Y. Crowell Co.); copyright © 1965 by Jean Craighead George. For "Icicles," from *Cold Stars and Fireflies: Poems of the Four Seasons* by Barbara Juster Esbensen (Thomas Y. Crowell Co.); copyright © 1984 by Barbara Juster Esbensen. For approximately 2200 words abridged from Chapters 13 and 14 (pages 82–95) in *Maria Luisa* by Winifred Madison; copyright © 1971 by Winifred Madison. For an excerpt abridged from pages 16–28 from *Sweetwater* by Laurence Yep; copyright © 1973 by Laurence Yep. For "Scene," from *River Winding* by Charlotte Zolotow; text copyright © 1970 by Charlotte Zolotow. John Hawkins & Associates, Inc.: For "My Friend Flicka" by Mary O'Hara, from *Story Magazine* of Jan./Feb., 1941; copyright 1941 by Mary O'Hara. Henry Holt and Company, Inc.: For "Dust of Snow," from *The Poetry of Robert Frost,* edited by Edward Connery Lathem; copyright 1923, © 1969 by Holt, Rinehart and Winston, Inc., copyright 1951 by Robert Frost. Macmillan Publishing Company: For "A Rare Provider," from *Magical Melons: More Stories About Caddie Woodlawn* by Carol Ryrie Brink; copyright 1939, 1940, 1944 by Macmillan Publishing Company, renewed 1967, 1968, 1972 by Carol Ryrie Brink. Scott Meredith Agency, Inc: For *Ghost of the Lagoon* by Armstrong Sperry, reprinted by permission of the author and the author's agent, Scott Meredith Literary Agency, Inc., 845 Third Avenue, New York, NY 10022. Houghton Mifflin Company: For "The Shark," from *Fast and Slow* by John Ciardi; copyright © 1975 by John Ciardi. For an excerpt from "All That Is Gold," from *The Fellowship of the Ring* by J.R.R. Tolkien; copyright ©

Staff Credits

Executive Editor, Language Arts: Carolyn McConnell

Editors: Sue Ellis, Patricia Opaskar

Associate Editors: Lisa Maria DeSloover, William McBride, Ph.D., Carol Kalas McMullen

Production Coordinator: Susan W. Nisson

Production Editor: Ronald G. Worman

Assistant Production Editors: Marion Chorvat, Catherine Hobbins

Copyeditor: Virginia Swanton

Senior Designer: Mary MacDonald